Liberalism under Siege

Liberalism under Siege

The Political Thought of the French Doctrinaires

Aurelian Craiutu

LEXINGTON BOOKS

Lanham • Boulder • New York • Oxford

LEXINGTON BOOKS

Published in the United States of America
by Lexington Books
an imprint of the Rowman & Littlefield Publishing Group, Inc.
4501 Forbes Boulevard, Suite 200, Lanham, Maryland 20706

PO Box 317
Oxford
OX2 9RU, UK

British Library Cataloguing in Publication Information Available

Library of Congress Cataloging-in-Publication Data

Craiutu, Aurelian.
    Liberalism under siege : the political thought of the French
doctrinaires / Aurelian Craiutu.
        p. cm. — (Applications of political theory)
    Includes bibliographical references and index.
    ISBN 0-7391-0657-0 (cloth : alk. paper) — ISBN 0-7391-0658-9
(pbk. : alk. paper)
    1. Liberalism—France—History—19th century. 2.
Democracy—France—History—19th century. 3. Representative
government and representation—France—History—19th century. 4.
France—Politics and government—19th century. I. Title. II. Series.
    JC574.2.F7C72 2003
    320.51'0944'09034—dc21
                                                        2003006256

Printed in the United States of America

∞™ The paper used in this publication meets the minimum requirements of
American National Standard for Information Sciences—Permanence of Paper for
Printed Library Materials, ANSI/NISO Z39.48-1992.

Il n'est rien de plus fécond en merveilles que l'art d'être libre; mais il n'y a rien de plus dur que l'apprentissage de la liberté.

—Tocqueville

Constituer la démocratie, c'est la modérer.

—Rémusat

Nous sommes du juste milieu, si la liberté unie à l'ordre est vraiment le milieu entre le despotisme et l'anarchie.

—Guizot

~

Contents

Foreword

Aurelian Craiutu's book comes at a very appropriate moment. For many years, students of liberalism have discussed the merits of Locke, Mill, and Kant as the sources of philosophical inspiration; and American readers of Tocqueville's *Democracy in America* have admired the more flattering parts of the portrait he painted of their country in its youth. Since the end of the Cold War, however, it has become clear that the building of a liberal political and legal order is a task of great difficulty, and one to which philosophy is less relevant than a strong sense of history and a tough sociological understanding of class conflict and its successful management.

Drawing historical parallels is a dangerous task, and Aurelian Craiutu leaves his readers to draw most of them for themselves; he has written a work of scholarship, not polemic. But this is a particularly appropriate moment to reach back behind the much-read Tocqueville and acquire a clearer understanding of the writers he learned from—many of them as active on the political stage as he, and some of them a great deal more successful than he. It was, indeed, a common complaint among Tocqueville's French critics that he saw the United States through François Guizot's eyes and knew what he would encounter before he left France; certainly, it is hard to think that the twenty-five-year-old Frenchman would have had so keen a vision if he had not attended Guizot's lectures before his famous visit.

Professor Craiutu's account reminds the reader how many more ways there are of instituting a liberal regime than those we have been familiar with for the past half century and that the connection between a liberal political regime (one that practices representative government and upholds the rule of law) and social liberalism (the minimization of unofficial restraints on private conduct) is less close than we have come to think. The writers on whom Aurelian Craiutu focuses had a very strong sense that France had started the revolutionary ball rolling in 1789 and that it had been, ever since, very hard to steer between revolutionary upheaval on the one side and counterrevolutionary dictatorship on the other. In times of peace, we may be tempted to think that they were overimpressed by the virtues of moderation and accommodation; watching a new Europe emerging on the other side of the vanished Iron Curtain and wondering how liberal values will fare elsewhere, we may well find ourselves sharing their sentiments as well as admiring their analyses.

—Alan Ryan
Oxford University

~

Preface

Writing a book about the political thought of the French Doctrinaires is a challenging task. With very few exceptions, French political theorists are usually not well-known in English-speaking academic circles, and often their ideas appear as unconventional and unnecessarily sophisticated. Moreover, they belong to a different political tradition whose principles are sometimes different from the main tenets of the Anglo-American political tradition. Finding an appropriate editor for a project on the French Doctrinaires was an even greater challenge, since very few presses these days are prepared to endorse proposals that might not bring an immediate profit or do not concentrate on canonical authors. Lexington Books, an imprint of The Rowman & Littlefield Publishing Group, wholeheartedly supported my project from the outset. I would like to extend special thanks to Serena Leigh Krombach, Jason Hallman, and Steve Wrinn for their encouragement and patience.

George Kateb and Alan Ryan welcomed my idea to write on early-nineteenth-century French political thought and kindly accepted to serve on my doctoral committee at Princeton University. They were joined by Patrick Deneen and Philip Nord. To all of them I owe a special debt. Shortly before his untimely death, François Furet read the chapter on Tocqueville and the Doctrinaires and made a few valuable suggestions. His "green light" encouraged me to continue the journey and gave me the reassurance that this work on the French Doctrinaires was worth completing.

Daniel Mahoney offered exceptional support and inspiration at various stages of this project, proving to be a fine connoisseur of things French. I am also extremely grateful to Catherine Coste for supporting my research on Guizot in many ways and suggesting that I include the photos of the Doctrinaires that figure in this book (they were scanned by Stéphane and Bertrand Coste and retouched by James Russell). Vladimir Protopopescu patiently read these pages and suggested valuable ways of improving the style, logic, and substance of my arguments. Virgil Nemoianu encouraged me to write on Guizot and provided generous insights on nineteenth-century philosophy, literature, and political thought. Special thanks also to Barbara Allen, John Burrow, Fred Fransen, Michael Gillespie, Stephen Holmes, Lucien Jaume, Jeremy Jennings, Alan Kahan, Charles Larmore, Chris Laursen, Pierre Manent, Carey McWilliams, Horst Mewes, Darío Roldán, Helena Rosenblatt, Filippo Sabetti, Paul Seaton, Vincent Starzinger, and K. Steven Vincent, who shared with me their expertise of nineteenth-century political thought.

I am also profoundly grateful to the members of the committee—Susan Shell, Mark Lilla, and Melissa Williams—that awarded my work on the French Doctrinaires the Leo Strauss Prize given by the American Political Science Association for the best doctoral dissertation in political philosophy (2000). My colleagues at Indiana University, in particular Jeffrey Isaac, Russell Hanson, and Timothy Tilton, the Workshop in Political Theory and Policy Analysis directed by Elinor and Vincent Ostrom, and our graduate students have created a congenial environment for studying, teaching, and discussing political theory and allowed me to work unhindered on allegedly "obscure" topics in the history of political thought. I would also like to express my warmest thanks to Liberty Fund for organizing two colloquia on Guizot and for publishing a new edition of the English translation of Guizot's *History of the Origins of Representative Government in Europe*. Finally, I would like to thank my former colleagues at Princeton who created a unique environment for studying political theory.

Various organizations provided financial assistance at different stages in the completion of this project. At Princeton University, I benefited from generous grants and fellowships from the University Center for Human Values, the Center for Regional Studies, and the Mellon Foundation. Also helpful was the financial support I received from Indiana University that gave me the opportunity to finish this project in a timely manner. I am also grateful for the assistance of the staff of the Interlibrary Loan Service at Princeton University, University of Northern Iowa, and Indiana University who helped me locate many rare or out-of-print books necessary for the timely completion of this project. I benefited from the opportunity to present chapters of this book at various academic seminars and conferences organized by the American Political Science Association; Institute Benjamin Constant and

University of California, Riverside; Princeton University; Indiana University's Workshop in Political Theory and Policy Analysis; Western Society for French History; New England Political Science Association; and the Midwest Political Science Association. I was also invited to present my work on Guizot and the other French Doctrinaires at many academic institutions in the United States and Europe, and it is my pleasure to thank all those who hosted me for their hospitality.

This book is dedicated to my parents, Adrian and Natalia, and my wife, Christina.

Bloomington, June 2003

~

Acknowledgments

The publisher and author gratefully acknowledge permission to reprint the following material:

Excerpts from *The History of Civilization in Europe* by François Guizot, translated by William Hazlitt, edited by Larry Siedentop. London: Penguin, 1997. Copyright © Penguin.

Excerpts from *The History of the Origins of Representative Government in Europe* by François Guizot, translated by Andrew R. Scoble, edited by Aurelian Craiutu. Indianapolis: Liberty Fund, 2002. Copyright © Liberty Fund.

"Between Scylla and Charybdis: The 'Strange' Liberalism of the French Doctrinaires," *History of European Ideas* 24, nos. 4–5 (1998): 243–65.

"Tocqueville and the Political Thought of the French Doctrinaires," *History of Political Thought* 20, no. 3 (Fall 1999): 456–94.

"The Battle For Legitimacy: Guizot and Constant on Sovereignty." *Historical Reflections/Reflexions historiques* 28, no. 3 (2002): 471–91.

"Rethinking Political Power: The Case of the French Doctrinaires." *European Journal of Political Theory* 2, no. 2 (2003): 125–55.

The engravings (pp. xviii and 79) and the portrait of Chateaubriand (p. 196) courtesy of Lilly Library, Indiana University, Bloomington.

The portrait of Guizot (p. 33) by Ary Sheffer courtesy of a private collection.

The portrait of Rémusat (p. 109) by Paul Delaroche, 1845.

The portrait of Barante (p. 164) from V. Frond, ed., *Panthéon des illustrations françaises an XIX e siède, 1865–1873*.

The portrait of Royer-Collard (p. 203) from Lahaye, ed., *Livre des orateurs*. Paris: Pagnerre, 1844.

P. G. Lamont fec 1790

Zusamenkunft der National-Versamlung im Ballspielhause, zu Versailles den 19 Jun. 1789

~

CHAPTER ONE

In Lieu of Introduction

Boredom with established truths is a great enemy of free men.

—B. Crick

A Strange and Unfair Neglect

This book is the outcome of a lasting interest in French political thought and the French idea of civilization. At a point in time when the concept of civilization has come to be identified only with material progress, sciences, and technology, the notion of civilization as it emerged in France challenges us to rethink this conventional view. It has been remarked that in France, the entire ordering of the day, the conversation, the meals, the correspondence, and the social relations have been subordinated to an aesthetic order seeking to achieve a harmonious fusion of social and private life. France proved to be simultaneously rich in ideas and powerful in politics and manifested a desire to improve the social order and to innovate in arts and sciences. As such, the French notion of civilization has successfully combined the taming of nature and material progress with respect for culture, refinement of manners, and humanism.[1]

Like many others, I first became interested in French *political* thought by reading Tocqueville's *De la démocratie en Amérique* and reflecting on the contemporary relevance of his ideas on self-government, individualism, free associations, despotism, equality, and liberty. The singularity of France was a favorite topic of Tocqueville, who traveled to the New World in order to better understand whether democracy could ever be built in his native country. As he argued in *L'Ancien Régime et la Révolution*, France was a country of paradoxes, "capable of everything, but excelling only at war; a lover of chance, of strength, of success, of fame and reputation, more than of true glory; more capable of heroism than of virtue, of genius than of common sense, ready to conceive vast plans rather than to complete great tasks" (Tocqueville 1998, 246). Indeed, what other country has simultaneously given the world the *Declaration of the Rights of Man and of Citizen* and the Terror of 1793? What other country had produced spirits as different as Descartes and Bossuet, Montaigne and Pascal, Rousseau and Constant, Robespierre and Napoléon? In all its incarnations, France emerged as "the most brilliant and dangerous nation of Europe, and the best suited to become by turns an object of admiration, of hatred, of pity, and of terror, but never of indifference" (Tocqueville 1998, 247).

How right he was! If Tocqueville's words seized my imagination, both his style and sociological acumen acted like a spell on me. Thus, I asked myself how it was possible for a young man like him to write such a wonderful book about democracy at such an incredibly early age. After all, Tocqueville was only twenty-six when he visited America and twenty-nine when he completed the first volume of *De la démocratie en Amérique*. This initial interest in Tocqueville's political philosophy eventually prompted me to inquire into his sources and to explore in further detail the intellectual milieu in which he was educated. In so doing, I came across a group of unduly neglected political theorists and politicians called the French Doctrinaires (a misnomer!), who were immensely influential in their epoch—the Bourbon Restoration (1814–30) and the July Monarchy (1830–48)—and whose ideas on a wide range of issues such as representative government, sovereignty, political power, publicity, and democracy significantly shaped the political debates of their age.

This is how I first heard about François Guizot, Pierre Royer-Collard, Charles de Rémusat, Prosper de Barante, Victor de Broglie, and Hercule de Serre.[2] Finding their books has proved to be a demanding task, since many of them have been out of print for a very long time in France and very few of their writings have been translated into English. Moreover, as I began reading Guizot and looked for bibliographical references about the Doctrinaires' works and lives, I noticed that their ideas had often been misinterpreted by the few historians who read their works. For the academic community of political theorists in the English-speaking world, the political thought of the Doctrinaires has remained to this day a terra incognita.[3] This is all the more surprising since their writings offer an excellent starting point for anyone interested in studying the origins of political liberalism and the difficult apprenticeship of liberty in postrevolutionary France.

While it is often tempting to claim that one's particular object of investigation has unduly been neglected before, it is also legitimate to ask whether this is anything more than an elegant form of *captatio benevolentiae* meant to convince one's readers that the subject of investigation is both new and important. In the case of the French Doctrinaires, however, the answer is simple: they have been systematically neglected by political theorists and historians of political thought. As I was discovering their writings, I derived special pleasure from reading books that in many cases had not been checked out for decades. But anyone working on a set of neglected or unconventional subjects or thinkers faces sooner or later a series of predictable questions. Why should we read allegedly second-rate political theorists whose works fall outside of the canon? What if the Doctrinaires were only seeking to justify a certain status quo without being able to see beyond the boundaries of their limited political environment? To what extent were their ideas time-bound? Are they still worth reading today? These are, of course, legitimate questions that ought to be seriously taken into account.

In this book which studies the liberalism of the French Doctrinaires, I shall demonstrate that their writings are still capable of surprising and instructing us in many ways. They help us rethink the nature of the political; invite us to reflect on the complex relation between liberalism, democracy, and parliamentarism; and offer a fascinating case study in political learning and institutional change that can teach us important lessons about success and failure in politics. These nineteenth-century French liberals set out to build the institutional framework of representative government in a conflict-ridden society that lacked a proper culture of accommodation and bargaining. To many of their contemporaries, the Doctrinaires' ideal of a *juste milieu* between Revolution and Reaction seemed either too vague or reactionary. Yet, it was this *juste milieu* that eventually led to the creation of a parliamentary regime that lasted longer than the Revolution and the First and the Second Empire; only the Third and the Fifth Republic lasted longer. After all, it can be argued—though it remains, of course, an open and contested issue—that the relative longevity of the Bourbon Restoration and the July Monarchy owed quite a lot to the Doctrinaires' ability to create the theoretical foundations of a liberalism of government, even if the Orléanist regime also owed its abrupt end to the Doctrinaires' later shortcomings as practical politicians, combined with a series of contingent factors such as Louis-Philippe's lack of vision and the revolutionary wave that swept over the entire Europe in the late 1840s.

In spite of the prominent place that they occupied within the French political tradition, the Doctrinaires often faced a tradition of scorn and distrust, sparked in part by their mixed legacy of success and failure but also by the very nature of their political agenda. Some of their contemporaries were put off by their appearance, above all by their alleged sense of superiority. Yet, the Doctrinaires became unpopular mostly because their image was associated with a centrist model of politics, which proved to be incapable of quenching the thirst for extremes that had often characterized French political life. The Doctrinaires were "trimmers" in politics, and their theories were consequently seen as a strange concoction of various ideas poorly mixed together and seasoned with a dose of rationalism and providentialism. Like any impure amalgam, the Doctrinaires' *juste milieu* was regarded by many as too austere or devoid of substance, but it had a very ambitious goal. It was supposed not only to educate the middle class and to transform it into a genuine political class, but also to lay down the foundations of representative government and to "end" the French Revolution.

If one opens any textbook or encyclopedia of political thought and looks for an entry on the French Doctrinaires, the result will be disappointing: Guizot and his colleagues are never mentioned. Not surprisingly, their writings are never taught in survey courses in modern political theory in the Anglo-American academic world. Moreover, the prestigious (alas, now discontinued) Cambridge series in the history of political thought did not find a place for the French Doctrinaires, even though a number of allegedly minor figures who do not belong to the canon (e.g., Loyseau, Lawson, Priestley, Bakunin, or Morris) were published in this collection. Not surprisingly, no mention of Guizot and the Doctrinaires can be found in the most recent edition of the famous Oxford World Encyclopedia, so generous with other "celebrities" whose names begin with G such as Andrei Gromyko, Germaine Greer, George Gallup, *et j'en passe*.

The few historians and writers who devoted some attention to the Doctrinaires often tended to distort their ideas and seemed to dislike their style and method.[4] The reasons for this *oublieuse proscription*, this strange combination of neglect, indifference, and hostility, are diverse and complex and have to do with politics and individual taste. First, political scientists and historians have a certain Hegelian tendency to worship success. Since the Doctrinaires were (are) not regarded as successful politicians, they were (are) not deemed worthy of scholarly attention. Second, the importance of the period in which the Doctrinaires lived has always been underestimated. It has been seen as an age that narrowed the scope of political theory and did not produce any significant political works deserving of inclusion in the canon (with the exception of Tocque-ville's *De la démocratie en Amérique*).

If many generations of historians relegated the Second Empire to the pur-gatory of history, the Bourbon Restoration (along with the July Monarchy) was always located in the *Inferno*. Furthermore, the French Doctrinaires were usually presented as inhabitants of one of its lowest circles, inhabited by atro-cious spirits worthy of universal derision and sarcasm. In fact, some histori-ans still regard the Doctrinaires as fraudulent counselors and are willing to place them in the eighth circle of Dante's *Inferno*—the infamous *Malebolge!*—along with hypocrites, sowers of scandals and schism, falsifiers, and thieves. Third, the Doctrinaires were regarded as dull, uninspiring apos-tles of the rising bourgeoisie and became the object of the most slanderous jokes. Their opposition to universal suffrage and popular sovereignty gained them the reputation of ultraconservatives hostile to democracy, and Marx went so far as to include Guizot into the infamous alliance of reactionaries, along with the (then) Pope, the Russian Czar, and Metternich.

It must be emphasized, however, that in the nineteenth century, Guizot's historical works were translated into English and were read by the general public. His *Histoire de la civilisation en Europe* became a best-seller sold in thousands of copies throughout Europe. Those who like to browse through secondhand bookstores can still find every now and then elegant leather-bound and nicely illustrated editions of the English translation of Guizot's eight-volume *Histoire de la France racontée à mes petits-enfants*.

Nonetheless, the existence of an original *political* theory in the Doctrinaires' writings has largely gone unnoticed, again with a few exceptions. In the 1920s, C.-H. Pouthas published an important book on Guizot under the Bourbon Restoration and affirmed that Guizot's political theory formed "a genuine sys-tem, a coherent ensemble" (Pouthas 1923a, 325). At about the same time, Or-tega y Gasset promised unexpected intellectual pleasures to those who ven-tured to read the Doctrinaires' works; in his view, the Doctrinaires created one the most admirable political theories of the entire nineteenth century. In Guizot, Ortega recognized a man who plunged into the depths of European his-tory: "It seems incredible that at the beginning of the nineteenth century, a time of rhetoric and confusion, there should have been written such a book as *The History of European Civilization*. Even a man of today can learn from it how liberty and plurality are reciprocal and between them constitute the permanent heart of Europe" (Ortega y Gasset 1962, 58). Ortega applauded the Doctri-naires' seriousness and their strong sense of intellectual responsibility and praised their style, which, in his view, had a classic clarity that contrasted sharply with the coarseness and frivolity of their age.[5]

In 1956, Spanish historian Diez del Corral published a pioneering study, *El liberalismo doctrinario*, in which he analyzed the main features of the liberalism of the French Doctrinaires and demonstrated the impact of their ideas on nineteenth-century Spanish thinkers. Seven years later, English historian Douglas Johnson published a biography of Guizot that provided an excellent account of his political career but downplayed to a certain extent the scope and originality of his political thought. In 1972, the University of Chicago Press published a selection from Guizot's historical writings edited (with an excellent introduction) by Stanley Mellon. The first colloquium on Guizot organized in 1974 in France focused mostly on his works during the July Monarchy but shed little light on his fundamental writings published during the Bourbon Restoration. Larry Siedentop's article "Two Liberal Traditions" (1979) drew attention to the richness of the political thought of the Doctrinaires. Six years later, Pierre Rosanvallon's *Le moment Guizot* highlighted the importance and originality of Guizot's *political* writings. Along with the rediscovery of the political writings of Benjamin Constant, the new interpretation of the French Revolution offered by Furet, and the renewed interest in Tocqueville, Rosanvallon's book signaled a spectacular comeback of political liberalism in France after many decades of neglect.

Thus, the old image of Guizot and his fellow Doctrinaires as unrepentant conservatives has eventually been replaced by a new paradigm that views their elitist liberalism in a more positive way and considers the Doctrinaires themselves as the founding fathers of many institutions of modern France. This issue was addressed by two colloquia[6] on Guizot organized in France in 1987 and 1993 and has recently been reinforced by the new interpretations of the French Doctrinaires offered by Lucien Jaume, Laurent Theis, Gabriel de Broglie, Jacques Billard, Christian Nique, Darío Roldán, Antoine Denis, and Jean-Miguel Pire. Perhaps as a curiosity, it is worth pointing out that the political thought of the French Doctrinaires is well-known in Italy, where there is a strong interest in the study of nineteenth-century French political thought.[7]

The current revival of interest in the Doctrinaires and French liberalism should not come as a surprise, since it was during the first half of the nineteenth century that important new principles of social organization and institutions emerged, along with many literary, artistic, and political movements. Like few others in history, that age itself abounded in great personalities, writers, artists, and philosophers. Not surprisingly, nineteenth-century French political thought displayed a bewildering and refreshing diversity, as illustrated by the writings of prominent thinkers such as Madame de Staël, Constant, Royer-Collard, Guizot, Rémusat, Chateaubriand, Lammenais, and Tocqueville. Although some of the Doctrinaires' works were written in response to immediate historical events that are no longer relevant today, their ideas can still teach us important lessons. They developed original theories of pluralism, civilization, democracy as social condition, sovereignty, political power, publicity, and representative government. Guizot and his friends investigated how clusters of beliefs, values, rules, and social norms operate and change in various historical, social, economic, and cultural contexts. Based on their analysis of the dependence of political institutions on social order, they studied how the transformations in social structure triggered correspondent changes in political institutions. Their rationalism belonged to an older tradition that sought to bridge the gulf between reason and history and saw in the latter the manifestation of reason in its essential forms.

The example of the Doctrinaires also illustrates the emergence of a new type of intellectual that, while remaining fully committed to the principles of rational inquiry, differed from the eighteenth-century *philosophes*. Unlike their predecessors, who formed an opposition of critical and passive spectators, the French Doctrinaires believed in the possibility of a happy marriage between politics and philosophy and sought to develop a "liberalism of government" suitable to the conditions of postrevolutionary France. The vagaries of political life during the Bourbon Restoration gave them the opportunity to experience the responsibility of power but also allowed them to familiarize themselves with the nature of political opposition. As such, the Doctrinaires' political careers were characterized by remarkable achievements, dramatic shifts, and tragic choices. The complex challenges they faced and the fact that they lived in a world in constant flux, beset by chronic social and political turmoil, explain the discontinuities and changes in emphasis that can be found in their writings.

It has been maintained that the Doctrinaires only reflected the spirit and dominant ideas of their epoch without adding anything new. However, how accurate is this claim? This book will demonstrate that Guizot was a prominent thinker whose theories of democracy as social condition, pluralism, civilization, and class struggle had a major influence on Tocqueville, J. S. Mill, and Marx. In order to understand the conceptual and methodological framework of Tocqueville's *De la démocratie en Amérique*, we need to read first Guizot's *Histoire de la civilisation en Europe*, the only book Tocqueville asked a friend to send him from France once he arrived in New York. Mill's ideas on systematic antagonism as the engine of progress and freedom owed a great debt to Guizot's theory of pluralism, and Marx's theory of class struggle was heavily influenced by Guizot's ideas on this topic developed in chapter seven of *Histoire de la civilisation en Europe*.

Furthermore, the richness of the Doctrinaires' political thought can be measured not only by the multifarious subjects they addressed in their writings, but also by the challenges their ideas pose to our traditional ways of thinking about liberalism, conservatism, freedom, parliamentarism, elites, and democracy. For example, those scholars working within the tradition of the Declaration of Independence and the American Constitution will be surprised by the Doctrinaires' refusal to idolize individual rights, as well as by their critique of certain forms of individualism. Those who cherish the principles of classical liberalism will be puzzled by the Doctrinaires' theories of political power and sovereignty that offered an original blend of political analysis, philosophical reflections, and historical investigations.

Arguably, some of their writings were time-bound, occasional pieces influenced by the debates of the epoch in which they lived. As such, the "strange" liberalism of the Doctrinaires owed a lot to the specific characteristics of their political environment, which was one of chronic crisis and constant change. Yet, the positive aspects of political crises should not be dismissed or underestimated, for they are often instrumental in fostering the emergence of new ideas and theories. It should not be forgotten that the most important political writings, from Plato's *Republic* and Augustine's *City of God* to Hobbes's *Leviathan* and Marx's *Communist Manifesto*, were written in times of crises and turmoil, when the institutions were in flux, the meanings of traditional concepts were vague, and the possibilities of political crafting seemed limitless. During those times, as Sheldon Wolin put it, "the political philosopher is not confined to criticism and interpretation; he must reconstruct a shattered world of meanings and their accompanying institutional expressions; he must, in short, fashion a political cosmos out of political chaos" (Wolin 1960, 8). In other words, political crises provide unexpected opportunities for rethinking the meaning of the major political concepts with which we attempt to make sense of the world around us.

This is precisely what the Bourbon Restoration and the legacy of the French Revolution did for the Doctrinaires. They lived, so to speak, under siege, and were constrained to find a middle ground between left-wing radicals who wanted to continue the Revolution and ultraconservatives who sought a return to the Old Regime. Challenged by a whirl of events that sometimes seemed out of their control, Guizot and his friends often felt trapped in a labyrinth of petty incidents and petty passions, too weak to successfully oppose the powerful forces that dominated the social and political life of their time. Nonetheless, they vigorously championed the principles of representative government and attempted to "end" the Revolution by building representative institutions in accord with the new spirit of the age. Their liberalism—I use here the term in the nineteenth-century sense of the word, as a *centrist* doctrine that opposed the revolutionary spirit in all its forms and promoted gradual political reforms[8]—was one of constant tension, a *liberalism under siege*, that had to prudently navigate between the Scylla of Revolution and the Charybdis of Reaction.

Between Archaeology and Renovation

Clarity is the form of courtesy that historians of political thought owe to their readers. Since the language of politics "is obviously not the language of a single disciplined mode of intellectual inquiry" (Pocock 1971, 17), an adequate interpretation of political texts requires textual analysis of a wide range of sources—political and historical writings, memoirs, essays—as well as a close interpretation of the historical context that sheds light on the complex interplay between ideas, institutions, and political practice.

The Doctrinaires' era was a period of great social and economic change. Hence, it is necessary that we carefully examine the environment in which they lived as well as the intellectual and political dialogue they had with their contemporaries. This book will place the Doctrinaires in their historical milieu and compare their works with the writings of prominent conservatives (Maistre, Bonald, Vitrolles, Chateaubriand, Ancillon, and Cortés) and liberals (Tocqueville, Constant, Cousin, Necker, Sieyès, and Madame de Staël). I shall draw upon a wide range of works that include not only the Doctrinaires' political texts, but also their historical writings, memoirs, essays, and correspondence.

The importance of their memoirs can hardly be overemphasized. It is not a mere coincidence that four of the most prominent Doctrinaires—Guizot, Rémusat, Barante, and Broglie—wrote memoirs that are an indispensable source of information for any student of nineteenth-century French politics and society. Their *souvenirs* also shed light on a series of questions that are central to our investigation. How did the Doctrinaires address the challenges posed by the French Revolution and its complex legacy? How did they attempt to reconcile freedom and order? How did they interpret the principles of representative government? How did they explain social and political change? How did they define important concepts such as representation, sovereignty, capacity, publicity, and power? And, last but not least, what kind of process of political learning did they undergo?

The focus of this study is inevitably limited and selective: It explores the Doctrinaires' *political* thought during the *Bourbon Restoration* (1814–30), although occasional references will also be made to their writings published after 1830. This choice is far from arbitrary and is imposed by their biography. If 1814 marked the beginning of the Doctrinaires' political careers, 1830 represented the closure of a significant period in their lives. Until 1830, they were involved in the process of laying down the theoretical foundations of a new "liberalism of government," while after 1830, they were called to govern the country and occupied prominent political positions in government, parliament, and diplomacy. Not surprisingly, the most important political works of the Doctrinaires were published during the Bourbon Restoration (1814–1830). Another study would be needed to give an adequate account of the evolution of their political ideas during the July Monarchy, the First Republic, and the Second Empire. The reader will also note that this book has little to say about Guizot's religious writings.[9] Once again, this choice was dictated by the period chosen as the main object of investigation. Guizot's religious works appeared after 1850 and ought to be part of separate treatment that focuses on Guizot's last two decades. It is true, however, that the implications of his religious views can be detected in his earlier writings published during the Restoration, in particular in regard to the theory of the sovereignty of reason.

The main emphasis of this book will be on the political, philosophical, and historical writings and discourses of François Guizot and Pierre-Paul Royer-Collard. It can be argued that by the time he became a minister under the July Monarchy, Guizot's liberalism had already crystallized into a coherent doctrine to which later writings added little in the way of new theoretical developments. The same conclusion applies to Royer-Collard, whose involvement in the politics of the July Monarchy was almost insignificant compared to his intense participation in the parliamentary debates of the Bourbon Restoration. Pierre Rosanvallon once argued that to offer a comprehensive analysis of Guizot amounts, in fact, to reconstituting a "virtual work"[10] that would attempt to bring together the small pieces of a large puzzle. Hence, this book will seek to reconstitute the Doctrinaires' political philosophy by concentrating on their theories of power, publicity, representative government, democracy, and sovereignty, which rested on a set of more or less similar assumptions and principles. This is not to deny, however, the existence of significant *differences* among the Doctrinaires, who never formed a political party in the proper sense of the word. Too much accustomed to act independently, in their relations among themselves as well as with their opponents, they were sometimes intemperate and miscalculated "the impediments, necessities, and practicable resources of the Government they sincerely wished to establish" (Guizot 1958b, 202).

This book will examine not only major writings such as Guizot's *Histoire de la civilisation en Europe*, *Histoire de la civilisation en France*, *Histoire des origines du gouvernement représentatif en Europe*, *Des moyens de gouvernement et d'opposition*, and Barante's *Des communes et de l'aristocratie*, but also lesser-known yet equally important texts such as Guizot's unfinished treatise *Philosophie politique: de la souveraineté*, Royer-Collard's parliamentary speeches, and Guizot's essays published in *Archives philosophiques, politiques et littéraires* and *Revue française*. A comprehensive study of the Doctrinaires will require, however, a more detailed analysis of Barante's, Rémusat's and Broglie's political writings than the one offered in these pages. For the purposes of this study, I shall use fragments from Barante's recollections in order to comment on various events that occurred during the Restoration. I shall also present some of the arguments of his book, *Des communes et de l'aristocratie*, which had a major impact upon its publication in 1821 (additional remarks will be made about Barante's other important political book, *Questions constitutionnelles*, published in 1849). Yet, anyone interested in Barante's *political* philosophy will have to reconstruct it from a variety of historical and political sources, some of which are beyond the scope of this study. Antoine Denis's recent biography of Barante is an indispensable instrument for anyone interested in Barante's historical and political works, although it does not provide a thorough analysis of his political thought.[11]

Darío Roldán's interpretation of Rémusat's political thought represents the most complete study of Rémusat to date in any language and contains valuable information about Guizot and Royer-Collard.[12] The least known of the Doctrinaires remains Victor de Broglie, whose political works are still waiting for an editor and interpreter. Last but not least, it must be pointed out that the most important works of Rémusat and Broglie were written and published only *after* the end of the Bourbon Restoration. Rémusat's *Politique libérale* appeared as late as 1860 (a new edition was published in 1875), while Broglie's *Vues sur le gouvernement de la France* became known to the public only posthumously in 1870.

It is appropriate to emphasize at the outset that this is *not* meant to be a partisan book, and the reader is politely invited to remember this detail as the story unfolds. The real issue is *not* to defend the Doctrinaires against real or imaginary critics, but to become familiar with their works, to understand them well, and, where appropriate, to point out their relevance to our contemporary debates regarding the foundations of parliamentarism, the mechanisms of institutional change, the role of intellectuals in politics, or the diversity of liberalism (in the nineteenth-century sense of the word). Needless to say, the task is not an easy one, since the Doctrinaires tend to have a negative image in academic circles, when they are not utterly neglected. This is due not only to their unconventional (and misleading) name, but also to the fact that, as defenders of the rising bourgeoisie, they opposed socialism and changed some of their views as political circumstances evolved. I should also mention here the negative impact of secondhand interpretations of the Doctrinaires' works, which often rest upon dubious exegeses or unrepresentative fragments from their writings.

Curiously, the ideological dislike of the Doctrinaires is often hidden behind more neutral doubts about their "originality" when compared to Montesquieu, Tocqueville, or Constant, or behind concerns regarding their alleged opportunism. Oddly enough, there is, however, a certain tendency to gloss over Constant's real opportunism; he became a supporter of Napoléon during the Hundred Days, after having previously vituperated against the emperor's despotism. Ever since I started working on the Doctrinaires, I have noticed a certain tendency among historians to regard any approach that seeks to challenge the clichés about the Doctrinaires as an ideological attempt to defend them, as if one must be a blind partisan of Guizot and his colleagues in order to be interested in reading their works and writing about them. Ideological blinders are not appropriate, however, to historians of political thought. My purpose is to offer a balanced presentation of both the virtues and limitations of the political thought of the Doctrinaires, an account that combines objective assessment, reasonable criticism, and congenial admiration and gives them due credit for their contribution to the development of a "liberalism of government" as well as for their theories of civilization, pluralism, and publicity.[13]

A few methodological observations are also necessary. Exploring the history of political thought should not amount to studying concepts and theories that are detached from our current problems. Pure archaeology must be combined with subtle self-inquiry and critical engagement with ideas that travel across time and space. "No important political theorist," George Armstrong Kelly once claimed (1986, 82), "can be submitted to simple archaeology, but should always serve as the groundwork and guide for renovative effort." Nevertheless, striking a sound balance between archaeology, interpretation, and renovation is a difficult task, because it must simultaneously avoid the pitfalls of pure archaeology and the obsession with "contemporary relevance" that might lead to misinterpretations of past authors and ideas.[14]

The assumption underlying this study is that by retrieving from oblivion the writings of the Doctrinaires, we stand to rediscover an original type of sociologically and historically minded liberalism whose ideas and principles can bring a valuable contribution to contemporary debates on liberalism, democracy, publicity, and power. An adequate form of liberalism needs not only a theory of individual rights and justice, but also a sound basis in sociology and history that examines the ways in which political ideas are embedded in a larger sociological and historical framework that changes over time. Not surprisingly, a growing number of contemporary political theorists have manifested their preference for a liberal political theory more entwined in politics, history, and sociology, and this book responds to this trend by highlighting the complex relations between social order and political institutions.[15]

More importantly, the writings of the Doctrinaires demonstrate what it means to think *politically* and give us a timely opportunity to reflect on the nature of the "political" and its relation to the social. Today, we tend to assume that there must be an abyss between the realm of ideas and the sphere of political action, but the situation was different two centuries ago. To grasp what it means to think *politically* requires that we always begin from the real situation and goals of real political actors, attempt to understand the choices they faced, and grasp the real antinomies defining modern politics. In other words, we must seek to understand what positions the Doctrinaires defended, who were their opponents, and how their contemporaries regarded them. Thus, we may be able to understand why Guizot and his friends often despaired of ever reaching the terra firma and compared themselves to a sailor navigating in the dark, without clear knowledge of the final port and constrained at each moment to make important choices based on his limited knowledge and gut feeling.

A larger point is worth making here. In order to be successful, historians of political thought need a good dose of empathy, a difficult and rare virtue. We must try to reenact within ourselves the states of mind of the Doctrinaires, their hopes and fears; we ought to "enter" into their thought in order to find a sound balance between *our* ideas and *their* concerns. As T. S. Eliot once said, the historical sense involves a perception not only of the "pastness" of the past, but also of its presence. This point deserves to be underscored, since one of the most common mistakes we are prone to make today is to use twentieth-century standards and criteria when studying and judging the ideas of past thinkers. Instead of asking what their original questions were, what motivated them to act the way they did, we often tend to ask them only our *own* questions, by simply reading into their political writings our own concerns and principles. Needless to say, in doing so, all we obtain is an array of more or less distorted answers, which are of little use in deciphering the past and understanding the evolution of political concepts.

Modern appropriations of past ideas are not a priori flawed, but they must not leave out of the picture our predecessors' understanding of their society and history.

One might argue that the story told in these pages is ultimately devoid of scholarly interest because the political project of the French Doctrinaires—a constitutional monarchy based on limited suffrage—lost its legitimacy in 1848 and was replaced by the Second Republic. But constitutional monarchy worked pretty well in England and gave that country a remarkable prosperity and stability that Guizot and his colleagues always admired. Needless to say, in politics success is a highly contested concept whose boundaries cannot be defined in an exact manner that would satisfy all parties. Was the *Declaration of the Rights of Man and of Citizen* "defeated" or discredited by the failure of the French Revolution to establish a stable political regime? The question is certainly rhetorical.

Furthermore, one should not forget that, despite their limitations, the Bourbon Restoration and the July Monarchy gave France more than three decades of peace and freedom that contributed to the political education of the bourgeoisie. The founding of the primary education system in France was the work of Guizot and his team, and the subsequent reforms carried out by Jules Ferry toward the end of the nineteenth century would have never been possible without Guizot's seminal contribution. If the ways in which Guizot and his fellow Doctrinaires justified their ideas might sometimes strike us as unorthodox or unsatisfactory, we must not forget, however, that they were engaged in an unprecedented political adventure, whose end was not always in sight.

The development of the main themes of this book can be followed by reading the ten chapters consecutively, but each chapter can also be read independently. I tried to keep the number of quotations in the main body of the text at a minimum and decided to give passages from the original French text in endnotes.[16] In chapters two and three, I present the group of the French Doctrinaires, comment on the differences between their individual ideas, highlight their method of inquiry, and discuss the main aspects of their *juste milieu* liberalism. Special attention is devoted to examining Guizot's theory of civilization and pluralism, which had a profound impact on both Tocqueville and Mill and can be described as a Whiggish theodicy that sought to justify God's justice in history. Arguably, the greatest contribution of Guizot to the understanding of politics (before Marx) was his insight that internal conflict and class struggle are the most important sources of change and innovation in modern society. I also analyze the Charter of 1814, which was the political bible of all Restoration liberals, and comment on the Doctrinaires' specific view of history and society, which combined insights from different disciplines such as history, law, philosophy, and theology.

Chapter four demonstrates the close intellectual affinity between the Doctrinaires and Tocqueville and explores the Doctrinaires' ideas on democracy as social condition and the French Revolution by drawing on a wide range of writings of Guizot, Royer-Collard, and Rémusat. Since they were often described as staunch opponents of democracy, this chapter seeks to nuance this view by drawing attention to the seminal distinction made by the Doctrinaires between democracy as social condition (*état social*) and political democracy. This distinction allows us to understand their ideas on the larger and more complex issue of "educating," "taming," and "moderating" democracy. Furthermore, I argue that in order to grasp all the nuances of Tocqueville's concepts and ideas, we must first become familiar with his intellectual dialogue with Guizot and Royer-Collard, whose ideas exercised a profound influence on Tocqueville. Guizot's theory of pluralism and civilization had a strong impact on Tocqueville's understanding of the virtues and limitations of democracy as well as on Mill's theory of antagonism and contestation as the engine of liberty and progress. It was not a mere accident that upon his arrival in New York, Tocqueville asked a friend to send him from France Guizot's lectures on the history of civilization in Europe, which were supposed to show him the most appropriate method of analyzing American democracy.

In chapter five, I discuss Guizot's theory of the sovereignty of reason that underpinned the Doctrinaires' theories of political power and representative government. The chapter begins with the examination of Guizot's rejection of the divine right of kings and his critique of Rousseau's theory of sovereignty. Then, it compares Guizot's ideas on sovereignty to those of Constant in order to point out the existence of important similarities between their approaches on this topic that have been overlooked thus far. I end by examining the claim that the Doctrinaires' theory of the sovereignty of reason was ultimately untenable and led in practice to emptying sovereignty of any political significance. I point out the concrete institutional implications of the sovereignty of reason and its relation to the Doctrinaires' theory of representative government and argue that the doctrine of the sovereignty of reason can help us rediscover what Charles Larmore called the heteronomous dimension of democracy.

One of the most striking features of the Doctrinaires' thought was their strong interest in rethinking the nature of the political, which will be examined in chapter six, which explores their theory of political power and the "new means of government" as illustrated by two books that stood out from the mass of political writings that appeared in the early 1820s: Guizot's *Des moyens de gouvernement et d'opposition dans l'état actuel de la France* and Barante's *De l'aristocratie et des communes*, both published in 1821. After presenting the Doctrinaires' views on decentralization and the role of intermediary bodies in protecting liberty, I comment on Guizot's claim that the growing complexity of social, political, and economic life in modern society requires a greater role for the executive power. In the final section, I critically examine the virtues and limitations of the Doctrinaires' elitist liberalism and point out that they, too, had too much confidence in the dignity of power and underestimated the problems created by the combination of unaccountable state power, legislative corruption, and incompetent bureaucracy.

Chapters seven and eight examine the Doctrinaires' theories of representative government, political capacity, rights, and elections. These chapters lay the groundwork for a reconsideration of the relation between parliamentarianism, liberalism, and democracy. The debates that took place during the Restoration, in particular the discussions on imperative mandates and capacity, demonstrate that representative government was originally conceived of as a mixture of both democratic and nondemocratic elements, which were supposed to "tame" and "moderate" democracy. I begin by tracing the evolution of Guizot's and Royer-Collard's ideas on the relation between the legislature and the executive power and comment on the responses they elicited from prominent contemporaries such as Vitrolles and Chateaubriand. Then, I devote special attention to the Doctrinaires' theory of elections as a means of selecting political elites by bringing to power distinguished individuals who have a sufficient amount of wealth and a certain level of education. Finally, I argue that the reexamination of nineteenth-century debates on representation gives us the opportunity to reassess the virtues and limitations of the literature on elites and representative government that has emerged in the past century (Schumpeter, Mosca, Laswell, Sartori, and Dahl).

The Doctrinaires' theory of publicity as the touchstone of representative government and their views on freedom of the press are examined in chapter nine. Along with his fellow Doctrinaires, Guizot defined representation as a dynamic process of collection of all the fragments of reason and knowledge from the bosom of society. In so doing, Guizot and his colleagues assigned an important role to publicity and freedom of the press in the context of the emergence of a new social condition characterized by high social mobility, freedom of inquiry, and civil equality. As such, the Doctrinaires reinforced the liberal definition of parliamentarism as government by discussion and highlighted the centrality of contestation and openness (publicity) to the functioning of representative institutions.

The concluding chapter sums up the findings of the book and places the ideas of the Doctrinaires in the larger context of French political thought and contemporary debates on liberalism. While the Doctrinaires defended the main principles usually associated with nineteenth-century (European) liberalism—opposition to absolute power, freedom of thought and freedom of movement, limited power, publicity, division of powers, civil rights, freedom of the press, freedom of speech, and trial by jury—their liberalism was also unconventional if compared to the ideas of classical liberals. Guizot's doctrine of sovereignty was related to a complex theory of social power and the "new means of government" based on an original understanding of the relation between state and society. I also comment on another striking feature of the Doctrinaires' thought, their sociological and historical imagination, underpinning their analysis of institutions, structures, practices, mores, beliefs, culture, property, and class relations. Then, I briefly compare the Doctrinaires' conception of the political with the views on this topic held by two prominent nineteenth-century English liberals, Jeremy Bentham and James Mill.

Finally, I argue that the foray into the history of nineteenth-century French liberalism invites us to reflect on the uneasy alliance between liberalism and democracy. The retrieval from oblivion of the liberalism of the Doctrinaires heightens our awareness of the internal diversity of liberalism. It also helps us avoid drawing a simplistic contrast between liberalism and conservatism in a way that not only neglects the richness of nineteenth-century liberal thought but also the extent to which certain liberal themes have been advanced by conservative or socialist thinkers. I conclude by pointing out that the study of the French Doctrinaires teaches us valuable lessons about how to "tame," "educate," and "moderate" democracy.

Notes

1. As Ernst Robert Curtius pointed out, French civilization rests upon an original philosophy and a set of shared beliefs that can be summed up as follows: "World history is the history of civilization; civilization is the development of freedom; France is the leader in the march of civilization" (Curtius 1932, 27). Curtius's book on civilization in France offers a comprehensive interpretation of the complex nature of French civilization, including its natural and historical basis, literature, intellectual life, religion, and educational system.

2. A detailed presentation of the Doctrinaires' group can be found in chapter 2.

3. The situation has not significantly changed in the last ten years. In 1997, Penguin published a new edition of Guizot's *History of Civilization in Europe*, but the book is currently out of print. The only available book of Guizot as I write is Liberty Fund's

new edition of Guizot's *History of the Origins of Representative Government in Europe* (Guizot 2002).

4. A few examples are worth pointing out: Faguet 1890, Michel 1896, Bagge 1952, Soltau 1959.

5. For more details, see Ortega y Gasset 1962, 59–61; also 1964, 251–54.

6. The publication of Pierre Rosanvallon's *Le moment Guizot* was followed by two colloquia dedicated to the political thought of Guizot and the French Doctrinaires in 1987 and 1993. The papers presented on those occasions were published in Valensise ed. 1991 and Roldán ed. 1994.

7. For more information on the reception of Guizot's works in Italy, see Griffo 2001.

8. For a detailed discussion of the liberalism of the Doctrinaires, see chapter 10.

9. For a comprehensive study of Guizot's religious views, see Kirschleger 1999.

10. For more details, see Rosanvallon 1985, 31.

11. Antoine Denis's biography of Barante has over a thousand pages and is based on an impressive research.

12. For more details, see Roldán 1999.

13. In this respect, the reader of these pages will encounter a more positive image of the Doctrinaires than the one offered by Jaume 1997a.

14. For a critique of the excessive obsession with contemporary relevance, see Palonen 2002. He defends an "indirect mode of theorizing" that consists of a "*Verfremdungseffekt* which helps us to distance ourselves from thinking in terms of contemporary paradigms, unquestioned conventions, given constellations of alternatives, or indirect value judgments" (Palonen 2002, 102).

15. For more details, see Siedentop 1979, Mansfield 1989, Merquior 1991, Bellamy 1992, Ryan 1993, Katznelson 1994, Gray 1995, Beiner 1996, and Wolin 1996.

16. Where possible, in the main body of the text I used the existing (nineteenth-century) English translations of the Doctrinaires' writings. The reader will note, however, that their quality is unequal. For example, Hazlitt's translation of Guizot's *History of Civilization in Europe* was excellent, while Cole's translation of Guizot's memoirs was mediocre. I also used Scoble's translation of Guizot's history of the origins of representative government. The translations of all fragments from Royer-Collard's, Rémusat's, and Barante's writings as well as from Guizot's articles published in *Archives philosophiques, politiques et littéraires*, and *Revue française* are mine.

~

CHAPTER TWO

The French Doctrinaires and Their Epoch

Il n'appartient qu'aux grands hommes d'avoir des grands défauts.

—La Rochefoucauld

Après la vérité, ce que j'aime mieux c'est la contradiction.

—Guizot

A Golden Age of Political Thought

The two Bourbon Restorations (April 1814–March 1815 and June 1815–July 1830) occupied a unique place in the history of modern France.[1] When Napoléon abdicated on April 6, 1814, it became clear that only the restoration of the Bourbon monarchy would offer a reasonable solution to the crisis of the country. But Louis XVIII could no longer rule the country as his predecessors had governed in the past. A new constitution was needed in order to give legal expression to the profound political and social transformations that had occurred in France since 1789.

Promulgated on June 4, the Charter of 1814 was seen as a much-needed peace treaty concluding a long civil war. Its ideas were regarded as the legitimate heir to the principles of 1789 and marked a clear departure from the theories that had inspired the Terror of 1793–94. The new constitution was "conceded" (octroyé) by Louis XVIII and was supposed to secure the peaceful enjoyment of civil rights and to create a new institutional framework that guaranteed political liberty and reflected the evolution of the new social and political interests. "Judged by itself," wrote Guizot, "notwithstanding its inherent defects and the objections of the opponents, the Charter was a very practicable political implement. Power and liberty found ample scope there for exercise and defense."[2] The Charter did not legitimize, however, the triumph of a philosophical school or political party: "It was, in truth, social liberty, the practical and legalized enjoyment of the rights, equally essential to the active life of the citizens and to the moral dignity of the nation" (Guizot 1858b, 31–2).

The first Restoration abruptly ended when Napoléon returned to France and entered Paris on March 20, 1815. France watched the event stupefied, and the emperor himself remarked: "They have allowed me to come just as they allowed me to go."[3] If vengeance loomed large on Napoléon's mind, he soon realized that he had to make a series of liberal concessions to those who advocated the principles of representative government and constitutional monarchy. In a private conversation, he acknowledged: "The taste for constitutions, debates, and speeches has revived. Authority is questioned."[4] Napoléon abolished censorship of the press and signed an "Additional Act to the Constitutions of the Empire" drafted by his former opponent, Benjamin Constant. The preamble of the act clearly indicated the new spirit that ruled over the country: "The emperor wishes to give to the representative system its full extension, while combining in the highest degree political liberty with the power necessary to secure respect abroad for the independence of the French people and the dignity of the throne."[5] Nonetheless, this marriage of convenience was anything but normal. "It presented a strange spectacle to intelligent men," claimed Guizot, "and one slightly tinged with the ridiculous, on both sides, to see Napoléon and the heads of the Liberal Party arranged against each other, not to quarrel openly, but mutually to persuade, seduce, and control" (Guizot 1858b, 66).

Promulgated on June 1, 1815, with great pomp at the Champ de Mai, the "Additional Act" was received, however, with general reservation and skepticism. The ultraroyalists saw in it a parody of the Charter of 1814, while left-wing radicals had no reasons to be satisfied with it, either, because they distrusted the emperor and feared that his moderate tone would soon be replaced by his old dictatorial habits. In the end, Napoléon could not heal the deep wounds of the country. After a few months of intense secret negotiations, on June 8, 1815, Louis XVIII entered Paris and was warmly welcomed by the population. In a risky attempt to save his life, Napoléon fled Paris and asked for the help of his former enemy, England. The appeal was unsuccessful. Caught prisoner, he was deported later to St. Helena, an island in the Atlantic Ocean, where he died six years later.

The return of Louis XVIII to France marked the beginning of the second Restoration, which lasted fifteen years and ended with the fall of the Bourbon dynasty in July 1830. When Napoléon's reign finally came to an end, France was embarking upon a long apprenticeship of liberty amid an uncertain and highly volatile political situation. All the major political questions raised by the Revolution were still open.[6] Humiliated by the defeat of its armies at Waterloo, France was placed under the supervision of the League of the Holy Alliance, represented by Russia, Austria, and Prussia, which had the right to interfere in the domestic affairs of other European countries. The Allies demanded that France surrender a considerable piece of its territory (depriving it of three key cities: Lille, Metz, and Strasbourg), pay an indemnity of 700 million francs, and accept a five-year military occupation (it was later reduced to three years). As a result of the Treaty of November 1815, France lost no less than 500,000 inhabitants and was required to accommodate foreign troops amounting to 800,000 soldiers who had to be supplied by means of requisitions.[7]

From its very beginning, the Bourbon Restoration became the ground of a fierce battle between the prophets of the past who wanted the restoration of the Old Regime, liberal defenders of the Charter of 1814, and radical revolutionaries who wanted to continue the Revolution. As such, this was not only a period of great change and great hopes but also an age in which the old battle between the Revolution and the Old Regime was waged once again by new political actors: "The parliamentary forms were new and the people were even newer" (Rémusat 1958, 236). As Guizot himself acknowledged, it was a struggle between two parties and forces—the party of the French Revolution and the party representing the old French society—that had little tolerance toward each other and espoused two radically different political visions.[8]

Although the old questions regarding the nature and legacy of the Revolution were reopened, a new set of issues dominated the political agenda of the country: How to create a representative government that would successfully reconcile freedom and order? How to deal with the complex legacy of the Terror? In the (in)famous *Chambre introuvable* (the "Prodigy Chamber") elected in July 1815 and dominated by the *ultras*,[9] those who had previously supported the emperor had to reconcile their views with Napoléon's staunchest opponents, while those who signed Louis XVI's death sentence had to sit next to the ultraroyalists who denounced the Revolution as God's punishment. The wounds of the Terror had not healed yet, and Napoléon's military defeat left in its wake a cumbersome institutional legacy that strengthened the long tradition of administrative centralization. The presence of foreign troops on the French soil only added to these tensions, and there was little consensus on what had to be done. Louis de Bonald grasped the magnitude of this unprecedented social and political change when arguing that "there was a greater change in the political and moral state of France between the beginning of 1814 and the end of 1815 than there had been between 1789 and 1814" (Bonald 1817, 53). His remark highlighted a new phenomenon that became visible during this period, the acceleration of social and political change, whose unprecedented magnitude was also noted by other thinkers such as Guizot and Tocqueville, who often felt that they were carried away by overwhelming forces that individuals could neither defy nor ignore.

The debates on the articles of the electoral law (1817), the law on the reorganization of the army (1818), and the laws of the press (1819) were among the most important moments of the Bourbon Restoration. The electoral law established a *régime censitaire* whose goal was to promote the interests of the rising bourgeoisie and to diminish the political influence of landowners, traditional supporters of the *ultras*.[10] The law on the reorganization of the army was the work of Marshal Gouvion Saint-Cyr; its main goal was to facilitate the rebuilding of the French army along new lines (Saint-Cyr's most important speech in defense of the bill was drafted by Guizot). The provisions of the new law triggered the strong opposition of ultraroyalists who had always regarded the army as the exclusive honor of the aristocracy. The law proposed limited conscription by drawing of lots, provided for the creation of a new legion of veterans (a reserve army after active service of six years), and stipulated new rules of promotion based on seniority that deprived the monarch of the right of choosing the officers, thus undermining the traditional military privileges of the nobles. Finally, the laws of the press passed in May and June 1819 relaxed the previous restrictions on the press and gave the latter the legal guarantees that it had previously lacked.[11]

This complex social and political situation created a unique environment that triggered an exceptional revival of arts and sciences. Nonetheless, until recently it has been assumed that the Restoration did not produce anything important or original at the level of political ideas in France. This view appeared, for example, in Henry Michel's *L'idée de l'état* and Roger Soltau's *French Political Thought in the Nineteenth Century*. Soltau argued that the incompleteness of the Revolution had narrowed the scope of political thought in France and produced contradictory theories of freedom, justice, and political obligation. The legacy of the Revolution "acted as a brake on political progress, as a check on political thought, and disastrously narrowed the field of political speculation" (Soltau 1959, xxix). By contrasting the alleged dullness of postrevolutionary thought with the brilliance of the Enlightenment,

Soltau presented Guizot and his contemporaries as limited and conformist minds, incapable of engaging in deep speculations about the nature of society and political change. In Soltau's view, none of the deep problems about the nature of state and society that preoccupied German or English thinkers could be found in Restoration France.[12]

This interpretation deserves to be challenged and revised. Anyone who takes time to study this period realizes that, far from being a time of intellectual stagnation, the Bourbon Restoration was, in fact, a remarkable golden age of political thought, a laboratory in which were tested many political doctrines: liberalism, the divine right of kings, Jacobinism, liberal Catholicism, Legitimism, positivism, and utilitarianism. The high quality and exceptional range of the articles published in the journals of the epoch, for example *Le Conservateur, Minerve, Tablettes universelles, Le Globe,* or *Archives philosophiques, politiques et littéraires,* impress even the most skeptical readers. Crucial political debates took place during the Restoration on important issues such as the electoral law, the reorganization of the army, freedom of the press, the nature of social change, the relationship between social structure and political order, and the prerequisites of representative government. Civil society also witnessed a revival as demonstrated by the many associations founded during this period. Furthermore, new forms of political and social rationality emerged along with novel ways of understanding the role of political institutions.

Not surprisingly, as Pierre Rosanvallon pointed out, this situation created a powerful cross-fertilization of various currents of thought and political ideas.[13] In a letter to his mentor Royer-Collard, Tocqueville himself called the Restoration a time of "great issues" and "great parties." A new vocabulary and agenda for political theory eventually emerged that found their most refined expression in Tocqueville's masterpiece, *De le démocratie en Amérique.* "During the Revolution," remembered Guizot, "there was contest; under the Empire, silence; but the Restoration introduced liberty into the bosom of silence" (Guizot 1858b, 54). Chateaubriand, who had harsh words for his "mutilated, exhausted, and despicable" generation, noted in his memoirs: "After the dignity of one man [Napoléon], the dignity of men was born again. If despotism was replaced by liberty, . . . if the rights of human nature are no longer unknown, we owe it to the Restoration" (Chateaubriand 1951, 4–5). Compared to the epoch that followed it (the July Monarchy), the Restoration, despite its limitations, appeared as an age of giants.[14]

To be sure, many personalities contributed to the flourishing of political and social thought during this period. The list is long and includes prestigious names such as Madame de Staël, Constant, Royer-Collard, Guizot, Rémusat,

Barante, Tocqueville, Lamennais, Bonald, Maistre, Saint-Simon, Chateaubriand, Cousin, Thierry, Leroux, Maine de Biran, Comte, Montlosier, Montalambert, and Vitrolles. But a cursory examination of almost any journal in the epoch, for example *Le Conservateur*, brings to surface a number of names that are certainly forgotten today but who deserve our admiration for the high quality of their theoretical contributions: Fiévée, Vicomte de Castelbajac, Marquis d'Herbouville, and Vicomte de Suleau. On the contributors list of *Le Globe* we find other important names such as Renouard, Guizard, and Farcy.

The flourishing of talent in arts and sciences was equally breathtaking: Hugo, Lamartine, Vigny, Musset, Stendhal, Balzac, Gauthier, Dumas, Daumier, Mérimée, Sainte-Beuve, Delacroix, Corot, Ingres, David d'Angers, Berlioz, Fresnel, Sadi Carnot, Ampère, Gay-Lussac, Cuvier, Lamarck, Laplace, and Galois.[15] Many important books in philosophy, history, and political thought were published during the Restoration. The list is long and includes Joseph de Maistre's *Les soirées de Saint-Petersbourg*, Madame de Staël's *Considérations sur les principaux événements de la Révolution française*, Victor Cousin's *Fragments philosophiques*, Chateaubriand's *De la monarchie selon la Charte*, and Guizot's *Histoire de la civilisation en Europe*, to name only the most famous titles.

The enthusiasm and energy of the new generation knew no bounds as new outlets opened for its seemingly inexhaustible creative energies. *Revue des deux mondes* attracted the collaboration of the most distinguished French intellectuals and became one of the most prestigious publications of its kind in Europe. Lamennais founded *L'Avenir* and Armand Carrel *Le National*. *Minerve* became the tribune of left-wing liberals such as Constant, while Chateaubriand's *Le Conservateur* disseminated the ideas of the conservative camp. The Doctrinaires founded *Archives philosophiques, politiques et littéraires* and contributed to two other influential journals, *Le Globe* and *Revue française*, which were also widely read abroad. "I count the *Globe*," Goethe confessed to Eckermann, "among the most interesting periodicals, and could not do without it."[16] A regular subscriber to the *Globe* since 1824, Goethe admired the boldness and lucidity of its French contributors, whom he compared favorably with their German colleagues across the Rhine.

The development of intellectual life and the rising standards of living during the Restoration were well documented by the statistics of that period. The population of Paris rose from 622,000 inhabitants in 1811 to 800,000 inhabitants in 1830. More impressive was the growth of the printing industry and the book trade. The number of booksellers in Paris tripled from 1815 to 1845, while the titles published soared from 3,357 in 1815 to 8,272 in

1827. In 1830, 61,000 copies of newspapers were sold every day in Paris. Writers thrived during the Restoration, helped by the growth of the printing industry. Victor Hugo earned 15,000 francs for a new book and 10,000 for reprints.[17] The fast pace of development of French society during this period was not an isolated phenomenon on the European scene. Major political and cultural developments occurred all over Europe, at a point in time when new resources in finance, management, science, and technology became available and the industrial revolution was about to transform the whole world. Social, political, and economic changes were accompanied by new currents in music, literature, painting, and philosophy; politics, literature, history, art, and science were enmeshed, reacting one upon another.

The feeling of living in a time of great change after decades of spiritual desolation was conveyed by many writings and memoirs of that period. Referring to the decade 1815–25, Edgar Quinet wrote: "It was a blind impatience to live, a feverish waiting, a premature aspiration for things to come, a sort of intoxication of reawakened thought, an unappeased thirst of the soul after years in the desert of the Empire."[18] A young Greek traveler to Paris, Mazier de Heaume, noted: "The love of study is the true spirit of the century, this is the dominant passion which has won all walks of life, all classes, all conditions. One could mistake the streets and boulevards for the doors to the Academy."[19] Inspiring professors, such as Guizot, Cousin, and Villemain, who formed a "sacred trinity," captured the imagination of the young generation. Balzac himself was seduced by Cousin's philosophical speculations and Guizot's reflections on the history of civilization. Balzac's sister, Laure Surville, remembered the pathos with which he read those authors, spoke about their ideas, and attended their lectures.[20] Referring to the Restoration, an independent mind and a sharp critic of the bourgeoisie such as Tocqueville confessed: "I had spent the best days of my youth amid a society which seemed to increase in greatness and prosperity as it increased in liberty; I had conceived the idea of a balanced, regulated liberty, held in check by religion, custom, and law; the attractions of this liberty had touched me; it had become the passion of my life" (Tocqueville 1959, 68).

Lamartine summed up the magnitude of these changes in the following words: "The constitutional government by the very novelty of a regime of freedom in a country that had undergone ten years of enforced silence accelerated more than at any other time in our history that expression of ideas."[21] As a result, France was full of restless and impatient young men ready to build a better future. "Scarcely out of absolutism," wrote Nettelheim, "they all plunged into the most difficult of all forms of government, that which demands the greatest wisdom, cleverness, moderation, controlled strength and intelligent compromise; each rushed headlong as passion led him, content with nothing and demanding everything."[22] Seen through Balzac's eyes, the social and political life during the Restoration appeared as "a ceaseless struggle between young and old for power, wealth and success, a battle between "a colorless youth and a senility bedizened in the attempt to look young."[23] There might have been some bitterness and irony in Balzac's words, but his impressions remind us how intensely competitive and unsettled life during the Restoration was. The Doctrinaires' political project emerged as a response to the complex challenges of that period.

Who Were the French Doctrinaires?

The origin of the word *Doctrinaires* has been the object of much speculation. What we know is that in 1816, in the middle of heated parliamentary debates, a right-wing deputy, exasperated by the numerous references to "principles," "theories," and "doctrines" in the speeches of Royer-Collard and his colleagues, contemptuously remarked: "*Voilà bien nos Doctrinaires.*"[24]

Nonetheless, the word was a misnomer, not only because it generated serious misinterpretations which (unfairly) portrayed Guizot and his colleagues as greedy opportunists or shameless hypocrites, but also because there were many differences among them that are not adequately conveyed by the word *Doctrinaires*. If the latter stands for rigidity, mediocrity, opportunism, greed, dullness, and shamelessness, then it can hardly be applied to Royer-Collard, Guizot, and their colleagues, who did not match this profile and were *not* inflexible and dogmatic spirits (at least, not during the Restoration!). Anyone who takes time to carefully read their writings and goes beyond superficial interpretations of their works realizes that Guizot, Royer-Collard, Rémusat, Broglie, and Barante were anything but stubborn, narrow, or rigid minds, as some of their political opponents wryly described them.

Although the Doctrinaires did not form a political party in the proper sense of the word, they held important positions in parliament, administration, and government during the Bourbon Restoration and the July Monarchy. Initially, the group included only a few members: Royer-Collard, Barante, de Serre, Beugnot, Jordan, and Guizot. In spite of its small size—they were once ironically described as *le parti sur le canapé*—the group was already surprisingly diverse. As Victor de Broglie recalled in his memoirs, "M. Royer-Collard possessed authority; M. de Serre eloquence; M. Guizot activity of mind in all matters, lofty views, and a great variety of knowledge; Camille Jordan was the most amiable and the most engaging" (Broglie 1887a, 389). Not surprisingly, their small number gave birth to various jokes and jests that poked fun at the Doctrinaires' alleged sense of superiority and uniqueness. The young Charles de Rémusat composed a poem that was sung in the salons of Paris with outbursts of laughter. "The day before yesterday," he wrote, "someone introduced me to it [the party of the Doctrinaires]; the whole party had assembled, and the thinking faction had found room on one sofa."[25] Quoting an ironic remark, Thureau-Dangin mentioned: "They are four, but sometimes they boast of being only three, because it appears impossible to them that there can be four men of such force in the entire world; and sometimes they claim that they are five, but that is when they wish to frighten their enemies by their number" (Thureau-Dangin 1876, 79). Lord Acton also remarked that the Doctrinaires were "the most intellectual group of statesmen in the country, but like the Peelites in England, they were "leaders without followers,"[26] and it was said of them that they were only four but pretended to be five, to strike terror by their number.

The initial leader of the Doctrinaires was Pierre-Paul Royer-Collard (1763–1845). A philosopher by formation, he taught at the Sorbonne and was influenced by Thomas Reid and the Scottish commonsense philosophy. Like other French liberals, Royer-Collard endorsed the principles of 1789, opposed absolute monarchy (power), and denounced the Terror of 1793–94. During the Bourbon Restoration, he enjoyed an enormous prestige that culminated on the eve of the July Revolution with his election as president of the Chamber of Deputies. In that capacity, he was one of the main authors of the important *Address of the 221* [*deputies*] adopted on March 16, 1830, that affirmed the right of the elected chamber to disagree with the opinion of the king on the nomination of his ministers. Royer-Collard combined a profound respect for authority and liberty with a strong spirit of independence.[27] A Cartesian spirit raised in the Catholic tradition of the Port-Royal, he was a great orator who possessed an unusual eloquence and elegant style that made a lasting impression on his audience. After the Revolution of 1830, he eventually became alienated from the politics of the July Monarchy. His famous parliamentary discourses of 1820s were collected and published posthumously by Prosper de Barante in 1861 (alas, they have not been re-edited to this day!). Royer-Collard's philosophical fragments were first collected by Théodore Jouffroy in 1836; a new edition was published by André Schimberg in 1913. In 1949, the Librairie de Médicis issued a new edition of Royer-Collard's most important speeches on liberty of the press.

"L'homme le plus grave et le plus autorisé de son temps,"[28] Royer-Collard enjoyed a huge popularity among his contemporaries. "As long as constitutional government will survive among us," argued Rémusat, "his discourses will remain its definitive commentary. He promulgated the spirit of our institutions,

wrote the justification of our laws, and founded the philosophy of the Charter" (Rémusat 1847, 350). From 1835 to 1845, Royer-Collard exchanged a series of important letters with Tocqueville, who was then writing the second
volume of De le démocratie en Amérique and was thinking about running for a
seat in the Chamber of Deputies.[29] Tocqueville saw in Royer a mentor and a
great politician whose integrity and vision he strongly admired. "M. Royer-
Collard," Tocqueville once wrote to J. S. Mill, "is a great judge, undoubtedly
the foremost in France today. . . . You recall the role the man played under the
Restoration. He was for a moment master of the country, and he still exercises
great power in the philosophical world" (Tocqueville 1985b, 149). Because
some of Royer-Collard's views changed over time, some critics accused him of
being an opportunist or saw in him nothing more than a "majestic egoist."
Madame de Staël, for example, who shared with Royer-Collard the same passion for liberty, found him to be too arrogant and pedantic. Nonetheless,
Royer was and remained a liberal whose liberal credentials were demonstrated
by his strong defense of pluralism, political liberty, and limited power.[30]

A prominent member of the new generation that came of age during the
early years of the Bourbon Restoration, Charles de Rémusat (1797–1875) became acquainted with the Doctrinaires in the late 1810s.[31] He was attracted
by the high intellectual level of the members of the group, who seemed to be
at home in both the realm of politics and the world of ideas. Rémusat also
admired the Doctrinaires' independence, ambition, and dedication to a noble cause and felt an affinity between his practical rationalism—"I am one of
the most stubborn practical rationalists that I have ever met,"[32] he once
said—and the Doctrinaires' method and style of inquiry.

A scion of a distinguished family, Rémusat was a gifted writer and politician. His numerous articles published in Le Globe from 1824 to 1830 brought
him wide recognition.[33] Rémusat held various ministerial positions during
the July Monarchy and the Third Republic; in March 1840, he became for a
short period minister of interior affairs in the Thiers cabinet. After the fall of
the government, Rémusat joined the opposition and distanced himself from
his former mentor, Guizot, who gradually veered to the right (they would re-
new their friendship a decade later). In 1846, Rémusat was elected a member of the French Academy to replace the late Royer-Collard, who had died
a year before. Neither the Revolution of 1848 nor the Second Empire was to
his taste. After a short exile in Belgium and England, he returned to France
in 1852, determined to fully dedicate his time to writing. Distressed by the
quarrels between the Bourbon and the Orléans families, he abandoned any
hope for the restoration of constitutional monarchy in France and eventually
became a supporter of the Republic. "I have never desired anything else than

the peaceful triumph of the great principles of the French Revolution," he wrote to his electors in 1873. "I hoped that the monarchy would bring it forth; today I put my hopes in the Republic, firmly maintained and wisely organized."[34] Rémusat returned to politics in 1871, when he was appointed minister of foreign affairs during the Third Republic. He passed away on June 6, 1875.

Rémusat was a prolific writer who wrote on an impressive array of literary, social, and political issues such as Bacon; English society, politics, and literature; German philosophy;[35] Abélard; and St. Anselm of Canterbury. He also wrote many influential articles in the prestigious *Revue des deux mondes* on topics as diverse as philosophy and society, the French Revolution, Protestantism, Burke, Tocqueville and Royer-Collard, political pessimism, and centralization in France. Rémusat took a special interest in English literature, politics and philosophy—he once confessed that his dream was to be the French Ambassador in London!—and was the author of *L'Angleterre au XVIIe siècle* (1856) and *Histoire de la philosophie en Angleterre* (1875). Rémusat's major political works were published only after the fall of the July Monarchy. His most significant book, *Politique libérale, ou Fragments pour servir à la defense de la Révolution française* appeared in 1860.[36] Rémusat's writings also include a collection of literary and political studies, *Passé et présent* (1847) and his important *Mémoires de ma vie*, an essential document for any student of nineteenth-century French political thought, posthumously published—alas, in an abbreviated form—by Charles H. Pouthas from 1958 to 1967.[37] While acknowledging the prominent role played by Rémusat in nineteenth-century French political and cultural life, most of his contemporaries were also quick to criticize him for his alleged frivolity. "M. de Rémusat," wrote Balzac, "can be explained by a single word: He is a serious little boy [who] makes efforts to appear grave" (Balzac 1869, 629). In turn, Royer-Collard claimed: "Rémusat is the first of the amateurs in everything."[38] He seemed to have had too many ideas and never managed to write a magnum opus comparable to Tocqueville's *De la démocratie en Amérique*, although they both worked on similar issues.

From his early youth, Prosper de Barante (1782–1866) displayed a strong propensity for historical studies. Real politics, notes his biographer Antoine Denis (2000, 866), did not interest him too much; moreover, he was not as gifted an orator as Guizot or Royer-Collard. Through his family connections, Barante was introduced to the circle of Coppet, where he had the opportunity to meet Madame de Staël in 1805; during the following years, he also became a close friend of Benjamin Constant.[39] In 1806, Barante started a long career in administration. In his first major writing, *De la littérature française au XVIIIe siècle* (1808), Barante criticized Voltaire and Mably for their allegedly biased and dogmatic attitude toward the past, which in his view had prevented them from genuinely understanding the spirit of older forms of government. Seven years later, he published an anonymous work, *Des divers projets de Constitution pour la France* (1814), in which he declared himself a strong supporter of constitutional monarchy and argued that the return of Louis XVIII to the throne of France was the only solution for ending the long social and political crisis of the country.

Elected into the Chamber of Deputies in 1815, Barante was also appointed member of the Conseil d'État and became general director in the Ministry of Finance in 1816. After the fall of the Decazes cabinet in July 1820, Barante was forced to resign from all his political and administrative positions and returned to his old love, Clio. The monumental twelve-volume *Histoire des ducs de Bourgogne* (1824–26) brought him wide recognition as one of the most distinguished representatives of the narrative historical school in France and Europe. At the same time, Barante's *Des communes et de l'aristocratie* (1821) came to be regarded as one of the most powerful and coherent critiques of the political project of the *ultras*. After the July Revolution, he held various diplomatic posts in Turin (1830–35) and St. Petersburg (1835–41).[40] Barante's other major political book, *Questions constitutionnelles*, was published in 1849. It offered in a condensed form a coherent presentation of all the major themes of the Doctrinaires, including the theory of the sovereignty of reason. His eight-volume *Souvenirs du baron de Barante*, published posthumously from 1890 to 1901, provide essential information about nineteenth-century French politics and society.[41] Barante's friends applauded his common sense and talent for conversation, a gift he developed and refined in the Coppet circle. According to Rémusat, Barante was "a Constant who lived well, a Constant with a good heart, conscience, purity, and perfect honesty, . . . the first man in our society whom I first heard calling himself, without any embarrassment or restriction, a liberal" (Rémusat 1958, 311). Nonetheless, as a writer Barante lacked the clarity of Guizot and his style was occasionally prosaic and heavy.

A close friend of Guizot, Achille Charles Leonce Victor, Duc de Broglie (1785–1870) was the scion of a distinguished aristocratic Catholic family. His father, Victor-Claude, Prince de Broglie, had joined the army corps sent to help the United States in 1782 (he was arrested and guillotined during the Terror). In 1814, Victor de Broglie was appointed to a seat in the House of Peers and joined the Doctrinaires' group three years later. He also frequented Madame de Staël's circle and married her daughter, Albertine Ida Gustavine de Staël. A lawyer by profession and a politician of high integrity and character, Victor de Broglie was primarily interested in the details of legislation. His distinguished profile was acknowledged by Rémusat, who once claimed that Royer-Collard and Broglie ought to be regarded as the two most original spirits of the so-called Doctrinaire school.[42] Broglie also had a grave and powerful eloquence that made him one of the most skillful orators of his time.

Like other French liberals, Broglie loved England, which he regarded as his second fatherland. During the July Monarchy, he was appointed president of the Conseil d'État and held important ministerial positions. Like Guizot, Broglie found himself opposed to the spirit and ideas of the Revolution of 1848 and feared that the premature introduction of universal suffrage would jeopardize the future of parliamentary government in France. The last two decades of his life were devoted to philosophical and literary pursuits. In 1855, he was elected member of the prestigious Académie Française and died on February 25, 1870. His most important political writings include the three-volume *Écrits et discours* (1863), *Vues sur le gouvernement de la France* (1870), and his memoirs, which cover the Bourbon Restoration.

A man of aristocratic extraction, Hercule de Serre (1776–1824) held high ministerial positions during the Restoration. A partisan of representative government, he combined a passion for liberty with a "royalism of honor or feeling,"[43] which was manifested by the firmness of his convictions and the intensity of his feelings. As Barante remembered in his memoirs, de Serre's speeches were enlightening and impressive and his thinking was particularly attracted to general ideas.[44] He acquired the image of an accomplished, passionate, and eloquent political orator capable of "seizing" his audience. But de Serre did not have all the qualities required to succeed in politics. He lacked, for example, the spirit of moderation that other Doctrinaires such as Guizot possessed. As Rémusat noted in his memoirs, de Serre's manner of thinking was powerful and simple, always searching for clarity and logic; his style of conversation was interesting, but not distinguished. Today, he is remembered mostly for his seminal contribution to the drafting of the laws of the press adopted by the Chamber of Deputies in 1819. A phrase from one of his parliamentary discourses, "democracy is in full spate," "*la démocratie coule à pleins bords*," became famous in the epoch. He left the Doctrinaires' group in 1820, when he broke with Guizot and Barante and eventually shifted his political allegiances to the right. He died in 1824 at the age of forty-eight.

On the fringes of the Doctrinaires' group we find figures such as Camille Jordan (1771–1821), Jean-Philibert Damiron (1794–1862), Théodore Jouffroy (1796–1842), and Pellegrino Rossi (1787–1848). A practical spirit,

Jordan was driven by a strong ambition to succeed. As Victor de Broglie remembered in his memoirs, "[Jordan's] mind was candid and elevated . . . his deep-seated tenderness of soul was united to a vein of sarcasm, at the same time ingenuous and stinging. . . . The turn of his mind was rather provincial, though refined; his heart was tender and generous; his eloquence real, though laborious and overelaborate."[45] Jordan's parliamentary discourses are difficult to find today. A collection of his speeches was published after his death, accompanied by an *éloge* of Ballanche and a letter of Baron de Gérando.[46] Jordan's analysis of the parliamentary session of 1817, *La Session de 1817, aux habitans de l'Ain et du Rhône*, triggered a long response from Bonald, who criticized Jordan's assessment in a long article published in *Le Conservateur*.

A former member of the Legislative Assembly, Beugnot was imprisoned during the Terror and barely escaped alive. His character was described by Victor de Broglie as follows: "A very upright and enlightened man, his views were broad, simple and sagacious. . . . But he had not altogether escaped the fatal effect of the successive revolutions whose crowning was the imperial government. His spirit was not on a par with his culture; . . . in a word, he belonged more or less to the race of functionaries" (Broglie 1887a, 248–49). In Rémusat's opinion, Beugnot shone in conversation but was a mediocre character, "a cultivated spirit, who understood many things and believed in very little" (Rémusat 1958, 369).

Jouffroy was the author of *Cours de droit naturel* (1834–35) and *Mélanges philosophiques* (1833). In 1823, he published an important essay, "Comment les dogmes finissent?" that became famous in the epoch and was hailed as the creed of a new generation of young philosophers and politicians. A student of Victor Cousin (1792–1867), Jouffroy was interested in the Scottish philosophy of common sense (Reid, Stewart) and believed that philosophy ought to become a genuine scientific discipline based on a careful examination of facts.[47] Finally, Pellegrino Rossi was the first holder of the chair of constitutional law at the Collège de France created by Guizot in 1834. He was author of an influential four-volume *Cours de droit constitutionnel* and *Mélanges d'économie politique, d'histoire et de philosophie* (1857).

"Lord Guizot"

François Guizot was born in Nîmes in 1787 to a Protestant family.[48] After his father was guillotined during the Terror, the whole family moved to Geneva, where the young Guizot received a solid education in history, philosophy, and classical languages under the close supervision of his mother. In 1805, he

François Guizot

left for Paris to study law. Stimulated by the rich cultural Parisian life, Guizot published his first article in 1807. It was the debut of a long and prodigious intellectual career that ended almost seven decades later. In Paris, the young Guizot attended one of the last famous salons, which met in the house of Paul-Albert Stapfer, a former minister of the Swiss Republic. Guizot became interested in Gibbon, whose masterpiece, *The Decline and Fall of the Roman Empire*, he translated into French.

In 1812, Guizot married Pauline de Meulan[49] and became a tenured professor of history at the Sorbonne at the age of twenty-five, a major achievement even by the standards of that romantic age, when talent flourished early. In his inaugural lecture, he expressed his strong belief in the power of the study of history to enlighten and to affect the course of human affairs. Guizot's object of study was not the extinct past, but that history which is capable of teaching various generations timely lessons about the enduring qualities of human nature and whose influence does not expire with a particular age.[50]

Guizot's public career began in 1814 when he accepted a position as secretary general of the Ministry of Interior. While acknowledging Bonaparte's political genius, his profound instincts in ruling, and extraordinary energy, Guizot did not forget that the emperor governed as an absolute ruler who admitted of no limit to his will. The spectacle of a highly atomized society having no common project for the future and no links between its citizens left a strong impression on the young Guizot. He remembered with sadness the image of France toward the end of Napoléon's reign: "There was no moral unity throughout the land, no common thought or passion, notwithstanding the common misfortunes and experience" (Guizot 1858b, 26).

Guizot welcomed the return of the Bourbons to the throne of France in April 1814. During the first years of the Restoration, too young to be eligible to run for a seat in parliament, he held high positions in the Ministry of Justice and the Conseil d'État that gave him unique opportunities to participate in the most important political debates of that age. Guizot's intense involvement in politics contributed to the crystallization of his own political philosophy, whose first sketch appeared in *Du gouvernement représentatif et de l'état actuel de la France* and his comments on his translation of Frederick Ancillon's *De la souveraineté et des formes de gouvernement* (1816). The same year, he also published an *Essai sur l'histoire et sur l'état actuel de l'instruction publique en France*, which contained in condensed form the philosophy of education that underpinned his educational policies in the 1830s.[51]

The years 1817–19 represented a watershed in the history of the Bourbon Restoration. Guizot and his fellow Doctrinaires were instrumental in drafting important bills such as the law on the reorganization of the army, the electoral law of 1817, and the laws of the press of 1819.[52] From July 1817 to December 1818, Guizot edited *Archives philosophiques, politiques et littéraires*, in which he commented on the writings of his contemporaries and discussed various issues ranging from freedom of the press to the meaning of the French Revolution. The assassination of the heir to the throne, the Duke of Berry, in February 1820 suddenly changed the political landscape of the country.

The inauguration of the Villèle ultraroyalist cabinet meant that the "Doctrinaire moment" was over. Guizot's first *saison en enfer*—the second one occurred after the Revolution of 1848—started with his dismissal from the Conseil d'État in 1820 (his friend Barante shared the same fate). Two years later, Guizot's lectures on the origins of representative government were officially suspended (they were published as *Histoire des origines du gouvernement représentatif en Europe* three decades later, in 1851). In his lectures, Guizot attempted to demonstrate the ancient roots of liberty and the legitimacy of representative government by surveying the long evolution of representative institutions in Europe, with special emphasis on England.

In spite of his political troubles, Guizot did not give up his faith in the future of liberal institutions in France.[53] While enjoying the temporary retreat from political life, he continued to write and published four important books that were well received in that epoch: *Du gouvernement de la France* (1820), *Des moyens de gouvernement et d'opposition dans l'état actuel de la France depuis la Restauration et du ministère actuel* (1821), *Des conspirations et de la justice politique* (1821), and *De la peine de mort en matière politique* (1822). He also began working on his treatise *Philosophie politique: de la souveraineté*, an important and dense philosophical text that purported to be a comprehensive treatise of political philosophy. Its first part was devoted to reexamining the concept of sovereignty that had occupied a central place in French political thought.[54] Unfortunately, Guizot never managed to finish the manuscript, which remained for a long time in the Guizot archives at Val-Richer. It was transferred to the Bibliothèque Nationale in Paris in 1975 and was published for the first time by Pierre Rosanvallon in 1985.

Ousted from political arena, Guizot looked for new ways of disseminating his ideas and turned to journalism and history. The most important publications to which he contributed during this period were *Le Globe* and *Revue française*. As always, Guizot's articles covered a wide array of philosophical, literary, historical, and political issues; at the same time, the study of the past remained a high priority for Guizot. Heir to a revolution that had gone astray in its attempt to remake society anew, he sought to reinterpret the lessons of history, convinced that the false knowledge or ignorance of the past amounted to a new form of barbarism. A clear idea led him during these years: that the inadequacies and uncertainties of the present can be compensated and overcome by the concentration upon the general trends of history and society.

Thus, Guizot began collecting a prodigious amount of documents regarding the history of France and England. In 1823, he started the publication of an impressive thirty-volume series entitled *Collection des mémoires relatifs à l'histoire de France, depuis la fondation de la monarchie française jusqu'au XIIIe siècle*; the same year his *Essais sur l'histoire de France* came out. In 1826, Guizot sent to press *Histoire de la révolution en Angleterre, depuis l'avènement de Charles I jusqu'à la restauration de Charles II*, preceded by another set of twenty-five volumes of *Mémoires relatifs à la révolution d'Angleterre*. During this period, Guizot also became involved in many civil and political associations, such as *La Société de la morale chrétienne* and *La Société Aide-toi, le ciel t'aidera*.[55] He contributed to *Le Globe* and founded another important journal, *Revue française*.

Guizot understood better than anyone else the profound needs of the young generation that came of age during the 1820s. He kept in touch with his younger friends and disciples and lifted their spirits when they felt discouraged or estranged from politics. His boundless energy, popularity within the younger generation, and unshaken hope in his mission were duly acknowledged by his contemporaries. In a letter to Barante dated July 1822, the Duchess of Broglie, one of the most astute observers of French political life during the Restoration, praised Guizot for all the aforementioned virtues and recognized his salient political qualities.[56]

Guizot returned to politics in 1827, after the fall of the ultraconservative cabinet led by Villèle. A year later, he resumed his teaching by giving a series of lectures on the history of civilization in Europe and France that drew a large audience.[57] These lectures marked the peak of Guizot's influence and prestige as a teacher and brought him many admirers all over Europe. Goethe applauded the depth and comprehensiveness of Guizot's historical vision, which shed new light on historical events and the links between them. He also had words of praise for the new intellectual movement in France led by Guizot, Villemain, and Cousin who, in his view, marked a real breakthrough in European cultural life. They combined a thorough knowledge of the past with a keen understanding of the spirit of the nineteenth century. "It is," Goethe told Eckermann, "as if now we had reached a garden through roundabout, crooked ways; these men, however, have been bold and free enough to pull down a wall, and put a door, so that we get at once into the broadest walk of the garden."[58] For the young Hippolyte Taine, Guizot's lectures on the history of European civilization were also a true revelation that inspired him to become a professional historian. The influential literary critic Sainte-Beuve warmly praised the three famous professors—Guizot, Villemain, and Cousin—and nostalgically evoked that "beautiful and brilliant period [the late 1820s], the most beautiful of public education in France."[59] Tocqueville also attended Guizot's lectures, took extensive notes, and admired his historical and sociological approach. As an unsigned note published in *Le Globe* in March 1828 claimed, Guizot's greatest talent lay in his exquisite ability to present historical characters that were real, *"des êtres de chair et d'os,"* with familiar faces and voices to which ordinary readers could easily relate.

Initially printed as a series of lectures, Guizot's history of civilization in Europe brought him well-deserved fame as a first-rate historian and philosopher of history and civilization. It was regarded as a great aid to students in forming the habit of reflecting upon the general laws and facts of history. A masterpiece of historical writing, Guizot's lectures—according to one commentator, "the most intelligent general history of Europe ever written" (Siedentop 1997, vii)—introduced a series of topics such as the class struggle, the idea of civilization, the role of antagonism in society, and the distinction between social and political order that were subsequently borrowed and refined by Tocqueville, Marx, and John Stuart Mill. A reviewer writing for the famous *Edinburgh Review* praised Guizot's consistency and comprehensiveness as well as his maturity and absence of haste in the explanation of historical phenomena.

Elected into the Chamber of Deputies in early 1830, Guizot quickly became a leading political figure and a master of parliamentary politics. Like other French liberals, he welcomed the Revolution of 1830[60] and, during the July Monarchy, he assumed various ministerial positions that made him one of the most influential and controversial political figures in France. This period can be divided in two parts.[61] During the first ten years of the July Monarchy, Guizot pursued a politics of resistance that sought to consolidate the achievements of the Restoration, while promoting a set of fundamental reforms such as the reform of primary education. After 1840, Guizot's politics of resistance was gradually replaced by a rigid form of conservatism which opposed further electoral reforms.

After serving as minister of interior affairs, Guizot was appointed minister of public education (1832–37) and became famous as the author of the Great Schools Law of 1833 that created the French national primary school system. In a letter sent to all teachers in July 1833, Guizot argued that no sectarian or party spirit must be allowed to reign in schools and invited all instructors to rise above the fleeting quarrels that agitate society in order to serve its general and long-term interests. Speaking of Guizot's achievement in the field of education, Matthew Arnold wrote: "Everywhere I found Monsieur Guizot's name held in honor for the justice and wisdom of his direction of popular education."[62] Jules Ferry's educational reforms carried out under the Third Republic would never have been possible without the foundations laid down by the Guizot Law of 1833.

Guizot's involvement in foreign policy from the late 1830s to 1848 marked a new phase in his political career. He sought to trigger a new debate on what type of government was suitable to the national interests of France in the new international context of the 1840s.[63] In his view, the vigor and success of constitutional government depended to a great extent on the ability of France to make its own will and power felt again on the international arena. At the same time, Guizot feared that any serious challenge to the settlement of 1815 would jeopardize the cause and future of constitutional government in France. Once again, his position was similar to that held by other French liberals of that period. Although Tocqueville eventually distanced himself from Guizot by the end of the July Monarchy, he expressed more or less the same views when confessing: "I want this monarchy to endure, but I am convinced that it will not last for long if the idea is allowed to grow that we, once a strong nation and great nation, accomplishing great things and making the world's affairs our own, now intervene nowhere, no longer take part in anything, and allow everything to go without us."[64]

In early 1840, Guizot was appointed ambassador to London, but remained in England only until October 1840, when he was recalled to Paris to help Louis-Philippe form a new government.[65] It was the beginning of the Soult-Guizot cabinet, which lasted, with a few changes, until 1848, thus breaking all the records for ministerial longevity in France (there had been fifteen governments between 1830 and 1840). Guizot occupied various positions during that period. He was minister of foreign affairs and chief spokesman of the government in the Chambers and even became for a brief period prime minister of France. As already mentioned, during the 1840s, his political views turned increasingly conservative, especially with regard to the extension of the suffrage and the question of socialism. Haunted by the specter of the Revolution starting again and again, Guizot rejected the extension of the suffrage to those who paid 100 francs in taxes. He also continued to oppose the doctrine of popular sovereignty and was unable to cope with the new social, economic, and political interests of the country at large.

More importantly, the mind-set and philosophy underpinning Guizot's "politics of resistance" fueled his increasing conservatism and took a high toll on his theoretical imagination. It is not a mere coincidence that Guizot produced no single major political work after 1830, with the exception of a few important parliamentary discourses. His long article on democracy in modern society published in *Revue française* in 1837 did not address the main themes raised by Tocqueville's *De la démocratie en Amérique* and only restated ideas that Guizot had already advanced in his previous articles of the 1820s. The Banquet Movement of 1847–48 expressed the growing popular discontent with Guizot's administration. The Revolution of February 1848 ended his political career, and his name became associated with the opposition to social and political reforms. In the streets of Paris, people marched shouting "Down with Guizot!" The former prime minister went to England and from there made one last attempt to return to French politics, but he was defeated at the polls a year later. The book he published in 1849, *De la démocratie en France*, was his political swan song; it had a strong conservative tone and brought no new ideas.

Guizot spent the last quarter of his life meditating on religious issues, writing history, and finishing his memoirs. He became one of the most influential figures in French Protestant circles and was regarded as a key figure in the renewed dialogue between Catholics and Protestants. Far from the political arena, enjoying the serene atmosphere of Val-Richer, the thinker Guizot came back to life, and his prodigious energy manifested itself once again in the realm of ideas. His magisterial *Histoire des origines du gouvernment représentatif en Europe*, based on the lectures given three decades before, was published in 1851. Also worth noting are the essays on George Washington,[66] *Trois générations*, *Histoire de la révolution en Angleterre* (III–IV), *Méditations et études morales*, *Méditations sur l'essence de la religion chrétienne*, *Méditations sur la religion chrétienne dans ses rapports avec l'état actuel des sociétés et des esprits*, and *Mélanges politiques et historiques*. Guizot died in 1874, at the age of eighty-seven.[67]

An Enigmatic Figure

Guizot's *political* thought has remained largely unknown to political theorists in the English-speaking world. To be sure, his name does not appear in any major anthology of political thought and most of his political writings are either not translated into English or out of print. Not a single reference to Guizot's political philosophy can be found, for example, in the prestigious *Blackwell Encyclopedia of Political Thought*, which includes generous entries on other equally unknown figures who do not belong to the canon.

Moreover, the occasional references to Guizot usually portray him as an insignificant political thinker and uncritically attribute to him the dogmatism characteristic of second-rate minds.[68] Even among his fellow countrymen, his image continues to be distorted, in spite of the publication of a few important books on Guizot in the last five years (Rosanvallon's *Le moment Guizot* appeared in 1985). To give only an example, in his most recent book that explores the idea of France, without seriously analyzing any of Guizot's writings, Pierre Birnbaum described Guizot (who was a Protestant!) as "a doctrinaire Catholic and unrepentant conservative who remained hostile to the ideals of democracy and equality to the end" (Birnbaum 2001, 101).

Nonetheless, the public dimness of Guizot's figure and the general lack of interest in his political thought should surprise us, since he was first and foremost a major political figure. This was demonstrated not only by his numerous political writings, but also by his memoirs, letters, historical works, and theological essays. "I have had three lives," Guizot once confessed to a friend, "a literary one, a political one, and a religious one. I hope there has been harmony between them and that this harmony will be clear."[69] Nonetheless, more than a century after his death, Guizot's hope has not been fulfilled. He has often been portrayed as a dull and uninspiring politician, while his political ideas have been misunderstood or distorted by unsympathetic readers, who viewed him as a rigid and extremely austere character, a staunch and uninspiring defender of the bourgeoisie, and an arrogant mind obsessed with power.

Equally important in creating a certain general feeling of uneasiness toward Guizot was his Calvinist background, which gave him the appearance of being estranged from the passions of the French Catholic majority, along with the image of an extremely austere and serious character, a fanatic of duty.[70] According to F. Guguel, the Calvinist tradition exercised a decisive influence on Guizot's mind. Not surprisingly, he was sometimes accused of transposing the categories of morality and religion straight into political and social life.[71] At the same time, other commentators pointed to Guizot's alleged versatility or portrayed him as an excessively cold and shallow man, incapable of deep feelings. Finally, when compared to some of his contemporaries such as Thiers, Tocqueville, or Michelet, his sober style as a historian was found wanting.

Forty years ago, Douglas Johnson summarized the conventional image of Guizot in the following terms. "At best," he wrote, "Guizot is thought of as a superior mediocrity, a dull dog, a man whose importance is only grudgingly admitted; at worst Guizot is thought to typify class oppression and corruption, and by his deliberate perversion of parliamentary institutions and deliberate encouragement of middle-class egoism, he is still considered, le mauvais génie de la bourgeoisie française" (Johnson 1963, 84–85). Guizot's philosophical vision was considered weak, inadequate, and uninspiring, and his eclecticism was seen as the product of weariness and conservatism. According to this view, Guizot seems to have lacked an original political vision and was not a great political thinker: "He was too fond of repeating himself, . . . too oblivious of new developments, and often used terms imprecisely."[72]

Today, Guizot is remembered mostly for a single phrase—*Enrichissez-vous!*—and is viewed as a classic example of an unsuccessful politician who failed to understand the evolution of modern society and the nature of political democracy. Marx saw in Guizot the perfect expression of "reactionary" conservatism and took his opposition to universal suffrage as a proof of his alleged political blindness. The first paragraph of the *Manifesto of the Communist Party* described Guizot as a member of the (in)famous holy alliance of reactionaries who wanted to exorcise the specter of communism. Guizot, who endorsed the order expelling Marx from France, shared this "honor" with the Pope, the Czar, and Metternich. Writing about the Doctrinaires in *The Holy Family*, Marx claimed that Guizot's single aim was to prevent the masses from acquiring political power, thereby suggesting that his political project was entirely reactionary and doomed to end in the recycle bin of history.

Upon closer scrutiny, this conventional image of Guizot stands in urgent need of revision. If the history of political thought could be compared to a stock market sui generis, Guizot is certainly one of the most underrated stocks, in which it would be wise to invest in the future. We love to hear about success stories in politics and tend to look down at those whom we (wrongly or rightly) perceive as "losers." Guizot, for one, is perceived as a classic case of failure. Politicians who eschew radicalism and choose the center are always liable to misinterpretations; Guizot, who took pride in being a member of the "party of the center" in Restoration France, shared this fate. Caught between two political extremes, he was often *la bête noire* of his opponents and enemies. As Protestant, he took pleasure in overtly opposing and challenging the ideas of his contemporaries and courageously maintained that the party of the center to which he belonged defended the good and the truth.[73] After all, he was a southern spirit, quick to react and catch fire, yet capable of disguising this nature under the figure of an austere and cold mind.

Left-wing radicals never forgave Guizot his strong opposition to universal suffrage, whereas ultraconservatives disliked his bourgeois outlook and the eclecticism of his *juste milieu* theory. Furthermore, the very phrase that had made Guizot famous—*Get rich*—was often misinterpreted and misquoted by commentators, who detached it from the larger context that alone can explain its true meaning. The exact quotation was: *"Éclairez-vous, enrichissez-vous, améliorez la condition morale et matérielle de notre France: voilà les vraies innovations."*[74] Viewed in this light, Guizot's true goal becomes clearer: he sought to improve *both* the material and the moral condition of the country by building the conditions for the orderly, peaceful, and honorable domination of the middle class.

As political thinker, Guizot is difficult to place on our conceptual map, because our conventional black-and-white categories are of little help when applied to such a complex and paradoxical figure. He loved struggle and contestation and was not afraid of contradicting himself. "After truth," he once said, "the thing I love most is contradiction." He began his political career as a liberal and ended as a conservative. An opponent of the sovereignty of the people, Guizot founded the system of primary education in France that created the necessary conditions for the general instruction of the masses. His writings on the history of civilization and representative government might have had occasional Burkean tones when praising ordered liberty, yet his sensibility was *not* Burkean. Born bourgeois and Protestant, he never forgot the debt he owed to the principles and ideas of 1789: political freedom, liberty of conscience, equality before the law, and the rule of law. "I had no previous tie, no personal motive to connect me with the Restoration," wrote Guizot, "I sprang from those who had been raised up by the impulse of 1789, and were little disposed to fall back again" (Guizot 1858b, 27). In his memoirs, he described himself as a liberal and antirevolutionary spirit, fully committed to the principles of the new French society, yet at the same time animated by a profound and affectionate respect for the old France, its traditions, and religion.[75]

Despite the popularity of those views which saw in Guizot nothing but a shallow and versatile mind, the facts seem to tell a rather *different* story, one that should invite us to read his writings (rather than satisfy ourselves with biased commentaries and interpretations) and to critically reevaluate the misconceptions surrounding Guizot's political vision. A man who was credited by his contemporaries with so many sins could hardly have been a mediocre mind.[76] An attentive reading of his works would persuade even the most skeptic interpreters that Guizot was anything but a second-rate character; he deserves to be seen as one of the founding fathers of the liberal state in France. In spite of its inherent limitations, Guizot's contribution to the building of parliamentary government was arguably more solid than that of Tocqueville, Constant, or Thiers. An article published in the prestigious *Edinburgh Review* acknowledged that Guizot had no equal in giving "the authority of a minister to the principles of a philosopher." In him more than anyone else, "the speculative genius of the one was united to the practical authority of the other."[77]

More importantly, Guizot's political philosophy did *not* remain a "virtual work," to borrow Rosanvallon's phrase (the latter is more appropriate to Royer-Collard and Barante). His political thought was articulated in substantial historical and political writings such as *Histoire de la civilisation en Eu-*

rope, Histoire des origines du gouvernement représentatif, Du gouvernement de la France, Des moyens de gouvernement et d'opposition, Philosophie politique, his memoirs, the article "Elections," and the numerous essays published in *Archives philosophiques, politiques et littéraires* and *Revue française.*

In a country where there had traditionally been a sharp divide between politics and public morality, Guizot was, to quote his biographer Douglas Johnson, "one of the examples of a statesman untouched by scandal" (Johnson 1963, 441), even when his personality was the subject of intense controversy. It should not be forgotten that Guizot refused to accept the aristocratic title offered by Queen Isabel of Spain and was never a very rich man. He always acted upon his belief that in order to be successful in politics, one must acquire from the earliest youth "habits of laborious and patient application, a certain strength of character."[78] In his view, the true politician must avoid the indolence of soul, the effeminate weakness, and the fickleness of mind that usually characterize opportunist politicians. The publication of Guizot's private correspondence shows him not only as a man of duty, but also as a warm and compassionate soul, capable of deep feelings toward his family and friends.

Moreover, Guizot's scientific honesty and seriousness left a strong impression on his contemporaries. Sainte-Beuve praised the unusual breadth of scholarship of Guizot: "this astonishing man about whom one could say so many things."[79] An omnivorous and quick reader given to meditative withdrawal, Guizot was an encyclopedic mind, steeped not only in history and political theory, but also in philosophy, theology, and literature. As a historian, he wrote about subjects as diverse as the origins of representative government, the history of European civilization, decentralization, Shakespeare, Cromwell and the English Revolution, Montaigne, Gibbon, and George Washington. As a political philosopher, he addressed topics as diverse as the nature of representation and sovereignty, the origins of political power, constitutionalism, publicity, and democracy. Guizot was also an outstanding orator, versed in the art of rhetoric and fully capable of dominating large audiences.

Many of Guizot's contemporaries acknowledged his prominent intellectual and political profile, even when their recognition went hand in hand with a strange combination of envy, uneasiness, and resentment. La Fayette, for example, confessed: "Guizot is more monarchical and less democratic than me, but he loves liberty. He knows a lot, writes and speaks with great talent, his character is of high quality and dignity."[80] The Duchess of Broglie admired Guizot's sagacity and depth: "He seems to live more in thought than in anything else."[81] Tocqueville found Guizot's lectures "prodigious in ideas" and read them with fervor before going to America. Edouard Laboulaye, the editor of Constant's constitutional writings, also remarked the difficult task assumed by the Doctrinaires who attempted to steer a *juste milieu* between Revolution and Reaction. In Laboulaye's opinion there was a certain system in the Doctrinaires' writings, which displayed an excessive confidence in the wisdom of executive power.[82]

Across the Channel, John Stuart Mill, who followed closely the politics of the July Monarchy, considered Guizot as "the man to whom perhaps more than to any other it is owing that Europe is now at peace," and praised his historical speculations which "may be ranked with the most valuable contributions yet made to universal history" (Mill 1985, 259). He added: "I have dinned into people's ears that Guizot is a great thinker and writer, till they are, though slowly, beginning to read him."[83] At some point, there were rumors that Guizot, who was regarded as a true Victorian spirit, might take up a chair in history at Cambridge.[84] Goethe, too, admired the depth and comprehensiveness of Guizot's historical vision. Of all French historians and philosophers of his time, he confessed that Guizot was the closest to his heart. "I am going on with his lectures which continue to be excellent; I know no historian more profound or more penetrating. Things of which no one thinks have the greatest significance in his eyes, as sources of important events" (Eckermann 1892, 389).

Furthermore, as Luis Diez del Corral demonstrated, the so-called *liberalismo doctrinario* was not a purely French phenomenon. In Spain, the writings of the French Doctrinaires were well-known and appreciated during the first half of the nineteenth century.[85] Writing from Paris in the 1830s, Donoso Cortés had high words of praise for Guizot, who in his view succeeded in channeling the desire for liberty into new institutions and consolidating liberty in the public sphere.[86] Cortés's *Lecciones de Derecho Político* show the strong influence of Guizot's theory of the sovereignty of reason and representative government on his Spanish disciple. A forthcoming book of Dutch historian Jan Drentje argues that the impact of the Doctrinaires' ideas was also felt in nineteenth-century Netherlands. Johan Rudolf Thorbecke, a professor of law in Leiden and one of the reformers of the Dutch constitution of 1848, was influenced by Guizot's ideas to which he added a touch of German Idealism.[87]

Last but not least, Guizot's ideas and books were also well-known in Central and Eastern Europe. In his major political treatise *The Dominant Ideas of the Nineteenth Century and Their Impact on the State* (written in German and completed in 1854), József Eötvös, one of the greatest reformist minds in nineteenth-century Hungary, devoted an entire twenty-page section to discussing Guizot's political ideas. "The minister of Louis-Philippe," wrote Eötvös, "saw more clearly than others what dangers encircle the peaceful development of the people if the majority in a single city can at every moment control the destiny of a whole State" (Eötvös 1996, 209–10). Guizot took on the obligation to defend the gains of the French Revolution against its enemies and held this position with "a manly candor" and "did everything he could, with rare steadfastness and self-denial, to see that the middle classes should remain in possession of the power they had at last come to enjoy" (Eötvös 1996, 212–13).

Between Pragmatism and Opportunism

The pragmatism of Guizot and his fellow Doctrinaires met with the skepticism of their contemporaries, who regarded their eclectic *juste milieu* as either too radical or too conservative. "My friends and I," wrote Guizot, "have often been represented as deep plotters, greedy for office, eager and shrewd in pushing our fortunes through every opening, and more intent on our own ascendancy than on the fate or wishes of the country, a vulgar and senseless estimate, both of human nature and of our contemporary history" (Guizot 1858b, 192–93). How accurate and fair was this image, after all?

The best way to answer this question is by examining the challenges faced by the Doctrinaires and placing their ideas in their original historical context. In his memoirs, Guizot wrote: "There was more than a new government to establish. It was necessary that a free government should be imbued with vigor [in order to] escape from that routine of alternate violence and falsehood, to place political power in the region within which the conservative interests of social order naturally predominate with enlightened independence."[88] Yet, the Doctrinaires' eclecticism and pragmatism made them vulnerable to the charge of opportunism or indecisiveness. Metternich, for example, believed that the center offers an untenable and unstable political platform that requires a good dose of flexibility in order to defend itself against the extremes. In turn, Bonald denounced the illusion of those who seek a *juste milieu* between opposed beliefs; sooner or later, their political belief will be seen by their opponents as weak and inadequate.[89]

Spanish historian Luis Diez del Corral once claimed that to be a Doctrinaire does not presuppose a rigid adherence to a certain set of principles and norms as the phrase might suggest, but a lack thereof. How can this paradox be explained? Were the Doctrinaires mere opportunists whose ideas and principles incessantly changed to suit their narrow personal interests? Their efforts to adjust themselves to shifting circumstances ought to be examined in light of the challenges that forced them to find solutions to urgent political problems in a social and political milieu marked by chronic instability and ideological intransigence. If one takes the word "*doctrine*" to mean a set of logically coherent and consistent principles, values, and rules to which one must strictly adhere regardless of circumstances, then the Doctrinaires, in Diez del Corral's opinion, owed their name precisely to the fact they did not have such a doctrine and were forced to invent one at almost every step.[90]

Needless to say, this is a controversial claim that must be critically reexamined, since a superficial reader of Diez del Corral, who otherwise was a sympathetic reader of the Doctrinaires, might easily misinterpret his words and ascribe to Guizot and his friends views which they never held, thus making them the prototype of opportunism. Commentators such as Michel, Soltau, and Bagge succumbed to this temptation. Guizot's opportunism, argued Soltau, manifested itself in two ways: "First in his use of power when in office, and his turning [his] back on positions adopted while in opposition; and secondly in the ingenuity by which he uses political philosophy to justify the ascendancy of a class" (Soltau 1959, 44). In Michel's view, the only principle followed by the Doctrinaires was to justify a certain state of affairs without ever challenging its legitimacy. They lacked any "positive" doctrine and were forced to improvise or advance incoherent, half-baked solutions that were bound to fail.[91] This negative view of the Doctrinaires was echoed by another French scholar, Dominique Bagge, who claimed that there had been no such thing as a "*doctrine doctrinaire.*" For Bagge, the Doctrinaires were nothing else than "sad heralds of circumstantial necessities" (Bagge 1952, 143), and their writings offer nothing else than a collection of disjointed and inconsistent ideas—that have little relevance to us today.[92]

It must be pointed out that there is a clear difference between Diez del Corral's argument and the strong accusations against the Doctrinaires advanced by Michel, Soltau, and Bagge. In fact, the late Spanish historian *denied* that the Doctrinaires were mere opportunists who adjusted to circumstances and changed their views solely for the purpose of their self-advancement.[93] In El liberalismo doctrinario, Diez del Corral demonstrated that the Doctrinaires developed a rational and systematic way of doing and thinking about politics based on a careful observation of the new social condition. He went to great length to show how they went about replacing the "politics of passion" carried out by radicals on both the left and the right with a politics of moderation, which aimed at creating and consolidating new institutions and laws without resorting to revolutionary means.[94]

While the issue of consistency in political life is not negligible, it is important to acknowledge that politics is a domain in which change and fluctuation are the rule rather than the exception. Political life requires a certain mixture of passion, restraint, ruthlessness, generosity, and vision that are not easily reconcilable with the desire to preserve one's purity and independence at all costs. After all, the successful politician ought to be a wise *trimmer,* who must not fear contradictions, often a sign of life and vitality. Moreover, political life thrives on ambivalence and constant approximations that are different from the axioms of natural sciences. Finding a synthesis between freedom and order always requires a series of difficult transactions.

The Doctrinaires brought an important contribution to the building of representative government in Restoration France. The significance of their enterprise consists in the seriousness with which they upheld a certain political and moral vision in a period of great uncertainty, confusion, and turmoil. If the Doctrinaires' ideas continue to speak to us today, it is precisely because of the modern conception of power that can be found in their political and historical writings. This point has recently been emphasized by Pierre Manent and Claude Lefort, who claimed that Guizot was among those who understood best the essence of government in modern society.[95] In the footsteps of Montesquieu, the Doctrinaires developed a systematic sociological approach to political theory, which relied upon the assumption that political questions cannot (and should not) be divorced from questions about social structure. But, unlike Montesquieu, their main concern was the government of society, which led them to develop a complex mode of argument that showed how various concepts such as democracy, freedom, and rights are related to specific social conditions characterized by unique constellations of mores, traditions, customs, and social and economic relations. As such, the Doctrinaires were among the first to describe the characteristics of democracy as social condition (*état social*), a theme whose full implications were spelled out a decade later by Tocqueville in *De la démocratie en Amérique*.

The next chapters of this book will explore in detail the Doctrinaires' contribution to modern political thought, most notably their theories of civilization, democracy, political power, sovereignty of reason, publicity, political capacity, and representative government. Let us begin by examining their political project during the Bourbon Restoration.

Notes

1. For a general view on the two Bourbon Restorations, see Vaulabelle 1855 and 1856, Gorce 1926 and 1928, Sauvigny 1966, Furet 1995, Jardin and Tudesq 1983, Charléty 1939, Lucas-Dubreton 1929, Hatin 1861. Important information about the

political thought during this period can be found in Rosanvallon 1985, Jaume 1997a, Bagge 1952, Jardin 1985, Girard 1985, and Roldán 1999.

2. Guizot 1858b, 36. For an analysis of the Charter of 1814, see chapters 3 and 7.

3. Napoléon as quoted by Guizot 1882, 165.

4. The detail appears in Lucas-Dubreton 1929, 13. Eugène Hatin gives the following account of a private conversation between Constant and Napoléon: "J'ai voulu l'empire du monde [said Napoléon], et pour me l'assurer un pouvoir sans bornes m'était nécessaire. Pour gouverner la France seule, il se peut qu'une Constitution vaille mieux. . . . Apportez-moi vos idées: des discussions publiques, des elections libres, des ministres responsables, *la liberté de la presse*, je veux tout cela . . . *la liberté de la presse surtout: l'étouffer est absurde*; je suis convaincu sur cet article" (Hatin 1861, 132; emphasis added).

5. See Guizot 1882, 197.

6. This feeling of uncertainty and powerlessness was conveyed by Charles de Rémusat, who recalled a conversation of his parents: "Et nous voilà, après dix-huit ans, encore au même point, ne pouvant voir clair dans l'avenir, ni nous confier au present. Tout est encore moins fini qu'au jour où notre enfant commençait à vivre" (Rémusat 1958, 202–3). Also see Rémusat 1958, 233–39.

7. For more details, see Lucas-Dubreton 1929, 1–15.

8. Guizot 1869, ix–x; xii–xiii.

9. For more details on the *Chambre introuvable*, see Barante 1892, 216–21, 236–55; Vaulabelle 1855, 175–212; Lucas-Dubreton 1929, 16–18; Gorce, 1926, 59–76; Charléty 1939, 89–107. In an article published in *Le Conservateur* in 1819, Bonald argued that the main reason for the unpopularity of the "Prodigy Chamber" was its hostility to the Revolution: "Ce n'est pas pour avoir banni quelques révolutionnaires, que la Chambre de 1815 est poursuivie par la calomnie, mais pour avoir arrêté la revolution, et l'avoir meme forcé de rétrograder" (Bonald 1819a, 158).

10. For more details on this issue, see Vaulabelle 1855, 392–401; Gorce 1926, 128–34. I discuss the electoral law of 1817 in chapter 8. For a statement that sums up the ultraroyalist position on elections, see the article published by Crignon d'Auzouer in the first issue of *Le Conservateur* (Crignon d'Auzouer 1818, 49–60).

11. For more details on the Gouvion Saint-Cyr law, see Vaulabelle 1855, 453–69; Furet 1995, 290. An anonymous conservative critique of the Saint-Cyr law and its effects was published in *Le Conservateur*, no. 5, 1819, pp. 399–411. For more details on the laws of the press of 1819, see chapter 9. Also see Hatin 1861, 315–36, and Avenel 1900, 254–65.

12. For more details, see Soltau 1959, 6–9. An English translation of Berthier de Sauvigny's history of the Bourbon Restoration was published in 1966.

13. See Rosanvallon 1985, 11–25, and Roldán 1999, 69–77.

14. For a detailed analysis of Tocqueville's important debt to the French Doctrinaires, see Diez del Corral 1989; Craiutu 1999; Manent 1991; and Siedentop 1994, 20–40. I discuss this issue in detail in chapter 4.

15. For more information, see Sauvigny 1966, 328–62.

16. Here is what Goethe actually said about *Le Globe*: "Ich zähle den *Globe* zu den interessantesten Zeitschriften und könnten ihn nich entbehren. . . . Was aber die Herren vom Globe für Menschen sind, wie die mit jedem Tage größer, bedeutender werden und alle wie von einem Sinne durchdrungen sind, davon hat man kaum einen Begriff. In Deutschland wäre ein solches Blatt rein unmöglich. Wir sind lauter Partikuliers; an Übereinstimmung ist nicht zu denken; jeder hat die Meinungen seiner Provinz, seiner Stadt, ja seines eigenen Individuums, und wir können noch lange warten, bis wir zu einer Art von allgemeiner Durchbildung kommen" (Eckermann 1949, 225). A detailed presentation of the *Globe*, its contributors, and philosophy can be found in Goblot 1995; also see Hatin 1861, 495–508; Avenel 1900, 292–94; Spitzer 1987, 97–128; Roldán 1999, 52–54.

17. I borrow these figures from Sauvigny 1966, 328–62, and P. Johnson 1991, 879–82. Hatin's book (1861) highlighted the richness of the press during the Restoration.

18. Quinet as quoted by Sauvigny 1966, 328–29.

19. De Heaume as quoted by P. Johnson 1991, 882.

20. Balzac's sister remembered: "Je me souviens encore de l'enthousiasme que lui causaient les éloquentes improvisations de Villemain, de Guizot, de Cousin. C'était la tête en feu qu'il nous les redisait pour nous associer à ses joies et nous les faire comprendre. Il courait dans les bibliothèques publiques afin de mieux profiter des enseignements de ses illustres professeurs" (Balzac as quoted in Guyon 1969, 35).

21. Lamartine as quoted in P. Johnson 1991, 141.

22. Nettelheim as quoted in Soltau 1959, 7.

23. Balzac as quoted in P. Johnson 1991, 967–68.

24. The detail is reported by Chevalier 1964, 13. A different story can be found in Rémusat: "On sait que l'ordre des Doctrinaires était pour l'instruction populaire ce qu'était l'Oratoire pour l'instruction secondaire. Un père Collard, grand-oncle de M. Royer-Collard, . . . était doctrinaire. . . . C'est par un souvenir vague de cette circonstance ou par un rapprochement fortuit que ce nom de doctrinaire lui fut donné, ainsi qu'à ses amis. Mail il fut plutôt entendu comme equivalent de *doctrinal,* adjective qui pouvait être regardé comme une qualification de leur *ton* et de leur *esprit*" (Rémusat 1958, 332; emphasis added). Rosanvallon offers an excellent overview of the Doctrinaires' writings (Rosanvallon 1985, 389–93). For more details on the initial group of the Doctrinaires as well as the temperamental differences between them, see Pouthas 1923a, 167–72; Gorce 1926, 144–59. Gorce commented on the diversity within the Doctrinaires' group as follows: "Comment réunir sous des traits communs des hommes si dissemblables et qui n'ont de tout à fait pareil que l'intensité de leurs amours-propres? Ce qui achève de déconcerter, c'est que parfois chez les doctrinaires, le philosophe, l'homme de lettres, l'historien se jette à la traverse du politique" (Gorce 1926, 152).

25. Here is the entire poem composed by Rémusat: "Aujourd'hui tout le monde pense. / En y pensant je me suis dit: / D'un parti chacun est en France; / Il m'en faut un grand ou petit / Or, il en est un fort paisible / Qui daigne m'ouvrir sa maison: /

C'est un parti peu visible / et presque un être de raison. / Avant-hier quelqu'un m'y présente / Le parti s'était attroupé; / Toute la faction pensante / Se tenait sur un canapé. / Nos majestés sont decidées, / Dit le doyen, je vous admets; / Sous la garde de nos idées, / Venez placer vos intérêts; / Mais, en suivant notre bannière, / Souvenez-vous de parler haut; / Répandez partout la lumière, / Sans être plus clair qu'il ne faut. / Faites de la métaphysique; / Tous les matins exactement; / Abstenez-vous de la pratique / Toute l'année étroitement; / Doutez fort de la théorie, / Afin de vivre longuement; / De notre abstraite confrérie, / C'est le triple commandement. / Notre parti, qui croît à l'ombre / A besoin d'un public discret; / Vous jouerez le rôle du nombre; / Placez-vous sur ce tabouret. / Monsieur, quand donc espérez-vous / Que notre règne nous arrive? / Monsieur, l'avenir est à nous. / Mais il n'y paraît pas encore. / N'importe le temps n'est pas mûr; / Mais il viendra. Quand? Je l'ignore, / Et voilà pour quoi j'en suis sûr" (Rémusat as quoted in Broglie 1887a, 391–92).

26. See Acton 2001, 306.

27. This is how Rémusat described Royer-Collard in his discourse of reception at L'Académie française in January 1847: "Nous comprendrions mieux en lui ce frappant mélange d'indépendance et de discipline, de témérité et de retenue, de respect pour l'ordre et de mépris pour toute autorité qui n'était pas la raison. . . . L'esprit du temps passé devait s'unir en lui à l'esprit moderne" (Rémusat 1847, 326). On Royer-Collard, also see Philippe 1857, Spuller 1895, and Langeron 1956. Pierre de la Gorce argued: "Nul ne fut illogique avec plus de dogmatisme et indécis avec plus d'apparente certitude. Nul n'excella mieux à soutenir d'une armature forte et magnifique, des idées fragiles" (Gorce 1926, 145).

28. The phrase belongs to Sainte-Beuve (quoted in Lamberti 1983, 168).

29. Their letters, chock-full of interesting insights on the politics of the July Monarchy, were published in Tocqueville 1970.

30. For a critical view of Royer-Collard, see Pouthas 1923a, 169; Faguet 1890; and Bagge 1952, 103–26. A different opinion can be found in Ortega y Gasset, who praised Royer-Collard's parliamentary speeches as "the last example of the finest Cartesian style" (1962, 61). The phrase "majestic egoist" belongs to Madame Guizot (as quoted in Brush 1974, 29). The detail about Madame de Staël's opinion of Royer-Collard can be found in Broglie 1887a, 361. For an interpretation of Royer-Collard as a precursor of modern pluralism, see Laski 1919, 303–5. A detailed interpretation of Royer-Collard's political thought can be found in Nesmes-Desmarets 1908 and G. Rémond 1979.

31. On Rémusat's life, see Roldán 1999, 11–30, and Gilberte de Coral-Rémusat's introduction to Rémusat 1958, xiii–xxvi.

32. Rémusat 1958, 366–67. Also see the following confession: "C'est donc à Guizot et en général aux doctrinaires que je m'attachais. . . . Là, je trouvais des communications intellectuelles libres et profitables, des esprits distingués, une certaine propaganda d'idées, une association formée par la communauté des principes. Parler et écrire était pour eux tous le grand moyen d'action. Ils se proposaient un but élevé et général, et leur ambition, si vive qu'on la supposât, avait cet element nécessaire de

désinteressement, une cause à servir. . . . La tentation était forte et je m'y adonnai" (Rémusat 1958, 366).

33. A comprehensive list of Rémusat's articles in *Le Globe* (1824–30) can be found in Roldán 1999. At the beginning, Rémusat published mostly literary articles; as the journal became more political in 1828, Rémusat's contributions included more political articles. On the profile of *Le Globe*, also see Goblot 1995.

34. This letter is quoted in Roldán 1999, 27.

35. Upon reading Rémusat's *De la philosophie allemande*, Victor Cousin exclaimed: "C'est un esprit essentiellement français, il va jusqu'à donner de la clarté aux Allemands" (Rémusat 1958, xix).

36. For a detailed analysis of Rémusat's political thought, see Roldán 1999, 69–245.

37. The five-volume edition of Rémusat's memoirs published by Pouthas in 1958 is incomplete. A comprehensive list of Rémusat's writings can be found in Roldán 1999, 317–28.

38. For more details, see J. Simon 1885, 319–20.

39. On the relations between Barante and de Staël, see Laurent 1972.

40. On this issue, see Denis 2000, 445–655.

41. On the historical works of Barante, see Reizov 1962, 190–267. For a general interpretation of Barante's writings, see Denis 2000, the only biography of Barante to date. Denis's book is full of details about Barante's life and political career and draws on many materials that have not been available before.

42. See Rémusat 1958, 368.

43. The portrait of Hercule de Serre is inspired from Rémusat 1958, 379–81. In Gorce's opinion, de Serre was arguably "the greatest" of the Doctrinaires (Gorce 1926, 147).

44. For mode details, see Barante 1892, 348–50, and Hatin 1861, 315–25.

45. Broglie 1887a, 360, 389; also see Gorce 1926, 146–47.

46. Jordan's book was reviewed by Rémusat in *Le Globe*, April 18, 1825.

47. A substantial selection from Jouffroy's and Cousin's writings can be found in Ripley ed. 1838. For more information on Damiron and Jouffroy, see Goblot 1995, 216–61.

48. For more details on Guizot's life and work, see G. Broglie 1990, Rosanvallon 1985, Pouthas 1923a, Pouthas 1923b, Johnston 1963, Bardoux 1894, and Coco 1983.

49. This was Guizot's first marriage; Pauline de Meulan died in 1827.

50. An English translation of Guizot's inaugural lecture at the Sorbonne (December 11, 1812) can be found in Guizot 1972, 3–17. For more details on Guizot's historical method, see chapters 3 and 4.

51. Interesting excerpts from Guizot's essay can be found in Nique 2000, 93–101.

52. For an overview of the debates on the electoral law of 1817, see Duvergier de Hauranne 1860, 25–61; Guizot 1858a, 165–71; Broglie 1887a, 362–414; Gorce 1926, 128–34; Vaulabelle 1855, 388–99; Furet 1995, 289–92. I discuss this issue in detail in chapter 8.

53. In this respect, Guizot echoed an idea that also appeared in a letter sent by the Duchess of Broglie to Barante in 1822: "Il me semble qu'à present *c'est le temps de semer des idées*; il n'y a que cette voie-là pour ceux qui ne se mettent pas dans les intrigues ou dans les folles tentatives" (Barante 1893, 26; emphasis added). The same belief was held by Royer-Collard. "On dit que vous travaillez," he wrote to Barante; "j'en suis charmé. . . . Le dernier ouvrage de Guizot m'a paru excellent. Écrivez, messieurs, faites de livres; il n'y a pas autre chose à faire en ce moment" (quoted in Barante 1893, 29).

54. Here is a fragment from a letter of Guizot (May 21, 1822), written to his friend, Prosper de Barante (quoted in Barante, 1893, 6), in which he referred to his treatise on sovereignty: "J'entreprendrai un grand travail sur les principes et la pratique du gouvernement représentatif." Three months later, in August 1822, Guizot told Barante that he had begun working on his project. A month later, he confessed that he had had to abandon it again. In a subsequent letter of October 1822, Guizot spoke one more time about the project, which remained, however, unfinished.

55. For more details on this issue, see Pouthas 1923a, 335–80; G. Broglie 1990, 76–108. Guizot was a member of various associations such as *Comité des prisons*, *Comité pour l'émancipation des catholiques d'Irlande*, and *Comité de charité et de prévoyance*.

56. The letter is quoted in Barante 1893, 26. A wonderful letter of Guizot to Rémusat nicely conveys his influence on the younger generation: "Je déplore le peu que vous faites de votre vie. . . . C'est la grande faiblesse de notre temps que les meilleurs hommes y sont, en fait d'idées et d'activité, comme les mauvais sujets en fait de plaisir, usés et blasés avant l'âge; . . . nous nous complaisons à étudier, à nous expliquer notre propre mollesse, nous jouissons encore par la pensée des forces que nous n'employons pas. Comment voulez-vous que je ne m'afflige pas de reconnaître en vous quelque chose de cette disposition? . . . Vous valez bien mieux, vous pouvez bien plus et vous ne faites rien. Je ne reproche jamais rien aux gens que j'aime, mais je m'en afflige. . . . Sachez que vous êtes pour moi une bonne part dans mon désir de voir changer l'état actuel des affaires et que le jour où vous ferez ce que vous pourrez et serez tout ce que vous êtes, sera un de ceux auxquels, dans ma vie, je penserai avec le plus profond plaisir" (letter of Guizot, August 27, 1824, quoted in Pouthas 1923a, 358). Guizot was not, however, a blind optimist. In a letter to Barante from October 1822, he confessed: "Jamais aucun temps n'a été marqué comme celui-ci de l'empreinte de la fatalité; pas un parti, pas un homme qui fasse ce qu'il veut, qui veuille ce qu'il fait" (Guizot's letter quoted in Barante 1893, 49).

57. The articles published in *Le Globe* convey the enthusiasm surrounding Guizot's lectures (as well as Cousin's and Villemain's). The unidentified author of a two-page article entitled "Ouverture du cours de M. Guizot," published in *Le Globe* in April 1828, wrote: "M. Guizot semble avoir gagné dans la retraite. Jamais il n'eut une allure si franche, une exposition si lucide, et une liberté d'expression si gracieuse. . . . Trois milles jeunes intelligences recevant trois fois par semaine le triple coup des leçons de M. Guizot, Cousin et Villemain. . . . Voilà la veritable énergie qui sied à

notre belle patrie; voilà ce qui, à côté des chambers et peut-être au-dessus des chambers, assure à la liberté son avenir, parce que par là il se fonde dans la conscience et dans la conviction" (*Le Globe*, April 1828, pp. 348–49).

58. Eckermann 1892, 369. The whole original passage is worth quoting: "Das Gespräch lenkte sich auf die Französen, auf die Vorlesungen von Guizot, Villemain und Cousin, und Goethe sprach mit hoher Achtung über den Standpunkt dieser Männer, und wie sie alles von einer freien and neuen Seite betrachteten . . . 'Es ist,' sagte Goethe, 'als wäre man bis jetzt in einen Garten auf Umwegen und durch Krümmungen gelangt; diese Männer aber sind kühn and frei genung, die Mauer dort einzureißen und eine Tür an derjenigen Stelle zu machen, wo man sogleich auf den breitesten weg des Gartens tritt . . . *Die Einsicht, Umsicht und Durchsicht dieser Männer ist groß*; sie verbinden vollkommne Kenntnis des Vergangenen mit dem Geist des neunzehnten Jahrhunderts, welches denn freilich Wunder tut . . . Statt des Voltairischen leichten oberflächlichen Wesens ist bei ihnen eine Gelehrsamkeit, wie man früher nur bei Deutschen fand. . . . Sie sind alle drei vortrefflich, *aber dem Herrn Guizot möchte ich den Vorzug geben, er ist mir der liebste*" (Eckermann 1949, 252, 253, 267; emphasis added). On Goethe and Guizot, see Nemoianu 2001.

59. See G. Broglie 1990, 102.

60. Guizot's views on the political situation prior to the Revolution of July can be found in Guizot 1830.

61. A similar argument is made by Nique 2000, 15–18.

62. For more details on Guizot's views on education, see D. Johnson 1963, 88–154; Rosanvallon 1985, 241–54; Nique 2000, 3–88; Terral 2000, 13–69. The entire text of the Guizot Law of June 1833, along with the memorable letter sent by Guizot to all primary educators in July 1833, can be found in Nique, 111–25. In this letter, Guizot explained the importance of the new law as follows: "C'est parce que la liberté n'est assurée et régulière que chez un people assez éclairé pour écouter, en toute circonstance, la voix de la raison. L'instruction primaire universelle est désormais une des garanties de l'ordre et de la stabilité sociale. . . . *Développer l'intelligence, propager les lumières, c'est assurer l'empire et la durée de la monarchie constitutionnelle*" (Guizot in Nique 2000, 119; emphasis added). I discuss Guizot's educational policy in connection to his conception of "gouvernement des esprits" in chapter 6.

63. Douglas Johnson disagrees with those who argued that under Guizot's government France was bent upon a policy of territorial advancement. Johnson claims that Guizot only tried "to fit his policy to the needs of France, and to make it appropriate to French requirements and to French power. . . . This approach to foreign affairs is in contrast to that of the opposition. When they discussed foreign affairs, they did so not always with an eye to the needs of France but with an eye to their audience both in the Chamber, and 'par la fenêtre,' in the country" (D. Johnson 1963, 318).

64. The letter is quoted by D. Johnson 1963, 225.

65. Guizot's diplomatic career was controversial; for example, Palmerston thought that Guizot lacked the experience necessary to a true diplomat. For an overview of Guizot's foreign policy, see D. Johnson 1963, 263–319.

66. An English translation of this study can be found in Guizot 1972. For a detailed analysis of Guizot's religious writings, see Kirschleger 1999.

67. For more information on Guizot's last years and his retreat at Val-Richer, see the special issue *Guizot et le Val-Richer* edited by Pierre-Jean Pénault and published by Association "Le Pays d'Auge" (August–September 1987). This superbly edited book contains many original photographs of Guizot's Val-Richer estate, his testament and last days, and other personal documents.

68. See, for example, Ruggiero 1959, 169.

69. This letter to Madame Jenormant dated October 1, 1865 is quoted in D. Johnson 1967, 84.

70. In the concluding chapter of his biography, Douglas Johnson dwells on this point (D. Johnson 1963, 433). Louis Girard also argued that in some respects Guizot was a "stranger" to the passions of the French (Girard in *Actes du colloque François Guizot*, 1976, 152). Ortega y Gasset once compared Guizot to . . . Buster Keaton, the man who ever laughed!

71. For more details, see the general discussion on this issue in *Actes du colloque François Guizot*, 1976, 150–53.

72. D. Johnson 1963, 86, 438. Also see the following portrait of Guizot drawn by J. Allier: "Ame hautaine, caractère impérieux, dédain des critiques, confiance imperturbable dans l'excellence de son jugement en toutes choses, eloquence froide faissant sans cesse appel à la logique, mais sous laquelle se cachent des convictions passionées, temperament dominateur, qui compte en toute circonstance sur la puissance exceptionelle de son esprit et sur son inépuisable capacité de travail. Et aussi volonté de réflexion et de méditation" (Allier 1976, 45).

73. "Vous ne vous hausserez jamais jusqu'à la hauteur de mon mépris," he once replied to a political opponent (Guizot as quoted in Allier 1976, 28).

74. The phrase is taken from *Le Moniteur*, March 2, 1843; see Allier 1976, 36.

75. Writes Guizot: "Je suis de ceux que l'élan de 1789 a élevés et qui ne consentiront point à descendre. Mais si je ne tiens à l'ancien régime par aucun intérêt, je n'ai jamais ressenti contre l'ancienne France aucune amertume. Né bourgeois et protestant, je suis profondément dévoué à la liberté de conscience, à l'égalité devant la loi, à toutes les grandes conquêtes de notre ordre social. Mais ma confiance dans ces conquêtes est pleine et tranquille, et je ne me crois point obligé, pour servir leur cause, de considérer la maison de Bourbon, la noblesse française et le clergé catholique comme des ennemis" (Guizot 1858a, 27–28). Also: "J'étais en même temps libéral et antirévolutionnaire, dévoué aux principes fondamentaux de la nouvelle société française, et animé, pour la vieille France, d'un respect affectueux" (Guizot 1858a, 315).

76. Louis Girard, author of a history of French nineteenth-century liberalism, holds a more nuanced—and, I believe, more accurate—view: "À *court terme*, les doctrinaires ont *échoué*. Leur project d'équilibre des pouvoirs au sein d'une monarchie mixte n'a pu se réaliser entre 1816 et 1820. . . . Pourtant ils ont conservé une place particulière, prestigieuse, au sein du libéralisme français. Leur personnalités sont séduisantes, par leur talent; leur prétention à constituer l'élite de leur époque n'apparaît pas rétrospectivement

trop outrecuidante. *Ils ont été libéraux de gouvernement*; ils ont séparé le libéralisme de l'esprit révolutionnaire sans désavouer la Révolution. . . . *Les doctrinaires ont tracé le schéma d'un gouvernement garant des libertés*, schéma qui, sans être le seul, conserve sa valeur, gouvernement de droit, pacifique et libre, non démocratique, mais capable d'adaptation" (Girard 1985, 78–79; emphasis added). Also see Burdeaux 1953, 410.

77. *Edinburgh Review*, CCXX, October 1858, 410.

78. The words are Guizot's. For more details, see Guizot 2002, 17–18.

79. The phrase belongs to Sainte-Beuve (as quoted by Johnson in *Actes du colloque François Guizot*, 1976, 484).

80. La Fayette as quoted in Pouthas 1923a, 407.

81. Duchess de Broglie's letter was published in Barante 1893, 462; also see Barante 1893, 26, 267, 275, 481. On Barante and the Duchess of Broglie, see Deguise 1989.

82. Writes Laboulaye: "Il y a toujours eu du système dans l'école doctrinaire. Elle s'est crue plus sage que les libéraux en cherchant une conciliation entre deux politiques contradictoires; elle a toujours été plus ou moins mêlé la prévention à la répression; elle n'a pas eu moins de confiance dans la sagesse de l'administration que dans le libre effort de l'individu" (Laboulaye in Constant 1861, xlvi).

83. Mill's letter is quoted in Varouxakis 1999, 292.

84. On Guizot's reputation in England, see Johnson 1976b and the summary of discussions published in *Actes du colloque François Guizot* (1976, 138–41).

85. For more details, see Diez del Corral 1956, 339–586.

86. See Diez del Corral 1956, 394. An English translation of Cortés's *Lecciones* was published in 1991. For an analysis of Cortés's political thought, see Diez del Corral 1956, Graham 1974, and Herrera 1996.

87. Thorbecke's most important book was *Over het hedendaagsch staatsburgerschap* (*On Modern Citizenship*) published in 1844; for an analysis of his political thought, see Drentje 2003. I would like to thank Dr. Jan Drentje for calling my attention to Thorbecke and the similarities between his ideas and Guizot's theories.

88. Guizot 1858b, 159. Also see Rémusat's confession: "J'avais en aversion ceux qui nient les principes, ceux qui traitent les pures idées de niaseries ou de chimère, ceux qui opposent l'expérience à la raison, et proclament un divorce eternal entre la théorie et la pratique. . . . Le mérite, ou si l'on veut la nouveauté, des doctrinaires a certainement été de chercher à réconcilier le fait avec le droit, à rendre les principes applicable, à trouver une philosophie de la réalité, une doctrine qui pût se combiner avec l'histoire et avec la politique" (Rémusat 1958, 367).

89. Here is what Metternich had to say about the Doctrinaires' *juste milieu*: "Cette pensée, rendue en chiffres, présente la formule arithmétique suivante: posez 1, 2 et 3; éffacez 1 et il restera 2 et 3. Toutefois, ce que la doctrine oublie, c'est qu'en effaçant le premier chiffre, le second ne représente plus le milieu. . . . Les efforts que fait la classe moyenne pour se débarrasser de celle qui la domine et en même temps pour empêcher la classe inférieure de s'élever jusqu'à sa hauteur aboutit à ce paradoxe . . . Telle est l'une des maladies du jour. Or que résulte-t-il de ce phénomène? . . . Nous voyons la

couche supérieure No. 1 se liguer avec la couche inférieure No. 3 et faire cause commune pour empêcher le triomphe de la classe moyenne. C'est effectivement ce qui a lieu en France et ce qui rend les doctrinaires si odieux aux yeux des restes de l'ancienne aristocratie qu'à ceux de la démocratie. Ce qui ajoute à la faiblesse de la doctrine, c'est qu'elle ne sait pas caractériser sa propre essence. . . . M. Guizot en a trouvé un caractère, c'est l'intelligence, mais *l'intelligence ne peut être l'apanage d'une classe*, elle ne peut être que celui d'individus" (Metternich as quoted by Sauvigny 1959, 74; emphasis added). Bonald's article was published in *Le Conservateur* (Bonald 1819b).

90. See Diez del Corral 1960, 60–62.

91. Writes Michel: "Si jamais école mérita peu son nom, c'est bien celle des doctrinaires. On est tenté de croire sur le vu du nom, qu'elle s'appuie sur des principes inflexibles, rigides, tout d'une pièce. Rien de moins conforme à la réalité. L'attitude des hommes, la hauteur du ton, le langage sentencieux, ne doivent pas faire illusion. Les doctrinaires sont pauvres de doctrine, ou si l'on aime mieux, leur doctrine consiste toute entière à expliquer et à justifier certains états de fait. . . . Toute la *doctrine* de Royer-Collard (ou de Guizot dans ses premiers écrits) se ramène à d'incessants compromis, à de majestueux marchandages entre le fait et le droit, au detriment du droit. Guizot y apparaît comme le théoricien par excellence de ce qu'on a appelé, plus tard, l'opportunisme" (Michel 1896, 291–92).

92. Bagge ironically remarks: "Royer-Collard, Guizot, tant d'autres, qui n'étaient que des brebis, et qui ont voulu jouer les pasteurs. . . . La doctrine des doctrinaires c'est de ne pas avoir de doctrine. Le seul principe qu'ils reconnaissent, c'est de ne reconnaître aucun principe. . . . Il n'est pas de doctrine 'doctrinaire.' Historiquement, il est des positions d'opportunités successives: elles se réclament le plus souvent du besoin d'autorité. . . . Beaucoup d'idées mal coordonnées, peu adaptables, rarement fécondes" (Bagge 1952, 99, 101).

93. Writes Diez del Corral: "Si se entiende por doctrina un conjunto de principios y reglas sólidamente establecidos y aceptados, resulta, pues, que los doctrinarios merecerían tal nombre justamente *por no tener doctrina*. Más la tendrían *sus antagonistas*, los ultras y liberales. En comparación con ellos, fuertemente atrincherados en sus posiciones, los llamados doctrinarios resultarán tornadizos, siempre andando en componendas, laboriosos en buscar justificaciones, precisamente por necesitarlas. Pero sería *exagerado* deducir de lo anterior que, efectivamente, como algunos creen, sean los doctrinarios verdaderos oportunistas. Para poner en claro el grado en que lo son, preciso es tener en cuenta la clase de principios, inusitadamente parciales y severos, que postulan sus antagonistas en un mundo político hondamente escindido. . . . Frente a la parcial inexorabilidad de los principios, los doctrinarios proclamarán un método unificador que *necesariamente será insinuante y acomodaticio*" (Diez del Corral 1956, 133; emphasis added).

94. See, for example, the following opinion of Louis Girard: "Guizot a élaboré une théorie du régime [parlamentaire], théorie qui a varié sur certains points, mais qui, *pour l'essentiel, est restée immuable* au cours de sa carrière politique" (Girard 1976, 121; emphasis added).

95. For more details, see Manent 1994, 93–102, and Lefort 1988.

~

CHAPTER THREE

Between Scylla and Charybdis

Il ne suffit pas d'être un homme, il faut être un système.

—Balzac

The Return of Clio

As we have already seen, the Bourbon Restoration provided an open arena for vigorous political debates between partisans of the Old Regime, supporters of constitutional monarchy and representative government, and radicals who wanted to continue the Revolution. The struggle, argued Guizot, was between rival and often incompatible interests and ideas that aroused the most ardent passions.[1] The legacy of the French Revolution made the entire situation extremely complex. The country had witnessed not only the "noble" moment of 1789 that marked the fall of absolute monarchy of divine right, but also the Terror of 1793–94.

While reopening the debate over the legitimacy of the principles of 1789, the Restoration had to come to terms with the violent episodes of French Revolution. In this context, the task of postrevolutionary liberals was to absorb the shock produced by 1793 and bring the Revolution to an end. They championed the main principles of 1789 and the civil liberties enshrined in the *Declaration of the Right of Man and of Citizen*—the rights of man, political liberty, freedom of association, and the like—and condemned the Terror and the ideas which, in their view, had made it possible. The liberals' challenge was to find the best means of protecting and defending the institutions and interests of the new France in the face of an avenging aristocracy, a resurgent clergy, and impatient revolutionaries. This was a real *travail de structure* that required building the institutional framework of representative government and replacing the old hierarchical society with a more egalitarian one in which the middle class played a leading role.

Thus, French liberals were confronted with the daunting task of finding the best ways of defending and legitimizing the Revolution in the face of its conservative opponents and left-wing critics.[2] On the one hand, liberals such as Constant, de Staël, Guizot, and Royer-Collard stressed again and again that there was no way back into the past and warned that any attempt to restore the Old Regime would be futile and dangerous. On the other hand, the liberals believed that their task was to bring the Revolution to an end by building viable representative institutions. "Let us confess without hesitation," claimed Guizot. "As a destructive [phenomenon], the Revolution is done and there is no question of returning to it; as a founding moment, it only commences now" (Guizot 1818a, 397).

The ultraroyalists rejected this position and interpreted the Revolution as a unique event in history that displayed a degree of destruction and human depravity never seen before. This thesis loomed large in Joseph de Maistre's *Considérations sur la France*: "No element of good disturbs the eye of the observer; it is the highest degree of corruption ever known; it is pure impurity. . . . What a horrible assemblage of baseness and cruelty! What profound immorality! What absence of all decency! Its general context has never varied, and from its birth there was evidence of what it would become" (Maistre 1994, 38–39). In Maistre's view, the radically negative character of the Revolution and its allegedly "satanic character"[3] were demonstrated by its attempt to overthrow religion and to violate individual property.

To answer their critics, many French liberals turned to history in order to find convincing proofs and arguments in favor of the legitimacy of the principles of 1789 and to explain the Terror of 1793–94. Needless to say, the interest in historical studies was not simply antiquarian but served a well-defined political agenda that marked a stark contrast to the ethos and method of previous historical studies. The difference was clearly explained by Guizot in the concluding chapter of volume two of *Histoire de la civilisation en France*. Up to the nineteenth century, the philosophical and scholarly study of history had been partial and limited. Learned books had been written on the origins and influence of laws, manners, sciences, religion, and arts, along with erudite political, literary, and religious histories. Yet, all these aspects of human life had never been regarded before in their fundamental union. Montesquieu, argued Guizot, confined his search to political institutions, while Bossuet limited his investigation to the study of religious beliefs. In spite of their undeniable and brilliant virtues, Montesquieu's analysis of the spirit of the laws and Bossuet's discourses on universal history did not yield a complete idea of the development of human nature, because of the partial foundation on which their books were built. In Guizot's opinion, the originality of the method used by nineteenth-century historians derived from the mission and challenges they faced. They were called to write a truly general history of civilization as "a summary of all histories" (Guizot 1859d, 368) that included an "immense variety" of political, legislative, religious, philosophical, and literary facts, which reflected the multifarious nature of human actions in history and sought to highlight their fundamental union.

A conflict-ridden society always appeals to the testimony of history in order to find reassurance and gain renewed confidence in its ability to reform itself. Given the contested legacy of the Revolution, its uncertainties and dilemmas, looking back into the past was also a way of looking forward into the future. As Douglas Johnson pointed out, far from being a mere form of escapism, turning to history was the only way of understanding what had to be done and what could be done in the complex political context of postrevolutionary France.[4] The initial moment of the Revolution had to be seen neither as a prelude to the Terror nor as a complete break with the past, but as the inevitable outcome of past trends that had been at work for a long time. In advancing this argument, liberal historians, including Tocqueville and Guizot, resorted to a selective reading of the past, one that insisted on discontinuities and long-term social, cultural, and political patterns. The new liberal catechism was memorably captured by Madame de Staël, who once said that in France liberty was ancient and despotism modern (Staël 1979, 273).

This hermeneutic strategy explains the liberals' emphasis on the Revolution's debt to the past and its continuity with the entire course of the history of France. The liberal historians realized that writing a *longue durée* history was the most efficient means of promoting the ideas and spirit of the Revolution. To this effect, they resorted—to quote Nietzsche's terms—to a combination of *monumental, antiquarian,* and *critical* history that used historical studies as a powerful means against resignation and inaction.[5] While looking for general patterns and causes in history, the high points that linked the previous centuries and brought the distant past into closer contact with the present, they did not forget that the analogies offered by the monumental type of history were sometimes deceiving. They searched into archives for old documents and records and argued that the knowledge of the past should serve the present and the future.

Almost overnight, history became one of the most popular forms of written communication in France. According to a note in the *Revue encyclopédique*, almost forty million pages of history had been published in France in 1825. Those who wrote history also tried to *make* history. "Our historians," argued Foustel de Coulanges, "have been men of a party. . . . Writing the history of France was a way of working for a party and fighting an adversary."[6] In turn, Jubé de la Perelle remarked that "the best way of giving the government your political opinions is to publish a good history of France."[7]

Hence, from a bookish and purely scholarly subject, history became again the *magistra vitae*. But the teaching of history turned out to be highly controversial, as zealous administrators carefully watched over and sometimes even censored the curriculum, fearing that the new interpretations of the history of France might surreptitiously or overtly advance unorthodox political claims. Opposing this trend, Thierry denounced the irrational behavior of those officials who wanted a tightly controlled curriculum in the teaching of history. In his view, the main purpose of rewriting the history of France was to contribute to the triumph of constitutionalism: "I turned to historical works to find corroboration of my political beliefs."[8] Thierry was convinced that only the rediscovery of the "true" history of towns, associations, and communes could bring the country back to the path from which "false" histories, which glossed over the considerable freedoms enjoyed by previous generations, had caused her to stray.

A similar belief was shared by Guizot, whose essays on the history of France and lectures on the origins of representative government in Europe sought to demonstrate the deep roots of liberty and the legitimacy of the principles of 1789. Starting from the assumption that a thorough knowledge of history should be harnessed to defend present political goals, he attempted to demonstrate the ancient roots of liberty and the inevitable rise of the third estate in Europe. Like Tocqueville, Guizot never wrote an entire book on the French Revolution, but he, too, was interested in understanding its origins and principles and explaining its accidents. Guizot argued that the Revolution had been the outcome of a class conflict which had been going on for many centuries. This idea appeared, for example, on the very first page of *Du gouvernement de la France depuis la Restauration et du ministère actuel* (1820), in which Guizot described the history of France as the chronicle of a protracted struggle between two peoples:

> The Revolution was a war, a true war. For more than thirteen centuries, France had contained two peoples: a victorious and a vanquished people. For more than thirteen centuries, the vanquished people had been fighting in order to

shake off the yoke of the victorious people. Our history is the history of this struggle. In our times, a decisive battle has been waged. It is called the Revolution.[9]

The reference to the struggle between the two peoples in the above passage carried strong symbolical connotations. Guizot's point was that the Revolution sanctioned the inevitable and legitimate triumph of the *tiers état* over aristocracy and clergy, a symbolic success which, in his view, marked the victory of liberty, right, and equality over privilege and absolute power and introduced the reign of justice and moral law into the social realm.[10] The triumph of representative government and constitutional monarchy sanctioned by the Charter of 1814 was seen as the final result of this long struggle. Guizot praised the medieval townsmen, those "champions of justice and liberty," precursors of modern bourgeoisie, whose courageous resistance to absolute power had contributed to the consolidation of ancient municipalities into strong bastions of local freedoms.

By placing the Revolution in a larger European political tradition, Guizot sought to demonstrate that, far from being merely a fortuitous event, the Revolution was both irreversible and invincible. "The Revolution," he argued, "was right in its principle and tendency. Seen from this point of view, it purported to introduce justice, that is to say the empire of the moral law in the relations between citizens as well as in the relations between government and citizens. This is what made it invincible" (Guizot 1820, 139). It is worth noting that Guizot advanced the thesis of class struggle a few decades *before* Marx, who explicitly acknowledged his debt to French "bourgeois historians" such as Guizot and Thierry.[11]

What is particularly interesting in the Doctrinaires' thought is their specific view of history and society, which combined insights from different disciplines such as history, law, philosophy, and theology and wove particular events and political ideas into larger historical and philosophical panoramas.[12] The Doctrinaires' theories of liberty, authority, representation, legitimacy, and sovereignty were not inferred from ahistorical, abstract principles, but were derived from a specific philosophy of history and social change that purported to explain the gradual rise of the third estate and the progress of the equality of conditions in the history of modern Europe. Unlike Rousseau, the Doctrinaires were not interested in advancing abstract theories about the origins of society, but they outlined the predominant principles and ideas that had shaped and altered the course of European civilization over time. In their view, the eighteenth century and the initial moment of the Revolution were elements of a long process of gradual emancipation from the shackles of the feudal past. The Enlightenment accomplished the work of the centuries that had preceded it, and the French Revolution was regarded as the last act in a drama that had started a long time before 1789.

To conclude, most of the historical writing published during the Bourbon Restoration displayed an unusual degree of political partisanship as historians sought to use the lessons of the past in order to justify their own political agenda. Not surprisingly, Guizot wrote a history of civilization in Europe and France in which the French Revolution figured as the climax of a Continental struggle for liberty. The Doctrinaires argued that the Revolution only adjusted the political institutions of France to a new social condition characterized by new mores, habits, and social relations. In advancing this claim, Guizot, Rémusat, and the other Doctrinaires made a seminal distinction between social condition and political order, a distinction that had a lasting influence on Tocqueville.

Pluralism, Liberty, and European Civilization

Guizot's historical works—*Histoire de la civilisation en Europe*, *Histoire de la civilisation en France*, *Histoire de la révolution en Angleterre*, along with his lectures on the origins of representative government in Europe—impressed his contemporaries with their "consistency, coherence, and comprehensiveness" (Mill 1985, 259). Like John Stuart Mill, Tocqueville also admired Guizot's many-sidedness and his ability to outline a general scheme, "so well wrought and digested beforehand."[13] Guizot sought for general hidden facts, but unlike Barante,[14] he was not primarily interested in narrative history. His talent consisted in articulating a philosophical and sociological history (not very different from the tradition of *Kulturgeschichte*), which attempted to identify those general patterns that would help his readers grasp the underlying causes and effects of particular events. If facts mattered a lot, their meanings were equally important, and Guizot tried to explain and connect them to general ideas, principles, and themes. He searched for those principles and ideas "which do not expire with a particular age, [and] form the destiny and glory of nations,"[15] and took historians to task for often being incapable of going beyond the bare facts in order to discern their hidden meanings.

As Guizot argued in *Histoire des origines du gouvernement représentatif en Europe*, the main limitation of what he called "the historic school" was that it lost sight of the general and fixed principles that alone can explain the meaning of facts. "It is deficient in general and fixed principles," wrote Guizot; "its judgments fluctuate according to chance; and accordingly it almost always hesitates to come to a conclusion, which the philosophic school, on the contrary, always impresses strongly, at the risk of leading it astray" (Guizot 2002, 366). Since history contains not only material (visible) facts such as wars, battles, and official acts of governments but also "moral" facts, the task of philosophical history is to throw light on those "general facts, without any particular designation, to which it is impossible to assign any precise date, but which are yet no less facts than the rest" (Guizot 1997a, 12).

Civilization was precisely the ensemble of those many "general, hidden, complex facts" which Guizot set out to explore in his historical writings. To be sure, for him civilization was "the fact par excellence, the general and definitive fact, in which all others terminate, into which they all resolve themselves" (Guizot 1997a, 13). But why did he attach such a great importance to the notion of civilization? A few words about the genealogy of this concept might be illuminating in this context. Littré's famous *Dictionnaire de la langue française* defined civilization as the action of civilizing and the ensemble of opinions and mores that result from the reciprocal action of industry, religion, arts, and sciences. The notion of *civility* was widely used in eighteenth-century France. "Politeness flatters the vices of others," wrote Montesquieu, "while civility prevents us from revealing ours."[16] Mirabeau used the concept of civilization in *l'Ami de l'homme* (1756). At about the same time, Voltaire opposed civilization to barbarism and wrote about Europe's civilizing mission in the world. In his view, the act of civilization was tantamount to becoming civilized, "*polir les mœurs.*" After 1800, civilization gradually became a synonym for the ensemble of the features—mores, ideas, sciences—of the collective life of a particular society. Nonetheless, the term was included in the *Dictionnaire de l'Académie* only in 1835.[17]

For Guizot, civilization was inseparable from the idea of *progress*, both social and moral. In the opening chapter of *Histoire de la civilisation en Europe*, he argued:

> It appears to me that the first act comprised in the word *civilization* . . . is the fact of progress, of development; it presents at once the idea of a people marching onward, not to change its place, but to change its condition. . . . The idea of progress, of development, appears to me the fundamental idea contained in the word, civilization. . . . It is the perfecting of civil life, the development of society, properly so called, of the relations of men among themselves. (Guizot 1997a, 16)

Guizot highlighted the role of institutions, wars, governments, individual facts, religious creeds, philosophical ideas, sciences, letters, and arts in the formation of the unity of European civilization.[18] In so doing, he concentrated on the simultaneous development of the (external) social life and the (internal) moral development of individuals, which are closely connected with each other. On the one hand, Guizot described the gradual and inevitable forward march of society, accompanied by the gradual rise of the third estate and the leveling of permanent distinctions between classes. On the other side, he pointed out that the word *civilization* comprehends "something more extensive, more complex, something superior to the simple perfection of the social relations, of social power and happiness (Guizot 1997a, 17).

Guizot claimed that a truly civilized society must have a prosperous social order *as well as* a developed intellectual and moral life. The latter includes the development of individual faculties, ideas, and sentiments that contribute to the great achievements in the realm of letters, sciences, and arts. Royer-Collard advanced a similar thesis. Man's social dimension, he argued, never exhausts his full humanity, and society can never contain the whole man. As beings "endowed with immortality," individuals have a different destiny from that of the states, because their highest allegiances are to forces superior to any power on earth. After we have engaged ourselves in social life, there remains to us the noblest part of ourselves, those high faculties by which we elevate ourselves to God and a future life, to unknown felicity in an invisible world.[19]

Not surprisingly, Guizot entertained a lofty image of the virtues of French civilization. He believed that France was unique among other European countries because it was in France that the idea of civilization as both social and moral (intellectual) progress was fully realized. The comparison he drew in *Histoire de la civilisation en France* between the French, English, German, and Italian civilization(s) is illuminating in this regard. The English, wrote Guizot, excel in "the amelioration of the external and public condition of men and the introduction of more justice, more prosperity into society." But in England, the development of society has been more extensive and more glorious than the evolution of arts and sciences. As a result, "social interests and social facts have . . . maintained a more conspicuous place, and have exercised more power than general ideas: the nation seems greater than the individual."[20] Famous English philosophers such as Bacon and Locke who founded the practical school of philosophy and relied exclusively on common sense reflected the practical cast of mind of their nation, as did English novelists.

In Germany, the situation was different. "The development of civilization has been slow and tardy; the brutality of German manners has been proverbial throughout Europe for centuries" (Guizot 1972, 273). The originality of Germany lay elsewhere: "Intellectual development has always surpassed and left behind social development" (Guizot 1972, 273). There was almost no comparison between the sophisticated theories of Luther, Melanchthon, and Leibniz and the contemporaneous manners of their times. The intellectual and the social order were "almost entirely separated," and the social condition did not advance at the same pace as the arts and sciences (philosophy, literature, music). In turn, Italian civilization has been neither essentially practical as that of England, nor almost exclusively speculative as that of Germany. "The leading men in the world of the intellect have not believed in the duty, perhaps not even in the right, of influencing society." At the same time, "men of action have held small account of universal ideas" and acted randomly, without any desire to regulate, according to fixed principles, the facts which came under their dominion." As a result, "the two powers have not lived in reciprocal confidence, . . . in continual action and reaction" (Guizot 1972, 274–75).

The unique nature of French civilization was, in part, due to its cult of reason that became a sort of national religion. For Guizot, the honor of reproducing more faithfully than any other country the fundamental idea of civilization must be ascribed to the country of Descartes, Montaigne, and Pascal. The essential fact of civilization, that is to say the intimate union and the harmonious development of ideas and facts, appeared only in France, the country of sophisticated ideas, refined arts, and noble civility:

> Indeed, as a general thing, in France ideas have preceded and impelled the progress of the social order; they have been prepared in doctrines, before being accomplished in things, and in the march of civilization mind has always taken the lead. This twofold character of intellectual activity and practical ability, of meditation and application, is shown in all the great events of French history, and in all the great classes of French society, and gives them an aspect which we do not find elsewhere. (Guizot 1972, 276)

France proved to be simultaneously rich in ideas and powerful in politics and manifested a desire to improve the social order and to innovate in arts and sciences. This was a current view in late-eighteenth-century and early-nineteenth-century Europe. Writing from a different political perspective, Joseph de Maistre described the singularity of France in more or less similar terms. "Providence," he wrote, "has given the French nation two instruments, two arms, so to speak, with which it stirs up the world—the French language and the spirit of proselytism. Consequently, France constantly has both the need and the power to influence men" (Maistre 1994, 20). In other words, because France "has addressed herself at once to the intellect of the nations, and to their desire for social amelioration," it became "the most civilized of civilizations" (Guizot 1997a, 279).

It would be inaccurate, however, to suggest that Guizot's history was supposed to be merely an apology for French civilization or a barely disguised form of nationalism. His true interest lay elsewhere. He wanted to write a *philosophical* history of European civilization conceived as a vast drama in which every people has its part to perform. He was impressed by the unity in diversity that he encountered in European civilization whose superiority vis-à-vis other civilizations was due (in his view) to both its cohesion and its vibrant pluralism of ideas, principles, and interests. Guizot emphasized "the unity and compactness of European civilization," its unique "community of ideas, feelings, aspirations, and efforts, in spite of territorial demarcations" (Guizot 2002, 221). This unity had been in the making for a very long time—to be precise, for more than twelve centuries. "This external and apparent community has not always existed," argued Guizot (2002, 221), "but such has been, at bottom, the unity of European civilization, that it is impossible thoroughly to understand the unity of any of the great modern peoples without considering the history of Europe as a whole."

Guizot's ideas on Europe and pluralism underpinned his theory of political freedom. In his view, the progress of European civilization was due to many factors, among which the most important were the development of Roman municipal institutions and civil law, freedom of thought, the Christian Church, the separation between temporal and spiritual authority, and the spirit of personal independence brought forth by the barbarians. The Roman Empire, the Christian Church, and the barbarians' tribes were organized and founded upon utterly different political and spiritual principles. Yet over time, the laws, principles, and customs of these different societies merged in the cauldron of European society and created a new civilization. The Romans bequeathed to European civilization "its municipal system, its habits, rules, the principle of freedom; [and] a general and uniform civil legislation, the idea of absolute power, of sacred majesty, of the emperor, the principle of order and subjection" (Guizot 1997a, 38–39). The barbarians who invaded and conquered the Roman Empire brought forth the noble spirit of "individual independence, the pleasure of enjoying oneself with vigor and liberty, . . . the taste for an adventurous career, full of uncertainty" (Guizot 1997a, 43–44). According to Guizot, this spirit of personal independence, the love of liberty displaying itself at all risks (as opposed to political, regulated freedom), was unknown to both the Roman and Christian societies.

The barbarians also introduced the hierarchical subordination, which eventually became the basis of aristocratic society, founded upon "the attachment of man to man, the fidelity of individual to individual, without external necessity, and without obligation based upon the general principles of society" (Guizot 1997a, 45). In turn, the Christian Church introduced the principle of equality into the political realm and "prepared the way for the independence of the individual intellectual world, the independence of thought" (Guizot 1997a, 96). The Reformation played a seminal role in promoting and giving a new impulse to freedom of inquiry and thought. In Guizot's view, Luther triggered a great insurrection of the human mind that affirmed "a new necessity for freely thinking and judging, on its own account, and with its own powers, of facts and ideas which hitherto Europe had received, or was bound to receive, from the hands of authority. It was a grand attempt at the enfranchisement of the human mind."[21]

Nonetheless, if left to themselves, all these factors would have never been able to create on their own the greatness of European civilization. The latter was based on the coexistence of rival principles of social organization and powers (monarchy, aristocracy, democracy, the Church), none of which had ever been able to reign absolutely and to stifle the development of others. "When we contemplate ancient civilizations," claimed Guizot (1997a, 28), "we find them stamped with a singular character of unity in their institutions, their ideas, and their manners; a sole, or, at least, a strongly preponderating force governs and determines all." There has never been a genuine coexistence of different and equally strong ideas and principles of social organization for a longer period of time. One principle managed to affirm itself absolutely and obstructed the development of its rivals, imposing a climate of intolerance, monotony, and stagnation. Elsewhere in the world, in countries such as Egypt or India, society also came under the absolute influence of one single principle of social organization that was responsible for social and political stagnation. But when society came under the exclusive domination of a single power, it sank into tyranny.

"It has been wholly otherwise with the civilization of modern Europe," added Guizot (1997a, 29). Unlike other civilizations, it has always been (and remained) varied, diverse, and stormy, a pluralist civilization in which all types of social organization—theocracy, monarchy, aristocracy, democracy— peacefully coexisted. Diverse powers, principles, and systems mingled, in a perpetual struggle, but none of them succeeded in stifling the development of others and taking absolute possession of society:

> In the ideas and sentiments of Europe there is the same variety, the same struggle. The theocratic, monarchic, aristocratic, and popular creeds cross, combat, limit, and modify each other. Open the boldest writings of the middle ages; never there is an idea followed out to its last consequences. . . . On neither part exists that imperturbable audacity, that blind determination of

logic, which show themselves in ancient civilizations. . . . With the prodigious diversity of the ideas and sentiments of European civilization, it has been much more difficult to arrive at this simplicity, this clearness. . . . Whilst, in other civilizations the exclusive, or, at least, the excessively preponderating dominion of a single principle, of a single form, has been the cause of tyranny, in modern Europe, the diversity of elements, which constitute the social order, the impossibility under which they have been placed of excluding each other, have given birth to the freedom which prevails in the present day. (Guizot 1997a, 30–31)

Guizot's message was that both absolute monarchy and pure theocracy are inimical to freedom, but so is absolute, unregulated democracy. In his opinion, freedom could survive only in a pluralist society in which various principles, ideas, and interests coexist and are engaged in a perpetual competition for power and influence. In other words, liberty was, and is, inseparable from "discordance, variety, and strife" (Guizot 1997a, 93). The history of Europe demonstrates these points with remarkable clarity: "In Europe liberty has been the result of the variety of the elements of civilization, and of the state of struggle in which they have constantly existed" (Guizot 1997a, 31).

By equating civilization with progress, Guizot suggested the existence of a telos in history, linked to the realization of the precepts of reason, truth, and justice on Earth. Whether or not he offered a full-fledged philosophy of history is beyond the scope of this chapter.[22] What is undeniable is that in his writings, Guizot hailed the triumph of the middle class and sought to offer a rational justification of its victory. The main limitation of this view, however, stems from the potential tension with the central idea of Guizot's political philosophy according to which the absolute domination of any single idea or principle of social organization would jeopardize political liberty. Why would a society characterized by the absolute triumph of the middle class be more capable of protecting liberty than any other society in which the interests of one single class have become predominant? Guizot's politics never manage to fully answer this.

Was Guizot a historical determinist, as some historians believed? After all, he claimed that social and political progress occurs *in spite* of the will of individuals, an idea that represented the gist of his critique of the anachronistic policies of the ultraconservatives in the 1820s. Phrases such as "*la force des choses,*" "necessary," "irreversible," "inevitable," the "nature of things" often appeared in his writings. Moreover, in his essay on George Washington, Guizot argued that there are some events, such as the French Revolution, so vast and complicated that "Providence does not permit those who live at the time of their occurrence to understand" (Guizot 1972, 407). Their causes remain hidden for a long time. On some occasions, Guizot even used the word *fatality* to describe the feeling of powerlessness he experienced when reflecting on the political challenges of his time. "No other time," he confessed to his friend Barante in 1822, "has ever been so marked with the imprint of fatality; [there is] no party, no man who does what he wills, who wills what he does. . . . Events happen as of themselves without the men who are associated with them being able to do or avoid them."[23]

Nevertheless, Guizot was *not* a fatalist and stopped short of falling prey to a vulgar historical or social form of determinism. The characters he described in his historical works were real ones, and their choices made a genuine difference in the sequence of events. It would be more accurate to argue that in Guizot's writings, the ideas of progress and necessity were more an expression of *providentialism* than determinism. The distinction between the two is important and ought not to be overlooked when studying Guizot's ideas on freedom and politics. He rejected pantheism and deism and was persuaded that people remain free even when they participate in the realization of a divine plan:

> Thus man advances in the execution of a plan that he has not himself conceived, or which, perhaps, he does not even understand. He is the intelligent and free artificer of a work that does not belong to him. He does not recognize or comprehend it until a later period, when it manifests itself outwardly and in realities; and even then he understands it but very incompletely. . . . So is the plan of Providence upon the world executed by the hand of mankind.[24]

Nonetheless, insisted Guizot, individuals were not passive agents of Providence; the plans and designs of God were always accomplished by the development of people's intellect and liberty. Guizot admired the role of great individuals in history such as Charlemagne, William the Conqueror, Luther, or Washington.[25] While it is undeniable that these superior men affected the course of events, it remains a mystery of Providence why they appeared at a particular point in time. Guizot had a particular affection for George Washington, whose courage, vision, and eloquence he praised in his essay "Character and Influence of Washington," written as an introduction to Jared Spark's *Life of George Washington* (1842). "Of all great men," Guizot wrote, "he was the most virtuous and the most fortunate. In the world, God has no higher favors to bestow" (Guizot 1972, 413).

Ultraconservatives rejected this interpretation of the role of great individuals in politics and history. Maistre believed that it was impossible to create a new constitution from scratch and denied that human beings had the creative ability to significantly change the course of history. "No constitution," he wrote (Maistre 1994, 49–50), "is the result of deliberation. . . . In the formation of constitutions circumstances do everything and men are only part of the circumstances." People, argued Maistre, are attached to the throne of a Supreme Being by "a supple chain" that restrains their freedom and limits their possibilities for action. In revolutionary periods, this chain is "abruptly shortened"[26] and individuals are carried along by overwhelming forces unknown to them. Thus, they become mere instruments led by circumstances and forces beyond their control.

The Charter of 1814

Ironically, it was a written constitution—the Charter of 1814—that turned out to be the object of intense controversies in the epoch. The new constitutional text became the "political Bible" of French liberals, whose motto was "The Charter, all the Charter, nothing but the Charter."[27] The document was described as an "insoluble alliance between the legitimate power from which it emanates and the national liberties which it recognizes and consecrates" (Royer-Collard 1861b, 16).

The new constitution sanctioned the triumph of liberal, forward-looking elements over those who wanted to undo the legacy of the Revolution. Without being a contract between the monarch and the people in the proper sense of the term, the Charter recognized the new rights of the nation, while the latter formally acknowledged the king's right to reign. The very phrase "De notre règne le dix-neuvième" that Louis XVIII used to date his declaration of Saint-Ouen on his return to France in 1814 was intent on claiming that the king's reign had started nineteen years earlier. This detail carried strong symbolic connotations because it suggested that all previous regimes since 1789, including the Empire, had been more or less illegitimate.[28]

The Charter provided for the creation of a two-chamber parliament, the Chamber of Deputies being elected by electoral colleges according to a narrow franchise. To be qualified to vote, individuals had to be at least thirty years of age and pay a direct tax of three hundred francs (Article 40). As a result, only approximately 100,000 French citizens out of a total population of approximately 23 million had the right to vote. The minimal age for being eligible for the Chamber of Deputies was set at thirty. Article 36 stipulated "the deputies shall be elected for five years and in such a manner that the Chamber may be renewed each year by a fifth," and Article 38 maintained that "no deputy can be admitted to the Chamber unless he is forty

years of age and pays a direct tax of one thousand francs." Article 37 stipulated that the Chamber of Deputies be composed of the deputies elected by
electoral colleges whose organization be determined by law.

The Charter sought to bring social peace in a country divided among rival factions and groups that were fiercely opposed to each other. This goal
was clearly conveyed by the language of reconciliation that loomed large in
the new constitutional text. It was illustrated by the symbolic references to
the "great family" of all French citizens who were expected to live as "brothers" in "love, peace and reconciliation," undisturbed by the recollection of
past tensions.[29]

Yet, in spite of the generous intentions of its authors (Beugnot, Ferrand,
Montesquieu), the new constitutional text contained many ambiguities that
stemmed from the twofold goal of the Charter as a document that sought to
formalize the victory of one camp over another and to bring social reconciliation. This point was conveyed by Guizot in his memoirs: "The Charter was
not alone the triumph of 1789 over the old institutions, but it was the victory of one of the Liberal sections of 1789 over its rivals as well as its enemies, a victory of the partisans of the English Constitution over the framers
of the Constitution of 1791, and over the republicans as well as the supporters of the ancient monarchy" (Guizot 1858b, 35).

The very term chosen for the new constitutional text—*charter* instead of
the more common notion *constitution*—carried equally important symbolic
connotations. For those involved in the drafting of the new document, the
latter evoked the constituent power of the nation which the Charter rejected
because of its potentially absolutist implications. The word *charter* was finally
preferred after a careful examination of the merits of other solutions such as
Acte constitutionnel, Ordonnance de réformation, Édit.[30]

The ultraroyalists adopted a twofold strategy that combined both liberal
and conservative themes in an inconsistent manner. On the one hand, they
accused the authors of the Charter of trying to artificially import and copy the
English (unwritten) constitution without paying due attention to the old traditions and mores of France. The motto of the *ultras* was: "*Restons Français et
ne soyons pas Anglais!*" On the other hand, they sought to downplay the novelty of the Charter by arguing that the latter was based on the same principles that had previously underpinned the institutions of the Old Regime.
This thesis appeared, for example, in Vitrolles's writings as well as in Montlosier's influential book *De la monarchie française* (1814).[31] On March 27,
1816, the ultraroyalist majority in the *Chambre introuvable* signed a declaration (drafted by Vitrolles) that contained the following statement: "We fully
adopt the principles of the constitutional Charter, the division of power that

it had established. We shall maintain its spirit and accept the consequences of this system as the most reasonable replacement of ancient institutions and liberties" (Vitrolles 1952, 303).

In turn, the liberal defenders of the Charter argued that the new political institutions and laws of France were in accord with the French political tradition and the evolution of European civilization as a whole. In other words, far from being an exotic plant, the Charter was deeply rooted in the soil of France. Speaking of the Charter, Royer-Collard maintained that it had its own prestigious genealogy and tradition.[32] In turn, Chateaubriand affirmed that France had previously had the same government as England, but it had gradually disappeared under the absolute rule of Louis XIV and his heirs.[33]

Hence, the function of the Charter was meant to be a *restorative* one, but even in this respect there was disagreement on what actually had to be restored. The liberals claimed that the new constitutional text did not seek to innovate or import principles and ideas foreign to the traditions of France. It only purported to restore what was considered to be the country's older constitution and to adjust it to the European trend toward limited, moderate monarchy. Echoes of this idea appeared even in the Declaration of Saint-Ouen, in which Louis XVIII proclaimed his determination to adopt a liberal constitution and endorsed the principles of representative government. Nonetheless, as already mentioned, the relative novelty of the term did not prevent Montlosier and Vitrolles from claiming that the Charter was nothing other than a return to the old French (absolutist) monarchical tradition. Thus, from the very beginning the debates on the legitimacy of the Charter involved a symbolic struggle between rival philosophies of history which, depending on each group's political agenda, highlighted different aspects of French history.

The eclectic nature of the document added to all these tensions instead of solving them. On the one hand, the Charter of 1814 acknowledged the legitimacy of the new civil liberties under the common title "the public law of the French" and gave legal recognition to the third estate. The opening paragraph reads as follows: "We have replaced by the Chamber of Deputies those former assemblies of the fields of March and May, and those chambers of the Third Estate, which so often gave at the same time proof of zeal for the interests of the people and of fidelity and respect for the authority of the king" (Anderson 1967, 458). On the other hand, the Charter was grounded in an ambiguous and problematic theory of royal sovereignty as evinced by its preamble, which maintained that the whole authority resided in the power of the king, the supreme authority that alone could grant the new institutions the force and majesty that they needed. The Charter stopped short of instituting a genuine constitutional monarchy based on the sovereignty of the nation. The sovereignty of the monarch was described as indivisible, inalienable, and imprescriptible, a language that recalled, to a certain extent, the old doctrine of *rex legibus solutus*. Yet, in practice the sovereignty of the king was limited by the prerogatives and power of the Chamber of Deputies.[34]

Unfortunately, the conceptual ambiguities did not end here. While the first twelve articles of the Charter of 1814 formally recognized a set of fundamental civil liberties, such as equality before the law, liberty of the press, liberty of opinion and association, freedom of religion, and the inviolability of private property, the first paragraph of the Charter stipulated that the new constitution was granted and conceded—*octroyé*—by the monarch, instead of being a contract or social pact between the monarch and his subjects.[35] The use of the word *octroi* (concession) that was imposed by Beugnot underscored both the royal sovereignty and the continuity with the French monarchical tradition and eliminated any possibility of conceiving of the Charter as a social contract or social pact.[36]

While the new constitution made no reference to the doctrine of divine right, it mentioned, however, that Providence had called Louis XVIII back to the throne of France. Since the monarch "conceded" the Charter to his subjects, the constitutional text gave the king considerable powers and wide prerogatives that were bound to eventually create insurmountable tensions between the executive and the legislative powers. Furthermore, according to Article 13, the executive power belonged to the king alone, while Article 16 added that the monarch also had the initiative of proposing laws; moreover, laws could not be amended if the changes were not also ratified by the king. Article 19 stipulated that the two chambers had the power to petition the monarch to propose new laws and to indicate their desirable content; yet the legislative power was limited by the fact that "the king alone sanctions and promulgates the laws" (Article 22). The wide prerogatives of the monarch also appeared in regard to the responsibility of the ministers. The following puzzle arose: If the king alone chooses the ministers, they are mere executors of his will and cannot be held politically responsible.[37]

In a letter to Louis de Kergolay, Tocqueville commented on the limitations of the Charter of 1814 which, in his view, was a short-lived constitution whose highly eclectic nature created a series of unsolvable contradictions in the long term. The Charter blended aristocratic and democratic principles without providing proper solutions for solving the tensions between them. The Bourbons, argued Tocqueville, should have paid more attention to the emerging democratic elements and principles rather than attempting to preserve old and inefficient institutions. They should have furthered administrative decentralization that would have strengthened the communal and departmental system in France.[38] Nonetheless, in spite of these shortcomings, the importance of the new constitutional text should be neither overlooked nor dismissed. A strong defender of the Charter, Guizot was candid about both its limitations and virtues:

> The Charter bore the impress of this impolitic conduct; timid and obstinate in its turn, . . . it replied to the pretensions of the revolutionary system by the pretensions of the ancient form, and presented itself as a purely royal concession, instead of proclaiming its true character, such as it really was, a treaty of peace after a protracted war, a series of new articles added by common accord to the old compact of union between the nation and the King.. . . . It was the outcome of the necessities and convictions of the hour. Judged by itself, notwithstanding its inherent defects and the objections of its opponents, the Charter was a very practicable political implement. Power and liberty found ample scope for exercise and defense. (Guizot 1858b, 33–34; 36)

The new constitution marked a clear break with the Old Regime and provided the foundations of a new political regime, a limited monarchy (*monarchie limitée, monarchie tempérée*) that eventually became a full-fledged constitutional monarchy and parliamentary regime.[39] The monarch was required to respect the interests and wishes of the French nation as represented and defended by its deputies in Parliament. At the same time, the king also had the legal power to dissolve the Chamber of Deputies under certain circumstances. This is what occurred in fact in September 1816, when Louis XVIII dissolved the ultraconservative *Chambre introuvable* at the recommendation of his liberal advisers, including Guizot. According to the Charter, the chambers were expected only to give advice to the king on various matters concerning legislation. What would happen, however, if the chambers disagreed with the opinion of the monarch? The answer to this question was finally given by the *Appeal of the 221 [deputies]*, which affirmed the power of the Chamber of Deputies vis-à-vis a king (Charles X) who abused the doctrine of royal sovereignty and was later forced to abdicate.

Time proved Tocqueville right. The authors of the Charter aimed high and had noble ideas, but, given the particular historical conditions of postrevolutionary France, they were unable to create in a few months what the history of England had achieved over a period of six hundred years. For all its virtues and in spite of the warm praise lavished upon it by many liberals, including the Doctrinaires, the Charter of 1814 remained a circumstantial work that did not create a genuine parliamentary regime. To a certain extent, the failure of the Charter proved the limitations of the liberals' project, including that of the Doctrinaires, who pinned their hopes in the virtues of the new constitutional text while downplaying its limitations. Nevertheless, the Charter and the debates around it allow us to grasp the peculiar nature of French liberalism as it emerged during the Bourbon Restoration.

What united all French liberals and distinguished them from their political opponents was above all their opposition to the political principles of the Old Regime and the common belief that political progress could be achieved only by means of free institutions and limited (constitutional) monarchy.[40] But during the Bourbon Restoration, the liberal camp was highly heterogeneous, and French liberalism acquired from the outset a protean quality that made it a complex and sometimes contradictory phenomenon. To be sure, there were many voices that claimed to be liberal, but each of them had its own definition of liberalism. Liberalism was equated with opposition to the Old Regime or, more broadly, with a certain open-mindedness and openness toward political reform. Most liberals advocated constitutional monarchy, a form of government in which the king acts as an indispensable moderating force and the two-chamber Parliament plays a key role in representing and defending the interests of the nation. Some liberals advocated a stronger role for the king and the executive power, while others accepted the full consequences of parliamentarism, including the political responsibility of ministers, the right of the elected chambers to propose new laws, and the dependence of government on the majority in the Chamber of Deputies.

The Doctrinaires' *Juste Milieu*

During the Restoration, the Doctrinaires pursued a liberal reformist agenda that advanced a set of ideas and principles that they shared with other nineteenth-century French liberals: opposition to absolute power, rejection of the Old Regime, civil equality, political capacity, freedom of movement, and freedom of thought. In the Doctrinaires' opinion, the most important means of limiting power were publicity, a sound division of powers, regular and free elections, civil rights, an independent judiciary, decentralization, and freedom of speech and expression. Yet, their elitist liberalism differed from the more individualistic liberalism of Tocqueville, Staël, and Constant with regard to important issues such as the limits of power and individual rights.[41]

The Doctrinaires became known as the leaders of the center—"the party of the moral sense" (Guizot 1867, 65)—in the Chamber of Deputies from

1816 to 1820 and played a significant role in the parliamentary debates of that period, without forming a political party in the proper sense of the word. As "moderate reformers,"[42] they advanced a political agenda that relied on the assumption that the new social condition that had arisen from the Revolution of 1789 demanded a new philosophy of government. As Charles de Rémusat noted in his memoirs, the main challenge was "to create a liberalism of government,"[43] and that remained the fundamental problem of the Restoration to its very end. The Doctrinaires attempted to provide the theoretical foundations of such a liberalism of government.

In order to understand their originality, we need to first examine their method and style of argument. In Rémusat's view, the word *Doctrinaire* designated more a quality of tone and spirit than a consistent set of political and philosophical principles and ideas. This opinion was also shared by C.-H. Pouthas, who argued that what distinguished Guizot and his fellow Doctrinaires from their contemporaries was above all their method, which always attempted to bring the facts back to abstract principles and general ideas.[44] The Doctrinaires insisted that when examining the validity of a law, one must first inquire into its underlying general principles and ideas; if the latter are unacceptable, then the law ought to be rejected as well. In a letter to Rémusat, Guizot described the true Doctrinaire as someone who always conducts himself according to a general idea on any particular matter, singles out the general principles underlying a specific policy proposal, and ends by proposing a certain course of action after having considered a large number of consequences likely to follow and after having carefully examined the merits of other alternative solutions.[45] The Doctrinaires also often referred to the power of circumstances, *"la force des choses,"* in order to justify their actions. Yet, they did not merely content themselves with asserting the irresistible power of social facts, but also sought to give them rational justification.[46]

In his memoirs, Guizot described the method and project of the Doctrinaires as follows:

> While frankly adopting the new state of French society, such as our entire history, and not alone the year 1789, had made it, they undertook to establish a government on rational foundations, but totally opposed to the theories in the name of which the old system had been overthrown, or the incoherent principles which some endeavoured to conjure up for its reconstruction. Alternately called on to combat and defend the Revolution, they boldly assumed from the outset an intellectual position, opposing ideas to ideas, and principles to principles, appealing at the same time to reason and experience, affirming rights instead of maintaining interests, and requiring France . . . to emerge from the

chaos into which she had plunged herself, and to raise her head once more towards heaven in search of light. (Guizot 1858b, 154)

Guizot pointed to the combination of philosophical sophistication, enlightened pragmatism, and political moderation that characterized the Doctrinaires' approach. Their project was a *juste milieu* between Revolution and Reaction that combined innovation and tradition. As such, their theories were at the same time new and conservative, antirevolutionary without being reactionary, "modest in fact although sometimes haughty in expression" (Guizot 1858b, 155).

Worth noting are the terms chosen by Guizot to illustrate the Doctrinaires' method. In his view, the Doctrinaires paid attention to both rights and facts, combined experience and enlightened pragmatism with reason and philosophical investigation, and showed respect to the past without underestimating the present or ignoring the future. They also maintained that in politics the passion for abstract ideas must always be accompanied by healthy respect for social facts and genuine commitment to social and political pluralism. Their theory of society rested on a moral and political philosophy that rendered homage to human reason without idolizing it. The Doctrinaires' method was animated by a spirit that carefully observed facts and only admitted generalizations slowly, progressively, concurrently with the ascertainment of facts. They maintained that no general idea could be of any real value unless founded upon—and supported by—the facts themselves.

The belief in the possibility of a happy marriage between philosophy and politics was another important idea in the Doctrinaires' writings. In a letter to Barante from December 1823, Guizot wrote: "Our situation demands that we act both as politicians in the Chambers and as philosophers" (Guizot 1884, 52). In other words, there is no a priori incompatibility between politics and philosophy: One must act like a philosopher *as well as* a politician. As such, the Doctrinaires' political project differed from that of their eighteenth-century predecessors, who had developed sophisticated theories about politics but played little attention to the practical consequences of their ideas.[47]

According to Guizot, until the eighteenth century, action had been linked to speculation and the heads of intellectual parties exercised a significant influence over the leaders of political parties. But in eighteenth-century France, writers and philosophers were only observers who wrote and spoke about politics without fully understanding the complex nature and demands of political life:

This movement, moreover, had a peculiar character; one which, perhaps, is not to be met elsewhere in the history of the world: it was purely speculative. Up to that time, in all great human revolutions, action had commingled itself with speculation. Thus, in the sixteenth century, the religious revolution began with ideas, with purely intellectual discussions, but it very soon terminated in events. The heads of intellectual parties soon became the heads of political parties; the realities of life were mixed with the labor of the understanding. Thus, too, it happened in the seventeenth century, in the English revolution. But in France, in the eighteenth century, you find the human spirit exercising itself upon all things, upon ideas. . . . Nevertheless, the leaders and actors of these great discussions remained strangers to all species of practical activity—mere spectators, who observed, judged, and spoke, without ever interfering in events. At no other time has the government of facts, of external realities, been so completely distinct from the government of minds. (Guizot 1997a, 242–43)

In France, men of letters took the lead in society and guided public opinion, but instead of developing theories of true statecraft, they indulged in imagining an ideal society in which everything is simple, coherent, uniform, and rational. Politics interested them only as an abstract subject of reflection, or to use Guizot's own words, *"comme étude, non comme affaire."*[48] Taking pride in the power of reason, the *philosophes* believed that their abstract speculations could offer valuable guidelines for reforming society. "Philosophy," wrote Guizot (1858b, 153), "had boasted that it would regulate politics, and that institutions, laws, and public authorities should exist only as the creatures and servants of instructed reason—an insane pride, but a startling homage to all that is most elevated in man, to his intellectual and moral attributes." French philosophers and writers indulged in abstract theories and generalizations regarding the nature and purpose of government and advanced bold speculations about the origins of society.

As Tocqueville remarked, the political ferment was channeled into literature, and French writers played for a while the part that usually fell to professional politicians in the free countries. Those writers cherished freedom of thought and speech but had little sense of the complex transactions and bargaining required by the nature of politics in modern society. "They criticized and opposed despotism," claimed Guizot (1858b, 6), "but theirs was an opposition of enlightened and independent lookers-on, who had neither the opportunity nor inclination to interfere as actors." Their "prodigious boldness"[49] was responsible for their hubris because it led them to believe that human reason could create a perfect society according to preestablished plans that assigned no role to tradition and religion.

Yet, in spite of the "weaknesses of its mores" and the "frivolity of its forms," the eighteenth century was also "a sincere and passionate century, full

Triomphe de Voltaire

of faith and enthusiasm. It had faith in truth and humanity" (Guizot 1829, 234–35). The most interesting and controversial case was Rousseau, the prototype of the eighteenth-century philosopher engaged in subtle but ultimately superfluous political speculations. Rousseau, claimed Constant, was "a blind architect"[60] unable to construct a new edifice out of the scattered rubble. Guizot held a similar view. In his opinion, Rousseau ignored the principles on which liberty was to be founded in practice, and, in spite of their theoretical brilliance, the ideas of the *Social Contract* could not be used to build true constitutional government.[51]

As nineteenth-century liberals, Guizot and his fellow Doctrinaires understood that theirs was a *political* task: They were called to "end" the Revolution that had started in 1789. "The philosophers," Madame de Staël once wrote, "have made the revolution and they will end it" (Staël 1979, 273). The Doctrinaires acted upon this belief and put their energy and talents in the service of this noble but difficult mission. "I entered upon all these questions," claimed Guizot (1858b, 301), "with a firm determination to sift thoroughly the ideas of our time, and to separate revolutionary excitement and fantasies from the advances of justice and liberty, reconcilable with the eternal laws of social order." This was a recurrent theme in the writings of all the Doctrinaires. The youngest of them, Charles de Rémusat, described the task of his generation in similar terms: "We shared one common thought: the idea of bringing the Revolution to an end by creating genuine representative government" (Rémusat 1959, 287).

Unlike their predecessors who had shone in aristocratic salons, the new generation was called to act in public assemblies and clubs, to draft new laws, and to build new institutions. Ideas and theories could no longer be separated from facts and practice, and the theoretical analysis of society was supposed to be put in the service of society. Abstract principles had to be tested at work, and broad generalizations, cut-and-dried legislative systems, and a thirst for perfection had to be replaced by intelligent and prudent political crafting. As the anonymous author of an interesting article published in *Revue française* in 1829 argued, for the new generation to criticize, theorize, and form an opposition became less important than to build representative government. Guizot endorsed this view:

> I was anxious to combat revolutionary theories, and to attach interest and respect to the past theory of France. . . . The time had come for clearing out that arena covered with ruins, and for substituting, in thought as in fact, equity for hostility, and the principles of liberty for the arms of Revolution. An edifice is not built with machines of war; neither can a free system be founded on ignorant principles and inveterate antipathies. (Guizot 1858b, 300)

The Doctrinaires lived in a historical context that forced them to rethink the nature and limits of liberty and power. They had to answer new questions among which the most challenging one was whether democracy could be educated, moderated, and purified of any trace of revolutionary spirit. To this effect, the Doctrinaires regarded the growing equality of conditions and the changes in the social condition as irreversible and understood that the real challenge was to demonstrate that the principles of 1789 could create stable and free government after being "purged" of anarchic elements.[52]

Finally, the Doctrinaires had to overcome the legacy of Napoléon, who wasted immense human and material resources and strengthened the French tradition of administrative and political centralization. Napoléon curtailed basic freedoms, ignored the rule of law, and had no tolerance for political dissent. Toward the end of the Empire, argued Guizot, there was neither a true public life nor a sound public morality: "Corrupt, he corrupted others; despotic, he subdued minds and debased consciences; all-powerful, he constantly made a bad use of his power. His glorious and bloodstained traces remained soiled not only by faults but by crimes" (Guizot 1882, 238). The dream with which Napoléon dazzled his compatriots proved to be nefarious, and the country eventually sunk into dejection and apathy.

"What we need," wrote Guizot in the first issue of *Archives philosophiques, politiques et littéraires*, "is internal peace, the union of all citizens around the throne, the stable functioning of institutions, the free development of public and civil virtues" (Guizot 1817a, 147). In his view, this goal could be achieved only if those who held power promoted the goals dictated by reason and public interest, fought the tyranny of factional interests, and furthered "the national interests, the moderate opinions, the truly patriotic sentiments."[53] To this effect, both the legislative and executive powers had to act in concert in order to advance the general interests of the country, and the monarch had to play a moderating and mediating role among competing social and political interests.

It must be emphasized that in defending their project during the Restoration, the Doctrinaires courageously opposed those popular theories and passions which, in their view, threatened or delayed the consolidation of representative government in France.[54] Their inability to accept, later, that democracy as social condition could be reconciled with popular sovereignty and universal suffrage is, however, indicative of the limitations of their agenda. But if there was any pride in the Doctrinaires' project, it was "a pride commencing with an act of humility, which proclaims the mistakes of yesterday with the desire and hope of not repeating them today" (Guizot 1858b, 154).

In this regard, the writings of the Doctrinaires illustrate both the virtues and limitations of any attempt to find a *juste milieu* between extremes. In a free system, wrote Guizot (1858b, 198), the center is "the fittest party to rule, the only one capable of maintaining order in the State, while tolerating the liberty of its rivals." As such, it must act as the definitive judge of government and ought to give or withhold the majority, not to conquer it. But the center is always under siege, and as such, it offers a fragile political platform highly exposed to the attacks of extremists. One of the most significant aspects of the Doctrinaires' *juste milieu* was their nuanced approach to democracy, a topic that will be explored in the next chapter.

Notes

1. See Guizot 1816, 59. Also see Guizot's article, "De la situation politique et de l'état des esprits en France en 1817," republished in Guizot 1869, 85–105.

2. On this topic, see Mellon 1958, 1–30; D. Johnson 1963, 323–25; Kelley 1984,

3–71.

3. I borrow the phrase from Maistre 1994, 41.

4. See D. Johnson 1963, 326.

5. Nietzsche elaborated on the distinction between the three types of history, "monumental," "antiquarian," and "critical" in *Vom Nutzen und Nachteil der Historie für das Leben,* first published in 1874 (part 2 of *Unzeitgemäße Betrachtungen*). For more details, see Nietzsche 1980, 14–22.

6. Coulanges as quoted in D. Johnson 1963, 321–22.

7. Jubé de la Perelle as quoted in Mellon 1958, 6. On this issue, also see Theis 1997, xl–xliv.

8. Stern 1956, 64. Thierry argued: "L'histoire qui porte le nom de notre pays n'est point la vraie histoire du pays. . . . La meilleure partie de nos annales, la plus grave, la plus instructive reste à écrire; il nous manque l'histoire des citoyens, l'histoire des sujets, l'histoire du public, l'histoire de la masses" (Thierry as quoted in Smithson 1972, 82). For a comprehensive view of Thierry's historical writings, see Smithson 1972.

9. Guizot 1820, 1–2; the translation is mine.

10. Writes Guizot: "La lutte a continué dans tous les âges, sous toutes les formes, avec toutes les armes; et lorsqu'en 1789, les députés de la France entière ont été réunis dans une seule assemblée, les deux peuple se sont hâtés de reprendre leur vieille querelle. . . . Le résultat de la révolution n'était pas douteux. L'ancien peuple vaincu était devenu le peuple vainqueur. À son tour, il avait conquis la France. En 1814 il la possédait sans débat. La charte reconnut sa possession, proclama que ce fait était le droit, et donna au droit le gouvernement représentatif pour garantie" (Guizot 1820, 2–3).

11. See Marx's letter to J. Weydemeyer (March 5, 1852); on this topic, also see Fossaert 1959.

12. On Guizot's historical writings, see Johnson 1963, 320–76; Reizov 1962, 268–352. On Barante's historical method, see Reizov 1962, 190–267.

13. This characterization appears in Mill 1985, 259.

14. Barante was one of the most distinguished representatives of the historical narrative school. For more information, see Reizov 1962, 190–267.

15. For an illustration of Guizot's historical method, see Guizot 1972, 7.

16. Montesquieu as quoted in Littré 1889, 633.

17. For more details, see the entries on *civilisation* and *civiliser* in Littré 1889, 632–33. The history of the concept is also discussed briefly by O'Connor 1955, 39–40. An excellent analysis can be found in Billard 1998, 36–65.

18. See Guizot 1997a, 13.

19. Royer-Collard was quoted by Guizot in the opening chapter of *Histoire de la civilisation en Europe*; for more details, see Guizot 1997a, 22–23.

20. Guizot 1972, 271; these quotes are from the first chapter of Guizot's *Histoire de la civilisation en France*.

21. Guizot 1997a, 203. On the other side of the political spectrum, Joseph de Maistre, no friend of Protestantism, also believed that the French Revolution was the

outcome of Luther's Reformation. But for him, Luther was not a hero.

22. On Guizot's philosophy of history, see O'Connor 1955, 71–81; Rosanvallon 1985, 204–12; D. Johnson 1963, 320–76; Hoeges 1974. A critique can be found in Balmes 1850.

23. The letter can be found in Barante's *Souvenirs*; here, I use the translation of O'Connor (1955, 74).

24. Guizot 1997a, 183. J. S. Mill, too, referred in similar terms to the force of circumstances. In his essay "The Spirit of the Age," he wrote: "Let us place our trust for the future, not in the wisdom of mankind, *but in something far surer—the force of circumstances*" (Mill 1986a, 245; emphasis added).

25. On Guizot's religious ideas, see Guizot 1864 and Kirschleger 1999; for his views on the role of great individuals in history, see O'Connor 1955, 77–81.

26. The first chapter of Maistre's *Considérations sur la France* is illuminating in this respect. For more details, see Maistre 1994, 3–8.

27. For more information on the Charter of 1814, also see chapter 7.

28. For more details, see Vaulabelle 1855, 60–4.

29. See, for example, Anderson (ed.) 1967, 458. On the elaboration of the Charter, see Rosanvallon 1994a, 15–43; Rials 1987, 102–3; Barante 1892, 38–50; Gorce 1926, 15–21; Vaulabelle 1855, 51–101.

30. For more details, see Rosanvallon 1994a, 49–50.

31. Montlosier's three-volume *De la monarchie française* was published in 1814. Guizot published an important review of this book in *Archives philosophiques, politiques et littéraires* (1818).

32. See Royer-Collard 1861b, 16.

33. In his *Réflexions politiques* (1814), Chateaubriand argued: "Nous avons eu autrefois le même gouvernement que l'Anglais; et nous conservons en nous . . . tous les principes de son gouvernement actuel. . . . Il n'est donc pas question, dans tout ceci, de se faire Anglais; l'Europe qui penche avec nous vers un système de monarchie modérée, ne se fera pas Anglaise: ce que l'on a, et que l'on va avoir, est le résultat naturel des anciennes monarchies. L'Angleterre a devancé la marche générale d'un peu plus d'un siècle: voilà tout" (Chateaubriand 1993a, 205–6).

34. In his study of the Charter of 1814, Rials argued that "la souveraineté royale . . . est une souveraineté limitée autant par les préceptes divins que par cette concrétisation de l'action de la providence que sont les coutumes fondamentales" (Rials 1987, 108). Referring to the allegedly contradictory nature of the Charter, Rials wrote: "La Charte octroyée est une simple loi édictée par le roi en vertu d'une souveraineté antérieure, traditionnellement exercée par lui dans le cadre des lois fondamentales du royaume. . . . La puissance royale qui avait octroyé la Charte du fait d'une puissance antérieure ne pouvait se trouver constitué par elle" (Rials 1987, 112). On this issue, also see Royer-Collard 1861b, 460; Gorce 1926, 15–21.

35. It is worth noting that Beugnot rejected the term *pacte social* proposed by Fontanes. Also see the following paragraph: "We have *voluntarily*, and by the free exercise of *our royal authority*, accorded and do *accord, grant, and concede* to our subjects,

as well for us as for our successors forever, the constitutional charter which follows" (Anderson 1967, 459; emphasis added). The Charter of 1830 was a true contract between the new king, Louis-Philippe d'Orléans, and the French nation. For more details, see Rosanvallon 1994a, 52–64 and Laquièze 2002, 38–76.

36. The word *octroi* (concession) has an interesting history. Sieyès, for example, strongly disliked the concept: "Le mot *octroyer* et tous ses dérivés doivent être banni à jamais de la science politique" (Sieyès as quoted in Rosanvallon 1994a, 48).

37. For more details, see Rials 1987, 105–12; Barbé 1904, 50–51; Anderson 1967, 461–62 and Laqièze 2002, 293–386. On the nature of the executive power during the Restoration, see Barbey 1936. According to Article 14 of the Charter, "the king is the supreme head of the state, commands the land and sea forces, declares war, appoints to all places of public administration, and makes the necessary regulations and ordinances for the execution of laws and the security of the state."

38. Writes Tocqueville: "La charte de Louis XVIII était une œuvre nécessairement sans durée; il avait créé des institutions aristocratiques dans les lois politiques et laissait dans les lois civiles un principe démocratique tellement actif qu'il devait détruire en peu de temps les bases de l'édifice qu'il élevait. . . . Les Bourbons au lieu de chercher à renforcer extensiblement un principe aristocratique qui meurt chez nous, auraient dû travailler de tout leur pouvoir à donner des intérêts d'ordre et de stabilité à la démocratie. Dans mon opinion, le système communal et départamental aurait dû dès le principe attirer toute leur attention. Au lieu de vivre au jour le jour avec les institutions communales de Bonaparte, ils auraient dû se hâter de les modifier, initier peu à peu les habitans dans leurs affaires, les y intéresser avec le temps, créer des intérêts locaux et surtout fonder s'il est possible ces habitudes et ces idées légales qui sont à mon avis le seul contrepoids possible à la démocratie" (1977, 234).

39. The fact that the Charter did not create a true parliamentary regime was also underscored by Chateaubriand in *De la monarchie selon la Charte*. The distinction between pure, limited, temperate, and constitutional monarchy is discussed in detail in Rials 1987. On this issue see also Laquièze 2002.

40. On the "liberal party" in Restoration France, see Thureau-Dangin 1876, 1–90, 191–264, 399–452; Harpaz 1968, 1–64, 249–82, 345–66; Kelly 1965, 509–30. I comment on the particular nature of French liberalism in chapter 10. For more details on this topic, see Jaume 1997a, 7–21, 537–54; Hazareesingh 1998, 3–28, 162–232; Judt 1992, 229–45; Rosanvallon, 1985, 44–46; Gunn 2000.

41. On the differences between these two types of liberalism, see Jaume 1997a.

42. The phrase belongs to Guizot 1858a, 159.

43. "Le problème de la politique était alors celui-ci: créer un libéralisme gouvernemental. Posé dès lors, il resta le problème fondamental jusqu'à la fin de la Restauration" (Rémusat 1958, 324). Also see Guizot 1869, 85–105.

44. See Pouthas 1923a, 168, 171, 230–32, 256–58; Reizov 1962, 198–204.

45. See Guizot 1884, 58. Also see the following passage from a parliamentary discourse of Hercule de Serre: "Le premier objet de l'examen dans une loi doit être son principe, l'idée dominante de laquelle dérivent toutes ses dispositions, sa convenance

en général. . . . Si le principe est inadmissible, si la loi en général est inconvenante, il est bien inutile de perdre des jours entiers à discuter et à voter des articles et des amendements destinés à être rejetés en masse avec le principe dont ils ne sont que le développement" (Serre as quoted in Guizot 1817b, 425).

46. Pouthas described this aspect of the Doctrinaires' method as follows: "Ils croient pénétrer dans l'essence des choses et se rendre maîtres de la conduite des évenements et des hommes, s'ils en ont degagé la philosophie" (Pouthas 1923a, 171).

47. On this issue, see Lough 1982 and Guizot 1829, 215–21.

48. Here is an interesting passage from an important article of Guizot originally published in *Revue française* (September 1829): "Le dix-huitième siècle aussi s'occupait fort de politique, mais comme étude, non comme affaire; en se promenant, pour ainsi dire, non en traînant la charrue; elle prenait beaucoup de place dans les esprits, peu dans la vie; on réfléchissait, on dissertait, on projetait beaucoup; *on agissait peu.* En aucun temps les matières politiques n'ont été l'objet d'une preoccupation intellectuelle si générale et si féconde; aucun temps peut-être n'a été plus étranger à l'esprit politique proprement dit, à cet esprit simple, prompt, judicieux, résolu, léger dans la pensée, sérieux dans l'action, qui ne voit que les faits et ne s'inquiete que dans les resultants. . . . Or l'école du dix-huitième siècle . . . était *essentiellement philosophique et littéraire*: la politique l'intéressait, mais comme l'un des objets, comme une application d'idées qui venaient de plus loin. . . . C'est là le caractère de l'esprit philosophique, bien différent de l'esprit politique qui ne s'attache aux idées que dans leur rapport avec les faits sociaux et pour les appliquer" (Guizot 1829, 215, 220–21; emphasis added).

49. I borrow the phrase from Guizot 1997a, 243.

50. Constant as quoted in Holmes 1984, 92.

51. See Guizot 1821, 358.

52. Here is a passage from an important parliamentary discourse of Guizot (March 1838) in which the same question appeared in a different form: "La vraie tâche de notre époque est de savoir si, des idées de 1789 et de l'état social qu'elles ont amené, il peut sortir un gouvernement *stable et régulier.* Pour y réussir, deux conditions nous sont absolument imposées. La première, c'est de *purger* les principes de 1789 de tout alliage anarchique: cet alliage a été naturel, inévitable. Ces idées ont servi à détruire ce qui existait alors, gouvernement et société; elles ont contracté dans ce travail un caractère révolutionnaire. Le moment est venu de les en dégager et de les ramener à leur sens vrai et pur" (Guizot 1863b, 153; emphasis added).

53. Guizot as quoted in Pouthas 1923a, 129.

54. Writes Guizot: "Les doctrinaires répondaient à un *besoin réel et profond*, quoique obscurément senti, des esprits en France; ils avaient à cœur l'honneur intellectuel comme le bon ordre de la société; leurs idées se présentaient comme propres à régénérer en même temps qu'à *clore la Révolution*. . . . Le côté droit les tenait pour des royalistes sincères, et le côté gauche, même en les combattant avec aigreur, savait bien qu'ils n'étaient les défenseurs ni de l'ancien régime, ni du pouvoir absolu" (Guizot 1858a, 159; emphasis added).

~

CHAPTER FOUR

Democracy, Civilization, and the French Revolution

Vous jugez la Démocratie en aristocrate vaincu et convaincu que son vainqueur a raison.

—Guizot to Tocqueville

The French Doctrinaires are usually described as staunch critics of democracy who rejected democratic principles and were hostile to its values. The present chapter will seek to *nuance* this image by exploring the Doctrinaires' views on two important topics that loomed large in their writings: the French Revolution and democracy as social condition. My intention is not, however, to present the Doctrinaires as enthusiastic champions of democracy, but to point out all the nuances of their arguments on the multifarious nature of modern democracy. Tocqueville had a more balanced and, ultimately, superior perspective on this issue, but he learned a lot from Guizot, Royer-Collard, and Rémusat. While democracy remained for the Doctrinaires a deeply ambiguous phenomenon, at the same time inevitable and potentially disruptive of the social and political order, Guizot and his colleagues made a seminal distinction between democracy as social condition (*état social*) and political democracy. This distiction allows us to understand their ideas on the larger and more complex issue of educating, taming, and moderating democracy.

Those who view Guizot as a conservative usually refer only to his book *De la démocratie en France* (1849) and tend to overlook his (more) important liberal writings published during the Bourbon Restoration. Yet, this volume was a circumstantial and, conceptually speaking, insignificant work, written in reaction to the Revolution of 1848, which marked the end of Guizot's political career. He feared that the premature introduction of popular sovereignty would jeopardize the new social order and would obstruct the proper functioning of representative institutions. Guizot equated political democracy with socialism, whose principles he strongly opposed (needless to say, he was *not* the only one to reject socialism in the epoch!).

Yet, we must not forget that Guizot had developed a much more nuanced and interesting theory of democracy as social condition (*état social*) in his political writings published during the Restoration, to which we shall turn our attention in this chapter. There is, perhaps, no better way of exploring the Doctrinaires' position on democracy and the French Revolution than by comparing their views with Tocqueville's ideas. By highlighting Tocqueville's often neglected debt to Guizot, Royer-Collard, and Rémusat, I shall also offer a contextual reinterpretation of the early phase in Tocqueville's life (1828–31) *prior* to his trip to America. The argument of this chapter is that in order to fully understand the conceptual framework of Tocqueville's *De la démocratie en Amérique*, we must first read Guizot's *Histoire de la civilisation en Europe* and Royer-Collard's parliamentary speeches.[1]

A Few Similarities and Differences

Sainte-Beuve[2] once prophesied that Tocqueville would become an inexhaustible subject of reflection for many generations of scholars fascinated by his "new science of politics." He was right. Political scientists who searched for Tocqueville's sources were often struck by a particular feature of his style. As Charles de Rémusat once remarked, Tocqueville rediscovered and reinterpreted in an original manner what others had said before him, but was very shy at disclosing his own sources.[3]

Not surprisingly, tracing these sources has proved to be a difficult task, because of Tocqueville's famous reluctance to acknowledge his debt and his inclination to look for truth on his own. Indeed, Tocqueville possessed an uncommon power of synthesis and generalization and also had a sharp sense of independence. Some scholars have tried an alternative approach by attempting to point out the *problems* from which Tocqueville started or those issues that were publicly debated in the 1820s in France.[4] In what follows, by drawing on his correspondence and notes from 1828 to 1831, I shall combine both approaches in order to demonstrate that Tocqueville had had plenty of opportunities to reflect on important themes that loom large in his masterpiece *before* traveling to America. Tocqueville's political outlook was significantly influenced by the parliamentary debates that took place during the Bourbon Restoration. Even if some changes in emphasis can be detected between the two volumes of *De la démocratie en Amérique*, it is likely that a significant part of Tocqueville's political vision had crystallized by the time he made his famous voyage. The French Doctrinaires—above all, Royer-Collard, Guizot, and Rémusat—exercised a crucial influence in this regard.[5]

The study of ideas, their origins, influence, and adaptations is an interesting but challenging and sometimes inconclusive endeavor. Given Tocqueville's unique style of thinking and writing, I shall analyze his adaptation of some of the Doctrinaires' ideas as a means of understanding how a great political philosopher made creative use of his predecessors' conceptual framework.[6] Without aiming at downplaying the originality of Tocqueville's *De la démocratie en Amérique* (Tocqueville remains my favorite author), it behooves us to demonstrate the ways in which his conceptual apparatus was shaped by the political debates between the Doctrinaires and ultraconservatives from 1815 to 1830. To this effect, I shall focus on three main issues: the interpretations of the origins of the French Revolution, democracy as social condition, and the fundamental distinction between social and political order.

Of all the French Doctrinaires, Tocqueville had a particularly close relation with Royer-Collard in the mid-1830s. Yet, before he became a close friend of Royer, he had passed through a Guizotian phase in the late 1820s and early 1830s and had also become acquainted with the writings of Rémusat, who was only eight years older than Tocqueville. We know that volume two of *De la démocratie en Amérique* was written in a period of intense correspondence between Tocqueville and Royer-Collard. Their letters bear witness to the affinities between the two men and demonstrate the extent to which Royer-Collard served as a model to his younger friend. The first letter of Tocqueville to his mentor was dated January 1835, on the eve of the publication of volume one of *De la démocratie en Amérique*. The exchange continued over the years and ended before Royer-Collard's death in 1845 (his last letter to Tocqueville was written on October 23, 1844). For us, the importance of these letters lies in the information they convey about Tocqueville's masterpiece and Royer-Collard's influence on his younger disciple.[7]

The affinity between the political ideas of Tocqueville and Royer-Collard was not a mere accident. Royer-Collard had words of high praise for volume one of *De la démocratie en Amérique*, which he favorably compared with Aristotle's *Politics* and Montesquieu's *De l'esprit des lois*. "I have read it five times," he confessed to his friend, Becquey; "it is for me an inexhaustible source of instruction and pleasure."[8] In turn, Tocqueville was thoroughly familiar with

Royer-Collard's parliamentary discourses and considered them as "seminal discourses, by their ideas, method, and style" (Tocqueville 1970, 103). Tocqueville cherished Royer-Collard for being one of the last representatives of a great generation and admired his dignity and strong spirit of independence.[9] He envied Royer-Collard's fortune in having lived at a crucial juncture in time when the foundations of a new regime were laid. He also shared the same concern with "ending" the Revolution and constitutionalizing its liberties. The fact that Tocqueville, like the Doctrinaires, was a defender of (constitutional) hereditary monarchy may surprise us, since political theorists have often glossed over this aspect of his political thought. Nonetheless, as his private correspondence demonstrates,[10] Tocqueville preferred a hereditary monarchy to a republic and regarded the first as suitable to the social and political condition of postrevolutionary France.

Furthermore, both Royer-Collard and Tocqueville vigorously defended liberty of the press, commented on the relation between liberty and legitimacy, and opposed absolute power. More importantly, both men felt a particular taste for great political actions that was stifled by the spirit of modern commercial society: "I do not miss the old form of society, but the type of people that lived then, the souls, and characters. I need greatness."[11] Royer-Collard's fears echoed Tocqueville's worries that, by furthering an endless and relentless quest for material success, the new regime would sow, in the end, the seeds of its own destruction. Politics, wrote Royer-Collard to his electors in 1837, is now devoid of its former greatness and individual interests prevail over more noble passions.[12] Last but not least, their views on democracy as social condition also shared many common points, to which we shall return in the final section of this chapter.

If the affinities between Tocqueville and Royer-Collard are more or less obvious from their correspondence, it is more difficult to accurately describe the relations between Tocqueville's political thought and the ideas of Guizot. At first glance, it seems easier to point out what *separated* Tocqueville from Guizot than what united them.[13] To be sure, by reading Tocqueville's private letters of 1835 to 1848 or the first chapter of his *Souvenirs*, one might be tempted to conclude that Guizot was the politician Tocqueville scorned the most during the last years of the July Monarchy. Tocqueville's correspondence conveys his skepticism toward Guizot the politician, whom he found "fundamentally alien"[14] to his own way of thinking and feeling. The bourgeois lifestyle of the July Monarchy seemed to the author of *De la démocratie en Amérique* marred by pettiness, egoism, and mediocrity with which Tocqueville could not reconcile himself. It was an age devoid of greatness, he noted in the *Souvenirs*, in which true politics became almost impossible and the government itself resembled more and more a huge industrial company. Tocqueville saw the cause of this predicament in the then widespread belief that politics had become nothing more than an arena for trivial ambitions and sordid political manipulations. He was dismayed by the increasing materialism of both private and public life in France and disliked political eclecticism.

This dissatisfaction with the regime led by Guizot was expressed by Tocqueville in a well-known parliamentary speech on the eve of the Revolution of 1848. "It seems to me," he argued, "that the present state of things, the state of opinion and of men's minds in France, gives cause for alarm and sorrow."[15] When his taste for great events remained unsatisfied, Tocqueville was not shy at disclosing his idiosyncrasy as well as his exasperation with "our little democratic and bourgeois pot of soup"[16] of the day. On September 27, 1841, he confessed to Royer-Collard that he felt an almost invincible repugnance to associate himself in a permanent manner with any of his contemporaries, by which he most likely referred to Thiers, Guizot, and their followers. Furthermore, he also wrote that among all the parties that divided France at that time, he did not see a single one to which he wanted to be tied. A few lines later, in a famous sentence, Tocqueville concluded: "The liberal and antirevolutionary party, which alone would suit me, does not exist and it is certainly not my task to create it" (Tocqueville 1970, 108).

But the differences between Tocqueville and Guizot do not stop here. Unlike the latter, Tocqueville was not an apostle of the bourgeoisie, and he refused to believe that the triumph of the middle class was the culminating point in the history of European civilization. For him, the rise of the middle class presupposed a combination of individualism and materialism that Tocqueville the aristocrat flatly rejected. Moreover, for Guizot, the value of representative government derived from its role as a mechanism of selection of natural superiorities, whereas Tocqueville admired it for the social and economic effervescence it spreads into the fabric of society.

More importantly perhaps, Guizot did not travel to America to catch a glimpse of the profile of the future society; instead, he looked across the Channel to England, whose institutions he admired (his opponents once ironically called him "Lord Guizot"). He also delved into the past and studied the development of European civilization by highlighting its diverse components in their perpetual struggle for supremacy. He worked mainly with concepts, such as *civilization*, that he inherited from his French and Scottish predecessors.[17] Tocqueville took a different tack. He did not share Guizot's obsession with the Glorious Revolution of 1688, nor was he sympathetic to the idea of mixed government or the doctrine of the sovereignty of reason.

He understood that the new democratic social condition characterized by the equality of conditions would make revolutions rarer in the future if the people were granted full political rights. Guizot failed to grasp this point and continued to fear the specter of the Revolution until his fall from power in 1848.

Tocqueville's interpreters often underestimated the lasting influence that Guizot exercised over Tocqueville between 1828 and 1831. What many historians overlooked was the striking fact that Guizot's *Histoire de la civilisation en Europe* was the *only* book that Tocqueville asked a friend to send him from France, a week after his arrival in New York in May 1831. "We cannot find here," he wrote to Chabrol, "a book which is very necessary in helping us to analyze American society; *these are the lectures of Guizot*, containing what he said and published three years ago about the society of Rome and the Middle Ages."[18] The fact that Tocqueville needed Guizot's lectures on the history of civilization in Europe in order to analyze American society is, indeed, puzzling. How can we explain this surprising detail?

If we examine the evolution of Tocqueville's ideas from 1828 to 1831, we realize that there were important *similarities* between Tocqueville's and Guizot's methods that have been neglected by those commentators who were too quick to highlight what separated the two French thinkers. Indeed, both Tocqueville and Guizot disliked socialism and were preoccupied with finding a way to "end the Revolution." Tocqueville believed that "the most rational government is not that in which all the interested parties take part, but that which the most enlightened and most moral classes of the society direct" (Tocqueville 1985b, 56). Guizot, too, shared this view and made it the cornerstone of his theory of representative government. They both argued that the French Revolution was the outcome of a long historical evolution and were keen on dissociating the spirit of 1789 from the Terror of 1793. In a letter to Eugène Stoffels that can be viewed as one of the best expressions of Tocqueville's political credo, he confessed his staunch opposition to revolutionary spirit in the following unambiguous terms: "I do not think that in France there is a man who is less revolutionary than I, nor one who has a more profound hatred for what is called the revolutionary spirit (a spirit which is very easily combined with the love of an absolute government)."[19] These words could have also been uttered by Guizot, who rarely disguised his fear of anarchy and his opposition to the revolutionary spirit in all its manifestations.

Guizot once wrote to Tocqueville: "You judge democracy like an aristocrat who has been vanquished and is convinced that his conqueror is right."[20] He wanted, in fact, to argue that, in spite of their apparent disagreements, their political ideas were surprisingly similar. This point was conveyed by Guizot in a discourse at the Académie française in 1861, in which he celebrated the memory of Tocqueville (who had died in 1859) and explicitly pointed to the affinity between their political ideas. The long-term goals that they pursued, claimed Guizot, were very much the same—the establishment of a liberal regime in postrevolutionary France—although the means they chose were sometimes different.[21] This was much more than a circumstantial or rhetorical acknowledgment of the merits of a deceased friend. To demonstrate this point, we shall explore next the impact of the Doctrinaires' writings on Tocqueville by concentrating on their interpretation of history and the nature of the French Revolution.

The Hidden Dialogue between Tocqueville and Guizot

Any reader of Tocqueville's masterpiece notes the important emphasis on the concept of the *equality of conditions* that lies at the core of what he called the "democratic revolution." The very first pages of the book are revealing. From the moment Tocqueville set foot on the American soil, nothing impressed him more than the equality of conditions in the New World. The equality of conditions, he noted, brings people together and creates new opinions, sentiments, and novel customs, thus engendering a new social condition. The barriers between classes are loosened, property is divided, and power is shared by many individuals. In other words, society becomes democratic, and the empire of democracy is slowly introduced into institutions and customs.

Given the key role played by this concept in Tocqueville's works, it is important for us to ask how Tocqueville reached this conclusion. Was it merely the result of observation or was it a part of a larger theoretical framework? My hypothesis is that when thinking about the equality of conditions, Tocqueville started from and adapted creatively Guizot's theory of "civilization"[22] that can be found in the very book he requested to be sent to him from France, a week after his arrival in New York. As we have already seen, the subject of Guizot's volume was the development of European civilization, which he identified with the slow rise of the equality of conditions and the third estate. Tocqueville discarded the concept of civilization altogether and concentrated on democracy as social condition, whose mainspring was the equality of conditions. In his eyes, *democracy* acquired almost the same meaning that *civilization* had for Guizot.

John Stuart Mill was quick to grasp this important point which, alas, many of Tocqueville's interpreters overlooked.[23] Mill carefully read Guizot's history of civilization, whose ideas he strongly admired. In a letter to Blanco White written on April 15, 1835, he drew an explicit parallel between Tocqueville and Guizot. It not a mere coincidence that Mill admired Tocqueville's capacity of drawing general conclusions regarding the history of society, a quality that he also praised in Guizot's case. In the letter sent to White, Mill confessed: "I have begun to read Tocqueville. It seems an excellent book: uniting considerable graphic power, with the capacity of generalizing on the history of society, which distinguishes the best French philosophers of the present day. . . . Did you ever read Guizot's Lectures? If not, I pray do."[24] Five years later, in his review of volume two of *De la démocratie en Amérique* (1840), Mill wrote:

> M. de Tocqueville, then, has at least apparently confounded the effects of Democracy with the effects of Civilization. He has bound up in one abstract idea the whole of the tendencies of modern commercial society, and given them one name—Democracy; thereby letting it be supposed that he ascribes to equality of conditions, several of the effects naturally rising from the mere progress of national prosperity, in the form in which that progress manifests itself in modern times.[25]

This passage points out the influence of Guizot's ideas on civilization on Mill's reading of Tocqueville. Mill understood that a great deal of what Tocqueville presented as the features of the modern democratic egalitarian society (as illustrated by American democracy) coincided to a significant degree with what Guizot had previously identified as traits of English mind and modern commercial society. The predominant philosophy of the latter is utilitarianism; its main goal is social perfection, the amelioration of the external and public condition of society. Modern democratic society displays the same characteristics: everywhere the principle of utility and its applications dominate, thus constituting at once its physiognomy and force.

It is worth noting that the influence of Guizot on Mill can also be detected in two of Mill's earlier essays, "The Spirit of the Age" (1831) and "Civilization" (1836). "The word *civilization*," wrote Mill, "is a word of double meaning. It sometimes stands for human improvement in general, and sometimes for certain kinds of improvement in particular" (Mill 1977, 119). The first meaning refers to advances in the road to perfection; in this view, a country is more civilized if it is happier, nobler, and wiser. A second meaning of civilization refers only to that kind of improvement which distinguishes a wealthy and powerful nation from savages and barbarians. The advent of civilization brings forth a new type of social power: "Power passes more and more from individuals, and small knots of individuals, to masses." As a result of the gradual equalization of conditions, "the importance of the masses becomes constantly greater, that of individuals less" (Mill 1977, 121). Mill argued that the characteristics of an advanced civilization are "the diffusion of property and intelligence, and the power of cooperation" (Mill 1977, 124), an idea that also loomed large in Guizot's lectures on the history of civilization in Europe and France.

In a letter to Louis de Kergolay written in January 1835, on the eve of the publication of *De la démocratie en Amérique*, Tocqueville acknowledged: "Nearly ten years ago I was already thinking about part of the things I have just now set forth. *I was in America only to become clear on this point.* The penitentiary system was a *pretext*: I took it only as a passport that would let me enter thoroughly into the United States."[26] For any interpreter of Tocqueville, this statement is of utmost importance because it helps place his masterpiece in a proper conceptual framework. To understand the profile of the new society, Tocqueville undertook in fact not one but *two* voyages. The first and best-known one—the voyage in space—took him to America, where he saw the new democracy at work. Volume one of *De la démocratie en Amérique* came out in 1835, followed five years later by volume two, in which Tocqueville offered a more abstract analysis of democracy and its mores. The second voyage was one in time and gave him the opportunity to analyze the political and social order of the Old Regime.

The fall and legacy of the Old Regime had long been, in fact, an obsession for Tocqueville with which he started wrestling *before* embarking for America. His ideas first crystallized in a less-known essay, *État social et politique de la France avant et depuis 1789 (The Social and Political Condition of France Before and Since 1789)*, which was published in 1836 and bore a title that foreshadowed his famous book on the Old Regime and the Revolution (1856). Tocqueville wrote only the first part of the study. His analysis stopped at 1789, which demonstrates that he was interested in writing neither a *histoire événementielle* nor a detailed chronicle of the Revolution. On the contrary, he was concerned with the *longue durée* and was intent on highlighting the obscure forces that had shaped the profile of his age.

Guizot espoused a similar approach in his historical books and lectures, above all in *Histoire de la civilisation en Europe* and *Histoire de la civilisation en France*, with which Tocqueville was entirely familiar (he attended Guizot's lectures). As we have already seen, Guizot's main project was to insert the history of France into the larger framework of European civilization, a path also followed in part by Tocqueville in *L'Ancien Régime et la Révolution*. The true object of Guizot's historical writings was the modern revolution, which he identified with the slow rise of the equality of conditions and the third estate. It is not a mere coincidence that Guizot himself valued highly Tocqueville's last book, which he considered to be his most beautiful work, albeit "less brilliant and confident" than *De la démocratie en Amérique*. The precision of ideas and the fine reflections on the prerequisites of liberty impressed Tocqueville's readers, including Guizot.[27]

All the major topics that loomed large in Tocqueville's last major book were already present in the short essay published in 1836: the division (segregation) of classes, aristocracy and political privileges, the connection between aristocracy and local government, democracy and centralization, liberty under the Old Regime, and the rise of the *tiers état*. In Tocqueville's view, the most important trend in the history of France had been neither the consolidation of monarchy nor the emergence of the French nation.[28] He pointed instead to the spontaneous march toward *civil equality*—or, to use his own phrase, the equality of conditions—that had emerged in the bosom of the old society. (Needless to say, this society continued to remain deeply inegalitarian in comparison with the United States.) This was a theme that also loomed large in Guizot's historical writings, above all in connection with his analysis of the rise of the third estate and the leveling of social conditions. "The earthquakes we call revolutions," Guizot once wrote, "are less the symptom of what is beginning than the declaration of what has already occurred" (Guizot 1884, 16). Tocqueville wholeheartedly endorsed this view.

In addition to discussing the leveling of conditions, Tocqueville also insisted on the divorce between the social condition of the country and its institutional superstructure, which had been based on political inequality and privilege. In France, claimed Tocqueville, the trend toward democracy understood as equality of conditions had had a long tradition. Nonetheless, in spite of this evolution, the institutions failed to adapt to the new social condition and continued to acknowledge the priority of privilege and social inequality.[29] Tocqueville's diagnosis foreshadowed his famous description of the Revolution as the outcome of a long historical process. To those who argued that the Revolution was an entirely new phenomenon, he pointed out that the period 1789–94 brought to fruition tendencies and developments that had, in fact, *preceded* the fall of the Old Regime. The Revolution was the effect of many hidden factors that had been at work for many centuries.

Therefore, Tocqueville concluded, the key to comprehending the Revolution should be looked for in the heart of the Old Regime, in the dark corners of the history of France. The real event was a truly European Revolution, which had started with the Reformation and continued with Bacon, Descartes, and the Enlightenment. The Revolution, argued Tocqueville, created a multitude of "secondary" things, but it only developed the kernel of the main things that had existed before it. "The Revolution regulated, coordinated, and legalized the effects of a great cause rather than being this cause itself. . . . All of what the Revolution did was done without it; it was only a violent and quick process by which the political order adjusted to the social order, the fact to ideas, and the laws to mores."[30]

L'Ancien Régime et la Révolution (1856) contained in a condensed form all the themes that occupied Tocqueville's attention during his life. The specter of the Revolution starting over and over again must have been one of the main reasons for writing this book. The political and social turmoil of the three years that separated the fall of the July Monarchy in 1848 from the Second Empire demonstrated that the age of revolution was far from over. Tocqueville addressed issues such as social leveling, administrative centralization, the rise of individualism and equality, and the segregation of classes in order to demonstrate that the Revolution had been the outcome of a long period of gestation, the work of six generations. It made far fewer changes than commonly admitted, though it furthered the modernization of the country by eliminating the legacy of feudal institutions. That is why, in order to understand the causes and meanings of the Revolution, one must place it in a larger historical and political context.

As already indicated, Tocqueville was not the first historian to have reached this conclusion. He only followed in the footsteps of Guizot, whose courses on the history of civilization in Europe and France had brought him well-deserved fame and recognition as one of the leading historians of his epoch. From the time when Tocqueville attended Guizot's lectures on the history of civilization in Europe, he entered into an intellectual and political dialogue with his teacher.[31] What united the two Frenchmen was a similar view of (monumental) history. Neither Guizot nor Tocqueville was primarily interested in writing a *histoire événementielle* of the French Revolution; instead, they concentrated on the factors and forces that had made possible the events of 1789.

By writing a history of the European civilization in light of the French Revolution, Guizot unearthed a whole tradition of representative institutions and local freedoms that were connected to the rise of the third estate in modern Europe. In the history of France, he discerned the march toward an ever more complex social organization, based on certain unifying principles. He pointed out the existence of a tradition of local liberties in pre-Revolution France and claimed that 1789 had not been a radical break with the past. The Old Regime had been characterized not only by a trend toward centralization, but also by a growing equality of conditions and the substitution of public powers (*pouvoirs publics*) for individual wills (Tocqueville addressed the same issues in the second part of *L'Ancien Régime et la Révolution*).

In *Histoire de la civilisation en Europe*, Guizot argued that the dissolution of feudalism eventually led to centralization, which emerged precisely in response to the disintegration of social ties and means of regular maintenance of order in the waning feudal world.[32] The fifteenth century witnessed the appearance of universal interests and ideas and marked the beginning of "the silent and concealed work of centralization, whether in social relations or ideas, a work accomplished by the natural course of events, without premeditation or design" (Guizot 1997a, 183). Traditional local liberties were gradually replaced by more concentrated and regular powers that led to "the centralization, unity, and preponderance of general interests and public powers" all over Europe (Guizot 1997a, 191). This ushered in a new epoch "when all [was] general facts and general ideas, the epoch of order and unity" (Guizot 1997a, 197). The centralization of social relations, power, and interests was inevitable and necessary,[33] but it was bound to clash with free inquiry (this is what happened in seventeenth-century England). Over time, the conflict between authority and liberty triggered the opposite tendency to dissolution by which the bonds of government were relaxed.

There are few references to Guizot's works in Tocqueville's early writings and letters, but the ones that we have demonstrate his strong admiration for Guizot, whose courses on the history of civilization in France and Europe he attended in 1829–30.[34] In a letter written on August 30, 1829, Tocqueville informed his friend, Gustave de Beaumont, that he had devoted all his time to reading the historical and political works of Guizot, whom he found "truly prodigious" in analysis of ideas and in choice of words; he also proposed that they reread Guizot the following winter.[35] When Tocqueville asked for a copy of Guizot's *Histoire de la civilisation en Europe* a week after his arrival in New York in May 1831, it was supposed to help him find the most suitable method for understanding American society. It is important to note Tocqueville's interest in Guizot's sociological *method* from which he drew inspiration when analyzing the spirit of (American) democracy as reflected in its mores, opinions, laws, and other "monuments of intelligence."

Tocqueville's notes demonstrate the impact of Guizot's lectures on his younger disciple, an influence that became more visible in his later writings, most notably in *L'Ancien Régime et la Révolution*. The course notes taken by Tocqueville in 1829 illustrate his search for a method that was reminiscent of Guizot's own historical approach. A history of civilization, noted Tocqueville, aims at a comprehensive understanding of the world by examining man and his social life; it explores and incorporates brute facts and opinions, mores and laws.[36] Tocqueville also elaborated on another theme that loomed large in Guizot's historical writings: the relation and interaction between society and the individual. The history of civilization, he argued, consists of both the history of society and the history of intellect (Tocqueville called it *l'histoire de l'intelligence*).[37] The first includes not only the history of civil society, with its facts and laws, but also the history of religion in society, while *l'histoire de l'intelligence* traces the development of both scholarly and popular literature. All these insights drawn from Guizot's course helped Tocqueville form his own original approach, which, as we shall see in the next section, was based on a seminal distinction between democracy as *état social* (social condition) and *political* democracy (popular sovereignty and universal suffrage).

Nonetheless, Tocqueville did not limit himself to refining his teacher's method, but also reformulated and qualified some of Guizot's political ideas. In *Histoire de la civilisation en Europe*, Guizot had argued that "wherever individuality predominates exclusively, wherever man considers no one but himself, and his ideas do not extend beyond himself, [permanent] society becomes for him almost impossible."[38] This idea fascinated Tocqueville. In an important (yet rarely quoted) letter to Charles Stoffels, dated April 21, 1830 (a year *before* his voyage to America), Tocqueville contrasted the social condition of a "semienlightened" people with that of a highly civilized people. In the latter case, the individual is gradually replaced by the social group and society becomes a new Leviathan that tends to take care of all the aspects of social life. The similarity between the message of this letter and the famous description of democratic despotism from volume two of *De la démocratie en Amérique* is striking and suggests the hypothesis that Tocqueville might have concieved of the idea of democratic despotism *before* visiting America, while meditating on Guizot's lectures on the history of European civilization.

Here is what Tocqueville wrote to Stoffels in 1830:

> Now, let us compare this semienlightened people with the one that had achieved a high degree of civilization. In the latter case, the social body has provided for everything; the individual barely takes the trouble of being born; beyond that, society takes him in his nourishing arms, watches over his education, opens up before him the paths of fortune, sustains him in his advance, and removes all dangers from his mind. [The individual] moves forward in peace under the eyes of this second Providence; this tutelary power which protects him during his life will also watch over the rest of his ashes: this is the fate of civilized man. The feeling and spectacle of happiness soon mollifies the wild roughness of his nature; he becomes mild, sociable, his passions calm down . . . the crimes become rare but, unfortunately, virtues, too, become more rare. The sleeping soul in its long repose no longer knows how to wake up when required; individual energy is almost extinguished; individuals rely on each other when they must act; in all other circumstances, one retreats into

one's shell. This is the reign of egoism, one's convictions are shaken at the same time. . . . The entire world becomes an insolvable problem for the individual who clings to the most tangible objects and ends by lying facedown on earth for fear of losing ground.[39]

What this seminal letter shows is that in 1830, a year *before* embarking for America, Tocqueville spoke of the reign of individualism[40] and referred to society as a second Providence, endowed with an immense power. The advance of civilization brings forth a new type of public administration, which eventually becomes not only more centralized, but also more inquisitive and minute. It tends to interfere to a greater extent with private concerns and to regulate more undertakings than ever before.

Tocqueville's ideas on this matter shared important affinities with Guizot's theory of the four states of societies presented in the first chapter of *Histoire de la civilisation en Europe*. In the first type of society, which can be found in small aristocratic republics, the people had a well-regulated material existence, but their "intellectual and moral existence [was] studiously kept in a state of torpor and inactivity" (Guizot 1997a, 15). In the second type of society that could be found in Asia, there was less material prosperity, but there existed at the same time a certain development in the moral and intellectual spheres. Yet, individual liberty was stifled and no one was allowed to seek truth for himself. The third type of society that characterized the early Middle Ages in Europe allowed a great degree of individual liberties, but also great inequalities. As such, it was the empire of force and the strongest, violence and arbitrariness being the most important features of the social state. In the fourth type of society, "the liberty of each individual is very great, inequality amongst them is rare. . . . Every man . . . differs little in power from his neighbour; but there are very few general interests, very few public ideas, very little society. . . . This is the state of savage tribes; liberty and equality are there, but assuredly not civilization" (Guizot 1997a, 16). Tocqueville was skeptical about the possibility of preserving freedom in this fourth type of society, characterized by equality of conditions and an extreme form of individualism. That is why he went to great length to emphasize the important role played by civil and political associations that bring people together in the public realm and allow them to pursue common goals that go beyond their private interests.

A Classic Comparison: France and England

In the *L'Ancien Régime et la Révolution*, Tocqueville drew a comparison between English and French political institutions and highlighted the different historical patterns that led to different political outcomes in the two countries. In doing so, Tocqueville followed a whole tradition of interpretation in nineteenth-century French political thought.[41] To be sure, attitudes toward England ranged from unrestrained to admiration to skepticism. In general, however, England was seen as the model that France had to imitate in its attempt to build representative institutions. The apogee of the liberal praise for England can be found in the third volume of Madame de Staël's *Considérations sur les principaux événements de la Révolution française* (1818) and Benjamin Constant's *Principes de politiques* (1815). But England and its political tradition also appealed to ultraconservatives, who praised the English Constitution for its wise balance between innovation and tradition and admired the English enlightened and active aristocracy.

Guizot was also a notorious Anglophile and remained a friend of England throughout his entire life. It will be recalled that he spent considerable time studying the roots of liberty in England, the subject of volume two of *Histoire des origines du gouvernement représentatif en Europe*. He also wrote a monumental history of the English Revolution that became a reference work for anyone interested in comparing the Revolutions of 1789, 1648, and 1688. "His [Guizot's] work on the English Revolution," claimed Lady Palmerston, "is regarded as the best and most impartial account written on this topic."[42] In the 1840s, as ambassador to London and prominent member of the Soult-Guizot cabinet, Guizot attempted to create an entente cordiale between France and England; after the Revolution of 1848, he sought refuge across the Channel.[43]

In an important essay on the history of the English Revolution written in 1850, Guizot commented on the importance of this event in the history of European civilization. It is worth pausing for a moment to examine this discourse, because it summarizes many important ideas that had loomed large in Guizot's writings published during the Bourbon Restoration. The opening lines of the text clearly convey the message underlying Guizot's interpretation of 1648: "The English Revolution succeeded. It succeeded twice. Its authors first founded constitutional monarchy in England; their descendants founded in America the republic of the United States."[44] Guizot interpreted 1648 and 1688 as two related episodes of a genuine revolution of liberty that successfully blended the spirit of political liberty and religion. It was a revolution that did not destroy the foundations of society and monarchy and did not tear down its old institutions (as it happened in 1789 in France). More importantly, the English revolution significantly changed the ways in which the country was ruled. The monarch was no longer able to govern independently from Parliament and the union between the crown and the latter became a true necessity. Moreover, the House of Commons acquired a prominent position in Parliament and came to exercise a considerable influence on public affairs. Finally, Anglicanism was instrumental in creating an intimate union between faith and liberty and a climate of toleration.

In *Histoire de la civilisation en Europe* and *Histoire des origines du gouvernement représentatif*, Guizot commented on the peculiar features of English society and its institutions. He stressed the absence of absolute power in England and attributed it to the sound division of powers, the strong public opinion and freedom of the press, and the strong tradition of self-government. He also praised the English unwritten constitution, which provided for a mixed form of government whose strength derived from the independence of judiciary and the freedom of municipal and provincial bodies. Guizot's analysis of 1648 and 1688 has to be interpreted in light of his liberal political agenda. In his view, the greatest merit of the Glorious Revolution consisted precisely in its peaceful, nonrevolutionary character. Guizot hoped that France, too, would eventually reach a settlement similar to that of 1688. Royer-Collard espoused a different approach. He challenged those who wanted to copy the English institutions and sought to transplant them onto the French soil. These institutions, argued Royer-Collard, were the outcome of a particular social condition and historical evolution, which created a unique balance of powers that could not be found in France.[45]

Tocqueville became involved in this debate at an early age and was a fervent Anglophile. He was interested in comparing the ways in which English and French political institutions developed over time, a preoccupation that arose early in his career, as a seminal letter to Beaumont written on October 5, 1828, attests. The result of this comparative analysis was part two of *L'Ancien Régime et la Révolution*. In fact, the whole book can be read as a comparison between France and England, which explains why Tocqueville considered England as his second *patrie*. His debt to Guizot, himself an admirer of the English system, must be duly underscored in this regard.

In the fourteenth chapter of *Histoire de la civilisation en Europe*, Guizot commented on the stark contrast between the relentless growth of administrative centralization in France and the nature of the English political system based on decentralization and local liberties. The key to explaining these divergent patterns lies in the different patterns of interaction between the monarch, aristocracy, and the commons. In France, the various elements of society—monarchy, aristocracy, and democracy—developed themselves not together, but in succession; each principle reigned in turn at the expense of the others. Feudalism reigned sovereign until the thirteenth century, while royalty and the democratic principle were more or less powerless during that time. This situation led to the predominance of local interests and was responsible for their lack of cooperation with the central power. A few centuries later, it was this sharp division of classes which paved the way for the consolidation of the royal power and the decay of nobility in France. The consequence of the struggle between the king and the nobles was the destruction of local autonomy and the appearance of a highly centralized administrative system.

On the contrary, in England, the feudal aristocracy allied itself with the commons, while seeking to limit the power of the monarch. This cooperation generated a unique balance of forces between aristocracy, royalty, and the commons, which created an original political system different from any other system on the Continent. The civil and religious orders, aristocracy, democracy, royalty, and local and central institutions developed hand in hand; never had any element wholly triumphed or attained to an exclusive preponderance over the others. There had always been a simultaneous and harmonious development of different forces that fostered a culture of compromise and bargaining between rival political powers.[46]

In turn, Tocqueville emphasized the different class patterns followed by the two countries and insisted on the close relation between local self-government and political liberty. He pointed out that in England the nobles had kept local affairs in their own hands and preserved their independence vis-à-vis the Crown by allying themselves with the commons. The outcome of this process was the emergence of a culture of compromise that furthered the cooperation between social classes. France took a different path. Each of the thousands of small groups of which the French nation was composed thought for itself alone and acted in isolation from other social groups and classes. Tocqueville blamed this isolation for having led to a form of "collective individualism" which paved the way for the emergence of a strongly centralized administrative and political system. This was, in fact, a new form of individualism that prepared people's minds for the thorough-paced individualism denounced by Tocqueville as the "rust" of democratic societies.[47]

The French nation was thus split into many compact groups living in isolation at the very moment when the egalitarian wave was drawing them together. The nation was an aggregate of different and incompatible social groups whose members had few links between themselves and were not concerned with public issues beyond the narrow sphere of their personal interests. As Turgot (quoted approvingly by Tocqueville) remarked, "nowhere is there any common interest visible [in France]" (Tocqueville 1998, 170). The French nobles stubbornly held aloof from the other classes and were keen only on increasing their immunities, thus following a different path from the third estate. The latter did nothing to prevent its own isolation and ended up cutting all contacts with the peasants.

In the end, the segregation of classes paved the way for the consolidation of absolutism. Though the nation came to be seen as a whole, concluded Tocqueville, its parts no longer held together. French society was made up of segregated classes loosely linked to each other that could not stop the growth of central government and administration. Thus emerged the atomized society, *la société en poussière*, denounced by Royer-Collard in one of his parliamentary discourses of the 1820s.

Democracy as *État Social*

It is time to explore the fundamental distinction between *political* democracy and democracy as *social condition* that appeared in the debates of the Revolution. Tocqueville was notorious for having worked with many definitions of democracy that have puzzled his numerous readers. More than half a century ago, George Wilson Pierson deplored Tocqueville's allegedly "inexact and confusing use of the word *démocratie*" and thought this was an "unconscious lack of precision"[48] on the part of the French author. In *De la démocratie en Amérique*, the term *democracy* refers primarily to *civil* equality of conditions but also designates political self-government, an inescapable (worldwide) phenomenon, and the government by the people.

Two decades ago, James Schleifer advanced a slightly different interpretation that attempted to explain this ambiguity. In his opinion, far from being a flaw in Tocqueville's argument, the imprecision in the definition of democracy should be viewed in a more positive light, as a token of his intention to offer a broader definition of democracy as a multifaceted social and political phenomenon.[49] The plural definitions of democracy in Tocqueville's work should not obscure the fact that one of his greatest merits was to have emphasized the importance of studying the *social* condition of a democratic regime. Democracy, claimed Tocqueville, represents the social condition, while the sovereignty of the people is primarily a political issue. In this view, democracy refers to a new type of society, whereas the sovereignty of people signifies a form of government.[50] This approach constitutes a significant departure from our present understanding of democracy, which tends to concentrate primarily on *political* democracy equated with sovereignty of people and majority rule.

In fact, it was the French Doctrinaires who referred for the first time to democracy as *état social* during the Bourbon Restoration, a significant conceptual innovation at that time. To understand the magnitude of this change, we must bear in mind that in eighteenth-century France, democracy was regarded neither as the best political regime nor as the future form of government and society. At least until Rousseau, democracy represented an obsolete form of government that was appropriate to the small polities of ancient Greece but was considered unsuitable to the conditions of modern, large-size states. Moreover, after the Terror of 1793, democracy was equated with anarchy, despotic rule, and a perverted form of popular sovereignty.

Throughout the first half of the nineteenth century, French liberals remained ambivalent toward democracy and wondered if its principles were compatible with political liberty.[51] While liberals agreed on the force and universality of the democratic movement and foresaw that the progressive equality of conditions could not be stopped, they were also keenly aware that the real challenge was to find the best ways of educating and purifying democracy in such a way that its perverse effects could be mitigated. As we have already seen, this skepticism stemmed from deep misgivings about the consequences of popular sovereignty and universal suffrage that, in the eyes of many survivors of the Revolution, contained the seeds of tyranny. Nineteenth-century French liberals feared that, if left to its own inclinations toward more and more equality, democracy would stifle liberty. Democracy, it was argued, tends to destroy the balance of opinions, interests, and classes; it interferes with the regular functioning of representative institutions and contributes to the expansion of the state. The *ultras*, no friends of democracy or popular sovereignty, also capitalized on the dark legacy of the Terror. Democracy, claimed Maistre, has a brilliant moment, but the price to pay for it far exceeds the benefits.

This historical context helps explain why the Doctrinaires' theory of representative government based on the sovereignty of reason and political capacity was presented as an alternative to popular self-rule. During the first years of the Restoration, reconciling democracy as a new type of society with representative government seemed a daunting task. The Doctrinaires took up this challenge and shifted the emphasis from the political to the social sphere by scrutinizing the social underpinnings of democracy—mores, ideas, habits of the heart—that fostered the growing equality of conditions. By democracy as social condition, Guizot, Rèmusat, and Royer-Collard referred to the advent of a new type of *society* which brought fourth a new configuration of mores, sentiments, laws, and institutions.[52] In other words, they used the term *democracy* to designate the new *egalitarian* society—democracy defined primarily as equality of conditions and equality before the law, *not* as sovereignty of people—rather than an old form of government suitable only to the small polities of the ancient world. The implications of this important conceptual change were fully fleshed out by Tocqueville in *De la démocratie en Amérique*, but its roots can be traced back to the famous parliamentary debates that took place during the Bourbon Restoration.

Obvious as these ideas may seem to us today, their true significance and origin have often been misrepresented or misunderstood by political theorists. The definition of democracy as *état social* is commonly attributed to Tocqueville,[53] whereas it was one of the many topoi in the debates during the Bourbon Restoration and figured prominently in the political writings of the French Doctrinaires. Tocqueville's contemporaries were mindful of the true genealogy of ideas. As Charles de Rémusat argued, Tocqueville owed a great debt to Royer-Collard's ideas on the irresistible nature of democracy.[54] "We ourselves are moving," wrote Tocqueville in 1831 to his friend Louis de Kergolay, "toward a democracy without limits. I am not saying that this is a good thing; but we are being pushed toward it by an *irresistible force*. All the efforts that will be made to stop this movement will only provide pause" (Tocqueville 1985b, 55; emphasis added).

The image of democracy as an irresistible phenomenon had appeared in the parliamentary speeches of the Doctrinaires a decade earlier. "In our country," Hercule de Serre said in 1820, "democracy is full of energy; one can find it in industry, property, laws, memories, people, and things. The flow is in full spate and the dikes can hardly contain it."[55] The phrase "democracy is in full spate," "*la démocratie coule à pleins bords*," instantly seized the attention of all Restoration liberals, who were concerned with "moderating" and "channeling" the social and political consequences of democracy. They were looking for means of reconciling democracy, liberty, and social order and were fearful of the potentially anarchical consequences of political democracy. Royer-Collard equated democracy with equality of rights[56] and argued that democracy had already become the universal form of society. Here is what he said in response to Serre:

> In turn, taking democracy as the opposite of aristocracy, I acknowledge that *democracy is in full spate in France*, such as the centuries have made it. . . . The middle classes have entered into the public affairs. . . . This is our democracy such as I see it and conceive of it. Yes, it is in full spate in this lovely France, more than ever favored by the heavens. . . . *We must either accept this state or destroy it*. And in order to destroy it, we would have to depopulate and impoverish . . . the middle classes. Aristocracy, democracy are not vain doctrines subject to our debates. . . . *The true work of wisdom is to observe and to direct them*. (Royer-Collard 1861b, 134–35; emphasis added)

Few passages illustrate better the originality of the Doctrinaires' approach to democracy as well as the error made by those who claimed that the Doctrinaires were hostile to the principles of modern democracy. Far from rejecting the latter, Royer-Collard pointed out the irresistible march of democracy and stressed the need for regulating and moderating it. He linked the emergence of democracy to the rise of the middle class and drew a sharp contrast between the aristocratic and democratic social condition. At the same time, he acknowledged the power of the social facts that the *ultras*, who held a holistic and obsolete view of society, failed to understand.[57] Along with his other Doctrinaires, Royer-Collard claimed that a new type of society had arisen from the ruins of the Revolution and described its profile by espousing an original sociological approach. He also analyzed the new social condition based on the equality of rights and public opinion.[58] This idea was refined and developed later by Tocqueville in volume one of *De la démocratie en Amérique*.

The Doctrinaires' interpretation of democracy and modern society was grounded in an original philosophy of history and civilization that sought to explain why democracy had become the unavoidable destiny of European civilization. To illustrate the originality of this sociological approach, let us examine briefly Guizot's ideas from *De la peine de mort en matière politique*, published in 1822 (the book was reedited in 1984). He opposed the death penalty by combining political and sociological arguments that were supposed to prove the futility of this type of punishment in the context of Restoration France. After drawing a sharp contrast between the fundamental principles of aristocratic and democratic societies, Guizot commented on the consequences of the disappearance of aristocratic elements and institutions. He emphasized the increasing uniformity in the fabric of society and the narrowing of the gap between various social classes:

> This common condition, this equality under the hand of God, is not the least powerful link uniting all individuals. It brings them toward one another and makes them one by experiencing the same feelings. It prevents them from isolating themselves . . . and constantly brings them together under similar laws and makes them feel that they are not very different and unlike each other. . . . They are given the same laws and opportunities; common ideas, feelings, and interests gain ground, spread, and become stronger. . . . Thus, on the one hand, many more individuals acquire a certain importance . . . ; on the other hand, all individuals are tightly intertwined. (Guizot 1984, 111)

Worth noting are the words Guizot used to describe the profile of the new egalitarian society. He referred to the "equality under the hand of God," and mentioned that people lived under the "same laws" and had the same chances, common interests, ideas, and sentiments. Guizot also remarked that individuals had more links in common with their fellow citizens than at any other point in history.

The larger point made by Guizot in *De la peine de mort en matière politique* is that the Revolution accelerated the trend toward social uniformity and the equality of conditions and created a new type of society that could no longer be governed with the aid of the institutions and principles of the Old Regime. The old aristocratic society had a low social mobility and a rigid hierarchy.[59] On the contrary, in a democratic regime, individual influences are scattered throughout the entire society and millions of people enjoy more or less similar conditions, think and feel in more or less the same way. Power leaves the old aristocratic families and spreads into the entire fabric of society. Strong personalities of aristocratic type give way to the empire of general ideas that are more influential and powerful. People, concluded Guizot, assent to prevailing public opinion, obey general impulses, and abide by the same common rules. They live under the empire of democracy and must learn how to benefit from it.[60]

Based on their analysis of the profile and constitution of French society, Guizot and his fellow Doctrinaires foresaw a decade *before* Tocqueville that nobody could control or stop the irresistible process toward more equality of conditions. In modern society, they argued, there is no longer an abyss between the superior classes and ordinary citizens; moreover, the force of the public is immense: "All the spheres of existence or action have expanded; what was particular has become general. . . . The social necessities, contained for some time, have regained their dominion" (Guizot 1984, 144; 170). In turn, Rémusat insisted on the invincibility of equality, which he related to the growing social homogeneity. In his view, the new mores, the ways in which individuals relate to each other, the distribution of properties, and the nature of private life were affected by the rising equality of conditions.[61] Yet, warned Rémusat, the increased power of individuals simultaneously furthered a tendency to isolation and growing individualism that needed, in turn, to be held in check if society were to remain civilized and to avoid new forms of despotism.[62]

The Doctrinaires' emphasis on the inevitability of democracy foreshadows Tocqueville's own religious awe, triggered by the spectacle of the march of democracy in the modern world. One cannot compete with social facts, argued Guizot; their roots lie beyond the reach of human beings. "A moving democracy," claimed Rémusat, "escapes all human efforts to contain it" (the concept of *démocratie mouvante* played a central role in Rémusat's

Charles de Rémusat

works).[63] If there is one single fact that is universally acknowledged in France, continued Rémusat, it is the fact that the new society, through its composition and mores, is impregnated by equality.[64] Hence, all that can be done in the new environment characterized by high social mobility is to learn how to live under the empire of social facts and to adjust to them.[65] Both the boldness and pertinence of the Doctrinaires' advice must be duly underscored. In a conflict-ridden country like postrevolutionary France, acknowledging the power of social facts as a first step toward social peace amounted to nothing else than declaring the definitive triumph of the new democratic society over the old aristocratic order.

Any reader of Tocqueville can easily realize the extent to which he followed in the footsteps of Guizot, Royer-Collard, and Rémusat in this regard. He refined and enriched their sociological arguments on the interaction between the social condition and the government of a free society. Guizot's picture of a new society in which millions of people enjoy the same social condition and have the same sentiments without ever meeting each other reminds us of Tocqueville's description of the democratic society in America.[66] The equality of conditions, the growth of individualism, and the rise of public opinion were also emphasized in the works of Guizot, Rémusat, and Tocqueville. The Doctrinaires claimed that the new democratic society requires new means of government entirely different from those employed by a centralized administration, which leaves no room for local government.[67]

Finally, I would like to argue that it was Guizot's theory of pluralism and civilization that suggested to Tocqueville (as well as to Mill) how democracy can be purified, "tamed," and channeled into stable institutions. We have already seen that the key idea of Guizot's *Histoire de la civilisation en Europe* was that the progress of society is predicated upon the existence of a systematic struggle for supremacy among rival powers, ideas, interests, and principles of social organization that naturally tend in different directions. In this view, diversity and pluralism are the essential ingredients of liberty. When society comes under the domination of a single principle, it sinks into tyranny and is condemned to stagnation. The cause can be the exclusive domination of a principle of social organization, such as absolute monarchy, aristocracy, or democracy, or of the spirit of commercial society, materialism, or industrialism.

By reflecting on Guizot's lectures on civilization in Europe and France, Tocqueville (and Mill) realized that if any one of these principles were ever allowed to reign absolutely, the competition between them would come to an end and society would be deprived of one of its leading principles of social improvement. To put it differently, if democratic or aristocratic elements and principles were allowed to dominate society unchallenged, social and moral progress would become impossible, because society would lack the necessary pluralism that makes political freedom possible. The same conclusion can be applied to the spirit of commercial society: if left unchecked, it would soon bring society to its ruin. That is why democratic society needs countervailing forces to the dominant (commercial) spirit of the age. Its survival depends on its ability to foster "systematic antagonism"[68] by creating the necessary conditions for a free competition for power between rival ideas, principles, forces, modes of life, and social interests.

This interpretation helps explain Tocqueville's misgivings about democracy that caught the attention of his interpreters and often puzzled them.[69] Tocqueville believed that if democracy were to survive and flourish, it would need to draw on "aristocratic" elements to countervail the predominant influence of democratic ideas, sentiments, and mores. Democratic institutions must also cultivate education, arts, and sciences in order to countervail the predominant influence of materialism, industrialism, and commercialism that tend to impose their own set of values and attitudes on the rest of society, thus engendering a pernicious form of social and cultural uniformity. Because modern society is ruled by public opinion that is unstable and in constant flux, it needs to foster ideas, opinions, and sentiments that are different from those of the public. This idea was memorably conveyed by the following fragment from Tocqueville's notes that explains best his views on how to "purify" democracy. "*Use Democracy to moderate Democracy*," wrote Tocqueville. "It is the only path to salvation that is open to us. To discern the feelings, the ideas, the laws which, without being hostile to the principle of Democracy, without having a natural incompatibility with democracy, can nonetheless correct its troublesome tendencies and will blend with it while modifying it."[70]

A variant of this idea can also be found in J. S. Mill's review of Tocqueville's *De la démocratie en Amérique*. In a passage that contains an explicit reference to Guizot, Mill wrote:

> It is profoundly remarked by M. Guizot that the short duration or stunted growth of earlier civilizations arose from this, that in each of them some one element of human improvement existed exclusively, or so preponderatingly as to overpower all the others. . . . The spirit of commerce and industry is one of the greatest instruments . . . of civilization. . . . So long as other coordinate elements of improvement existed beside it, doing what is left undone, and *keeping its exclusive tendencies in equipoise by an opposite order of sentiments, principles of action, and modes of thought*—so long the benefits which it conferred on humanity were unqualified. (Mill 1977, 197; emphasis added)

In modern democratic society, the rising influence of the commercial spirit and the modes of thought that it promotes must be countervailed by a rich cultural life. Liberty can survive only if accompanied by genuine social, cultural, and political pluralism:

> It is not the uncontrolled ascendancy of popular power, but of any power, which is formidable. There is no power in society, or capable of being constituted in

it, of which the influences do not become mischievous as soon as it reigns un-controlled—as soon as it becomes exempted from any necessity of being in the right, by being able to make its will prevail, without the conditions of a previ-ous struggle. To render its ascendancy safe, it must be fitted with correctives and counteractives, possessing the qualities opposite to its characteristic de-fects.[71]

It would be a mistake, however, to believe that there were no differences between Tocqueville and the Doctrinaires on the issue of moderating and educating democracy. In fact, the Doctrinaires were less optimistic than Tocqueville about the possibility of "moderating" democracy and more pes-simistic than he about the sovereignty of people. The Terror of 1793, they ar-gued, was precisely the sovereignty of the people in action, the consequence of an illegitimate attempt to create an infallible sovereign that turned out to be an extreme case of political idolatry.[72] In Guizot's view, the four cardinal sins of democracy as manifested in the French Revolution had been the rev-olutionary despotism, the lack of any protection of rights, the centralization of power, and the despotism of majority.[73] After the revolution of 1848, which ended his political career, Guizot went so far as to equate political de-mocracy with chaos by resorting to one of the classical instruments of con-servative rhetoric, the jeopardy thesis, warning that attempts at social and political reform would jeopardize the existing social and political order.[74] Guizot's use of the jeopardy thesis was not a novelty in his epoch, since ul-traconservatives had already denounced the Revolution by resorting to a combination of jeopardy and futility theses that were meant to demonstrate the radically negative character of the French Revolution.

In Lieu of Conclusion

The importance of defining democracy as social condition can hardly be overestimated. It enriches our contemporary discussions on democracy and sheds additional light on the fundamental distinction between social and po-litical order. The Doctrinaires considered the egalitarian social condition as the core of the new democratic regime and the prime cause of its institutions. As we have already seen, they believed that political institutions and laws were the expression of the social condition, the outcome of mores, ideas, cus-toms, habits, and traditions. The conclusion of their analysis of democracy as social condition should be of interest to all students of democratic theory. In the fourth essay included in his book *Essais sur l'histoire de France* (originally published in 1823 and then reedited in numerous editions), Guizot highlighted the dependence of the political institutions of each society on the social condition, as follows:

> It is by the study of political institutions that most writers have sought to understand the state of a society, the degree or type of its civilization. It would have been wiser to study first the society itself in order to understand its political institutions. Before becoming a cause, political institutions are an effect; a society produces them before being modified by them. Thus, instead of looking to the system or forms of government in order to understand the state of the people, it is the state of the people that must be examined first in order to know what must have been, what could have been its government. . . . Society, its composition, the manner of life of individuals according to their position, the relation of the different classes, the condition of persons—that is the first question which demands attention from the inquirer who seeks to understand how a people are governed.[75]

A decade later, Tocqueville elaborated on this topic and spelled out its full consequences. He drew on the method and ideas of the Doctrinaires, who, as Rémusat argued, had been the first to reflect in a systematic way on the fundamental distinction between social and political order during the Restoration:

> Then emerged more clearly than ever before the fundamental distinction between social and political order. The Doctrinaires were those who revealed this distinction and who, with more insistence than anyone else, paid particular attention to emphasizing all of its consequences. The social order is not identical with the political order because society is different from the government. Yet, the social order acts on the political order: if society is not a power, it is an influence. Or, what the French revolution wanted, tried, and achieved, and what makes it greater perhaps than any other revolution, is to have conscientiously changed the social order. . . . This social order which has its own opinions, habits, mores, interests, and civil legislation is founded on equality and in this sense, one can affirm that democracy is in the social order. This is the most certain, the most astonishing outcome of the Revolution. It is an irrevocable fact, independent of the will of men and governments. The constitution of the state remains under our discretion up to a certain point. The constitution of society does not depend on us; it is given to us by the force of things, or to elevate our language, it is the work of Providence.[76]

The Tocquevillian ring of this passage should not surprise anyone by now. Tocqueville saw democracy in America through preexisting lenses or conceptual frames that not only yielded a well-crafted image of America, but also a *precrafted* one. In other words, he did not contemplate the spectacle of American democracy with the innocence of a dazzled traveler to an exotic new continent. He tested live some of the ideas that had been debated during the Bourbon Restoration, such as the inevitability of equality and democracy defined as social condition. In America, he saw such processes at work amid many other different strands of reality; his perception was, to a great extent, a *selective* one. Had he come out of a different theoretical background, he might have perceived and emphasized other equally powerful social patterns, which in turn might have generated a different book, with different conceptual and political implications. To put it differently, one can argue that Tocqueville did not give an objective and neutral perception of America, but rather one that was significantly shaped by the preexisting conceptual lenses through which he saw the nation, and which many commentators embraced and magnified over time. This is *not* to say, however, that the American experience did not teach him anything new. On the contrary, the important role of civil and political associations convinced him that the sovereignty of the people can be purified of its destructive tendencies. America also taught Tocqueville that religion can serve as a bulwark of liberty, a lesson that his compatriots had forgotten.[77]

For the Doctrinaires, democracy remained to the very end an ambivalent phenomenon, at the same time inevitable and menacing. They hailed some of its aspects, while continuing to fear its potentially destructive and anarchic elements. During the July Monarchy, Guizot, for example, continued to consider democracy as social condition as a fait accompli,[78] but stopped short of endorsing the principles of *political* democracy, namely universal suffrage and popular sovereignty. His description of democracy, in an important text on democracy in modern societies published in *Revue française* in 1837, clearly conveys this ambivalence. He referred to democracy as "the banner raised sometimes in the name of the most sacred rights, sometimes in the name of the most absurd passions; a banner raised sometimes against the most unfair inequalities, sometimes against the most legitimate superiorities" (Guizot 1837, 197). While hailing the definitive triumph of democratic principles over aristocratic privileges and the divine right of kings, Guizot opposed "personal sovereignty" (or the sovereignty of individual will) and the "sovereignty of the number" (Guizot 1937, 203) on which political democracy was based.

The dual nature of democracy—as a social and political phenomenon—explains why the Doctrinaires put so much emphasis on the distinction between representative government, whose principles they wholeheartedly championed, and political democracy, equated with the sovereignty of the people and universal suffrage. In their opinion, far from deriving its existence from the principle of the sovereignty of the people, representative government disowned this principle and was based upon an entirely different idea, the sovereignty of reason.[79] A true representative form of government, argued Guizot, regards political life from a point of view different from political democracy. The latter admits that the right of sovereignty resides in numerical majorities, whereas representative government denies the validity of this claim and grants political rights only to those individuals who are presumed to have the required political capacity to exercise the right to vote. In other words, political democracy attributes power and right to numerical majorities, while representative government is predicated upon the twofold assumption that simple majorities might not always be right and often fail to respect individual rights and liberties.[80]

Of all the Doctrinaires, it was arguably Charles de Rémusat[81] who went as far as Tocqueville to reconcile himself with the advent of political democracy. In his private correspondence, Tocqueville acknowledged that he feared that Rémusat, who was working on similar themes, would publish the definitive book on democracy (alas, Rémusat never wrote such a book).[82] An indefatigable optimist, he invited his contemporaries, much as Tocqueville did, to contemplate democracy and to try to understand its nature and principles. To constitute democracy, Rémusat once said, means to moderate and purify it of any trace of revolutionary spirit.[83] The difficult and long apprenticeship of liberty in nineteenth-century France shows how prophetic his words were. In the next chapters, we shall explore the ways in which the French Doctrinaires sought to moderate democracy in order to reconcile its principles with liberal ideas.

Notes

1. Tocqueville also carefully read and annotated Guizot's *Histoire de la civilisation en France*.

2. See Sainte-Beuve 1874, 330.

3. Writes Rémusat: "M. de Tocqueville a suivi dans son travail une habitude qu'il s'est faite. . . . Il a écarté tout ce que d'autres avaient trouvé, écrit, pensé. Il a marché droit aux choses mêmes, consultant les pièces et non les livres, s'enquérant des faits et non des réflexions d'autrui" (Rémusat 1856, 655). In *The Humane Comedy*, George Armstrong Kelly (1992, 3–4) also discussed Tocqueville's strange silence on his sources. In a letter to Duvergier de Hauranne, Tocqueville observed: "Quand j'ai un sujet quelconque à traiter, il m'est quasi impossible de lire aucun des livres qui ont été composés sur la même matière; le contact des idées des autres m'agite et me trouble. Je m'abstiens donc, autant que je le puis, de savoir comment leurs auteurs

ont interprété après coup les faits dont je m'occupe, le jugement qu'ils en ont porté. Je me donne, au contraire, une peine incroyable pour retrouver moi-même les faits dans les documents du temps; souvent j'obtiens ainsi, avec un immense labeur, ce que j'aurais trouvé aisément en suivant une autre route" (Tocqueville as quoted by Nolla 1990, xxxviii). For a description of Tocqueville as a "restless mind," see Lawler 1993.

4. François Furet invited Tocqueville's interpreters to concentrate on the very problems that brought Tocqueville to America in order to find answers to the problems of the Old World. For more details, see Furet 1985–86, 117–27.

5. Drescher 1964, 201–16, and Lamberti 1983 insisted on the existence of a clear shift between the two halves of De la démocratie en Amérique. The opposite view can be found in Schleifer 1980 and Pierson 1996.

6. For a chart of Tocqueville's intellectual affinities and debts, see Pierson 1996, 761–62. An excellent discussion of Tocqueville's writings and milieu can be found in Mélonio 1993.

7. On this topic, also see Laborie 1930; Lamberti 1983, 167–84; Hayward 1991, 142–49. Royer-Collard's intellectual authority over his younger friend reached a peak in 1836–37 and declined thereafter.

8. Royer-Collard's letters to Tocqueville were published in Tocqueville 1970. This passage can be found in Tocqueville 1970, v.

9. Writes Royer: "En aucun temps je n'ai fait profession d'être auxiliaire; je cherche, selon mes lumières, la vérité et la justice." Tocqueville comments sadly: "Position qui n'est possible que dans des époques exceptionnelles, par des hommes exceptionnels" (Royer-Collard in Tocqueville 1970, 104).

10. Tocqueville's preference for hereditary monarchy has somewhat escaped the attention of political theorists. Here is what he had to say on this subject in a letter to E. Stoffels in 1836, after the publication of volume one of De la démocratie en Amérique: "Ce que je veux, ce n'est pas une république, mais une monarchie héréditaire. Je l'aimerais même mieux légitime qu'élue aussi que celle que nous avons" (Tocqueville as quoted in Lamberti 1983, 160). It seems that Tocqueville did not change his views on this topic thereafter. For more information about Tocqueville's political career, see Tocqueville 1985a.

11. Writes Tocqueville: "Le sentiment du grand me manque et on dirait que l'imagination du grand s'éteint" (Tocqueville 1970, 61). Royer-Collard answered: "Ce n'est pas la vieille forme de la société que je regrette, mais les hommes qui en sortaient, les esprits, les âmes, les caractères. Il me faut de la grandeur, n'en fût-il plus au monde; je ne redemande pas assurément les privilèges de la noblesse, mais je redemande le gentilhomme, et je ne le retrouve pas dans notre société" (Royer-Collard in Tocqueville 1970, 117).

12. Royer-Collard parted company with Guizot around 1835. The two Doctrinaires would be reconciled only ten years later, shortly before Royer-Collard's death in 1845. The whole passage is worth quoting: "La politique est maintenant dépouillée de sa grandeur; les intérêts qu'on appelle matériels la dominent. Je ne dédaigne

point ces intérêts; ils ont leur prix et ils méritent l'attention favorable des gouverne-ments, mais ils ne viennent dans mon estime qu'après d'autres intérêts bien supérieurs où les nations doivent chercher leur véritable prospérité et leur solide gloire" (Royer-Collard 1861b, 523).

13. Both Furet 1985–86 and Manent 1991, 147–59, insisted on the differences between Tocqueville and Guizot. On the relations between the Doctrinaires and Tocqueville, also see Rémusat 1861, 803; Diez del Corral 1989, 33–39, 46–52, 353–92; Girard 1985, 69–79, 93–103; Hayward 1991, 142–49.

14. The letter to Royer-Collard was published in Tocqueville 1985b, 154.

15. Tocqueville's speech pronounced in the Chamber of Deputies on January 27, 1848, during the discussion of the proposed answer to the speech of the throne, re-published as an appendix to Tocqueville 1969, 749–58.

16. Tocqueville 1985b, 143. The passage is taken from a letter to his friend, Gus-tave de Beaumont, written on August 9, 1840.

17. On this issue, see Manent 1991, 147–48.

18. Tocqueville's letter is quoted in Gargan 1955, 13; emphasis added.

19. This revealing letter to E. Stoffels on October 5, 1836 was originally published in Tocqueville's *Œuvres*, edited by Beaumont (Tocqueville 1866, 436–38). The let-ter was translated into English and published in Tocqueville 1985b, 112–15. Nonetheless, in spite of his political ambitions, Tocqueville was *not* a gifted politi-cian. He lacked a certain willingness to compromise and the authority necessary to dominate a chaotic assembly. Guizot had all these gifts. Tocqueville's speeches were collected in Tocqueville 1985a.

20. Guizot's letter to Tocqueville as quoted in Marcel 1910, 69.

21. In 1861, Guizot argued: "Ce que souhaitait, ce que cherchait pour notre pa-trie M. de Tocqueville, je le souhaitais, je le cherchais comme lui; nous portions aux libertés publiques et aux institutions qui les fondent, le même amour, inspiré par des idées et des sentiments à tout prendre *très semblables*" (emphasis added). This passage is taken from "Réponse de M. Guizot," published in Tocqueville 1989, 343.

22. A detailed analysis of Guizot's theory of civilization can be found in chapter 3.

23. Varouxakis (1999) is a notable exception. His essay nicely highlights the in-tellectual dialogue between Mill, Tocqueville, and Guizot.

24. The letter can be found in Mill 1963, 259; also see 1963, 280.

25. Mill 1977, 191–92. On the influence of Guizot on Mill's interpretation of Tocqueville, see Varouxakis 1999.

26. Tocqueville to Kergolay in Tocqueville 1985b, 95; emphasis added.

27. This is how Guizot referred to *L'Ancien Régime et la Révolution*: "Livre moins brillant, moins confiant, plus sévère que le premier [*De la démocratie en Amérique*], mais supérieur par l'élévation et la précision des idées, par la fermeté du jugement politique et l'intelligence des conditions impérieuses de la liberté" ("Réponse de M. Guizot," in Tocqueville 1989, 343–44).

28. Also see Mélonio's introduction in Tocqueville 1988, 11.

29. Writes Tocqueville: "En France, ce pendant, tout marchait déjà depuis longtemps vers la démocratie. . . . Celui qui eût rassemblé tous ces objets divers, n'eût pu manquer de conclure que la France d'alors avec sa noblesse, sa religion d'État, ses lois et ses usages aristocratiques, était déjà, à tout prendre, la nation la plus véritablement démocratique de l'Europe; et que les Français de la fin du XVIIIe siècle, par leur état social, leur constitution civile, leurs idées et leurs mœurs, avaient dévancé de très loin ceux même des peuples de nos jours qui tendent le plus visiblement vers la démocratie" (Tocqueville 1988, 69).

30. Here is the passage in full: "La révolution a crée une multitude de choses accessoires et secondaires, *mais elle n'a fait que développer le germe des choses principales; celles-là existaient avant elle.* Elle a reglé, coordonné et legalisé les effets d'une grande cause, plutôt qu'elle n' été cette cause elle-même. En France les conditions étaient plus égales qu'ailleurs; *la Révolution a augmenté l'égalité des conditions* et introduit dans les lois la doctrine de l'égalité. Chez les Français, le pouvoir central s'était déjà emparé, plus qu'en aucun pays du monde, de l'administration locale. La Révolution a rendu ce pouvoir plus habile, plus fort, plus entreprenant. Les Français avaient conçu avant et plus clairement que tous l'idée démocratique de la liberté; la Révolution a donné à la nation elle-même, sinon encore toute la realité, du moins toute l'apparence du souverain pouvoir. Tout ce que la Révolution a fait se fût fait, je n'en doute pas, *sans elle*; elle n'a été qu'un procédé violent et rapide à l'aide duquel *on a adapté l'état politique à l'état social, les faits aux idées et les lois aux mœurs*" (Tocqueville 1988, 84; emphasis added).

31. On this topic, also see Furet 1978, 177–80.

32. Guizot summarized the general characteristics of feudal society in the eleventh chapter of volume four of *Histoire de la civilisation en France* (Guizot 1859f, 62–83). They were: necessity of individual consent for the formation of society; simplicity of the conditions of association; intervention of society in judgments; right of resistance formally acknowledged. Among the vices of feudalism, Guizot mentioned excessive predominance of individuality; progress of inequality of force among the possessors of fiefs, and of inequality of rights.

33. In Pierre Rosanvallon's view (1985, 60; emphasis added), "la perspective des doctrinaires n'est donc pas tant de combattre la centralization que de réaliser *une centralization de type nouveau.*" While it is true that for Guizot the predominance of local institutions was a characteristic of the beginning of civilization, Rosanvallon's formulation does not fully capture the complexity of Guizot's subtle understanding of the positive and negative aspects of centralization and decentralization. I elaborate on this issue in chapter 5.

34. For more details, see Jardin 1984, 80–82, and Gargan 1955, 1–20. On the similarities between Guizot and Tocqueville, see Siedentop 1994, 20–40, and Hoeges 1974, 338–53.

35. The letter is discussed by Jardin 1984, 81, and Gargan 1955, 4.

36. Writes Tocqueville: "L'histoire de la civilisation veut et doit vouloir embrasser tout en même temps. Il faut examiner l'homme dans toutes les positions de son exis-

tence sociale. Il faut qu'elle suive ses développements intellectuels dans les *faits*, dans les *mœurs*, dans les *opinions*, dans les *lois* et dans les monuments de l'intelligence" (Tocqueville as quoted by Jardin 1984, 81; emphasis added). Tocqueville's course notes were published as *Notes sur les cours d'histoire de la civilisation en France de Guizot* in Tocqueville 1989, 439–534. The affinity with Guizot's method is striking (see Guizot 1859d, 367–69).

37. See Tocqueville 1989, 485.

38. Guizot 1997a, 56. A similar argument appeared in *Histoire de la civilisation en France*; see Guizot 1859f, 62–83.

39. Tocqueville's letter to Charles Stoffels, Versailles, April 21, 1830 in the Tocqueville Collection, Beinecke Library, Yale University. The full text is in Toqueville 2003, 145–48.

40. The word used by Tocqueville is *égoïsme*, but it seems that what he describes here is individualism, as defined in volume two of *De la démocratie en Amérique*.

41. On this issue, see Reboul 1962 and Raynaud 1991.

42. Lady Palmerston quoted in Theis 1997, liii. Macaulay was also very impressed by Guizot's profound knowledge of English history.

43. For more details, see Theis 1997, xxxvi–xxxviii.

44. Guizot 1997b, 15. For more details, see Theis 1997, liv–lvii.

45. As already indicated, Rémusat, too, was an Anglophile. In addition to the book on eighteenth-century English philosophy, he authored two important essays in which he critically discussed the legacy of Burke (Rémusat 1853a and 1853b).

46. See Guizot 1997a, 229.

47. Tocqueville 1998, 162–63. On Tocqueville's comparative analysis of France and England, see Drescher 1964, 193–223. On Guizot's attitude toward England, see Guizot 2002, 89, 221–30, 357–58, 377–81, 433–35. Also see D. Johnson 1976b, Theis 1997, and Kahan 1991.

48. See Pierson 1996, 158–59.

49. For more details, see chapter 19, "Some Meanings of *Démocratie*," in Schleifer 2000, 325–39. For a discussion of Tocqueville's views on democracy, also see Manent 1993.

50. For more details, see Lamberti 1983, 33.

51. For a typical nineteenth-century view on the relation between democracy and liberalism, see Lecky 1981. On the history of the word democracy in France, see Rosanvallon 1993.

52. On democracy as social condition, also see Rémusat 1861, 797–98. In his book on Rémusat, Roldán quotes from a few unpublished manuscripts of Rémusat from the 1820s, in which he elaborated on the distinction between social and political order. For more details, see Roldán 1999, 72–92.

53. See, for example, Zuckert 1993. According to Zuckert, "Tocqueville speaks of social condition as though it were a well-known concept, but in fact it was not so. He is, so far as I know, the first to use it" (Zuckert 1993, 4). When attempting to trace this idea back to Tocqueville's precursors, Zuckert invokes Rousseau but ignores

Royer-Collard and the other Doctrinaires: "Social state is Tocqueville's great discovery, but he seems to owe a great debt to Rousseau" (Zuckert 1993, 15).

54. Writes Rémusat: "Nous ne voulons ici le [Tocqueville] considérer que comme une sorte de continuateur de Royer-Collard par rapport à cette grande question de la démocratie" (Rémusat 1861, 801).

55. "La démocratie, chez nous," Serre said, "est partout pleine de sève et d'énergie; elle est dans l'industrie, dans la propriété, dans les lois, dans les souvenirs, dans les hommes, dans les choses. *Le torrent coule à pleins bords dans de faibles digues qui le contiennent à peine*" (Serre as quoted in Rémusat 1861, 797; emphasis added). Also see Rémusat 1959, 61.

56. Royer-Collard 1861b, 134–35. He also argued: "À travers beaucoup de malheurs, *l'égalité des droits (c'est le vrai nom de la démocratie*, et je le lui rends) a prévalu; reconnue, consacrée, garantie par la Charte, elle est aujourd'hui *la forme universelle de la société*, et c'est ainsi que la démocratie est partout. Elle n'a plus de conquêtes à faire" (Royer-Collard 1861b, 137; emphasis added).

57. See Royer-Collard 1861b, 135. Also see Rémusat: "C'est là le point fondamental que les séparait de leurs adversaires du côté droit. Sur ce point, [les doctrinaires] se montraient absolus et intraitables. . . . Lorsqu'on les pressait d'établir ou de supposer dans la société un classement fixe, une hiérarchie immobile qui s'opposait à la libre ascension des individus, ils résistaient impérieusement, ils répondaient que le problème politique était d'accommoder le gouvernement à la société et non de refaire arbitrairement la société pour la commodité du gouvernement" (Rémusat 1861, 795–96).

58. The Doctrinaires were familiar with Montesquieu's sociological approach. They criticized some aspects of his political theory, most notably his classification of political regimes and his understanding of the separation of powers as the cornerstone of free government. For a clear statement about the fundamental difference between Guizot's comprehensive history of civilization and Montesquieu's limited political history, see Guizot 1859d, 367–68, and chapter 3.

59. See Guizot 1821, 8, 119–20; also Guizot 1984, 102–5. It is worth noting that J. S. Mill paid considerable attention to the transition to democratic society as described in Guizot's historical works; for more details, see Mill 1985, 286.

60. The whole passage is worth quoting for its sociological acumen: "Où sont maintenant ces chefs éminents, avoués, qu'il suffit de détruire pour détruire un parti? Peu d'hommes ont un nom, et ceux-là même sont peu de chose. La puissance a quitté les individus, les familles; elles est sortie des foyers qu'elle habitait jadis; elle s'est répandue dans la société tout entière; elle y circule rapidement, à peine visible en chaque lieu, mais partout présente. Elle s'attache à des intérêts, à des idées, à des sentiments publics dont personne ne dispose, que personne même ne représente assez pleinement pour que leur sort dépende un moment du sien" (Guizot 1984, 102). Also see Guizot 1984, 106, 110–12, 144–45, 166–69.

61. Writes Rémusat: "*Nos mœurs sont emprunts d'égalité*. . . . C'est là, c'est surtout dans l'intimité de la vie privée, qu'elle réside, *cette égalité tout attaquée, tout prônée*,

mais definitivement invincible" (quoted in Roldán 1999, 91; emphasis added). This passage is taken from an unpublished manuscript written in the 1820s, in which Rémusat commented on the political ideas of Lammenais and Bonald.

62. In the manuscript on Lamennais and Bonald, Rémusat argued: "L'individu est entré en possession d'une independence qu'il regarde comme son premier bien et son premier besoin. [Il y en a quelque-uns qui vont] jusqu'à la confondre avec l'isolement et à se refuser à toutes ses associations" (quoted in Roldán 1999, 88). The affinity with Tocqueville's ideas is worth noting.

63. This passage is from Rémusat's essay "De l'égalité," as quoted in Roldán 1999, 84.

64. This revealing passage is taken from Rémusat's unpublished manuscript on Lamennais and Bonald. Here is the original version: "*S'il existe un fait universellement convenu, c'est que la société française et par sa composition comme par ses mœurs ne respire que l'égalité.* Toutes les classifications hiérarchiques se sont effaces; toutes les habitudes de subordination se sont affaiblies" (quoted in Roldán 1999, 84; emphasis added).

65. Writes Guizot: "*On ne lutte point avec les faits sociaux*; ils ont des racines où la main de l'homme ne saurait atteindre, et quand ils ont pris possession du sol, il faut savoir y vivre sous leur empire" (Guizot 1984, 114; emphasis added).

66. Guizot referred to "cette société électrique où des millions d'hommes de condition pareille, de sentimens analogues, sans s'être jamais vus ni parlé, connaissent réciproquement leur sort" (Guizot 1984, 113–14).

67. Writes Guizot: "Regardons la question sous son autre face; de l'établissement de la liberté passons à celui du pouvoir. Sa tâche est immense; des forces lui sont indispensables pour y suffire; il doit les trouver dans les institutions, dans les lois, dans les dispositions de la société à son égard" (Guizot 1821, 13). At the same time, I should point out that Tocqueville's main theme was the condition of a democratic people as torn between two conflicting tendencies: toward forming associations and withdrawal from public life. This issue did not occupy a similar place in Guizot's writings.

68. The phrase is Mill's. For more details, see Varouxakis 1999, 299.

69. For an excellent example, see Boesche 1987.

70. Tocqueville as quoted in Schleifer 2000, 234; emphasis added. The phrase "to moderate democracy" also appeared in Rémusat's writings.

71. Mill 1977, 202; also see Varouxakis 1999, 296–305. For more details on Mill's sociological essays written in the 1830s, see chapter 8.

72. On political idolatry, see Guizot 1985, 319–27; I discuss this issue in chapter 5.

73. See Guizot 1849, 43–44. For an earlier and more important statement on democracy, see Guizot 1837.

74. Guizot 1849, 9; 65. For an analysis of the rhetoric of conservatism, see Hirschman 1991.

75. Guizot 1836, 83–84. Also see Guizot 1859c, 30–31, 98–101.

76. Rémusat 1861, 795. This passage is from an important article of Rémusat published in *Revue des deux mondes.* In his memoirs, referring to the difficulty of reconciling

the demands for political liberty and social stability, Rémusat argued: "Les doctrinaires avaient fait de cette question spéciale leur question. Avant Tocqueville, avant personne, ils ont observe et défini avec hardiesse et vérité la démocratie moderne, et ce n'est qu'après 1830 qu'ils ont commence à prendre peur" (Rémusat 1959, 61).

77. I would like to thank Larry Dodd for his suggestions on this point.

78. The phrase is from Guizot 1837, 195. For an analysis of the ambivalence of democracy in the Doctrinaires' writings, see Rosanvallon 1985, 80–86. Guizot's article on democracy in modern society (published in 1837 in *Revue française*) is also important. It is surprising that in his long article, Guizot neither reviewed nor commented on Tocqueville's *De la démocratie en Amérique* (volume one had appeared in 1835). Instead, he referred to two other books on democracy, *De la démocratie nouvelle, ou des mœurs et de la puissance des classes moyennes en France* by Edouard Alletz and *Essai sur l'organisation démocratique de la France* by Auguste Billiard, both published in 1837. For a critique of Guizot, see Benjam 1838, 11–31.

79. For more details, see Guizot 2002, 52–53.

80. For more details on this topic, see chapters 7 and 8.

81. On Rémusat's conception of democracy, see Roldán 1999, 72–124. Rémusat's text, written a decade before *De la démocratie en Amérique*, contains a subtle analysis of the political consequences of the equality of conditions in modern society, the central theme of Tocqueville.

82. Here is a revealing passage from a letter of Tocqueville to Rémusat: "Vous étiez l'homme du monde qui m'avez fait le plus peur et avez le plus précipité neon travail. Je pressentais que vous marchiez sur la même route, et je voyais que vous jetiez chaque jour dans la circulation les idées-mères sur lesquelles je voulais établir mon œuvre" (quoted in Rosanvallon 1985, 54).

83. Writes Rémusat: "La démocratie n'est pas cette monstruosité qui scandalise tant de bonnes âmes, mais enfin elle place le monde dans une situation nouvelle et inconnue; l'expérience nous manque ou n'est pas suffisante pour nous éclairer sur ses besoins, ses lacunes, ses difficultés, ses ressources. . . . *Constituer la démocratie, c'est la modérer*. . . . Contemplez la démocratie, en songeant que vous devez y vivre, qu'elle est l'affaire de tout le monde, et que ses destins sont les vôtres" (Rémusat 1861, 810, 812, 813; emphasis added).

CHAPTER FIVE

The Sovereignty of Reason

Il n'y a point de souverains sur la terre.

—Guizot

The key concept of the political philosophy of the French Doctrinaires was the sovereignty of reason, which underpinned their theories of political power and representative government. In this chapter, we shall study in detail what Guizot and his colleagues understood by *la souveraineté de la raison*. The focus will be on Guizot's works, namely, *Philosophie politique, Histoire des origines du gouvernement représentatif en Europe,* and the essay "Élections," all written in the 1820s.

We shall begin by examining Guizot's rejection of the divine right of kings and his critique of Rousseau's theory of sovereignty, which can be found in Guizot's unfinished treatise on sovereignty and his history of representative government. Then, we'll compare Guizot's ideas on sovereignty to those of Constant in order to point out the existence of important similarities between their approaches on sovereignty that have been overlooked thus far. We'll end by examining the claim that the Doctrinaires' theory of the sovereignty of reason was ultimately untenable and led in practice to the emptying of sovereignty of any political significance.[1] The final section of this chapter will highlight the concrete *institutional* implications of the sovereignty of reason and its relation to other aspects of the Doctrinaires' theory of representative government.

Sovereignty in French Political Thought

It might seem surprising that Constant and Guizot spent so much time writing about sovereignty, an issue that has almost vanished from the writings of political theorists today. The reasons for this declining interest in the issue of sovereignty are complex and diverse. Fifty years ago, in *Man and the State*, Jacques Maritain argued that political philosophers should dispense altogether with the concept of sovereignty, not only because it is an antiquated notion, but also because "this concept is intrinsically wrong and bound to mislead us if we keep on using it" (Maritain 1951, 29). In other words, while sovereignty is a legitimate concept in the spiritual sphere, it should have no place in the political sphere. Because sovereignty is defined as the power to do all things without accountability, it shares an inherent affinity with absolutism. On this view, it is ultimately impossible to reconcile sovereignty with limited power and accountability. Furthermore, the sovereign state is invested with a power that is always exercised without accountability from above. Hence, "the concept of sovereignty," concluded Maritain, "is but one with the concept of Absolutism. . . . The two concepts of sovereignty and absolutism have been forged together on the same anvil. They must be scrapped together. . . . Political philosophy must get rid of the word, as well as the concept of sovereignty" (Maritain 1951, 49; 53; 29).

To be sure, today we take political democracy for granted and no longer feel compelled to question the validity of popular sovereignty, the very principle that lies at the core of our democratic regimes. This was *not* the case in early-nineteenth-century Europe. Moreover, the relation between political power and sovereignty seems to have undergone an important transformation in the field of political science in the past five decades or so. The upshot of this trend is that concepts such as power, legitimacy, and domination have been privileged at the expense of sovereignty,[2] with the notable exception of the field of international relations and international law, in which notions such as sovereignty and supreme power are still frequently used (the current debates on national sovereignty and the European Union have contributed to the reemergence of sovereignty as a key political concept).

The entry in the *Blackwell Encyclopedia of Political Thought* defines sovereignty as "the power or authority that comprises the attributes of an ultimate arbitral agent—whether a person or a body of persons—entitled to make decisions and settle disputes within a political hierarchy" (King 1987, 492). The importance of sovereignty derives from its association with the right to command, legitimacy, political obligation, and, more importantly, the power to make and enforce laws. The main characteristic of any legitimate sovereign power is the right to make laws and to change the norms and rules that preside over the actions of the individuals without their explicit consent. As such, sovereignty is a property that is indivisible and admits of no degrees, yet it must not be a priori equated with arbitrariness. As Bertrand de Jouvenel pointed out, there is a fundamental distinction between absolute power (*sit pro voluntate ratio*) and arbitrary power (*sit pro ratione voluntas*). An absolute monarchy, is "a government in which the sovereign will is absolute, but in which every precaution, moral or material, has been taken to ensure that this will coincides with reason. In theory, the monarch can do whatever he wills; but he is allowed to will only what is just and reasonable" (de Jouvenel 1997, 251).

The complex nature of the concept of sovereignty was underscored by political philosophers and jurists alike. As Hans Kelsen pointed out, "the term sovereignty, while denoting one of the most important concepts of the theory of national and international law, has a variety of meanings, a fact that causes regrettable confusion in this theory" (Kelsen 1969, 115). Political philosophers such as Althusius, Grotius, Hobbes, Bossuet, and Rousseau defined sovereignty as the highest power to administer the affairs concerning the safety and welfare of the members of the state. They derived the legitimacy of the sovereign power from individual will and stressed the inalienable, indivisible, and infallible character of the sovereign's authority. It has been remarked that these theories (with the exception of Bossuet's) had in common the hypothesis of a social contract as the foundation of sovereign power and derived the legitimacy of power from individual will. Nonetheless, the social contract theory was not sufficient for effectively limiting sovereignty and power. It led in practice to the vesting of absolute, indivisible, and inalienable sovereignty in a fictitious body created by a hypothetical social contract, a body that sometimes acted against the interests and liberties of the members of political community.[3]

Bodin defined sovereignty as a unified, unlimited, and supreme power to govern and to make laws without the consent of the subjects. In his view, the sovereign was "*legibus solutus*" and sovereignty was to be conceived of as autonomous and indivisible. In France, the legacy of absolutism and the violent episodes of the French Revolution made the issue of sovereignty more salient than anywhere else. A cursory look at the historical context shows that political life during the Bourbon Restoration was dominated by an unprecedented battle between competing theories of sovereignty and political obligation that created a rich cross-fertilization of ideas, as illustrated by the works of Constant, Guizot, and Maistre.

Benjamin Constant emphasized the salience of the issue of sovereignty when arguing that "the first question [that must be solved] is that of the competence and limitation of sovereignty. Before we organize something, we must have determined its nature and extension" (Constant 1988, 182). The same point was made by Guizot in his historical and political writings of the 1820s. Unwilling to forget the darkest moments of the French Revolution, Guizot and his fellow Doctrinaires questioned the validity of those theories that granted sovereignty to individual will. They were particularly concerned with the political implications of the principle that individuals have the right to make and unmake political institutions as they please. While rejecting the idea that society as a whole is ever entitled to exercise unlimited sovereignty over its members, Guizot and the other Doctrinaires warned that the rule of the people would turn into a new form of despotism and maintained that popular sovereignty was not a reliable safeguard of individual freedom. The main question that had to be answered was in whose hands should power be placed in order to prevent the usurpation of the sovereignty of right. Since the fall of the Old Regime and the Terror of 1793–94 had showed the illegitimacy of the divine right of kings and cast doubt on the practical implications of the sovereignty of the people, there was a pressing need for finding new ways of conceptualizing sovereignty, political power, and authority.

Constant and Guizot offered two different, yet related, ways of addressing this challenge. In *Principes de politique* (1815), Constant explained the darkest episodes of the Revolution by arguing that instead of destroying absolute power once and forever, the people only thought of displacing it. The general will, opined Constant, contains in itself the seeds of despotism if it is unlimited. In other words, all the precautions against absolute power are futile if sovereignty is not properly divided: "You can try a division of powers, but if the sum total of powers is unlimited the divided powers have only to form a coalition for despotism to be installed without remedy." Constant went on to add that "the important truth, the eternal principle to be established is that sovereignty is limited, and that there are desires that neither the people nor their delegates have the right to entertain."[4] Again, when sovereignty is unlimited, there is no means of protecting individuals from any potential encroachment on their liberties.

The emphasis on limiting individual will and the general skepticism toward general will require further clarification. As already mentioned, the return of the Bourbons to the throne of France rekindled the interest in sovereignty and other related topics such as legitimacy, authority, distribution of powers, political responsibility (of the king's ministers), and the limits of political obligation. Constant believed that the abstract limitation of sovereignty was not sufficient and argued that new political institutions must be built that would "combine the interest of the different holders of power so that their most apparent, most durable, and most certain advantage would be to remain within the limits of their respective attributions" (Constant 1988, 182). His theory of constitutional monarchy is particularly relevant in this context. Constant conceived of royal power as a neutral power (*pouvoir neutre*), whose main goal was to facilitate a cooperation between the executive, legislative, and judicial powers. The royal power ought to be placed in the middle, yet above the four other powers (the hereditary assembly, the elective assembly, the cabinet, and the tribunals), and must not disturb the balance between them.[5]

Mutatis mutandis, it can be argued that the real intention of Constant was more or less similar to Guizot's with respect to the relation between political freedom and limited sovereignty. Both thinkers searched for "a fixed, unassailable point which passions cannot reach."[6] Like Guizot, Constant claimed that no authority upon earth—neither that of the people, nor that of the monarchs or of the representatives of the people—can be unlimited, which was tantamount to denying that the consent of the majority suffices to give legitimacy to all of its decisions. In an essay written in 1818 as a companion to *Principes de politique*, Constant wrote that "if it is recognized that sovereignty is not without limits, that is to say, that there is no unlimited power on earth, then nobody will ever dare to claim such a power."[7] This important idea underscored his belief that "the boundaries within which the authority must be kept are fixed by *justice* and by the *rights of individuals*."[8]

The emphasis on justice in this passage is particularly important, because it proves the existence of a certain overlap between Constant's ideas on sovereignty and Guizot's theory of the sovereignty of reason. This similarity has been ignored thus far. It is well-known that Constant did not advance a full-fledged theory of the sovereignty of reason and put great(er) emphasis on individual rights as effective means of limiting sovereignty. Yet, both Constant and Guizot believed that public opinion, publicity, and a wise distribution of powers should be used to limit sovereignty. They also claimed that popular sovereignty—indeed, any form of sovereignty—should be circumscribed within the limits traced by justice (Guizot's exact terms were *reason, justice,* and *truth*). More importantly, both thinkers emphasized the need to find a fixed point that passions cannot reach. For Guizot, however, neither the monarch nor the hereditary chamber was able to provide such a fixed, unassailable point, which could be reached only by granting sovereignty to reason. Guizot started from the assumption that both popular sovereignty and the sovereignty of divine right were two different forms of usurping the sovereignty of right and concluded that the best means of limiting sovereignty and power was to grant *de iure* sovereignty neither to individual will nor to general will, but only to reason, truth, and justice.

A few words about the history of the concept of the sovereignty of reason are also necessary.[9] The concept of reason as the highest authority and final court of appeal supposed to judge all standards of truth was one of the central tenets of the Enlightenment. Kant granted reason the power and right to examine all beliefs and claims to truth, yet this idea preceded him and can be traced back to seventeenth-century England where, as Frederick Beiser demonstrated, reason came to be regarded as "the only legitimate rule of faith by almost all parties" (Beiser 1996, 7). *Reason* was defined as the source of universal, self-evident moral principles and was related to the activity of giving and evaluating the evidence in support of various claims to truth. It was also supposed to establish a universally accepted criterion of morality and to produce a set of self-evident principles.

French political thinkers retained this second meaning but had little interest in exploring the epistemological questions regarding reason. In *De la Révolution française* (1796), Jacques Necker claimed that true sovereignty belongs only to "eternal" reason and justice. The supremacy of reason also appeared, albeit in a different form, in Destutt de Tracy's *Commentaire sur l'Esprit des lois* (1819) as well as in Victor Cousin's philosophical lectures, especially in his *Cours d'histoire de la philosophie morale au dix-huitième siècle* (1819–20). Cousin, who played a particularly important role in the shaping of the young generation that came of age in the 1820s, believed that man must endlessly search for truth and legitimate authority located in transcendent reason. In his view, reason was a sovereign power that did not reside anywhere on Earth.[10] Against Rousseau, he claimed that the general will could not constitute abstract right and argued that reason ought to replace will and force as the foundation of legitimate sovereignty and the guarantee of political liberty.

Kant's influence on Guizot should also be underscored. Guizot became familiar with his philosophical writings early on and admired not only Kant's moral philosophy with its strong emphasis on duty, but also his theory of a noumenal world that "traced a clear demarcation line between sky and earth, soul and body."[11] Nonetheless, Guizot parted company with Kant in several important ways. He opposed the autonomy of human will that plays such a prominent role in Kant's philosophical and political writings and rejected the idea that morality can ever exist apart from religion. Furthermore, Guizot opposed Kant's belief that human beings can lay down a moral law for themselves, a law that does not transcend the boundaries of reason. For Guizot, human reason was not an infallible yardstick and could never become a source of right.

Reason and Will

Raised in the Calvinist tradition, Guizot relied upon the assumption that one of the most important and politically significant characteristics of human nature is the tendency to worship idols. In his view, this was an unambiguous sign of the fallibility and limitations of the human mind, "biased by passion and limited by frailty" (Guizot 2002, 51). In the course of human history, argued Guizot, human beings built idols to which they afterward granted absolute sovereignty and promised unconditional obedience. Nonetheless, they found themselves obliged to defend their freedom against the same idols to which they had previously surrendered their will. By wandering from one idol to another in search of certainty, human beings only changed the object of their adoration, being incapable of breaking the chains of bondage or quenching their insatiable thirst for transcendence, security, and certainty.[12]

In Guizot's view, political idolatry is the origin of tyranny. In their quest for certainty and salvation, human beings search for a legitimate sovereign, yet they are unable to find such a sovereign here on Earth. The endless search for an infallible and legitimate sovereign defines both the greatness and the misery of human condition.[13] Human beings have an insatiable need to worship. They desire freedom and seek to transcend the limitations of human nature; they try to overcome their own mortality by aspiring to partake in the transcendence of the idols they adore. Nonetheless, they often pay a high price for the costly illusion to have found the true sovereign on Earth. They grant sovereignty of right either to monarchs or to the people, only to discover soon that ruthless individuals seek to usurp political power by shrewdly playing with the people's insatiable need for idols, security, and certainty:

> As he made his own gods, man also made his own masters. He tried to place the sovereignty and divinity on Earth. He wanted to be ruled by a power to which he owed a permanent and certain right of obedience. He did not succeed, however, in fully establishing the limits of his faith and obedience. This original and infinite sovereignty was invested sometimes in one man, sometimes in several people; occasionally, man granted it to a caste, or even to an entire people. He barely attributed this sovereignty to them before he saw himself constrained to contest or take sovereignty away from them.[14]

Echoing a point made by Constant a few years earlier, Guizot argued that during the French Revolution, instead of destroying absolute power once and forever, the people only thought of displacing it, thus making possible the appearance of a new form of despotism; that is, the despotism of the majority and the general will. By worshiping false and dangerous idols, the people opened the door to new forms of oppression. In the end, both the divine right of kings and the sovereignty of the people proved to be two disguised forms of tyranny:

> We have heard the sovereignty of the people proclaimed on the ruins of the divine right of kings. Even when disavowing their dethroned master, men have not lost, however, the hope of finally finding a master who would never fall, the master whom they would never need to reject nor have the right to repudiate. There has been no reform of ideas that did not grant infallibility to someone. There has been no revolution in the name of liberty that did not promote in the end the rights of a new tyranny. . . . At the height of their enthusiasm, the people have always bent their knees in front of a new idol. In their pride, they believed that this new idol was the true God; in their weakness, they needed to rely upon this belief. (Guizot 1985, 320)

The important point made by Guizot is that liberty survives only where the conditions exist for a "laborious and unremitting search after reason and justice" (Guizot 2002, 52); that is, only where there is a sound division of powers that imposes on all powers the obligation to search in common for reason, truth, and justice. At the same time, all claims to power and sovereignty are subject to strict public scrutiny and must constantly be justified under the eyes of public opinion. Also worth noting is Guizot's appeal to skepticism toward any claim to power and *de iure* sovereignty.[15] Sovereignty of *right* cannot be granted to any individual or collective being, because no one can rightfully claim to fully possess or represent reason, truth, and justice. Given the imperfection and limitations of human nature, no individual will can or should be granted sovereignty of right:

> No power here on Earth can be unique and inalienable because no power is or can be invested with the sovereignty of right. . . . The only sovereign that is legitimate by nature and in all eternity is reason, truth, and justice; it is the unchanging Being whose laws are reason, justice, and truth. . . . No absolute power can ever be legitimate. Hence, there is no sovereignty on Earth, no sovereign [power].[16]

Yet, while neither the people nor the monarch can ever have sovereignty of right, those who exercise political power must be granted de facto sovereignty on the condition that they should publicly and constantly demonstrate the conformity of their actions to the precepts of reason, truth, and justice.[17]

Not surprisingly, Guizot's own religious beliefs had an important impact on his political ideas. In his private letters, he confessed to his closest friends his firm belief in the existence of a real or noumenal world which always remains beyond the reach of our knowledge. Yet, stressed Guizot, although God is the true and only actor on the stage of history, human beings are free and responsible for their actions. True wisdom lies in the ability to go beyond apparent contradictions and perceive the necessary relations between grace and liberty, between Providence and human action in history.[18]

The emphasis on the radical fallibility of man led Guizot to criticize those eighteenth-century writers—Condorcet was the most notorious representative of this tradition of thought—who displayed an overly optimistic belief in the possibility of unlimited progress and the perfectibility of mankind. It will be recalled that eighteenth-century philosophers conceived of human agency as autonomous and self-sufficient and affirmed its independence vis-à-vis tradition and religion. Guizot rejected this view and regarded reason as a moral rule superior to individual will as well as a manifestation of a divine law to which all must equally obey. While rejecting Rousseau's belief in general will as man's only legitimate sovereign, Guizot stressed the fallibility and arbitrariness of individual will and opposed Rousseau's claim that individuals can become free only upon entering into a social contract, through which each individual alienates his natural freedom to the collective body in order to gain an allegedly superior form of freedom, civil liberty.[19]

As already mentioned, other liberal thinkers such as Germaine de Staël[20] and Benjamin Constant also took issue with Rousseau's ideas on liberty and sovereignty and stressed their anachronistic elements along with their nefarious political implications. Nothing illustrates better the fascinating dialogue between Rousseau and the postrevolutionary mind than the contrast between his republican ideal based on "positive" liberty and Constant's defense of the autonomy of the private sphere and of the sacredness of individual rights. While agreeing with Rousseau that all authority must emanate from the will of the people and the consent of the nation, Constant criticized Rousseau's failure to limit popular sovereignty, a failure that allowed unscrupulous leaders to use the sovereignty of the people and the doctrine of the general will to legitimize their own claims to power.

For both Constant and Guizot, the main lesson of the Terror was that a semblance of popular sovereignty could be easily misused in order to create a tyranny of the "enlightened" or the "virtuous" ones in the name of the common good. Like Rousseau, Guizot wanted to create a political order in which citizens would no longer be dependent upon the potentially arbitrary will of other individuals. Yet, unlike Rousseau, Guizot believed that, if transformed from de facto into *de iure* sovereignty, popular sovereignty would pave the way to despotism instead of liberty. He rejected what he took to be Rousseau's extreme form of individualism and accused him of not having spelled out all the logical consequences of his ideas that would have led to the dissolution of the social order.

Constant took a different tack. He criticized Rousseau's extreme form of collectivism (incompatible with liberty) and his idea that individuals should surrender their inalienable rights to the general will.[21] The difference between the two interpretations of Rousseau is puzzling and points to a fundamental ambiguity in Rousseau's theory. Guizot believed that the specter of anarchy was more menacing than the alienation of (individual) rights: "Rousseau's only fault was that he did not push it far enough. Going as far as this would lead him, . . . he would have condemned all constitutions—he would have affirmed the illegitimacy of all law and all power" (Guizot 2002, 287–88). In Guizot's view, the radical nature of Rousseau's theory of sovereignty prevents individuals from contracting real political and social obligations. Moreover, Guizot pointed out another significant tension in Rousseau's theory between, on the one hand, the principle claiming that every individual has absolute sovereignty over himself and, on the other hand, the alleged supremacy of the general will over the individual will. Guizot questioned Rousseau's idea that the only legitimate sovereign is the individual will and argued that we receive the laws from a higher source than our will.[22] These laws come from a sphere which "is above the region of his liberty, where the question is not whether a thing is willed or not willed, but whether it is true or false, just or unjust, conformable or contrary to reason" (Guizot 2002, 292).

What are the political implications of this theory? "The right to power," argued Guizot (2002, 294), "is always derived from reason, never from will." No one has a right to impose a law because he wills it. Hence, no one has a right to refuse submission to it because his will is opposed to it; the legitimacy of power rests in its conformity to the precepts of eternal reason. Reason, not will, is the true foundation of social order and the only source of political legitimacy:

> What is true concerning the child and the fool is true of man in general: the right to power is always derived from reason, never from will. No one has the right to impose a law because he wills it; no one has the right to refuse submission to it because his will is opposed to it; the legitimacy of power rests in the conformity of its laws to eternal reason, not in the will of the man who exercises, nor of him who submits to power. (Guizot 2002, 294)

Hence, since the right to power is derived neither from the individual will nor from the general will, may no power can be seen as legitimate unless it constantly proves the conformity of its actions to the precepts of reason, truth, and justice. In Guizot's opinion, Rousseau's definition of liberty as obedience to the laws we have prescribed to ourselves was flawed, since the individual will is not be man's legitimate sovereign. By equally subjecting all individual wills to a unique sovereign—reason, truth, and justice—we proclaim that no one may rightfully refuse to obey reason, justice, and truth.[23] Guizot referred to a "divine contract" according to which all human beings must abide by the laws of reason, justice, and truth.[24]

Mutatis mutandis, the same ideas can be found in St. Thomas Aquinas's political writings, most notably in his famous treatise on law in which he discussed four types of laws (divine, eternal, natural, civil) and the relations between them. It will be recalled that Aquinas defined "just" laws as the ordination of reason for the common good and interpreted them as the applications of the eternal law governing the entire universe to the field of political life. Aquinas stressed the fallible and sinful nature of the individual will and emphasized the need to restrain the latter by subordinating it to the precepts of eternal reason. As the Spanish Catholic writer Jaime Balmes pointed out (Balmes was a strong critic of Guizot), this theory based on a fundamental skepticism toward unrestrained individual will was a traditional principle, "as ancient as the world, acknowledged by ancient philosophers, inculcated and applied by Christianity" (Balmes 1850, 347). The main idea was that "when reason commands there is legitimacy, justice, and liberty; when the will alone commands, there is illegitimacy, injustice, despotism" (Balmes 1850, 319). In other words, the power of the sovereign must be the personification of the sovereignty of reason, which rises above all individual wills.

It must be remarked that this principle had an interesting genealogy that was outlined by Bertrand de Jouvenel in his book on sovereignty (de Jouvenel 1997). The French Doctrinaires worked with the idea that authority and power must be independent of any human will and applied it to a new social and political context, which prompted them to reflect again and again on the nature, origin, and limits of sovereignty.[25]

The Sovereignty of Reason and the Sovereignty of the People

The most important offshoot of Guizot's approach was a new way of thinking about the role of sovereignty in assessing the nature and legitimacy of political regimes. We may surmise that Guizot first encountered this idea, albeit in a slightly different form, in Frederick Ancillon's study of sovereignty, which he translated into French in 1816. An influential nineteenth-century Prussian political thinker, Ancillon maintained that sovereignty is the only criterion that enables us to offer a valid and pertinent classification of ancient and modern governments. Other classifications of political regimes such as the one proposed by Montesquieu were deemed unsatisfactory, because they failed to take into account the concept of sovereignty and did not look beneath the surface of political phenomena. A similar point had also been made, in a different manner, by Sieyès, who argued that Montesquieu was wrong in classifying the different governments "under names which do not indicate their nature, and in having systematically believed each of them to be reducible to a single principle."[26]

In the footsteps of Ancillon, Guizot claimed that the principle lying at the heart of each political regime must first be examined before considering the exterior forms of governments.[27] Appearances, argued Guizot, had deceived Montesquieu, because he only considered the exterior characteristics of political regimes, not their true principles and tendencies. Montesquieu's classification of political regimes had little to say about the issue of sovereignty and only took into account the shape that power assumes, thus glossing over the most important question that ought to be answered when reflecting upon the nature of a political regime: What is the source of sovereign power and what are its limits? In Guizot's opinion,

> That is a superficial and false method which classifies governments according to their exterior characteristics; making monarchy, government by one individual; aristocracy, government by several; democracy, government by the people, the sovereignty of all. This classification, which is based only upon one particular fact, and upon a certain material shape which power assumes, does not go to the heart of those questions, or rather of that question, by the solution of which the nature and tendency of governments is determined. This question is, "What is the source of the sovereign power, and what is its limit? Whence does it come, and where does it stop?" In the answer to this question is involved the real principle of government. (Guizot 2002, 48)

Guizot's ambition was to offer a new method of classifying political regimes, which, unlike Montesquieu's approach, assigned a central place to the concept of sovereignty. He argued that only by studying the extent to which each political system defines the nature and limits of sovereignty it is possible to properly identify and effectively denounce all the forms of tyranny, as a first step toward laying down the foundations of a legitimate and rational type of government.[28]

An important article published in *Archives philosophiques, politiques et littéraires* in 1818 explained why in the modern age the ancient idea of the best form of government had become virtually irrelevant and vanished from the agenda of modern political philosophers. Rather than inquiring into the best or ideal type of government, a favorite topic of ancient political philosophers, modern thinkers should ask which is the government that best corresponds to the modern social condition and conforms most to the precepts of reason, truth, and justice. This was a particularly important question for Guizot, who claimed that political institutions depend to a large extent on the particular social order of each society as illustrated by its mores, customs, traditions, and property relations.[29]

Guizot's classification of political regimes must be placed in the larger context provided by his theory of the sovereignty of reason. In his view, all regimes could be classified according to two different principles, depending on whether sovereignty was vested in human agency (will) or in a transcendent entity (reason, justice, and truth). On the one hand, claimed Guizot, there are those political regimes which recognize justice, reason, and truth as their true sovereign and are founded on the assumption that sovereignty does not belong as a right to any individual. These governments were reluctant to concede sovereignty of right to individual will, because human beings are fallible and prone to usurp sovereignty in order to exercise power for their own interest. On the other hand, there are governments that attribute sovereignty of right to individuals and admitt that human beings have certain prerogatives and rights that, in Guizot's view, could only belong to justice and reason.

Guizot's theory of representative government was based on the assumption that only the first aforementioned type of government is legitimate. This amounts to arguing that it would be impossible to attribute to one man or to several individuals an inherent right to sovereignty, because this would defy the rules of eternal reason as well as the "true law of society."[30] Hence, concluded Guizot, representative government must not attribute sovereignty of right to any individual will; "its powers are directed to the discovery and faithful fulfillment of that rule which ought ever to govern their action" (Guizot 2002, 52). The sovereignty of fact is only recognized on the condition that it has to be continually justified on the basis of its compliance with the precepts of reason, justice, and truth.

Also worth noting is the way in which Guizot reinterpreted the notion of legitimacy. In his view, the classical scheme of classifying governments according to the number of those who hold power—the one, the few, or the many—could not offer adequate solutions to the problems of absolute power and political legitimacy. For Guizot, legitimacy was no longer the prerogative of a single form of government, be that monarchy, republic, or democracy. Any type of government can be regarded as legitimate insofar as its principles do not contradict the sovereignty of reason and are in accord with the interest of society expressed by its representatives.

But, one might ask, how are we to assess whether or not the actions of those who hold power are or are not in accord with the precepts of reason? At first glance, Guizot's formulation strikes us as excessively ambiguous. Would it be sufficient then to claim that political legitimacy is based on a moral idea of right, justice, and reason that all human beings are able to recognize and follow?[31] Guizot's answer to this question was that no power can ever be judged to fully possess legitimacy and no individual is ever capable of fully knowing and applying into practice the principles of reason, justice, and truth. No body of human beings can fully know and perform all that is required by reason, justice, and truth: "The right to sovereignty vested in men, whether in one, in many, or in all, is an iniquitous lie" (Guizot 2002, 51).

Thus, the doctrine of the sovereignty of reason must be understood as a *liberal* strategy to divide and limit sovereignty. It expresses the fundamental difference between that power whose conduct is predetermined by preexisting moral imperatives (or by the rule of reason) and the idea of a sovereign without any guiding rule or norm other than its own will.[32] As an article published in *Le Globe* argued, the theory of the sovereignty of reason was considered as "the theory of the century"[33] that offered a new and coherent conception of political representation and representative government. The "middling" nature of this theory was conveyed by Guizot in the opening pages of *Du gouvernement de la France* (1820):

> I believe neither in divine right nor in the sovereignty of the people. I cannot see in them anything else than usurpation of force. I believe instead in the sovereignty of reason, justice, and right: this is the legitimate sovereign that people search and will always search for, because reason, truth, and justice do not reside anywhere on Earth in a complete and infallible form. No man, no assembly of men can have them or possess them without failure or limits. (Guizot 1820, 201)

As this passage clearly shows, for Guizot, both popular sovereignty and the divine right were *incompatible* with genuine political liberty. It bears repeating that his position on this issue was strikingly similar to Constant's critique of popular sovereignty and the divine right of kings. In a lesser-known text on sovereignty that was discovered and published by Éphraïm Harpaz in 1989, Constant arrived at a similar conclusion: The will of all is not *a priori* more legitimate than the divine right of kings. Both of them (might) jeopardize liberty and are not incompatible with absolute sovereignty:

> Two systems have always dominated the world: the sovereignty of the people which I deny and the divine right which I detest. . . . The divine right destroys both legitimacy and liberty. . . . The will of all is not more legitimate than the will of one man simply because it is—or claims to be—the will of all. There is no unlimited sovereignty. There is only limited sovereignty and sovereignty becomes usurpation when it exceeds its competence. (Constant 1989, 176–77)

Guizot's opposition to popular sovereignty—which he also called *"la souveraineté du nombre"*[34]—led some commentators to argue that he was a reactionary conservative hostile to the principles of democracy. In reality, as we have already seen, Guizot's main concern was to denounce arbitrary and absolute power. He made a clear distinction between democracy as *social condition* (*état social*), whose consequences he accepted, and *political* democracy as universal suffrage, which he opposed (the same point applies to the other Doctrinaires as well). Guizot understood the inevitability of the new democratic social condition and its most salient characteristic, the equality of conditions. At the same time, he rejected the idea that the legitimacy of power does necessarily result from the number of the voices that support a certain course of action at a certain point in time. "Justice and wisdom," concluded Guizot, "are not always present in the will of the majority."[35]

Also worth noting here is the contrast between representative government and democracy. According to Guizot the latter admits that the right of sovereignty resides in the people, while representative government denies that the sovereignty of right can ever be granted to anyone on Earth.[36] Guizot went on to qualify his view by pointing out that in spite of its limitations, the sovereignty of the people is a "great force" (Guizot 2002, 64) that played an important role in the struggle against excessive forms of inequality and absolute power. Nonetheless, the darkest episodes of the Revolution sounded a cautionary note against idolizing the sovereignty of the people. Popular sovereignty was used as a pretext for imposing an uncommon degree of social homogeneity and an unrealistic conception of civic virtue incompatible with liberty and individual rights.[37] Guizot explicitly referred to the

Montagnard Constitution of 1793 which made unity and unanimity the very conditions of sovereignty. He also denounced the authorization of arbitrary acts in the name of the people and pointed to the nefarious consequences of any theory that grants absolute sovereignty to the people bound by no other rule than its own will.

As already mentioned, there are a few striking similarities between Guizot's opposition to popular sovereignty and Ancillon's ideas. The Prussian thinker referred to the sovereignty of the people as a "principle of political death" on which no enduring political institution can ever be built.[38] During the French Revolution, those who advocated popular sovereignty displayed a disquieting propensity to violence and, thriving on ambition, egoism, and vanity, eventually acquired an awesome power that triggered an unprecedented degree of destruction. As such, the doctrine of popular sovereignty became a threat to political order and made possible a "despotism of liberty" (Ancillon 1816, 107) never seen before. By using the doctrine of popular sovereignty as a pretext for pursuing their own interests, ruthless leaders committed the most heinous crimes, discredited moral principles, and confounded virtue and vice, crimes, and duties.[39] Guizot's own position on this matter was more nuanced, if equally forceful and uncompromising. In his opinion, according to the principle of the sovereignty of the people, absolute right resides with the majority. This was a flawed idea that made possible the oppression of the minority and imprinted in the minds of the people a "shameful respect for the number and a false humility toward the multitude."[40]

Moreover, Guizot denied that the whole people could ever exercise political power in the proper sense of the word. As the Revolution demonstrated, power ultimately remained in hands of a few individuals who defended popular sovereignty only to impose their own ruthless rule in the name of the "people." The self-proclaimed leaders of the people invoked the concept of popular sovereignty to denounce "corrupt" representatives and the alleged "enemies" of the people. Similar points were also made by Barante, who denounced the "divine right of revolutionaries" in the following unequivocal terms:

> This is how one can identify the deadly vice of this doctrine of absolute popular sovereignty. Indeed, the people themselves have never exerted it properly speaking; this sovereignty has only become real in the hands of those who have taken hold of it. They alone have said that it was absolute, in order to better justify their absolute rule. This is the birth of tyranny; no other doctrine justifies it better: [absolute popular sovereignty] is the divine right of revolutionaries.[41]

Barante's point needs little additional commentary. He rejected popular sovereignty on the grounds that those who defended the doctrine of popular sovereignty did not grant sovereignty to the real people who worked in the fields and traded in the streets, but only to the *idea* of the people that did not exist in reality. The "people" that the theory referred to had neither form, nor residence, nor majesty; it was only an abstract concept, a mere figment of imagination.[42]

To conclude, the French Doctrinaires opposed popular sovereignty because in their view, the latter was an impracticable and flawed political principle that postulated the equal right of all individuals to exercise sovereignty and rested on the false assumption that each man possesses as his birthright an equal right of governing others. "Like aristocratic governments," writes Guizot, "[popular sovereignty] connects the right to govern, not with capacity, but with birth" (Guizot 2002, 60) and overlooks or denies the presence of *legitimate* forms of inequality established by nature between the capacities, abilities, and skills of different individuals.[43] Under the pretext of establishing legitimate equality, the doctrine of popular sovereignty violently introduced equality where it did not exist and proved to be "a weapon of attack and destruction, never an instrument for the foundation of liberty" (Guizot 2002, 64).

A Surprising Affinity: Guizot and Cortés

If we leave aside for a moment the Doctrinaires' fundamental opposition to the divine right of kings, their critique of individual will and popular sovereignty appears to have important similarities with the position held by some French ultraroyalists. Nonetheless, a closer look at the Doctrinaires' writings demonstrates the existence of significant differences in the ways in which the two groups approached the issue of sovereignty.

The *ultras* argued that every form of sovereignty is absolute by nature, regardless of how the system of power is structured. In the last analysis, claimed Joseph de Maistre (1971, 113), "it will always be an absolute power which is able to commit evil with impunity." That is why the absolute nature of sovereignty must be recognized as a necessity of political life. As Maistre wrote in a famous passage (1971, 108–109), "government is a true religion; it has its dogmas, its mysteries, its priests; to submit to individual discussion is to destroy it; it has life only through the national mind, that is to say, political faith, which is a creed." In his view, the true origin of political obligation was not individual consent, which might be revoked and cannot absolutely bind future generations, but a superior divine will that commands universal obedience. Furthermore, man-made laws can never replace the "natural constitution" of society, which exists prior to any written laws and underpins all forms of social life.

While Guizot opposed the idea that government could be compared to a true religion, he, too, acknowledged that the true law of society is not the work of any individual. Its origin is transcendent. In volume one of *Histoire des origines du gouvernement représentatif*, Guizot explicitly referred to the existence of a natural or divine law to which all individuals must unconditionally obey:

> In his interior life . . . as well as in his exterior life, and in his dealings with his fellows, the man who feels himself free and capable of action, has ever a glimpse of a natural law by which his action is regulated. He recognizes a something which is not his own will, and which must regulate his will. He feels himself bound by reason or morality to do certain things; he sees, or he feels that there are certain things which he ought or ought not to do. This something is the law which is superior to man, and made for him—the divine law. The true law of man is not the work of man; he receives, but does not create it; even when he submits to it, it is not his own—it is beyond and above him. (Guizot 2002, 51)

Given the existence of a transcendent law that governs man's will, all individuals must strive to discover this eternal law and should apply its precepts in practice.

Nonetheless, in spite of their common critique of the hubris of individual will, the French Doctrinaires and the ultraroyalists held in fact utterly *different* views of sovereignty as illustrated by their general political agendas. The political ideal of the Doctrinaires, a liberal constitutional monarchy based on constitutionalism, division of powers, rule of law, a two-chamber Parliament, and publicity, was entirely opposed to the theocracy advocated by Maistre and Bonald, based on a close alliance between throne and altar. Unlike the *ultras*, the Doctrinaires believed in the effectiveness of written constitutions and advocated a sound balance of powers. An interesting parallel can be drawn, however, between the Doctrinaires' theory of sovereignty and Donoso Cortés's ideas on this issue.[44] Before veering to the extreme right in the late 1840s, when he abandoned his earlier moderate liberalism for a radical version of ultramontanism, Cortés passed through a (lesser-known) "Doctrinaire" phase in the mid-1830s, when he advanced a set of ideas that bore striking similarities to Guizot's political philosophy, to which he frequently referred in his writings. Cortés's own lectures on political right delivered in 1836 in Madrid, *Lecciones de Derecho Político*, translated into English under the (misleading) title *A Defense of Representative Government*, demonstrate the strong impact of French *juste milieu* liberalism on his own political philosophy.

These lectures were "the magnum opus of Donoso's liberal years"[45] and provided the first systematic treatment of sovereignty in Spain. Cortés elaborated a Spanish version of Doctrinaire liberalism[46] that drew heavily on Guizot's theory of the sovereignty of reason, to which he also referred as "the sovereignty of intelligence." Cortés chose the term *intelligence* to distance himself from the abstract rationalism of his age, with which he eventually became disenchanted and against which he launched a fierce crusade toward the end of his short but tumultuous life. In the mid-1830s, Cortés's critics took him to task for being a "Guizotian" and a plagiarist of Royer-Collard's eclecticism. They were not far from the truth, although Cortés's own version of "Doctrinaire" liberalism seems to have been in many respects more coherent, but also more dogmatic and rigid, than the original one of Guizot and his colleagues.[47]

In the footsteps of Guizot, Cortés drew a seminal distinction between two types of sovereignty—sovereignty of fact and sovereignty of right—and rejected both the divine right of kings and popular sovereignty. "It is generally believed," argued Cortés, "that the dogma of popular sovereignty is essentially contrary to the dogma of the divine right of kings. This belief is an error" (Cortés 1991, 46). In reality, the two theories were nothing else than "dogmas of social omnipotence," advanced by two equally "decrepit and sterile schools" (Cortés 1991, 47) competing for political power. Popular sovereignty is a manifestation of pride, hubris, and force that jeopardizes the civilizing legacy of previous centuries. Cortés contrasted the sovereignty of the people to the sovereignty of "intelligence," which, in his view, was the "sublime expression of right and justice" (Cortés 1991, 17).

Hence, concluded Cortés, to ground sovereignty in the individual will was a mistake pregnant with serious political consequences. To rule is a function of reason, not will:

> All facts which serve as a basis in order to locate sovereignty in the human will have to be necessarily moral crimes or political crimes, public crimes or private crimes. Either the will has to obey the reason, and thus the sovereignty cannot be located in the will because it cannot be localized in obedience, or the will has to disobey the reason, and then sovereignty is localized in disobedience and in crime.[48]

The sovereignty of intelligence is inseparable from justice and acts as a banner of liberty and progress: "The banner of reason was put by Providence on the horizon of peoples as the ensign of salvation" (Cortés 1991, 58). In order to achieve a balance between intelligence, order, and freedom, the most intelligent must have the right to command in society. Cortés's conclusion deserves to be quoted in full, not only because of his excellent rhetoric (he was an exceptionally gifted writer), but also because of a few surprising similarities with the ideas of the French Doctrinaires:

> Two banners have been waved, Gentlemen, since the origin of human societies on the horizon of peoples; the banner of popular sovereignty and the banner of divine right. A sea of blood separates them, and this sea of blood testifies what is the destiny of societies that adopt them, and what is the fortune of societies that follow them. But a new banner, candid, resplendent, immaculate, has appeared in the world, and whose theme is the sovereignty of the intelligence, the sovereignty of justice. Let us follow it, Gentlemen, since its appearance, it alone is the banner of liberty, the others of slavery; it alone is the banner of progress, the others of reaction; it alone is the banner of the future, the others of the past; it alone is the banner of humanity, the others of factions. (Cortés 1991, 21).

The Guizotian ring of this passage can be explained by the fact that Cortés had carefully studied and meditated on Guizot's writings while living in Paris in the 1830s. Nonetheless, he eventually became disenchanted with *juste milieu* liberalism and ended his flirtation with the French Doctrinaires' ideas. Cortés's dogmatism, gloomy dualism, and unique inclination to hyperbole became evident in *Ensayo sobre el Catolicismo, el Liberalismo, y el Socialismo* (1851). This work full of "piquante originality"[49] advanced a theocratic view of authority and an eclectic view of history, combining insights from authors as diverse as St. Augustine, Bossuet, Vico, and Comte.

The Institutional Implications of the Sovereignty of Reason

As both Maurice Barbé and Paul Bénichou argued, Guizot's theory of the sovereignty of reason had a distinctive *liberal* character. It affirmed the idea that human beings are fallible and inclined to abuse power if allowed to do so. Equally important were Guizot's emphasis on the relativity of *all* claims to authority and his strong belief that the legitimacy of those who held power is contingent upon their demonstrating the conformity of their actions to the precepts of reason, truth, and justice.

Hence, Guizot's doctrine of the sovereignty of reason and Constant's theory of limited sovereignty can be regarded as two overlapping strategies that sought to limit sovereignty in order to prevent arbitrary power exercised either by an absolute monarch or in the name of the people. Both thinkers argued that the will of the many was not a priori more legitimate than the will of one. Both of them agreed that no unlimited sovereignty should be allowed to exist on earth. Yet, there were also important differences between Constant and Guizot. While the latter stressed the fallibility of all powers and had greater confidence in the virtues of properly limited executive power, Constant emphasized the inviolability and sacredness of individual rights, a theme which loomed large in his writings.[50]

The question remains: Can Guizot's theory of the sovereignty of reason, which emerged out of a particular historical context, have any relevance to our contemporary debates in political theory? Needless to say, the sovereignty of reason is a notoriously ambiguous concept when it comes to identifying the concrete attributes of reason. To claim that only reason is capable of restraining individual will does not lead us too far, since there can be no genuine agreement on what the characteristics of reason are or what the precepts of reason, truth, and justice exactly require in practice. Even if reason can be used as an effective tool of philosophical or political criticism, it cannot be universally acknowledged as the source of self-evident moral and political principles, since there can be no single "rational" set of moral, political, and religious principles on which we all can agree.[51]

In his history of the theories of sovereignty after Rousseau, Charles Merriam claimed that the affirmation of sovereignty of reason led in practice to the emptying of sovereignty of any political significance.[52] In Merriam's opinion, the doctrine of the sovereignty of reason made sense only in the limited historical context from which it originally emerged as a middle ground between the divine right of kings and the sovereignty of the people. From a theoretical point of view, the doctrine of the sovereignty of reason renders it difficult or ultimately impossible to find a concrete location for a legitimate sovereign power. Merriam concluded that the Doctrinaires were not really concerned with solving the problem of sovereignty, but only wanted to demonstrate that the concept of sovereignty must be stricken from political science altogether. "Their answer to the question of sovereignty was that there is no question to answer. . . . On the whole, the progress of the French theory during this period offers little of importance in the development of sovereignty" (Merriam 1900, 79; 84).

Charles Merriam was not alone in holding this view. In Douglas Johnson's opinion, the doctrine of the sovereignty of reason did not allow any constitutional body to possess true constituent power. Guizot failed to locate any one center of power in the state, refused to establish any body as supreme, and misunderstood the role of the Chamber of Deputies while seeking to limit its influence and prerogatives.[53] A related critique can be found in Vincent Starzinger's comparative analysis of *juste milieu* theories in nineteenth-century France and England and Guy Dodge's study of Constant. Starzinger maintained that the sovereignty of reason seems to contradict the principles of constitutionalism and empties the notion of sovereignty of any practical content.[54] Finally, in Guy Dodge's view, the Doctrinaires' main limitation came from their belief that the limitation of power in the abstract was sufficient. As such, they failed to consider how particular institutions—not just abstract reason—could establish an effective division of powers.

These views are worth revisiting because they draw questionable and, ultimately, misleading conclusions about the alleged incompatibility between constitutionalism and the sovereignty of reason. Above all, the thesis according to which the Doctrinaires' theory led to eliminating the concept of sovereignty from political debates stands in need of urgent revision. A closer look at the writings of Guizot and the other Doctrinaires suggests, in fact, a rather different conclusion.[55] Not only were they persuaded that it was impossible to dispense with the concept of sovereignty in politics, but they did not shy away from wrestling with a few fundamental questions in political theory. How can sovereignty and accountability be reconciled? Is it possible to have a sovereign invested with supreme power who can also be held accountable for his actions?

The distinction between *de iure* and de facto sovereignty allowed the Doctrinaires to answer these questions. While admitting that the sovereignty of *right* should be granted only to reason, truth, and justice, they pointed out that in a constitutional monarchy the sovereignty of *fact* was in practice divided between the executive and the legislative power, which had to work together to promote and defend the general interests of the nation. Guizot and his colleagues maintained that the limitation and division of sovereignty of fact ought to be supplemented by a set of concrete political institutions and principles such as the rule of law, publicity, and freedom of the press. Furthermore, they insisted that, according to the doctrine of the sovereignty of reason, those who rise to positions of power in society must be required to justify the legitimacy of their actions under the eyes of public opinion and under the penalty of being ousted from power if their actions do not conform to the precepts of reason and justice.

Hence, far from being a mere theoretical statement, the doctrine of the sovereignty of reason led in practice to a series of important institutional arrangements mediated by free press, publicity, the rule of law, and open parliamentary debates. In the Doctrinaires' opinion, the regime that corresponded best to the principle of the sovereignty of reason was a limited monarchy, *une monarchie temperée*, in which the king reigned but did not govern. The institutions of representative government characterized by publicity, popular elections, parliamentary debates, and free press were considered to be the concrete expression of the political principles derived from the doctrine of the sovereignty of reason.[56]

It must be stressed that for Guizot, representative government was first and foremost a means of limiting power (constitutionalism) based on the following principles: (a) no de facto power can be considered a priori a power of right; (b) those who hold power may never claim the right to be the unique and infallible source of right in the state; (c) they must constantly prove the legitimacy of their actions by demonstrating that they are in accord with (and do not deviate from) the precepts of reason, truth, and justice. As Charles de Rémusat once wrote, the best political constitution was that which recognized that no power is infallible and granted power to those who were presumed capable of promoting the general interests of the country in accord with the principles of reason and justice.[57]

Surprisingly, it was an antiliberal thinker such as Carl Schmitt who understood better than anyone else the *liberal* nature of the Doctrinaires' theory of the sovereignty of reason. In *Die geistesgeschichtliche Lage des heutigen Parlamentarismus* (translated into English under the inaccurate title *The Crisis of Parliamentary Democracy*), Schmitt referred to Guizot as a classic defender of the liberal theory of the rule of law and applauded his correct insight that a norm can be sovereign only insofar as it represented rational justice, reason, and right. Yet, in Schmitt's opinion, Guizot appeared as the typical representative of bourgeois liberalism, which relied on an absolute and ultimately problematic belief in Parliament as the representative of reason on Earth.[58] Guizot's theory of sovereignty, concluded Schmitt, was ultimately untenable, because it contained a few important and unsolvable contradictions. It failed to provide a clear solution to the most pressing political problem of the first half of the nineteenth century, namely, the rising power of the demos and the issue of universal suffrage.

From our vantage point today, the debates around universal suffrage and popular sovereignty can no longer arouse the same passions as they did two centuries ago. We are no longer interested in attacking the sovereignty of the people or defending popular sovereignty against its enemies. Like universal suffrage, this principle has become central to our understanding of liberal democracy, and any attempt to question it would certainly be absurd and illegitimate. In this regard, one might rightly argue that the Doctrinaires' theory of the sovereignty of reason is obsolete.

Yet, the *liberal* character of their theory predicated upon the seminal distinction between sovereignty of *fact* and sovereignty of *right* must be duly underscored. As nineteenth-century liberals, the Doctrinaires argued that political democracy ought to be made subordinate to liberal principles and insisted that even democratic principles must acknowledge the existence of *pregiven* moral norms, the most important of which was the sovereignty of reason, truth, and justice. In their view, democratic principles depended on an antecedent moral commitment to a superior norm that could not be the outcome of popular consent or deliberation.

This amounts to arguing that even democracy, the best form of government, needs outside guidance in the form of principles and values that individuals do not create but, rather, discover by reflection. In other words, democratic self-rule cannot serve as the sole normative foundation of the modern state. Instead, this principle must also acknowledge the existence of certain *pregiven* moral norms, without which common life in liberal-democratic societies would become impossible or anarchic. To put it differently, political liberty cannot be fully guaranteed unless we recognize what Charles Larmore once called the "heteronomous dimension" of liberal democracy; that is, the existence of certain norms and principles that are not created by individuals and do not depend on their consent.

This idea has reappeared in contemporary debates on liberalism and democracy with respect to the proper relation between will and reason. In Jürgen Habermas's opinion, only those action norms are valid to which all those who might be affected by their implementation could assent as the result of rational discussion. In his more recent works, Habermas demonstrated the limitations of an overly concrete reading of sovereignty and argued for a less concrete notion of popular sovereignty, mediated by publicity. "Public discourse," he argued, "must mediate between reason and will, between the opinion-formation of all and the majoritarian will-formation of the representatives" (Habermas 1998, 473). It is worth pointing out that Habermas's position remained, however, distinct from that of nineteenth-century liberals in one important respect. He took issue with a central tenet of liberalism—the belief that individual rights enjoy normative priority over democracy—and claimed that "the exercise of popular sovereignty simultaneously secures human rights . . . [which] are identical with the constitutive conditions of a self-limiting practice of publicly discursive will-formation" (Habermas 1998, 473; 477).

Habermas's position on this issue triggered an interesting response from Charles Larmore, who claimed that, while it is true that the principles that justify the conditional use of coercive force should be the object of rational justification and must be acceptable to—and accepted by—all citizens, this conclusion does *not* apply to all moral norms and principles. "In this century," wrote Larmore, "there has been a tendency to suppose that the ideas of democratic self-rule must aim to stand on its own, that popular sovereignty must present itself as the ultimate source of political principles. This view of democracy does not in the end make sense."[59] The rediscovery of what Larmore called the heteronomous dimension of democracy might help us correct this view. The doctrine of the sovereignty of reason reminds us that popular sovereignty and democratic will, too, must be subject to *pregiven* moral principles and values.

The French Doctrinaires would have wholeheartedly endorsed Maritain's claim that sovereignty becomes dangerous when transplanted from the religious to the political realm. They would have also agreed with Maritain and Habermas on the need to avoid an overly concrete interpretation of sovereignty. Nonetheless, they would have opposed the idea that the concept of sovereignty is similar to absolutism and must be discarded from political science. It is not a mere coincidence that Guizot thought highly of the *Federalist Papers,* which he considered the greatest work known to him on the application of elementary principles of government to practical administration.[60] In turn, Barante insisted that, in order to protect liberty and rights, no power could ever be allowed to reign absolutely and sovereignty must be divided between all the powers in the state.[61] Staunch opponents of any form of absolute power, the Doctrinaires praised the virtues of English constitutional monarchy, which successfully combined liberty, tradition, and innovation. They affirmed that at the core of the theory of representative government lies the responsibility of power under penalty of being taxed with illegitimacy. The doctrine of the sovereignty of reason was meant to denounce the radical illegitimacy of arbitrary power and was seen as compatible in practice with the principles of constitutionalism.[62] The next chapters of this book will examine in further detail the Doctrinaires' theory of power and the "new means of government," along with their views on publicity as the cornerstone of representative government.

Notes

1. See, for example, Soltau 1959, Dodge 1980, and Neidleman 2001.
2. See Beaud 1996, 626.
3. For more details, see Rees 1969, 210. On the relation between sovereignty and authority, see de Jouvenel 1997, 31–47, 222–37.
4. Constant in Simon 1972, 67.

5. For more details, see "The nature of royal power in a constitutional monarchy," in Constant 1988 (chapter 2), 183–93.

6. Constant 1988, 190. A detailed study on the theories of sovereignty in Restoration France can be found in Barbé 1904.

7. Constant in Simon 1972, 68.

8. Constant in Simon 1972, 67; emphasis added.

9. For a comprehensive intellectual history of the sovereignty of reason, see Beiser 1996. In a true tour de force covering the period from 1594 to 1737, Beiser examined the ramifications of this concept in the works of Hooker, the Cambridge Platonists, Toland, and Hume.

10. For a good presentation of Cousin's influence on the new generation, see Spitzer 1987, 71–96. On Cousin's theoretical contribution, see Jaume 1994b, 249–51; Jaume 1997a, 459–72; Diez del Corral 1956, 193–94; Billard 1998, 106–93. Writes Cousin: "Le vrai révélateur des droits de l'homme, c'est la Raison, . . . puissance souveraine, mais invisible qui ne revêt aucune forme, n'habite aucun lieu, mais qu'il faut bien se garder de nier, car elle est dans l'humanité comme Dieu est dans l'univers, partout et nulle part" (Cousin as quoted in Barbé 1904, 125).

11. A letter of Guizot to his mother conveys his strong and sincere admiration for Kant: "Kant est le seul philosophe qui ait tracé la ligne de démarcation entre le ciel et la terre, l'âme et le corps; j'espère que je parviendrai à connaître à fond et dans toutes ses branches le système le plus beau, le mieux établi qu'ait enfanté l'esprit humain" (quoted in Jaume 1992, 142–43). On the influence of Kant on Guizot, also see Kirschleger, 1999, 50–52; Thadden 1991.

12. Here is a revealing passage from Guizot's *Philosophie politique*: "L'homme s'est fait des idoles; il les a appelé dieux et les a adorées. À mesure que l'homme a grandi, que son esprit s'est ouvert sur un horizon plus vaste et pur, il a reconnu la vanité de ses idoles et les a brisées. Mais aussitôt il a porté son adoration ailleurs. De progrès en progrès, déplaçant sans cesse son dieu visible, il l'a toujours placé quelque part, ne pouvant ni s'en passer ni s'en tenir à sa première foi, également incapable d'enfermer Dieu dans une image terrestre et de se résigner à ne le voir jamais face à face, sous une forme et des traits apparents" (Guizot 1985, 319).

13. See Guizot 1985, 320, and Guizot 2002, 50–53.

14. Guizot 1985, 319–20; the translation is mine. Also: "Il voulait un maître constamment et parfaitement légitime. Nulle part et en aucun temps il n'a pu le rencontrer. Cependant il n'a pas cessé de le chercher ou de croire qu'enfin il l'avait trouvé. C'est l'histoire des sociétés humaines. On s'étonne de leurs révoltes contre des pouvoirs anciens et longtemps révérés. Fréquemment déplacé, le pouvoir absolu a toujours obtenu un asile, un trône" (Guizot 1985, 319–20).

15. See, for example, Guizot 1985, 372. Also see the following paragraph: "Que la souveraineté de fait, la volonté qui, en définitif, doit commander, soit donc le résultat d'un effort, du rapprochement et de la collision de pouvoirs indépendants, égaux, et capable de s'imposer réciproquement l'obligation de chercher en commun la vérité" (Guizot 1985, 343). A similar argument about the division of sovereignty can

be found in Frederick Ancillon's *De la souveraineté et des formes de gouvernement* (1816), a work translated into French by Guizot. In Ancillon's view, the division of powers was a fundamental political principle: "Diviser la souveraineté de manière à opposer pouvoir à pouvoir. . . . De l'action opposée de plusieurs forces, dont chacune peut être funeste à l'État, naissent la liberté et la sûreté" (Ancillon 1816, 50).

16. Guizot 1985, 321, 327, 341. Also see the following passage: "L'homme étant, de sa nature, imparfait et sujet à l'erreur, il ne peut tomber aux mains de l'homme, ni sortir du sein des hommes, nul pouvoir infaillible et parfait, partant nul pouvoir investi de la souveraineté de droit" (Guizot 1985, 325).

17. This idea was quite popular in nineteenth-century Europe. One can find it, mutatis mutandis, in Giuseppe Mazzini's *The Duties of Man*: "O dobbiamo obbedire a Dio, o servire ad uomini, uno o piú non importa. Se non regna una Mente suprema su tutte le menti umane, chi può salvarci dall'arbitrio dei nostri simili, quando si trovino piú potenti di noi? Se non esiste una Legge santa inviolabile, non creata dagli uomini, qual norma avremo per giudicare se un atto è giusto o non è?" (Mazzini 1984, 40).

18. Here is what Guizot said in a letter to Barante in November 1826: "Mais plus j'avance, plus je me confirme dans cette double certitude qu'il y a là un monde réel, auquel nous tenons par des rapports assurés, et que ce monde est interdit à la connaissance humaine, que nous n'en pouvons jouir ici-bas, de cette possession claire et satisfaisante qui s'attache à la science. . . . Je suis comme un aveugle avide de lumière, tourmenté de n'en jamais jouir, et qui marche pourtant avec une pleine et intime confiance dans la main qui le conduit" (Guizot 1884, 64–66). Also essential for the understanding of Guizot's religious beliefs is a superb letter to Laure de Gasparin (June 19, 1836). "Il y a de Dieu et de l'homme en toutes choses," wrote Guizot, "dans l'histoire de chaque individu, dans celle du genre humain, dans notre avenir eternal. Soit qu'il s'agisse de ce petit drame qu'on appelle une vie d'homme ou de ce grand drame qui est l'histoire du monde, Dieu est le premier et le souverain auteur. . . . Mais nous, acteurs de Dieu, acteurs intelligens et libres, nous inventons, nous créons à chaque instant une partie de notre role; et c'est pourquoi nous en sommes responsible. . . . À mon avis, non seulement toute partialité, mais toute contradiction disparaît dans le système qui admet en meme temps Dieu et l'homme, la Providence et l'action humaine, la grace et la liberté" (quoted in Kirschleger 1999, 242). For Guizot's meditations on the essence of Christianity, see Guizot 1864.

19. Writes Guizot: "Quand les philosophes ont considéré l'homme en lui-même, nul n'a prétendu que sa volonté fût, pour lui, la seule loi légitime, c'est-à-dire que toute action fût raisonnable ou juste dès qu'elle est libre et volontaire. Tous ont reconnu qu'au-dessus de la volonté de l'individu plane une certaine loi appelée raison, sagesse, morale ou verité, et à laquelle il ne peut soustraire sa conduite sans faire, de sa liberté, un emploi absurde ou coupable" (Guizot 1985, 366–67). Also see Guizot 1864, 45–47.

20. I refer to Madame de Staël's *Des circonstances actuelles qui peuvent terminer la Révolution et des principes qui doivent fonder la république en France*, written in 1798 and first published in an incomplete edition in 1906. The full text was published in 1979.

21. For more details, see Guizot 1863a, 32–61; Guizot 2002, 288–89; Jaume 1997a, 127–28.

22. See Guizot 2002, 285–94; also Guizot 1863a, 32–36.

23. See, for example, Guizot 2002, 293–94.

24. Writes Guizot: "Le contrat qui lie les hommes aux lois de la justice et de la vérité n'est point leur ouvrage, pas plus que les lois elles-mêmes. C'est un contrat divin où sont écrites, de la main du Très-Haut, les vraies règles de toutes les relations humaines et qui oblige l'un envers l'autre le gouvernement et le peuple, précisément parce qu'il leur est supérieur à tous deux, parce qu'il ne tomba sous l'empire de leur volonté" (Guizot 1820, 84). On the theological background of Guizot's sovereignty of reason, see Griffo 2001, 98–101.

25. For more details, see Guizot 1985, 369–70. An interesting parallel can be drawn between Guizot and his Spanish Catholic critic, Jaime Balmes. For more details, see Balmes 1852, 319–20; 347. Balmes attacked Guizot's Protestant interpretation of the evolution of European civilization. On the fundamental distinction between absolute and arbitrary power, see de Jouvenel 1997, 238–57.

26. For more details on Sieyès's attitude toward Montesquieu, see Forsyth 1987, 58–59.

27. Writes Ancillon: "La notion de souveraineté est la seule mesure commune d'après laquelle on puisse juger les gouvernements anciens et modernes, et le seul principe qui puisse servir de base à une classification exacte des constitutions politiques" (Ancillon 1816, 37). For more details, also see Ancillon 1816, 38–39.

28. Fore more details, see Guizot 1985, 339.

29. The (unidentified) author of the article published in *Archives philosophiques, politiques et littéraires* in 1818 wrote: "La question si vaine et si débattue, quel est le meilleur gouvernement? doit être remplacée par celle-ci: quel est le gouvernement le mieux en harmonie avec la raison humaine dans un pays et dans un temps donnés? Ou, en d'autres termes, quel est le gouvernement rationnel relatif?" (*APPL*, vol. 5, p. 32). According to Pouthas (1923b, 19–23), the author of this article was not Guizot.

30. Guizot 2002, 51. For more details on Guizot's classification of governments, see Guizot 2002, 49–52, 64–65.

31. Guizot 1985, 349. For more details on Guizot's theory of legitimacy, also see Guizot 1997a, 49–51.

32. See the following statement of Émile Faguet: "L'idée libérale a été très lente à naître en Europe. Elle est essentiellement moderne; elle est d'hier. Elle consiste à croire qu'il n'y a pas de souveraineté; qu'il y a un aménagement social qui établit une autorité qui, pour qu'elle ne soit qu'une fonction, doit être limitée, contrôlée, divisée" (quoted in Derathé 1950, 347). On the idea of limited sovereignty as resistance to political arbitrariness, also see de Jouvenel 1997, 253–56.

33. *Le Globe*, November 25, 1826 (quoted in Rosanvallon 1985, 87). Also see Guizot 1820, 201.

34. Guizot spoke of "la souveraineté du nombre, si absurdement appelée la souveraineté du peuple" (Guizot 1858a, 167).

35. Guizot 1863a, 36. Also see the following passage: "*Le grand nombre s'égare souvent. Et il s'égare d'autant plus que les questions soumises à sa décision sont plus hautes. . . . Que de charlatanerie et d'inconséquence, que de mensonge et de péril dans cette prétendue intronisation de la multitude*" (Guizot 1985, 377; emphasis added). This idea also appeared, though in a different form, in Ancillon's treatise on sovereignty. For more details, see Ancillon 1816, 30.

36. The principles of representative government are discussed in Guizot 2002, 47–65, 345–448, 371–72. On the nature of political representation, see Guizot 2002, 52–53, 295–97.

37. For a good discussion of this topic, see Baker 1989, 856–58.

38. Ancillon 1816, 101; also see Ancillon 1816, 103.

39. "Avec le mot *souveraineté du peuple,* ils commirent, voilèrent, excusèrent, justifièrent des forfaits inouïs; c'est à la faveur de cette doctrine qu'ils ont perverti toutes les idées, dénaturé toutes les expressions, attaqué les principes moraux comme la moralité publique, chassé la religion des cœurs commes des temples, confondus les vertus et les vices, donné au crime le nom de devoir, au devoir le nom de crime" (Ancillon 1816, 114–15; emphasis added).

40. Guizot 1821, 147–48. On this point, also see Guizot 2002, 62–63, and Guizot 1985, 374.

41. Barante 1849, 9–10. Although published in 1849, Barante's *Questions constitutionnelles* contained many themes that had already appeared in his writings published during the Restoration.

42. Guizot's words are worth quoting again: "Ce souverain collectif n'a ni forme, ni résidence, ni majesté. Ce n'est pas même ce peuple visible et animé qui laboure, travaille, circule dans les champs et dans les rues. C'est le peuple, mais seulement en idée, un peuple abstrait qui ne se laisse ni entendre ni voir, à qui la théorie seule attribue l'être et la volonté" (Guizot 1985, 339).

43. On legitimate forms of inequality, see Guizot 2002, 61, 369–70. In Guizot's opinion, two opposite tendencies dominate society. The first one tends to produce inequality, while the second one works to create and maintain equality. Both of them, claimed Guizot, are natural and indestructible. Moreover, their effects are salutary, since without legitimate inequality, society would be inert and lifeless, while in the absence of equality naked force would dominate in society. I comment on this issue in relation with the Doctrinaires' theory of political capacity in chapter 8.

44. Roldán (1999, 103–4) draws a parallel between the Doctrinaires' views on sovereignty and individual will and Lamennais's ideas on these topics.

45. See Graham 1974, 42.

46. For a comprehensive presentation of the Spanish Doctrinaires, see Diez del Corral 1956, 399–586. On Cortés's political thought, see Diez del Corral 1956, 479–514; Herrera 1996; Graham 1974; McNamara 1992.

47. See Graham 1974, 42–43.

48. Cortés 1991, 57. The religious background of Cortés's political works was much stronger than in Guizot's case.

49. I borrow the phrase from Albert de Broglie's 1852 essay on Cortés (quoted by Graham 1974, 285, fn. 44). On the relations between Cortés and Guizot, see Graham 1974, 284–85.

50. Writes Bénichou: "La démonstration de Guizot se présente autrement que celle de Constant; au lieu de se fonder sur l'inviolabilité des droits intrinsèques de l'individu, elle évoque surtout la faillibilité des autorités humaines, et la distance qui sépare inévitablement la pratique des gouvernements de l'idéal moral dont les hommes se réclament dans le même temps. . . . *Cette argumentation, si différente qu'elle apparaisse de celle de Constant, n'est qu'un autre aspect de la même doctrine.* Toute politique libérale se fonde aussi bien sur les droits inhérents à l'individu que sur la relativité des titres du pouvoir" (Bénichou 1977, 38; emphasis added). On this topic, also see Roldán 1999, 107–9, and de Jouvenel 1997, 253–77.

51. On this issue, see Beiser 1996, 323–27.

52. For more details, see Merriam 1900, 77. The same point was also made, in a slightly different form, by Starzinger 1991 and Dodge 1980. Dodge argued that "Royer-Collard thought that as long as the idea of sovereignty is retained, the problem of limiting the power of the state by law becomes insoluble" (Dodge 1980, 70). I disagree with this interpretation.

53. See Johnson 1963, 86.

54. See Starzinger 1991, 22–23.

55. See Merriam 1900, 80.

56. See Guizot 2002, 295–97. For an excellent discussion on this issue, see Roldán 1999, 162–67; Diez del Corral 1956, 202–9; Griffo 2001. In chapters 7, 8, and 9, I examine in detail the concrete *institutional* implications of the doctrine of the sovereignty of reason.

57. Writes Rémusat: "Nous professons qu'aucune souveraineté humaine n'est absolue, c'est-à-dire que l'infaillibilité n'existe pas sur la terre. La loi souveraine, la raison infaillible, est donc la loi, la raison, la sagesse divine, ou Dieu même. Mais cette loi cependant se révèle en ce monde; cette raison s'y communique à des intelligences qui la reconnaissent et la proclament. . . . Ainsi nulle souveraineté absolue n'est realisée en ce monde; mais, invisible et présente, la raison suprême parle à la raison humaine, et ne parle qu'à elle. Tous entendent sa voix, non pas pour la suivre également, mais assez pour être également obligés de la suivre. . . . Aux plus capables de faire prévaloir la loi commune de la société, savoir la justice, la raison, la vérité. Quelle est la meilleure constitution politique? La plus propre à mettre en lumière la vérité sur chaque chose, et à faire arriver le pouvoir dans les mains de ceux qui sauront le mieux l'exercer" (Rémusat 1829, 156–57, as quoted in Rosanvallon 1985, 92–93).

58. For more details, see Schmitt 1996 (1928). Referring to the liberal character of Guizot's theory, Schmitt wrote: "Das ganze politische Pathos von Guizot, dieses typischen Vertreters einer bürgerlichen Liberalismus, liegt in dem Glauben an das Parlament als eine Repräsentation der Vernunft" (Schmitt 1928, 311).

59. Larmore 1996, 182. Larmore's critique of Habermas was first articulated in *The Morals of Modernity* (1996) and, more recently, in Larmore 2000. Referring to the heteronomous dimension of liberal democracy, Larmore argued: "Dans nos démocraties modernes, la volonté collective ne peut donc pas former la source suprême de l'autorité, à l'opposé de ce qu'on croit communément. . . . Dans le passé, on s'est souvent accroché, cela se comprend, à la notion de la souveraineté du peuple pour s'opposer à la souveraineté de Dieu. Mais il est temps de s'affranchir de cette vieille problématique théologico-politique et des positions primaires qu'elle produit. S'il faut absolument parler de souveraineté, on ferait mieux de dire, avec François Guizot, qu'elle réside, ni dans l'homme ni en Dieu, mais dans la 'raison,' par laquelle il entendait en fait les vérités objectives de la morale" (Larmore 2000, 233; the text was originally written in French). It is interesting to note in passing the affinity between Larmore's liberal position and de Jouvenel's views on sovereignty.

60. See Guizot's letter to Richard Rush quoted in Fasnacht 1952, 102. A former U.S. Attorney General from 1815 to 1817, Rush was appointed minister to Great Britain. Later (1847–49), he served as United States minister to France. Guizot met him in the 1840s. I would like to thank Fred Fransen for this information on Rush.

61. See Barante 1849, 44.

62. See Guizot 2002, 227. In his study of Acton's political philosophy, Fasnacht pointed out a few similarities between Lord Acton's ideas and Guizot's political philosophy (see Fasnacht 1952, 45–46).

CHAPTER SIX

Political Power and the "New Means of Government"

J'aime le pouvoir parce que j'aime la lutte.

—Guizot

One of the most striking features of the Doctrinaires' thought was their strong interest in rethinking the nature of the political. This chapter will examine their theory of power and the "new means of government" as illustrated by two books that stood out from the mass of writings that appeared in the early 1820s: Guizot's *Des moyens de gouvernement et d'opposition dans l'état actuel de la France* and Barante's *Des communes et de l'aristocratie*, both published in 1821.

Written almost two centuries ago, *Des moyens de gouvernement et d'opposition*, a true manifesto of government, established Guizot's reputation as a prominent theoretician of the role of executive power in modern society. While inviting his readers to rediscover the nature and dignity of political power, Guizot predicted that the development of representative government would lead to a considerable extension of the scope of government in modern society and argued that this extension was made possible by a social demand unseen before.[1]

A New Way of Conceptualizing Political Power

It seems appropriate to begin with a short historical detour that will take us back to the Constitution of 1791, which marked an important moment in the history of revolutionary France. By postulating the existence of natural rights that ought to be protected by political institutions and laws, the constitution reiterated a famous idea from Article 2 of the *Declaration of the Rights of Man and of the Citizen*, according to which "the aim of every political association is the conservation of the natural and imprescriptible rights of man; these rights are liberty, property, security, and resistance to oppression."[2] Nonetheless, the text of the constitution contained an important conceptual ambiguity that was bound to have significant political consequences. Positive laws were made responsible for determining the very conditions under which rights could be guaranteed and enforced. As such, the constitution signaled a fundamental and often insurmountable tension between citizenship and liberty defined as independence. Rights were, in fact, subordinated to the legislature's idea of what public order required for the preservation of society. As a result, rights were "saddled with the ghost of duties" (Gauchet 1989, 824), a conceptual transformation whose full implications were demonstrated by the darkest episodes of the Terror.[3]

The second principle that occupied a central place in the *Declaration of the Rights of Man and of the Citizen* as well as in the Constitution of 1791 was the separation of powers. It has been remarked that Article 16 of the Constitution of 1791—"any society in which the guarantee of the rights is not secured, or the separation of powers not determined, has no constitution at all" (Anderson ed. 1967, 71)—was more or less similar to Article 16 of the *Declaration*. In its original form, the principle of the separation of powers had a strong antimonarchical character, because it attempted to transform the king into a simple magistrate—that is, the head of the executive—entirely dependent on the legislative power. The skeptical attitude toward executive power was motivated by the extreme confidence in the virtues of legislative power. An example of this attitude was Mounier's claim that "the most beautiful functions of sovereignty are those of the legislative body" (Mounier 1789, 26). The preeminence of the legislative power was also affirmed by the Constitution of 1791 and reappeared in the constitutions of 1793 (Year I) and 1795 (Year III), which relegated the executive power to a secondary position and conceived of the government as a mere agent of the legislative power that was supposed to execute what the legislature—the soul and mind of the commonwealth—had decided.

Necker's *Du pouvoir exécutif dans les grands états* (1792) offered a novel perspective on the complex role played by executive power in modern society. The government, claimed Necker, represents that power which unites action to will in the moral individual. To establish its scope, means, and influence, along with the proper relation between the legislature and the executive power, constitutes one of the most important political problems, infinitely more complicated than the formation of the legislative body.[4] Far from being a secondary power and a mere agent of the legislature, the government, argued Necker, is in reality *le chef de la société*, which ought to command general obedience and respect. By drawing on the example of England, Necker advocated the *union* between executive and legislative powers and criticized those who endorsed a radical version of the principle of the separation of powers. The total subordination or annihilation of executive power, remarked Necker, could not be seen as the triumph of liberty, because it would grant an almost unlimited power to the legislature: "There is no real liberty if there is in the middle of the state an authority without balance" (Necker 1792, 209). Moreover, an all-powerful legislative assembly cannot properly fulfill the functions of the executive power, because it lacks the latter's ability to take into consideration the specificity of particular cases.[5] Following in the footsteps of her father, Madame de Staël held a similar position on this issue. "There is much talk about the division of powers," she once wrote, "and yet *the most difficult problem is probably their union*. An executive power which has no rapport with the making of the laws is the natural enemy of those who wish to impose upon it decrees that go against its views and its means."[6]

Perhaps the most interesting element in both Staël's and Necker's arguments was the claim that the extreme separation of powers would contribute in reality to the fragmentation of power if it overlooked the fundamental fact that decision and execution stem from the same source. In making this claim, Necker and Staël had in mind the limitations of the Constitution of 1791, which, in their view, was marred by a serious error—Necker called it, in fact, a "*défaut de proportion*" (Necker 1792, 206). It regarded the total subordination of executive power to the legislature as a momentous triumph of liberty over oppression and sought to gain protection from the abuses of the government by attempting to annihilate the latter, thus paving the way for the emergence of the absolute power of the legislative body. Furthermore, while isolating and separating the powers, the Constitution of 1791 did not provide for efficient ways of resolving the conflicts that were bound to arise between the monarch and the elected assembly. Their deep disagreements and the chronic inability to compromise triggered the open conflict that eventually led to the execution of Louis XVI and the fall of the Bourbon dynasty.

Hence, unlike the American founding fathers, who *simultaneously* stressed the importance of executive power and upheld the principle of the separation of powers, the French affirmed the absolute primacy of the legislature seen as the sole guarantor of liberty and judge of all matters impinging on it. Inspired by Rousseau's political ideas, the text of the *Declaration* of 1789 adumbrated the idea of a legislative body enacting the will of the nation and denied anyone the right to censor the decisions of the legislature. By giving a blank check to the legislative power, it contributed to the emergence of a parliamentary absolutism sui generis,[7] a tradition of thinking grounded in the Rousseauian belief in the infallibility of the law and the wisdom of a legislator endowed with extraordinary powers. It was this absolute confidence in the virtues and capacity of the legislative body or, to put it differently, this unwarranted optimism in the goodness and righteousness of the legislator's intentions that eventually led the French to reject the idea of a nonparliamentary judicial control of the constitutionality of the laws passed by Parliament. Unlike the Americans, they did not see it necessary to create a special court whose main role was to exercise a strict and permanent control of the constitutionality of the laws. Moreover, whereas the French held that factions could be neutralized only through their submission to the general will, the American founding fathers grounded their political theories in a more realistic view of human nature.[8] They sought to tame factions by assigning and guaranteeing them a real, if limited, place in the institutional framework of representative government.

Critical of their predecessors' approach to government and political power, Guizot and the other Doctrinaires elaborated a theory of power and government whose principles marked a significant departure from the previous attitude espoused by eighteenth-century thinkers, who fought against the absolute sovereignty of the king and the political power of the Church. The Doctrinaires no longer postulated a "natural" individual against the social order and did not work within the framework of social contract theory and natural rights. Instead, they stressed the *natural* character of power and maintained that there is no a priori opposition between individual rights and state power. They also insisted on the necessary union of powers and criticized those who were ready to abuse the principles of the separation of powers and the supremacy of the legislative body. It is worth pointing out that Guizot often used the words *power, government*, and *executive power* interchangeably.

As such, Guizot and the other Doctrinaires approached the problem of power and government in a manner different from that of their English and French predecessors, such as Hobbes, Locke, Montesquieu, and Rousseau. Because liberal ideas had previously been used to challenge the authority of the established powers, Guizot sought to create a new liberalism of government appropriate to the particular social and political condition of modern

French society.[9] He started from the assumption that power is generated within the social realm and maintained that society ought to be studied first before attempting to explain the nature of political institutions. In other words, to understand the functioning of government, one must first examine the social condition, which includes the mores, customs, the manner of life of individuals, the relations of the different classes, and the distribution of property in society. In emphasizing the dependence of power on *l'état social*, the Doctrinaires rejected the claim that society is (entirely) constituted by power, a thesis defended by Lamennais and Bonald.[10]

The contrast between the Doctrinaires' views on power and sovereignty and Rousseau's political ideas deserves special consideration. As already mentioned, the Doctrinaires rejected two fundamental principles of Rousseau's political philosophy, which equated liberty with man's sovereignty over himself and affirmed that the only legitimate law for every individual is given by one's individual will.[11] In Guizot's view, it is mistaken to attribute to any individual or group an inherent right to sovereignty. Instead, legitimate sovereignty must be endlessly sought out and should remain subject to public scrutiny at all times. Against Rousseau, Guizot claimed that the true contract that brought individuals together in society and allowed them to cooperate and live in peace could only be a "divine contract" that creates a new form of political obligation to the immutable laws of reason, truth, and justice. In this view, Rousseau's social contract was nothing else than a figment of imagination, because it is impossible to distinguish and separate the origin of society from that of government. Government and society appeared at once when individuals felt united by bonds that were no longer based on force and violence.

Hence, concluded Guizot, it would be meaningless to imagine a hypothetical situation in which individuals, living in an alleged state of nature, were to come together and agree to form a government. By virtue of a natural law sui generis, the bravest and the most skillful individuals always managed to assert their will in society. In other words, power is a *natural* phenomenon that manifests and accompanies "natural superiorities"; that is, exceptional leadership skills, abilities, and achievement. As long as no external or violent cause occurs to upset the natural course of society, power will always be placed in the hands of the bravest ones who demonstrate the highest capacity to exercise it.

It is worth noting, however, that Guizot did *not* equate superior force with superior capacity and virtue.[12] The upshot of his view was twofold. First, pace Hobbes and Rousseau, Guizot maintained that power and government did not arise out of a social contract between individuals seeking to place their lives under the protection of a sovereign. Second, the true origin of political obligation is the recognition of—and acquiescence to—"natural superiorities," a theme that returned time and again in Guizot's writings:

> Power accompanies and reveals superiority. In making itself recognized, power makes itself obeyed. . . . This is the origin of power; there is no other one. Power would have never been born between equals. The superiority that is felt and accepted [by others] represents the original and legitimate link in human societies. It is both the fact and the right; it is the true and only social contract.[13]

It is worth noting that Guizot's position asserted that the characteristics of human nature could be reconciled with the evolution of history and civilization defined as progress. In this view, the authority of history becomes identical with that of nature and tends to replace it.

All these ideas loomed large in Guizot's *Des moyens de gouvernment et d'opposition*, written and published in 1821, in the aftermath of the inauguration of the Villèle ultraroyalist government.[14] In this book, Guizot demonstrated an unparalleled awareness of the complex nature of power in modern society and appeared as the spokesman of *la France nouvelle* that had arisen from the ruins of the Revolution. He described the most important political actors, identified their chief motives, and indicated the causes of the inefficiency of the policies carried out by the ultraroyalist government. Guizot took the *ultras* to task for advancing an obsolete model of government that was anachronistic and did not suit the spirit of that age, which demanded representative government, political accountability, and publicity. Furthermore, he elaborated an original theory of the "new means of government" and predicted that in modern society the development of liberty would inevitably be accompanied by the extension of state power.

A closer look at Guizot's argument reveals the extent to which he was preoccupied with articulating a new doctrine of government suitable to the particular conditions of Restoration France. He began by pointing out that reconciling liberty and power (authority) is "the eternal problem of human societies" (Guizot 1821, 6). Too often, notwithstanding their generous intentions, many friends of liberty failed to find viable solutions and advanced grandiose schemes and plans that proved to be highly unrealistic. That is why, added Guizot, those who govern in modern society must acquaint themselves with the nature of power and should cast away their old prejudices against government:

We must found an entire constitutional order and reject the Old Regime: this is the essence of our situation. The revolution had destroyed the government of the Old Regime, but had not built its own government yet. The true government of the Revolution is a system of institutions and influences that guarantee constitutional equality and legal liberty. . . . The Revolution, so to speak, continues to live in the air; . . . the principles it had proclaimed have not been converted into practical institutions and efficient laws yet; the interests it had founded are still dispersed and badly linked to each other. (Guizot 1821, 2–3)

This passage sheds light on the ambitious political project of the Doctrinaires. The Revolution, argued Guizot, brought forth the fall of the Old Regime but failed to create a regular and well-ordered government capable of guaranteeing the definitive triumph of representative institutions. As such, the Revolution continued "to live in the air," and the mission of the new generation to which the Doctrinaires belonged was to replace the principles and institutions bequeathed by the Revolution and the Empire with new representative institutions, "liberal principles," and "fixed rules" that promoted the general interests of the nation. To this effect, Guizot emphasized that both the government and society ought to work together and must be engaged in a constant dialogue mediated by publicity, free press, and the other institutions of representative government.[15]

This sociological approach to power enabled Guizot to advance a powerful critique of laissez-faire liberalism, whose proponents believed that the scope of state intervention could be increased *only* at the expense of individual liberty. Guizot rejected this interpretation and argued that state power properly exercised and limited could be an effective means of protecting and strengthening individual freedoms. While endorsing the principles of constitutionalism and limited government, Guizot criticized those who argued that the government—in this case, the executive power—ought to be nothing else than a humble agent in the state. To this effect, he denounced the (then) widespread belief that compared the government to a hired servant to be paid at a bargain rate. For Guizot, to require that the government be nothing else than a passive umpire among rival social and economic interests was tantamount to subverting both political authority and the foundations of society. The idea of government as a passive umpire is not suitable to the task of building a new political order, because it misunderstands the complex nature of power in modern society:

What are you doing then, you who proclaim that power is only a hired servant who can be paid at a bargain rate, who must be reduced to the lowest degree in activity as in wages? Do you not see that you misunderstand completely the dignity of its nature? . . . Are nations made up of superior beings who, in order to attend freely to more sublime work, would have inferior creatures responsible for the material aspects of life under the name of government? This is an absurd and shameful theory. . . . True superiorities do not always rule, and even when they do, they do not always make a legitimate use of their position. . . . Also, with institutions and laws, there must be guarantees on the one hand against the reign of false superiorities, and on the other hand against the corruption of the most authentic ones. . . . Generally speaking, power belongs to superiority.[16]

To claim that the only task of government is to prevent and punish those who disobey the laws amounts to misunderstanding the nobility of governing, because it confounds power with top-down command. In reality, power provides the necessary centers of decision required for the maintenance and stability of society.[17] Guizot's opposition to laissez-faire was an upshot of his belief in the positive role that the executive power could—and should—play in modern society. "The axiom *laissez faire, laissez passer*," he wrote, "is one of those vague axioms, true or false depending on how it is applied; it can warn us against dangers, but it gives us no guidance" (Guizot 1821, 172–73). Like Necker, Guizot maintained that the executive power ought to be regarded as the "leader of society" and must promote the general interests of the country. But, added Guizot, only the power that is respected by society and has adequate means of intervention in society can properly fulfill its tasks. Hence, a weak and unstable power is likely to be inefficient and to be usurped by those who seek power. What should be feared then, concluded Guizot, is not power per se, but only weak and unaccountable power, which might be easily tempted to resort to arbitrary means in order to extend its prerogatives and influence.

The "New Means of Government"

At the core of the Doctrinaires' ideas on political power also lay an interesting theory of the "new means of government." It has become a commonplace to assume that the Doctrinaires' liberalism through the state presupposed a more or less rigid form of centralization that failed to recognize the importance of local liberties and institutions. Take, for example, the argument advanced by Pierre Rosanvallon in *Le moment Guizot*. After pointing out that, for Guizot, local institutions and individual independence flourished in the early stages of European civilization, Rosanvallon went on to claim that Guizot sought in fact to create a new form of centralization in accord with the progress of civilization. A more radical version of this argument was offered by Lucien Jaume in his recent history of nineteenth-century French political thought. Jaume contrasted the Doctrinaires' political ideas with those of the Coppet circle (Benjamin Constant, Madame de Staël) and argued that the Doctrinaires played a seminal role in the creation of an oligarchic state and a corrupt administration that delayed the consolidation of parliamentary government in nineteenth-century France. The Doctrinaires, claimed Jaume, often acted as if they believed in the infallibility of power, and many of their political initiatives were reminiscent of Napoléon's antiliberal policies.[18]

Does this mean, then, that the Doctrinaires had no objections to absolute power and centralized government? Did they advocate or pursue authoritarian policies that contradicted the principles of the Charter of 1814? Like many of their contemporaries, the Doctrinaires tried to explain the factors that had contributed to the growth of administrative centralization and absolutism in France, a topic that found its locus classicus in Tocqueville's writings. It will be recalled that in *De la démocratie en Amérique*, Tocqueville distinguished between centralized government and centralized administration. The existence of a centralized government requires that the power that directs political affairs be concentrated in one single place. Yet, a centralized administration is neither inevitable nor essential for the preservation of the country. It concentrates under the umbrella of a huge bureaucratic apparatus the direction of all local interests and, as a result, stifles self-government and fosters political apathy.[19]

More than a decade before Tocqueville, the Doctrinaires struggled with much the same problems, albeit in a different way. Guizot, for example, did not draw a clear distinction between centralized government and centralized administration. Instead, his framework of analysis was the development of European civilization, which, in his opinion, had been characterized by a tendency toward political centralization and the predominance of general interests. As Guizot explained in *Histoire de la civilisation en Europe*, the fifteenth century marked the beginning of the "silent and concealed work of centralization" (Guizot 1997, 183) that led to the creation of what had hitherto never existed, nations and governments.

Yet, the Doctrinaires were also aware of the nefarious consequences of political and administrative centralization. In one of his parliamentary speeches from 1821, Royer-Collard explicitly linked the art of being free to the preservation of local independent institutions, "true republics in the bosom of monarchy" (Royer-Collard 1861b, 130–31) that had provided effective opposition to the power of the kings. A similar point can be found in Barante's *Des communes et de l'aristocratie*. In his opinion, the local institutions were

Prosper de Barante

"fragments of a constitution" (Barante 1821, 7) that had never been fully established or recognized in legal terms but had played an important role in bringing citizens together and allowing them to form common bonds.

The interesting point made by the Doctrinaires was that, under the Old Regime, the communes formed a surprisingly diverse society characterized by diverse customs, unwritten laws, and local associations—Barante referred to them as *communal societies*—all of which were destroyed under the rule of Louis XIV and the administration of Richelieu. The disappearance of these institutions was an event of great significance, because it paved the way for the irresistible growth of absolute power and administrative centralization in France. The French Revolution completed the process of social leveling, destroyed intermediary bodies, and ended the tradition of local freedoms and local institutions that had served as countervailing forces to the power of the monarchs. The outcome of this process was the emergence of an atomized society, "*la société en poussière*," and the destruction of local communal societies that were swallowed up in the centralized nation. As Barante remarked, the "rule of administrators" began when the communes disappeared and were replaced by a new system in which prevailed the absolute will of the king.

For Royer-Collard, too, the factor that had made possible the rise of absolutism in France was the vanishing of intermediary bodies, which had traditionally opposed the growth of centralized administration and protected local liberties by acting as a buffer between the king, the nobles, and the commons. In the absence of these intermediary bodies, the trend toward centralization was both inevitable and irresistible. In a famous speech on freedom of the press (1822), Royer-Collard explained:

> We have seen the old society perish, and with it that crowd of domestic institutions and independent magistracies which it carried within it, strong bundle of private rights, true republics within the monarchy. These institutions, these magistracies did not, it is true, share sovereignty; but they opposed to it everywhere limits which honor defended obstinately. Not one of them has survived and nothing else appeared to replace them. The revolution left only isolated individuals standing. The dictatorship that ended it consummated, in this regard, its own work. From an atomized society has emerged centralization. (Royer-Collard 1861a, 130–31)

In his discourse, Royer-Collard referred to the emergence of a nation of solitary and powerless individuals governed by an incompetent bureaucracy. When only isolated individuals are left standing, with few ties among themselves, the state inevitably acquires a huge power and its authority and sphere of influence significantly increase.[20] Thus, concluded Royer-Collard (1861b, 131), "we have become a nation of administered people, under the hand of irresponsible civil servants, themselves centralized by the power of which they are agents."

With the benefit of hindsight, it can be argued that one of the main obstacles to the establishment of a free and stable government in France had been the gradual disappearance of local and intermediary institutions that conjured up "a monstrous and dysfunctional power."[21] The similarity between the Doctrinaires' ideas and Tocqueville's points about local institutions is worth noting. It was a decade *before* Tocqueville that Guizot, Royer-Collard, Rémusat, and Barante highlighted the connection between administrative centralization, the process of atomization of society, and the social leveling that completed the destruction of intermediary bodies. They reached the conclusion that democracy is compatible with new forms of despotism that, instead of using soldiers and prisons, would resort to new, "softer" means of power and domination. The Doctrinaires also warned that centralization would be the natural government of a democratic society, a rather paradoxical idea that had a strong impact on Tocqueville. "I think," argued Royer-Collard (1861b, 131), "that in the democratic centuries to come, individual independence and local liberties will always be a product of art and culture, while centralization will be the natural government." Royer-Collard's emphasis on individual independence and local liberties foreshadowed Tocqueville's description of the art of being free in *De la démocratie en Amérique*.

Because Guizot's critique of centralization has often been neglected by his interpreters, it is important that we pay attention to all the nuances of his arguments on power in modern society. Let us begin with the following passage from a letter sent to Charles de Rémusat in June 1821:

> Providence did not place in the middle of the world a great basin from which thousands of channels originate; Providence placed in thousands of places live sources which flow naturally. It is useless to pretend to distribute political and moral life through a system of "administrative navigation" which originates solely from Paris. *To trigger action, spontaneity, this is the condition of liberty.* This is the only way to obtain the real influences that you need in order to govern. These influences exist here [in society] more than anywhere else; but they languish in obscurity and perish by inaction.[22]

In this letter, Guizot claimed that all individuals must be allowed to shine freely in their sphere and maintained that the key role of government is not to create a network of bureaucrats and central institutions that would supplant the local ones, but, broadly speaking, "to trigger action, spontaneity." A new form of absolute power would only strengthen the long and nefarious tradition of administrative centralization. Reason, Guizot wrote to Barante in 1821, can only come from above, but life can only rise from below; it exists in the roots of society as much as in the roots of a tree. "There is everywhere [in society] *a government already made*, we must accept and regulate it:"[23] this is a government that is born in society and is provided by society itself.

Guizot made a similar argument in *Des moyens de gouvernement et d'opposition*. He claimed that society contained numerous "capable" individuals, property owners, lawyers, notaries, entrepreneurs, manufacturers, and merchants who represented the backbone of the emerging middle class. While visiting the small towns and villages of France, Guizot met such individuals capable of undertaking many enterprises, but, much to his surprise, he observed that they rarely cooperated with each other, lacked mutual bonds, and were condemned to political powerlessness and apathy. He heard them speaking of their local affairs and noticed that they acted as if local matters were entirely foreign to their own interests and daily preoccupations. The art of association was unknown to them, since they lacked a public sphere in which they could meet and cooperate with each other to promote their common interests.[24] In spite of their growing force, opined Guizot, these talented individuals lived isolated, separated from each other, with no close ties between them:

> I lived in the counties, in the bosom of this society which, it is said, contains only scattered, isolated individuals, without any links between them. . . . I found everywhere ignored links, lost influences, unemployed superiorities. I met individuals who had money, but had nothing to do with it, who could have done many things, but who were nothing in reality. I heard them talking about public affairs, local affairs, but it was as if they were talking about things that were irrelevant, if not to their destiny, at least to their interests. They were talking about them as if they were talking in a coffeehouse or in theater; not as if they were discussing their own affairs. (Guizot 1821, 266–67)

Guizot proceeded from this point to formulate a trenchant critique of the ultraroyalist government that came to power in 1820, after three years of liberal reforms carried out by the Decazes cabinet. Outraged by the policies of the conservative government, Guizot denounced the blindness of the *ultras* who mistakenly believed that it was possible to oppose or ignore the power of "social facts" that demanded representative and constitutional government. The new government found itself in a paradoxical situation:

> Why does a new government show itself from the very beginning stagnant and powerless? Everything moves around it; the social movement has not ceased, its direction has not changed; the classes that follow it continue to rise, while those which refuse to take part in this movement remain behind. The division of properties, the development of industry, the rapid circulation of wealth, the

diffusion of ideas, all these elements that constitute the new order grow and develop every day. (Guizot 1821, 119)

Stagnant and *powerless* were the two words that Guizot chose to characterize the new government. He claimed that those who held power showed themselves incapable of understanding and following the momentous social and economic changes that occurred during the Restoration. The main reason was that the ultraconservative government did not work with the proper means of government, failed to elicit the cooperation of the new social forces and interests, and was out of touch with public opinion.[25] The government mistakenly believed that it could govern solely from above, as if society were a large and deserted field in the hands of a powerful landlord, or a huge mass of anonymous individuals wanting everything from their government and lacking the power to change their lives.

Yet, continued Guizot, society can be compared neither to an obedient herd nor to a barren field. It contains its own means of government that political leaders ought to take into account and learn how to work with.[26] In other words, those who exercise political power must open and institutionalize new channels of communication with society in keeping with the demands of publicity. Because this dialogue did not exist, the government was unable to cope with the new ideas and social interests. It confounded power and command and mistakenly conceived itself as foreign to—or above—the interests of society. As a result, it tended to interpret most social initiatives as immediate threats to its stability and legitimacy.

Caught between the fear of revolution and the specter of the counterrevolution, the ultraconservative government relied on a policy of temporary survival, personal intrigues, and ministerial arbitrariness. It believed that the only way of intervening in society was by increasing the number of civil servants and policemen. In Guizot's opinion, the villèle government consisted of agents who pretended to be omniscient, believed that their sole duty was to keep a watchful eye on society, and conceived of the state as an armed missionary. Not surprisingly, the government was unable to benefit from the new ideas and social interests because it distrusted them as soon as it felt itself incapable of controlling and supervising their evolution. In reality, these new liberal interests and ideas were not a hotbed of anarchy but a genuine source of social order and progress. As property became more widespread in society, more individuals were expected to acquire a stake in the system by becoming, to use Barante's inspired phrase (Barante 1821, 111–12), "stockholders in this great association of public interests," whose interests were legitimate, peaceful, and strong.[27]

That is why, argued Guizot, to resort only to traditional agents of power, such as policemen, tax collectors, soldiers, and civil servants, to govern modern society was a costly illusion. In each department, town, or village, added Guizot, lived many individuals who could form an essential part of the government of society but remained uninvolved in public life because they lacked the opportunity to participate in the direction of local affairs. These small entrepreneurs, lawyers, notaries, and tradesmen represented a huge potential that ought to be used and channeled into appropriate institutions:

> The true means of government are not these direct and visible instruments of power. They reside in the bosom of society and cannot be separated from the latter . . . In each county, each town, each place there are individuals who have nothing to do with the government, who have no close relation among themselves, but who exercise around them a more or less decisive and extended influence. These are small owners, lawyers, notaries, capitalists, manufacturers, and tradesmen who stay away from public affairs in order to devote themselves to their own business, but who have nonetheless a considerable influence. (Guizot 1821, 129; 264–65)[28]

Those who hold power must actively look for these "natural superiorities" and, with the aid of the new laws and institutions, should give them opportunities to participate in public life and local government.[29] Since French society had become more complex and diverse, continued Guizot, the government must give up the ludicrous pretension to control everything and ought to foster the circulation of property and industry as well as the diffusion of new ideas and interests that are the constitutive elements of the new social order:

> It is necessary that the lie vanish, that central power give up its pretension to be everything, and soon it will cease to be alone. Soon, it will notice that our society does not lack individuals capable of participating in its government by virtue of their position, preeminence, and credit. . . . In order that the superiorities and natural influences that exist in a country do not disappear, it is necessary that they be employed. . . . They render themselves useful only where they feel that they are necessary. . . . Hence, if you want to benefit from all the means of government that individual superiorities contain, involve them in the government of society. (Guizot 1821, 268; 270–71)

Thus, Guizot's *sociological* approach to political power offered a reinterpretation of the relation between power and society based on an original theory of the "new means of government." To make of power what a miser makes of gold, claimed Guizot, would be a great and irreparable mistake. The true art of governing does not consist in accumulating as much power as possible, but in locating and employing all the fragments of power, knowledge, and reason that already exist in the bosom of society.[30] Those who hold power must try to understand the ways in which the public is inclined to act reasonably and to cultivate good principles and legitimate tendencies. They must not conceive of power as mere top-down command relying on a large army of bureaucrats; instead, they ought to see it as an element in flux that should constantly adapt itself to the changing needs and interests of society.[31] To put it differently, those who exercise power must become familiar with the ideas and interests of society as well as with "the instincts and sentiments of the people"[32] in order to grasp the direction of social change. If they fail to do that, they will inevitably pursue anachronistic policies.

To conclude, the Doctrinaires believed that the true task of government was to rally around its banners the new social interests and forces, to foster the emergence of new talents and skills in society, and to elevate the moral condition of the country. This ambitious task conveys the image of an active executive power that governs, civilizes, and disseminates "capacity" in society by playing an active role in the intellectual and moral development of individuals. In modern society, Guizot once said, the greatest challenge is the "*le gouvernement des esprits*," the government of minds:[33]

> It has frequently been said in the last century . . . that minds ought not to be fettered, that they should be left to their free operation, and that society has neither the right nor the necessity of interference. Experience has protested against this haughty and precipitate solution. It has shown what it was to suffer minds to be unchecked, and has roughly demonstrated that even in intellectual order, guides and bridles are necessary. . . . But if, for the advantage of progress, as well as for good order in society, a certain government of minds is necessary, the conditions and means of this government are neither at all times nor in all places the same. (Guizot 1860b, 14)

How are we to interpret this conception of political power that sought to combine the seemingly illiberal and paternalistic idea of a government acting as the guardian of the long-term interests of the nation with the liberal commitment to political freedom and limited power? What can prevent an activist state that has at its disposal a considerable range of means of intervention in society from trying to promote the interests of a single social class at the expense of all others? An adequate answer to these questions would require that we refer not only to the Doctrinaires' theory of civilization and the sovereignty of reason, but also to their ideas on publicity and political capacity that will be discussed in detail in the next three chapters of this book. Guizot and his fellow Doctrinaires acknowledged that in modern society the government can no longer play the role that the Church had previously had in controlling the human mind. At the same time, they believed that the government must not be careless or ignorant of the intellectual and moral development of future generations. Instead, it ought to create the conditions for progress in the intellectual order by promoting great establishments for science and schools for public instruction.

It is important to stress that, to Guizot, the complex task of government in modern society was justified by the progress of *civilization*. The argument was surprisingly simple. It is because civilization has not only a material element, but also a spiritual (intellectual, moral) component, that the government must *simultaneously* foster the material development of society and its intellectual and moral life. Without playing the role of a new Church, it must seek to civilize and instruct; this explains Guizot's emphasis on primary education as a key element of the apprenticeship of freedom.[34] "Liberty," Guizot wrote in his letter addressed to all instructors on July 18, 1833, "can neither be assured nor regulated except with a people sufficiently enlightened to listen, under all circumstances, to the voice of reason. Universal elementary education will become henceforward a guarantee for order and social stability."[35] Guizot saw no contradiction between the "government of minds" and freedom of thought as long as liberty of conscience and freedom of the press were duly protected and the government did not seek to become a new Church.[36]

More importantly, Guizot foresaw that the social, economic, and political trends at work in modern society would trigger a two-way process. The government would gain more power over society, while public opinion would simultaneously acquire a greater influence over those who exercise power. Guizot elaborated a complex theory of publicity that was supposed to act as the most important link between government and society. The originality of his approach lay in defining publicity as the key feature of representative government. The object of publicity, maintained Guizot, was to call upon all individuals who possess rights as well as those who exercise power to seek in common the principles of reason, justice, and truth, the source and rule of legitimate sovereignty.[37] On this view, only publicity could correct the malfunction of political institutions by creating the conditions for public debate, establishing the space for the exercise of citizenship, and opening new channels of communication between government and society. Guizot predicted that the scope of government intervention would *increase* as a result of the profound changes in the social condition triggered by a combination of economic, political, cultural, and social factors.

Finally, in keeping with his theory of publicity, Guizot stressed the need for more *transparency* and a tighter connection between society and government, a point that returned time and again in his writings. He was persuaded that society itself remained weak as long as a sharp division continued to exist between the government and the predominant social forces and interests. When society does not respond to the appeal of government, claimed Guizot, it is because the latter "has lied" to society.[38] Hence, the statesman's task is to constitute the government through the action of society and society through the action of government. In a seminal passage from *De la peine de mort*, Guizot wrote:

> If power no longer has any secrets for society, this is because society no longer has any secrets for power. If authority meets everywhere minds claiming to judge it, this is because it has something to ask or to do everywhere. If power is always asked to legitimize its conduct, this is because it can use all its force and has a right over all citizens. . . . If you are in harmony with society, the whole society concentrates and contemplates itself in you. . . . Now, politics must be true, that is to say national, and this restrains the capricious action or the arbitrary opinions of individuals.[39]

Guizot's paradoxical conclusion is that in modern society, the growth of liberty and the development of representative institutions inevitably lead to a considerable extension of the authority of government, an extension made possible by a social demand unseen before, in the context of a process of growing "social complexification"[40] and homogenization. The two tendencies are not contradictory but represent the two sides of the same phenomenon.

The Doctrinaires' Liberalism of Government

It is time to move on from Guizot's theory of the "new means of government" to more general considerations about the elitist liberalism of the Doctrinaires and its place in the liberal tradition. Liberal thinkers have traditionally been skeptical toward political power and made "don't cross the line" their ultimate battle cry against the state. This attitude has dominated the Anglo-American liberal tradition and has deep roots that go back to Locke and the Declaration of Independence. As a result, contemporary political philosophers have concentrated first and foremost on the protection of individual rights and individual autonomy against the encroachment of the state, turning liberalism, to quote Benjamin Barber (1989, 59), into "a politics of negativity, which enthrones not simply the individual but the individual defined by his perimeters, his parapets, and his entrenched solitude."

The French liberal tradition, with its emphasis on the importance of executive power and its own version of constitutionalism, poses a set of interesting challenges to this dominant view.[41] The fact that the Doctrinaires lived in a period of transition in the aftermath of a great revolution allowed them to reach a set of conclusions about the nature of social change, political reform, and the relation between social and political order. Their theory of political power was meant to offer an answer to the daunting question that preoccupied all nineteenth-century French political thinkers: How to "end" the Revolution? The Doctrinaires' elitist liberalism of government based on the theory of the "new means of government" was their response to this question.

Des moyens de gouvernement et d'opposition is a distinctively French book. Its style is French and its ideas can be understood only if placed within the larger tradition of French political thought. Guizot sought to demonstrate the need for an active executive power that opens and institutionalizes new channels of communication with society in a process of what we would call today "mutual empowerment." At the same time, while emphasizing the need for an effective union of powers, the book highlighted the seminal role played by limited power in protecting civil liberties and rights.[42] Last but not least, *Des moyens de gouvernement et d'opposition* demonstrates that Guizot deserves to be seen as one of the most astute theoreticians of executive power in modern society.

If the Doctrinaires' political project failed in the short term (their constitutional monarchy was replaced by the First Republic in 1848), it is fair to say that in the long term some of their ideas, most notably their theories of education, publicity, and parliamentarism, had a profound (positive) impact on French politics.[43] Their critics claimed, however, that the Doctrinaires had too much confidence in the dignity of power and underestimated the problems created by the combination of unaccountable state power, legislative corruption, and incompetent bureaucracy.

Even if the political careers of Guizot and his fellow Doctrinaires during the July Monarchy are beyond the scope of this chapter and book, a few words about their record in power are necessary. Historians who dislike Guizot's *juste milieu* often accused him and his colleagues of having created a corrupt, unstable, and antidemocratic system (one is also entitled to ask whether they ever read his writings published during the Restoration). Needless to say, this charge overlooks the Doctrinaires' contribution to the building of representative government, in particular to the drafting and passing of important laws such as the electoral law of 1817, the law on the reorganization of the army, and the laws of the press of 1819.[44]

Furthermore, if France experienced a good deal of political instability in the 1830s and 1840s, the Doctrinaires were not the only ones to be blamed for it. Unpredictable and foreseen historical circumstances, temporary political alliances, and personal ambitions played a significant role in creating a general climate of turmoil and uncertainty. "Time will still belong to anarchy for many years to come," Royer-Collard is reported to have said to Victor de Broglie upon his nomination in the cabinet formed on October 11, 1832.[45] He was right. "In the parliamentary field," argued Guizot (1858b, 217), "all was uncertainty and confused opposition; a phantom appeared at each extremity, revolution and counterrevolution, exchanging mutual menaces." To combat the influence of extremists, the Doctrinaires adopted a defensive *politique de résistance* that sometimes led them to think in black-and-white categories, which left little room for nuances: "The Charter *or* the revolution; the constitutional spirit *or* the revolutionary spirit."[46] Their greatest illusion was that the principles enshrined in the Charter of 1814 (and, later, the Charter of 1830) offered the definitive solution to the problems of modern French society.

Anyone who seeks to understand how Guizot's theory of power relates to his political practice will have to consider his activity as minister of public education from 1832 to 1837. Guizot had a long-standing interest in educational issues. His first significant articles on this topic, "Rapport au Roi pour la réforme de l'instruction publique" (1815) and "Essai sur l'histoire et sur l'état actuel de l'instruction publique en France" (1816), were published during the first years of the Restoration. A few years earlier, he had co-edited with his first wife, Pauline de Meulan, *Annales de l'éducation*.[47] In regard to education, it will be difficult to claim that his record in power was a negative one. Guizot believed that the pursuit of material wealth was only a means that furnished little intrinsic satisfaction. Far from being a residual aristocratic prejudice, his belief was a direct offshoot of his theory of civilization predicated upon the idea of an active state which, through its educational and cultural policies, explicitly undertakes the creation of the conditions necessary for the full development of individuality.

To this effect, Guizot launched a comprehensive *politique de mémoire nationale*, which, along with his ambitious educational reform, was an essential component of his conception of "*le gouvernement des esprits*."[48] In Guizot's view, the state ought to fulfill the function of a public educator and must be, to use Pierre Rosanvallon's phrase, an "*état sociologue*"[49] that promotes and disseminates knowledge ("light") in society and seeks to comprehend its general needs and interests. Guizot's notion of the "government of minds" was qualitatively different from the political ideal of thinkers such as Saint-Simon, Comte, and their followers. Guizot disliked Comte's technocratic elitism and drew a clear distinction between "scientific government" and "government by science."[50]

The famous Law of June 1833 was the best illustration of Guizot's philosophy of education. Drawing on an impressive number of surveys and detailed statistics about the state of education in France,[51] Guizot and his team drafted the law that founded universal primary education in France, an exceptional achievement measured by the standards of that time. The figures speak for themselves. In 1830 there were only 31,000 primary schools in France; in 1847 their number rose to 43,514, and the number of students doubled from 1,200,000 in 1833 to 2,450,000 in 1836. The budget for public education (including the universities) was 7,883,803 francs in 1832. Three years later, it rose to 12,371,527 francs and reached 13,826,460 francs in 1837 when Guizot left the Ministry of Public Education.[52]

In Guizot's and Royer-Collard's view, the universality of elementary education was one of the most important consequences of the Charter. "As all the principles of our government are sound and rational, to develop intellect and propagate light is to confirm the empire and durability of our constitutional monarchy" (Guizot 1860b, 327). Unfortunately, Guizot lacked the time, energy, and political support to complete the reform of superior education. In order to countervail the preponderant influence of Paris, he envisaged the creation of a few major universities in the province (Strasbourg, Rennes, Toulouse, and Montpellier). As the political context changed and his position became weaker in the chamber, Guizot did not manage to bring his reformist plans to fruition.

As minister of public education, Guizot also reestablished the prestigious *Académie des sciences morales et politiques* and gave generous financial assistance to publishing houses (such as Hachette), libraries, and publications. Lamartine, Hugo, and Thiers received considerable funds from the Ministry of Education that sought to establish a new relation with the "republic of letters." In January 1834, Guizot founded *La Société de l'histoire de France* whose task was to coordinate the publication of scholarly historical materials in conjunction with the newly established *Comité des travaux historiques* (founded on July 18, 1834). The same year, Guizot created the first chair in constitutional law in France, held by Pellegrino Rossi. In a report to the king written on August 22, 1834, Guizot justified the need for this chair in the following terms: "It is the exposition of the Charter, and individual guarantees, as well as political institutions that it consecrates. It will no longer comprise for us a simple system of philosophy, given over to the disputes of men; it will become a written and acknowledged law, which can and ought to be explained and reasoned on. . . . Such a course of instruction

. . . ought to substitute for the errors of ignorance and the temerity of superficial ideas powerful and positive knowledge."[53]

Second, it should be pointed out that the Doctrinaires' politics of resistance was, in fact, neither negative nor arbitrary.[54] Theirs was a liberalism *through* the state that was predicated upon the assumption that in modern society the executive power must play an important role in the direction of political affairs. "We seriously wished to introduce a liberal system," wrote Guizot (referring to the Périer cabinet that came to power in 1832), "with the effectual guarantees of sound legislation. It was in truth political liberty which we sought to exercise ourselves and to establish for our country" (Guizot 1860b, 4). Guizot insisted that "no really existing power can be a rightful power, except in so far as it acts according to reason and truth, the only source of right. . . . No actual power is, or can be, in itself a power by inherent right."[55] He also maintained that the essence of free society lay in the endless questioning of power through publicity, elections, civil associations, and the free press. In his view, the greatest challenge was to bring the various powers of society into harmony, a task that needed constant attention and adjustment, since the balance of powers was fragile and always likely to be disturbed (Guizot 1972, 398).

Third, the Doctrinaires' ideas about the role of civil society have also escaped the attention of many historians, who concentrated instead on the laws that restricted freedom of association during the Restoration and the July Monarchy. In the 1820s, Guizot and his friends were actively involved in the creation of many civil associations such as *Aide-toi et le ciel t'aidera*, *Comité des prisons*, *Comité pour l'émancipation des catholiques d'Irlande*, and *Comité de charité et de prévoyance*.[56] They maintained that it would be a great mistake to encourage modern individuals to channel all their energies into the pursuit of private interests at the expense of getting involved in public affairs (a slightly different and more elaborated version of this idea appeared in Constant's essay on the liberty of the moderns). The Doctrinaires warned that this tendency might foster, in fact, new and perverse forms of despotism that would encourage even further the privatization of life.

Since the Doctrinaires' theory of power and the "new means of government" was not devoid of paradoxes and inconsistencies, to ignore the latter would be as unfair as to neglect its virtues. My presentation of the Doctrinaires' theory of the new means of government must *not* be taken to imply that their political ideas were always coherent and consistent. The best characterization of their limitations was given by no one else than Guizot, who wrote in his memoirs:

[The Doctrinaires] had in reality . . . neither the ambition nor the vanity of a co-
terie; they possessed open, generous, and expanded minds, extremely accessible
to sympathy; but, too much accustomed to live alone and depend on themselves,
they scarcely thought of the effect which their words and actions produced beyond their circle. . . . In their relations with power, they were sometimes intemperate and offensive in language, unnecessarily impatient, not knowing how to
be contented with what was possible, or how to wait for amelioration without
too visible an effort. These causes led them to miscalculate the impediments, necessities, and practicable resources of the Government they sincerely wished to
establish. In the Chambers, they were too exclusive and pugnatious, more intent
on proving their own opinions than on gaining converts, despising rather than
desiring recruits, and little gifted with the talent of attraction and combination
so essential to the leaders of a party. (Guizot 1858b, 202)

Critics of arbitrary power, the Doctrinaires advocated an elitist liberalism
that was not immune to corruption and politicking. They highlighted the inevitability of the new democratic social condition, but in practice refrained
from recognizing the existence of natural rights and rejected universal suffrage (it is true, however, that all French liberals did the same, including
Tocqueville and Constant). The Doctrinaires championed the principles of
representative government, but were initially reluctant to accept, for example, the autonomy of the elected chamber. Guizot once claimed that the
most important element of the art of governing is the ability to acquire
l'intelligence du social. Yet, in the end, he misunderstood the general trend of
French society and failed to implement an adequate social policy on the
model of the Poor Laws in England. Guizot believed in the need for social
and political pluralism, but he never fully tried to understand the deep roots
of the conflict between the middle and the lower classes and proved unable
to cope with the rise of new social and economic forces toward the end of the
July Monarchy. A proud bourgeois, Guizot presided over an administration
that showed a "blind and arrogant indifference" (Rémusat 1962, 245) not
only toward the working classes, but also the small bourgeoisie that could
have become a stronger supporter of the Orléanist regime.[57]

The words chosen by Tocqueville in his *Recollections* to describe Duvergier
de Hauranne might also apply, mutatis mutandis, to Guizot himself: "An intellect which, while seeing clearly and in detail all that is on the horizon, is
incapable of conceiving that the horizon may change" (Tocqueville 1959,
18). In the end, however, the horizon did change and a powerful wave of social discontent triggered Guizot's fall from power during the Revolution of
1848. Nonetheless, these charges against Guizot, important as they are,

should be taken with a grain of salt. As Jacques Billard reminded us, much depends on what *we* would have liked Guizot to have seen and done. Unlike him, we have the benefit of hindsight, which may sometimes distort our perspective and objectivity.

If, for example, we consider the building of representative government to have been the true priority of his time rather than the coming to terms with socialism, then it can be argued that Guizot's politics was not a failure.[58] His regime did not create any new taxes and succeeded in reducing the tax burden on citizens. It increased the revenues collected by the state through indirect contributions and carried out an impressive number of public projects.[59] "Qui de nos jours n'est pas tombé?" Guizot once asked. If the electoral system of 1817 disappeared in the tempest of 1848, he wrote in his memoirs,

> [i]t conferred on France thirty years of regular and free government, systematically sustained and controlled; and amidst all the varying influences of parties, and the shock of a revolution, this system sufficed to maintain peace, to develop national prosperity, and to preserve respect for all legal rights. In this age of ephemeral and futile experiments, it is the only political enactment which has enjoyed a long and powerful life. At least it was a work which may be acknowledged, and which deserves to be correctly estimated, even after its overthrow. (Guizot 1858b, 161)

Finally, what can contemporary political theorists learn from the Doctrinaires' ideas on power? This chapter highlighted the modern conception of social power underpinning Guizot's analysis of the role of government in *Des moyens de gouvernement et d'opposition*. Guizot questioned the validity of one of the main tenets of classical liberalism that identified individual freedom with the absence of government involvement in society. In so doing, he warned against the one-sided view of the state as a Leviathan ready to usurp our rights and liberties and stressed the importance of communication between government and society as well as the role of government in the education of society. *Des moyens de gouvernement et d'opposition* shows that an adequate understanding of liberalism must include a renewed appreciation for the nature and dignity of limited power.[60] It also sheds light on the importance of creating institutions capable of tapping into the resources, knowledge, and reason that exist in society. The key question then becomes how to gather this decentralized knowledge, how to mobilize and channel the scattered individual energies and influences in order to constitute with them the government of society.

Finally, another lesson that we can draw from the writings of the Doctrinaires is that power is always born in society and the means of government include the dominant opinions, interests, and ideas that can be found in the social sphere. A power that is not rooted in society is condemned to sterility and inefficiency. Guizot and his colleagues learned this lesson the hard way when their political project came to an end in 1848 and it was proven that they, too, had chosen the wrong means of government. Nevertheless, their liberal writings published during the Bourbon Restoration retain a surprising freshness and continue to speak to us today through their valuable insights into the nature of social power in modern society.

Notes

1. On the originality and reception of Guizot's *Des moyens de gouvernement et d'opposition*, see Lefort 1988, 7–31; Manent 1994, 93–102; G. Broglie 1990, 83–84.

2. See Beik ed. 1970, 95. The *Declaration*, voted on August 26, 1789, was on the frontispiece of the Constitution of 1791.

3. Article 4 of the *Declaration* reads as follows: "Liberty consists in being able to do anything that does not harm another person. Thus the exercise of the natural rights of each man has no limits except those which assure to the other members of society the enjoyment of these same rights; these limits can be determined only by law" (Beik ed. 1970, 95).

4. See Necker 1792, 1–6. He writes: "On peut donc advancer sans légereté que la constitution du pouvoir exécutif compose la principle et peut-être l'unique difficulté de tous les systèmes de gouvernement" (Necker 1792, 3).

5. For more details, see Necker 1792, 195–217.

6. Letter to Roederer from June 1795 quoted in Fontana 1991, 62; emphasis added. The need for a sound "union" of powers also appeared in other writings of Madame de Staël: "Un penseur éloquent l'a dit, c'est à *l'union des pouvoirs* qu'il faut tendre; et *l'on confond sans cesse la séparation nécessaire des fonctions avec une division des pouvoirs qui les rend forcément ennemies les uns des autres*" (Staël 1979, 179; emphasis added).

7. Another possible term is *légiscentrisme français* (Lacorne 1993, 18). Article 6 of the *Declaration* reads as follows: "The law is the expression of the general will; all citizens have the rights to concur personally or through their representatives in its formation" (Beik ed. 1970, 95).

8. On this issue, see Raynaud 1989, 595–98.

9. On this issue, see Manent 1994, 94–95.

10. Lamennais wrote: "Ce qui constitue la société, c'est le pouvoir." In turn, Bonald argued: "Le pouvoir est préexistant à toute société, puisque le pouvoir constitue la société" (as quoted in Roldán 1999, 79, 116). One of Rémusat's unpublished manuscripts was conceived of as a refutation of Lamennais's and Bonald's ideas. Rémusat's essay put forward a set of ideas that had many interesting affinities with Guizot's theories.

11. On Guizot's critique of Rousseau, see chapter 5; also see Guizot 2002, 285–97, and Guizot 1985, 363–70.

12. See Guizot 1821, 163–64. Guizot defined capacity as "the capacity to act according to reason, truth, and justice" (Guizot 2002, 61). For more details, see chapter 8.

13. Guizot 1821, 164; all the translations from Guizot's book are mine. I would like to thank Charles Hoffman for his valuable suggestions.

14. For more details on the place of Guizot's book in modern French political thought, see Lefort 1988, 7–31, and Manent 1994, 93–102.

15. See Guizot 1821, 4–5, 17; Guizot 1984, 146–47, 170–71.

16. Guizot 1821, 166–67. For more details on Guizot's defense of limited power, see Guizot 1821, 171–73; for Guizot's views on the dignity of political power, see Guizot 1821, 142–43. For a general view of Guizot's constitutionalism, see note 42.

17. Writes Guizot: "Qu'on dirige toute cette théorie contre un pouvoir qu'on veut démolir, je le conçois; l'instrument est bon et d'un effet sûr. Mais qu'on prétende la prendre pour règle lorsqu'il s'agit de fonder un ordre nouveau, de constituer un pouvoir durable; l'erreur est bien grande" (Guizot 1821, 172).

18. It is worth noting that Jaume quotes Faguet, one of the most polemical and, ultimately, unfair critics of the Doctrinaires. Here is a passage that combines both Jaume's and Faguet's views: "Dans cette optique, *le meilleur portrait de Guizot*, mais non dénué d'ironie, a été tracé par Faguet. Il vaut la peine de citer ce passage malgré sa longueur: '*Très autoritaire*, très persuadé non seulement qu'on ne gouverne *que de haut en bas*, mais encore que l'individualisme n'est qu'un égoisme, . . . et, sans l'avoir jamais dit formellement, évidemment très enclin à croire que l'homme ne vaut que groupé, qu'associé, . . . jamais il n'a envisagé, même un instant, la liberté comme un droit personnel, inhérent à l'homme, consubstantiel à lui et étant parce que l'homme existe. *Personne n'a plus ignoré que Guizot la Déclaration des droits de l'homme.* . . . Sur quoi se fonde le droit de l'homme à la liberté, et comment se tracent les limites où la liberté doit rester contenue, sont choses dont il s'est occupé moins encore'" (Jaume 1997a, 122; all emphasis added). Faguet's message comes close to arguing that Guizot was the greatest enemy of freedom in nineteenth-century France! The allusion to an alleged affinity between the Doctrinaires and Napoléon can be found in Jaume 1997a, 136. Yet, Guizot and his fellow Doctrinaires were critical of Napoléon's legacy.

19. See Tocqueville 1958, 89–101.

20. In turn, Rémusat argued: "Je ne vois que des individus. Plus on regarde l'état de la population en France, moins on y trouve les elements d'une classification tranchée" (quoted in Roldán 1999, 84–85).

21. Royer-Collard 1861b, 230. Also: "C'est parce que les institutions se sont écroulées que vous avez la centralisation; c'est parce que les magistratures ont péri avec elles que vous n'avez que des fonctionnaires" (Royer-Collard 1861b, 226). On this topic, also see Barante 1821, 8, and Rémusat 1861, 804.

22. Guizot 1884, 13; emphasis added. The translation is mine.

23. Guizot 1884, 11; the emphasis is mine. Here is the entire passage from this revealing, yet rarely quoted, letter to Barante (July 7, 1821): "Il faut sortir de cette ornière, appeler les influences au pouvoir et permettre à la vie de se manifester là où elle est; la raison ne peut venir que d'en haut, cela est sûr; *mais la vie ne peut monter que d'en bas*; elle est dans les racines de la société commes dans celles de l'arbre; notre problème est la creation d'un gouvernement; *or il y a partout un gouvernement tout fait*: il faut l'accepter et le régler. Nous avons beau broyer et faire fermenter à Paris des députés et des ministres, il ne sort de ce laboratoire unique ni de chaleur, ni lumière" (Guizot 1884, 10–11; emphasis added).

24. On the role of local associations in preserving freedom, see Guizot 1821, 268–69, and Barante 1821, 16–17. Barante, too, criticized the "complete isolation of each citizen in his own interest" as a result of the growing privatization of life and denounced the ensuing atrophy of public life (Barante 1821, 17).

25. See Guizot 1984, 143–49.

26. See Guizot 1821, 130–34.

27. See Barante 1821, 88–89.

28. Also see Guizot 1821, 128–29; Guizot 1984, 144–47.

29. See Guizot 1821, 129–30; Barante 1821, 72–73, 249.

30. See Guizot 1821, 224–25, 270–72.

31. For more details, see Guizot 1821, 122, 132–34. For Guizot's emphasis on "social necessities," see Guizot 1984, 165–74.

32. Barante 1821, 122; 72. According to Barante, "Une administration des intérêts locaux instituée sur de telles bases ferait naître et perpétuerait les deux élémens les plus moraux et les plus salutaires qui puissant garantir la liberté d'une nation: l'esprit d'association entre les citoyens et l'emploi des superiorities sociales à l'intérêt general" (Barante 1821, 22). For Guizot, the government must "s'unir plus profondément à la France, rallier les intérêts qui se méfient d'elle, de changer enfin, dans l'état moral, dans les instincts et les pressentimens de ce peuple, ce qui la rend elle-même, sinon étrangère, du moins trop extérieure à l'existence publique, trop peu ancrée dans les besoins et dans les forces qui semblent appelés à décider du sort futur de tous. . . . [Etre] à l'affût de toutes les existences un peu importantes qui se formaient, de tous les talents qui s'élevaient, de toutes les considérations naissantes, de toutes les activités qui aspiraient à se déployer. Là aussi sont les auxiliaires du pouvoir" (Guizot 1821, 121). Hence, the task of government is to "recueillir les vraies et naturelles influences de la société pour les mettre à profit en les réglant, pour les consolider en leur donnant une part dans les affaires. . . . S'emparer des principes féconds, des intérêts permanents, des passions fortes et légitimes. . . . *Le public, la nation, le pays*, c'est donc là qu'est la force, là qu'on peut la prendre" (Guizot 1821, 68, 133, 225–26; emphasis added).

33. Guizot also used the phrase "gouverner par le maniement des esprits et non par le bouleversement des existences" (quoted in Rosanvallon 1985, 223). The phrase "le gouvernement des esprits" can be found in Guizot 1860a, 14. For a detailed analysis of the sociological aspects of Guizot's theory of *gouvernement des esprits*, see Pire 2002.

34. See Billard 1998, 62–69, 85–92. For an analysis of executive power, see Mansfield 1989.

35. Guizot 1860b, 327. This letter was published as an appendix (*Pièces historiques*) to volume three of Guizot's memoirs. A comprehensive discussion of Guizot's theory of education can be found in Terral 2000 and Nique 2000.

36. For a similar argument, see Billard 1998, 87.

37. On Guizot's theory of publicity as the cornerstone of representative government, see chapter 9.

38. I borrow the phrase from Guizot 1821, 267–68.

39. Guizot 1984, 145; my translation.

40. The phrase "complexification du social" is used by both Rosanvallon 1985 and Roldán 1999. On this issue, also see Manent 1994, 93–102.

41. On the original features of French constitutionalism, see Keohane 1980, 3–53, 392–419, 451–64; Jaume 1997a, 7–21; Judt 1992, 229–45. I discuss the complex nature of French liberalism in chapter 10.

42. Guizot memorably described the Doctrinaires' *juste milieu* in Guizot 1858a, 156–59. For Guizot's defense of free movement of persons and ideas, see Guizot 1821, 157–58. For Guizot's constitutionalism, see Guizot 1821, 172, 277–99; Guizot 1985, 326–27, 343–45, 359, 379; Guizot 2002, 54–57, 66–70, 328–29, 345–48, 370–76.

43. On this issue, see Girard 1985, 78–79, and Burdeaux 1953, 410.

44. On the laws on the press passed in 1819, see chapter 9.

45. See G. Broglie 1990, 143.

46. See G. Broglie 1990, 136–37.

47. For an analysis of Guizot's *Essai sur l'histoire et sur l'état actuel de l'instruction publique en France*, see Nique 2000, 31–37.

48. See Guizot 1860a, 1–184, 341–82, 399–423. The success of Guizot's educational policy has often been downplayed by historians. Yet, in the past five years, there has been a renewed interest in Guizot's educational policies. Four important new studies of Guizot's philosophy of education have been published in France: Billard 1998, Terral 2000, Nique 2000, Pire 2002.

49. Rosanvallon 1985, 255. Victor de Broglie claimed: "On ne peut pas dépouiller le gouvernement du double caractère d'instituteur public et de pouvoir exécutif" (Victor de Broglie as quoted in Rosanvallon 1985, 232).

50. Commenting on the ideas underpinning the Doctrinaires' theory of government, Rosanvallon pointed out: "Parler de politique rationnelle, c'est enfin de chercher à sonder les entrailles de la société pour comprendre et guérir les maux cachés qui l'agitent" (Rosanvallon 1985, 256). Also see Nique 2000, 38–41, 76–77.

51. Important documents that shed light on this issue can be found in the final section (*Pièces historiques*) published as an addendum to volume three of Guizot's memoirs (1860a; 1860b).

52. On Guizot's educational reforms, see Rosanvallon 1985, 223–62; D. Johnson 1963, 88–154; Reboul 1991, 163–85; G. Broglie 1990, 157–63; Nique 2000, 21–88; Terral 2000, 13–69.

53. Guizot 1860b, 360. Guizot's report was published as an appendix (*Pièces historiques*) to volume three of his memoirs. For more details, see G. Broglie 1990, 168–74.

54. Gabriel Broglie holds a similar view: "La position qu'il défendait n'était en effet pas negative. C'était celle d'un gouvernement qui se voulait libéral et légal, qui travaillait à l'extension des libertés publiques, par l'élection des maires, des officiers de la garde nationale, par la liberté de la presse et de l'enseignement, qui voulait procéder en tout par la voie legislative" (G. Broglie 1990, 148). I borrow the phrase *libéralisme par l'état* from Jaume 1997a.

55. Guizot 2002, 67; on this point, also see Guizot 1985, 375–80.

56. For more details, see Pouthas 1923a, 335–80, and G. Broglie 1990, 76–108.

57. An excellent overview of the causes of the fall of the July Monarchy—in many ways more balanced than Tocqueville's—was offered by Rémusat in volume four of his memoirs (Rémusat 1962, 241–52). It would be interesting to compare the two accounts of Rémusat and Tocqueville with Guizot's own summary of the policies carried out during the July Monarchy (Guizot 1867, 596–627). For an account of the last years of the regime, also see Guizot 1867, 518–95. Guizot's summary offers a detailed presentation of social and political legislation, finance, education, and public works from 1830 to 1848.

58. See Billard 1998, 26–27.

59. For more details, see Guizot 1867, 616–17.

60. Writes Guizot: "Je pense que l'autorité n'est pas bonne à tout, ni toujours salutaire; mais je répète qu'il est vain en pratique et absurde en principe de prétendre réduire le gouvernement à un role subordonné et presque inactif. Il est le chef de la société. C'est à lui qu'appartient et qu'échoit naturellement l'initiative de tout ce qui est objet d'intérêt public ou occasion de mouvement general" (Guizot 1821, 175).

~

CHAPTER SEVEN

The Battle for Representative Government

La représentation n'existe nulle part dans notre gouvernement.

—Royer-Collard

Representative Government in an Eclectic Age

In his book on parliamentary democracy originally published in 1923, Carl Schmitt identified the concept of parliamentarism—government by discussion—as an essential component of the intellectual world of liberalism, based on the idea that the truth can be found through an unrestrained clash of opinions that produces a harmony of social and political interests. According to the liberal catechism, remarked Schmitt (1996, 35), truth becomes "a mere function of the eternal competition of opinions," and the essence of political life is the confrontation of differences and opinions, public deliberation of argument and counterargument made possible by openness (publicity), discussion, and freedom of the press. Not surprisingly, Schmitt referred to Guizot as one of the most important representatives of this tradition of thinking based on the idea that political freedom depends on openness, debate, and a sound balance of powers.

This position, which was also held by other Doctrinaires such as Royer-Collard and Rémusat, contained a few puzzling elements, most notably the extreme confdence in—one would almost be tempted to compare it to a liberal dogma sui generis—the virtues of openness and discussion. It seems that today this belief has partially eroded and we have come to doubt that

185

reasonable laws arise out of a clash of opinions in Parliament and the press. Oddly, the argument made by Schmitt almost a century ago has a strange resonance today. The emergence of mass democracy has made argumentative public discussion a more or less "empty formality," a "superfluous decoration" (Schmitt 1996, 6). The reason for the erosion of the belief in public debates is that political parties no longer "face each other today discussing opinions, but as social or economic power-groups calculating their mutual interests and opportunities for power. The masses are won over through a propaganda apparatus whose maximum effect relies on an appeal to immediate interests and passions" (Schmitt 1996, 6). Hence, Parliament is no longer seen today as an arena in which ideas and opinions clash and truth arises out of their competition for power. Instead "Parliament itself appears a gigantic antechamber in front of the bureaus or committees of invisible rulers" (Schmitt 1996, 7). This development challenges one of the fundamental principles of liberalism and representative government.

As Bernard Manin has reminded us in the conclusion to his recent book on the principles of representative government, the latter remains "a perplexing phenomenon, even though its routine presence in our everyday world makes us think we know it well. Conceived in explicit opposition to democracy, today it is seen as one of its forms. . . . We are thus left with the paradox that, without having in any obvious way evolved, the relationship between representatives and those they represent is today perceived as democratic, whereas it was originally seen as undemocratic" (Manin 1997, 236). To account for this paradox, we must rethink the relation between parliamentarism, liberalism, and democracy. To this effect, a reexamination of nineteenth-century debates on political representation is both timely and necessary.

The Bourbon Restoration offers an ideal starting point for our investigation of the meanings of representation and representative government. The parliamentary debates that took place during this period, in particular the debates on imperative mandate and capacity, demonstrate that representative government was originally conceived of as a form of mixed government; that is, as a mixture of both democratic and nondemocratic elements, which were supposed to "tame" and "moderate" democracy. Election was regarded as a means of selecting political elites by bringing to power distinguished individuals who had a sufficient amount of wealth and a certain level of education that made them capable of recognizing and promoting the general interests of the nation.

As such, the study of nineteenth-century debates on representation also gives us the opportunity to reassess the literature on elites and democracy that has emerged in the past century (Bryce, Schumpeter, Mosca, Laswell, Bachrach, Sartori, Dahl, Etzioni-Halevy).[1] We stand to gain a more realistic understanding of democracy that stresses the important role elites play in shaping and reforming political institutions. It will be recalled that for the Doctrinaires, the central question of politics was how to design a stable and legitimate political system capable not only of governing effectively and coherently, but also of fostering the development of human faculties in a harmonious manner.

Guizot's first book on the nature, principles, and goals of representative government, *Du gouvernement représentatif et de l'état actuel de la France,* was published in 1816. The ideas of this volume were influenced by (and written in response to) the particular political context of the first years of the Restoration, characterized by a fierce battle between liberals and the ultraroyalist majority in the *Chambre introuvable.* That is why *Du gouvernement représentatif* should not be interpreted as Guizot's definitive statement on this topic. He subsequently revised his views on the nature of representative government in two of his later books, *Du gouvernement de la France* and *Histoire des origines du gouvernement représentatif en Europe,* as well as in his important essay "Élections," all written during the Bourbon Restoration. The principles of representative government were also discussed by Royer-Collard in his parliamentary speeches and by Rémusat in his essays written during the Restoration, which were never published.[2] The evolution of the Doctrinaires' ideas on this topic represents an interesting case study in political learning and gives us the opportunity to reflect once again on the particular nature of their liberalism.

Of all the Doctrinaires, Guizot provided the most coherent theory of representative government that was a direct offshoot of his theory of publicity and the sovereignty of reason. Along with John Stuart Mill's *Considerations on Representative Government,* Guizot's *Histoire des origines du gouvernement représentatif* ought to be regarded as one of the most important books on the principles of representative government published in nineteenth-century Europe. Guizot provided the classical definition of publicity as the touchstone of representative government and demonstrated the limitations of those theories that considered election as the essence of representative government. Unfortunately, Guizot's theory of representative government is rarely, if ever, discussed by contemporary political theorists interested in political representation. To give just two well-known examples, neither Bernard Manin's *The Principles of Representative Government* nor Hannah Pitkin's *Concept of Representation* devoted any attention to Guizot's theory of representative government. Although Manin mentioned Guizot in a footnote (that actually referred to Carl Schmitt's critique of parliamentarism), Guizot did not even appear in the index of Pitkin's book, one of the most influential works on the nature of political representation. This neglect is both unfair and regrettable.

By writing and reflecting on the origins and evolution of representative government, Guizot sought to demonstrate the legitimacy of representative institutions in postrevolutionary France and their deep roots in the history of European civilization. In so doing, he advanced a set of ideas that opposed the views held by the majority of ultraroyalists. It will be recalled that in *Considérations sur la France,* Joseph de Maistre argued that representative government is "by no means a modern discovery, but a *production,* or better, a *piece* of feudal government" (Maistre 1994, 34; emphasis added). In his opinion, national representation was not peculiar to England but was virtually present in every European monarchy. Maistre saw no incompatibility between the divine right of kings and national representation, and maintained that the type of representative government advocated by the French liberals was nothing else than a tautology, because it made impossible the exercise of sovereignty in the proper sense of the word.[3]

As we have already seen, those who supported the principles of representative government understood that the best way to promote and legitimize them was by demonstrating that representative institutions were, in fact, the outcome of a long political and social evolution that could be neither stopped nor reversed by any individual.[4] A thorough acquaintance with the history of representative government, in particular with the development of representative institutions in England, was more than a scholarly or antiquarian endeavor. Guizot underscored this point when remarking that an adequate knowledge of history, and especially of the history of free peoples, was "not merely an accomplishment of cultivated minds, it [was] a necessity to every citizen who feels desirous to take part in the affairs of his country, or to appreciate them" (Guizot 2002, 225). Nonetheless, while praising the virtues of English representative institutions, Guizot stopped short of arguing that they ought to be transplanted onto the French soil. Instead, he claimed that representative government has no unique and universal type in conformity to which it should be instituted. He also maintained that each nation is called to find its own proper balance between liberty, order, and authority.

As already noted, the debates on representative government in Restoration France focused on the principles and articles of the Charter of 1814, whose mixed nature was seen as a strength rather than a weakness.[5] Eclecticism and moderation were regarded as the two key elements of a new public philosophy suitable to an age of uncertainty and transition from despotism to freedom. As Victor Cousin argued:

> If the French Charter contains all opposed elements founded in a harmony more or less perfect, the spirit of the Charter is a *true eclecticism*. . . . Eclecticism is *moderation* in philosophic order; and moderation which can do nothing in the days of crisis, is afterwards a necessity. Eclecticism is the necessary philosophy of the age, for it is the only one that can conform to its wants and to its spirit; and every age terminates in a philosophy which represents it. . . . A mixed government is the only one appropriate to a great nation like France.[6]

The eclecticism advocated by Cousin was, in fact, a salient feature of the new constitutional text. The latter lay down the foundations of a mixed regime consisting of a monarch who ruled but did not reign, a chamber of peers surrounded by universal veneration and playing a limited political function, and an elected chamber of deputies. Commenting on the originality of the Charter of 1814, Cousin criticized the "vain abstractions" of the former constitutions, which had failed to provide a much-needed basis for reconciling the various social and political interests of the country. "Our glorious Constitution," he wrote, "is no mathematical fiction of the artificial equilibrium of the legislative and executive powers. [The Charter is] a real union of the king and the people."[7] While Cousin criticized those who supported only the democratic elements of the constitution and rejected the rest of the Charter, he also took to task those who vigorously opposed the presence of democratic elements and principles in the Charter. Both camps, argued Cousin, failed to understand that France needed a true eclecticism; that is, a combination of monarchy (order) and democracy (liberty) demanded by the new social condition and the spirit of the age: "All around us is mixed, complex, and mingled together."[8]

Concepts such as "national representation" and "natural rights," which had occupied a central place in the previous constitutions of 1791 and 1793 (Year I) as well as in the *Declaration of the Rights of Man and of the Citizen*, were conspicuously missing from the Charter of 1814. It will be recalled that the constitutional text adopted in 1791 explicitly endorsed the principle of national representation and stipulated that the representatives of the French nation were the elected chamber and the king. Articles 1, 2, and 3 of Title III ("Of the Public Powers") of the Constitution of 1791 read as follows: "Sovereignty is one, indivisible, inalienable, and imprescriptible: it belongs to the nation: no section of the people nor any individual can attribute to himself the exercise thereof. The nation, from which alone emanate all the powers, can exercise them only by delegation. The French constitution is representative; the representatives are the legislative bodies and the king" (Anderson ed. 1967, 64–65). The constitutional text also mentioned that the supreme authority belonged to the law and affirmed that nobody was above the law. According to Article 3, the source of all sovereignty was placed in the *nation* and the laws were supposed to express the general will of the nation.[9]

Given these antecedents, it is legitimate to ask why the Charter of 1814 was silent on the issue of "national representation." The complex legacy and memory of the Revolution loomed large in the mind of all political actors. During the Restoration, it was believed that the darkest episodes of the French Revolution had been made possible by the general confusion generated by false views of representation, sovereignty, and liberty.[10] This argument appeared, for example, in Guizot's writings of the period. "The source of all this confusion," he wrote, "is to be found in a wrong apprehension of the word representation; and the word has been misunderstood because false ideas have been entertained regarding sovereignty and liberty" (Guizot 2002, 287). Chateaubriand echoed Guizot's point when denouncing the mischief done by popular assemblies dominated by demagogues, adventurers, and radicals: "Deliberative assemblies have done so much mischief to France that we cannot too carefully guard ourselves against them" (Chateaubriand 1816, 14). In one of his most important parliamentary discourses, Royer-Collard also criticized the theories of representation and sovereignty that emerged during the Revolution: "We had the sad advantage of having learned what nations gain in being 'fully' represented," argued Royer-Collard (1861a, 231). "The Revolution, as it developed, was the doctrine of representation in action." The premature introduction of the doctrine of popular sovereignty made possible a pernicious form of despotism by creating a "degree of power in human society too great by definition . . . an evil no matter in whose hands it is placed."[11]

The widespread skepticism toward previous theories of representation and sovereignty stands in need of further clarification. Once again, an encounter with Rousseau's ideas is inevitable. As we have already seen, Restoration liberals claimed that Rousseau failed to provide an adequate theory of sovereignty and inspired the "crudest sophistries of the most ardent apostles of the Terror."[12] In their view, Rousseau did not recognize the dangers inherent in the notion of unlimited popular sovereignty and did not take into account the possibility that the people might legalize, directly or through their own representatives, a new form of tyranny that posed a significant threat to individual freedoms and rights.

Nonetheless, Rousseau's own position on representation was no less ambiguous than his ideas on the possibility of direct citizen participation in politics. As Richard Fralin demonstrated in an important study published three decades ago, Rousseau was not always hostile toward representation, and in his later writings he came close to acknowledging the importance of representative institutions. In *Du contrat social*, he rejected the possibility of representation in the legislative power on the basis that individual will can never be represented. "The cooling off of love of country," wrote Rousseau, "the activity of private interest, the immensity of states, conquests, and the abuse of government have suggested the device of sending deputies or representatives of the people to the assemblies of the nation. . . . As soon as a people give itself representatives, it is no longer free, and no longer exists."[13] Rousseau nuanced his position in *Considérations sur le gouvernement de Pologne*. He acknowledged the need for a mandate-based system of representation and made an important distinction between representatives and deputies. He insisted that the deputies of the people ought to be subject to imperative mandates and claimed that they should never be regarded as the true representatives of the people, because sovereignty can neither be represented nor alienated.

Rousseau's rejection of representative government did not prevent other French thinkers of that period from defending the legitimacy of political representation. An interesting case was Sieyès, whose pamphlet *Vues sur les moyens d'exécution dont les représentants de la France pourront disposer en 1789* ought to considered as one of the founding texts of modern representative government. Sieyès regarded deliberation and the "competition of opinions" as key features of representative government. In another text on Adam Smith, he argued that the development of society has three epochs, the third of which is characterized by "a representative common will"[14] that makes representative government—the "government by agents"—necessary. Underpinning Sieyès's defense of representation was the assumption that both the scope of government and the role of civil society evolve as a result of changes in the division of labor and the distribution of professions and trades in modern commercial societies.

Sieyès argued that representation is "the only source of civil prosperity"[15] and the consequence of the complex division of labor in modern society: "The division of labor, of professions is simply the representative system establishing itself spontaneously; it goes hand in hand with the progress of the society it animates."[16] Against Rousseau, Sieyès claimed that representation does not restrict political liberty: "To have oneself represented in the most things possible *increases* one's liberty."[17] As such, added Sieyès, representative government ought to be regarded as superior to direct democracy, because it is the only form of government suitable to the complex nature of modern commercial society. Sieyès denied that political representation is a form of alienation and insisted that direct democracy and representative government "grow from the same stem."[18]

Furthermore, Sieyès opposed imperative mandates in categorical terms: "For the deputy there is, and can be, no imperative mandate, or indeed no positive will, except that of the national will. He needs to defer to the councils of those who directly elect him only insofar as these councils are in conformity with the *national will*. And where else can this will exist, where else can it be recognized except in the National Assembly itself?"[19] Worth noting here is the reference to the concept of "national will" in a passage that in principle was critical of Rousseau's glorification of direct democracy.

It is interesting to ask to what extent Sieyès's theory of representation was a radical departure from Rousseau's ideas. While for Sieyès the will of the nation could not transcend particular interests, both thinkers relied on the hypothesis that the laws must be the manifestation of the general or national will. They also conceived of representation as a relation between two elements that are supposed to make present something which is, in fact, absent. As Keith Baker pointed out (1989a, 318), Sieyès's famous pamphlet *Qu'est-ce que le Tiers État* added "to a definition of society as a productive entity satisfying the various needs and interests of its members . . . a political definition of the nation as a unitary body of citizens exercising an inalienable common will." As such, Sieyès was unable to fully purge the idea of a unitary common will from its inherent illiberal connotations.[20]

The *"Principium et Fons"* of Representative Government

During the Bourbon Restoration, representative government came to be regarded as a necessary and effective means of reconciling freedom and authority. Those who supported representative government were ready to learn from the mistakes of the past.

Not surprisingly, England became the object of special praise and admiration on the part of many French liberals (and conservatives), who often contrasted the sound practical sense of the English to the propensity to abstract speculation that characterized French thinkers.[21] French liberals liked England for its its liberal spirit and solid institutions; the utilitarian spirit of the English appeared as an additional advantage. The English, wrote Madame de

Staël, often engage in utilitarian pursuits that have a clearly defined practical aim. Their books seek utility or entertainment, while the French apply a "literary spirit" to politics and search only for what is novel and ingenuous rather than for what is possible to achieve in practice. The English, added Germaine de Staël, rarely fall prey to abstract ideas and speculations and distrust those thinkers who are not concerned with the practical implications of their ideas.

As already noted, Guizot also admired the English practical school of philosophy that successfully blended liberty and authority and made a wise and wide use of the principle of utility. The English pragmatic spirit and common sense managed to achieve a sound balance between all classes and social interests; it also underpinned efforts to improve the English political system and social relations. Guizot studied with interest both the Revolution of 1648 and the Glorious Revolution of 1688. He admired the harmonious development of English political institutions, the influence of public opinion, and freedom of the press that led to the creation of a genuine system of checks and balances across the Channel.

The principles of English constitutional monarchy appealed not only to French liberals but also to conservatives of various persuasions, who praised England for its successful combination of tradition, religion, aristocracy, monarchy, and liberty. Voices as different as Vitrolles, Chateaubriand, and Maistre admired the English unwritten constitution, although each of them interpreted its principles in different ways. A believer in the futility of any attempt to write constitutions, Maistre found in the example of England a living proof of his theory that institutions cannot be created from scratch by the pen of the legislator. Far from being the outcome of the deliberations of a Constituent Assembly, the English constitution was the product of time and customs that allowed for incremental changes in the "natural" constitution of society.[22] In turn, Chateaubriand admired England for its wise middle ground between aristocracy and democracy and emphasized the important role played by the English aristocracy in the government of the country.[23]

Not surprisingly, the issue of the legitimacy of representative government along with its practical and institutional implications generated strong controversies in the French Parliament and the press. In the *Chambre introuvable*, prominent ultraroyalists opposed the legitimacy of the Charter of 1814 because, in their view, it sought to establish a questionable contractual relation between the monarch and his subjects.[24] Nonetheless, the majority of conservatives lukewarmly supported representative government and interpreted the Charter of 1814 as a replacement for ancient French institutions.

"We entirely adopt the principles of the Charter and the division of powers that it established," claimed Villèle. "We shall maintain its spirit and accept the consequences of this system as the most reasonable replacement of the ancient French institutions."[25]

What is interesting is that the theory of representative government defended by the *ultras* assigned a prominent role to the elected chamber in the direction of political affairs and affirmed the political responsibility of the king's ministers. It is legitimate to ask, however, to what extent this position was an expression of a genuine conversion to parliamentarism or nothing but a manifestation of political opportunism. It will be recalled that the parliamentary elections held in August 1815 brought to power a significant conservative majority in the Chamber of Deputies (more than two thirds of the seats belonged to the right and the extreme right). This surprising result was made possible by the existence of two types of electoral colleges, *collèges d'arrondissement* and *collèges de département*, elected in turn by county assemblies in which landlords, traditional supporters of the *ultras*, occupied a prominent role. This comfortable majority in the elected chamber helps explain why many ultraroyalists were unwilling to bargain and moderate their claims.[26]

Nonetheless, it would be an exaggeration to assume that the conservative camp was entirely "reactionary." To demonstrate its diversity, we shall examine two influential books on representative government, written by Vitrolles and Chateaubriand. In *Du ministère dans la gouvernement représentatif* (1815), Vitrolles put forward an interesting theory of representative government which, paradoxically, was more modern than the ideas on representation advanced by the Doctrinaires during the first years of the Restoration. Although it is difficult to draw a sharp line between political opportunism and sincere convictions, at first glance Vitrolles's ideas seem anything but reactionary, especially if one takes into consideration his praise of English institutions.

Vitrolles believed that the opposition between two main parties and their contest for power bring to light the true public interests; he favored a two-party system which, in his view, was the only effective way of adequately representing various social interests.[27] He argued that the principles of representative government, properly understood, require that ministers be held politically responsible for their actions, which amounted to claiming that the government must have the majority in the elected chamber and ought to be dependent on holding this majority at all times under the penalty of being ousted from power. Vitrolles was skeptical toward those theories which gave priority to executive power, downplayed the role of the elected chamber, and denied the principle of political responsibility.

In a tone reminiscent of Burke's plea for a choice of another inheritance,[28] he maintained that the power of the French monarchs had traditionally been limited by the General Estates, the Assembly of Notables, and the old *parlements*. More importantly, Vitrolles identified the essence of representative government as "the legal expression of public opinion" (Vitrolles 1815, 4) and defined representative government as a form of *mixed* government predicated upon the cooperation between the monarch ("*le premier mobile du pouvoir*"), the hereditary chamber (as a conservative body), and the elective chamber representing public opinion. Using a liberal tone, he championed a system of checks and balances sui generis, "*un système de contre-poids*" (Vitrolles 1815, 7) based on the separation of powers and the political responsibility of the king's ministers. Commenting on Article 13 of the Charter of 1814 stipulating that the person of the king was inviolable and sacred and that the executive power belonged to the monarch alone, Vitrolles emphasized that each minister ought to be held responsible to both chambers, which had the right to judge their acts.[29]

By admitting the principle of political responsibility, Vitrolles went even further than the Charter of 1814, whose Article 55 specified that the Chamber of Peers alone had the right to try the ministers of the king. Vitrolles claimed that the choice of ministers that the law described as a prerogative of the king could not be made in practice without the advice of the elected chamber. The monarch must, in fact, consult with the latter and select only those individuals "that the opinion of the Chamber would have designated if it were called to choose them directly."[30] Last but not least, Vitrolles's idea that the government must have the majority of votes in the Chamber of Deputies implied that the executive power should always follow public opinion and pursue only those policies that reflect the true interests of the nation. The implication of this view was that if the government were to lose the majority in the elected chamber, it must resign and enter in opposition.

Chateaubriand's case was not very different from Vitrolles. If today Chateaubriand's political thought is generally neglected by political theorists, the situation was different two centuries ago. *De la monarchie selon la Charte* (1816) was regarded as a "constitutional catechism,"[31] which advanced a set of ideas that had surprising affinities with Benjamin Constant's *Principes de politique* (1815). In *Réflexions politiques sur quelques écrits du jour* (1814), Chateaubriand made a strong argument for liberty of the press and championed the legislative independence of the two chambers vis-à-vis the executive power. In chapter thirteen of *Réflexions*, he defended the legitimacy of the Charter of 1814 and praised it for having provided a much-needed reconciliation between the past, the present, and the future.[32]

Chateaubriand argued that the new constitution satisfied the interests of all Frenchmen and was *not* an exotic plant artificially transplanted onto the French soil. On the contrary, the Charter was the political expression of French mores, traditions, and institutions that had gradually developed over time; it also reflected the "change in manners and the progress of the human mind."[33]

In *De la monarchie selon la Charte*, Chateaubriand defined representative government as follows: "By *Representative Government*, I understand Monar-

Vicomte de Chateaubriand

chy, such as it at present exists in France, in England, and in the Nether-lands. . . . We start with this fact: we have a Charter, and we can have noth-ing but this Charter" (Chateaubriand 1816, vii, 3; emphasis added). An im-portant part of the book was devoted to examining the division of powers, the principle of political responsibility, and the right of the legislature to ini-tiate and propose new laws. Chateaubriand claimed that in a constitutional monarchy "nothing is done directly by the King himself; every act of gov-ernment is in truth his Ministers', though the thing be done in his Majesty's name, or the document signed by his Majesty's hand" (Chateaubriand 1816, 6). He also championed the right of the elected chamber to initiate and pro-pose laws in concert with the king. Oddly enough, many reformist liberals, including the Doctrinaires, opposed this, because they feared that it would strengthen the influence of the *ultras* in the elected chamber. "Common sense," argued Chateaubriand (1816, 14), "requires that the Chambers, that are employed in the framing of a law, should have the right of proposing whatever amendments they shall think necessary to its perfection."

Furthermore, Chateaubriand insisted that the political responsibility of ministers be strictly enforced: "The Chambers have a right of putting to the ministers what questions they please and the ministers ought always to at-tend and to answer whenever the Chambers desire it" (Chateaubriand 1816, 34). He maintained that the government must rely and depend on the ma-jority in the elected chamber and denounced the "political heresy" accord-ing to which a government could survive only with the support of a minor-ity. This heresy, explained Chateaubriand (1816, 84), "was the device of a moment of despair, to justify false systems and imprudent pledges."

Hence, those who hold power, claimed Chateaubriand, must either strive to change the opinion of the majority or should submit to it. In making this point, Chateaubriand acknowledged the growing role played by public opin-ion, "*principium et fons*" of representative government. In a constitutional monarchy, he concluded, public opinion is the legitimate source and funda-mental principle of administration. The king's ministers must be selected from the majority in the Chamber of Deputies and should always defer to public opinion as expressed by the majority of elected deputies.[34]

Guizot's Early Views on Representative Government

It is interesting to note that both Guizot and Vitrolles portrayed themselves as supporters of representative government but interpreted its principles in different ways. Guizot's early views on representative government were shaped by the particular political context of the first years of the Bourbon

Restoration (1815–16) that brought to power an ultraroyalist majority in the elected chamber. Guizot questioned the applicability of a fundamental principle advocated by Vitrolles: the dependence of government on the majority in the Chamber of Deputies. A year later, along with other liberals, Guizot supported the decision of the king to dissolve the chamber and to call for new elections.

At first glance, such a position seems to challenge two fundamental principles of representative government: the separation of powers and the centrality of the legislature. Yet, once again we need to take into account the specific historical context of the early years of the Restoration in order to understand the rationale of Guizot's argument. We must also remember that, during the French Revolution, the legislature acquired an almost absolute power, which led in practice to a "parliamentary absolutism"[35] that, in the name of democracy and popular sovereignty, paved the way for a new form of arbitrary power. The image of an omnipotent and uncontrollable legislature enacting the general will of the nation haunted the Doctrinaires. In their attempt to bring the Revolution to a peaceful end, they sought to avoid at all costs the formation of an excessively powerful elected chamber whose authority knew no bounds.

Yet, their maneuvering ability was limited by the political context of the first years of the Restoration, when the "liberal party" itself was highly heterogeneous and the country itself was divided between two major systems of principles and interests engaged in a fierce battle for power.[36] Neither of the two groups was, in fact, homogeneous. The first group included not only radical revolutionaries, but also supporters of the Charter who saw in the new constitution an effective means of staving off a new revolutionary wave. To this group also belonged those who sought above all order and social peace.[37] In turn, the conservative camp had its own diversity and included both theocrats and legitimists who agreed on some principles and disagreed on a number of other issues.

The battle against the partisans of the Old Regime was the most salient characteristic of the legislature elected in 1815. The *ultras* championed a greater role for the Chamber of Deputies and argued that the institutional framework of representative government was formed by the king, the executive power, and public opinion acting through a fourth power, the majority of the chamber. Guizot, who regarded the Charter of 1814 as the legitimate heir to the principles of 1789, interpreted the debate on representative government as part of a larger struggle between those who sought to "end" the French Revolution and those who opposed the principles of 1789 and wanted to undo the legacy of the Revolution.[38] Guizot supported the dissolution of the ultraroyalist chamber by the king in 1816 and maintained that the ultraconservative majority in the elected chamber was *not* the true representative of the French people.[39] Referring to the ideas of Vitrolles, Guizot warned that, if implemented literally, they would destroy the delicate balance of power in the state by placing an almost unlimited power in the hands of the Chamber of Deputies. During the Revolution, legislative assemblies obstructed the functioning of the government and sought to drastically limit the authority of the latter. Hence, Guizot feared that the elected chamber would wage a new war against the government in order to weaken the authority of the king and his ministers.[40]

Du gouvernement représentatif also partly challenged another classical principle of representative government: majority rule. Here again, we must draw attention to the nuances of Guizot's argument. He maintained that the majority in the elected chamber ought to be regarded as "an uncertain and mobile quantity" (Guizot 1816, 41–42), an "undetermined force" disputed by rival parties and factions likely to change from one camp to another in a short period of time, without faithfully reflecting the evolution of the true interests of the country.[41] Guizot's argument was twofold. On the one hand, he acknowledged that in a representative government, the executive power is never at liberty to ignore or disregard the claims of the majority. On the other hand, he maintained that the majority might easily become an instrument used to legitimize the most appalling forms of tyranny.

The perception of this potential threat led Guizot to initially reject the idea that the survival of the government must always depend on an uncertain and volatile majority in the elected chamber. In other words, the Chamber of Deputies should not be entrusted with the right to make and unmake governments according to its whims and temporary interests that might contradict the public interest. On the contrary, claimed Guizot, the essence of representative government is to impose on the government and the chambers the obligation to be "*assez juste, assez sage, assez habile, assez national*" (Guizot 1816, 44–45) and to promote the general, long-term interests of the country.

My intention is neither to endorse Guizot's views nor to suggest that he was entirely justified in challenging some of the fundamental principles of representative government. Following a Machiavellian suggestion, I would like to suggest that he might be "excused" for having done so, while not being "justified" in temporarily departing from the principles of representative government. In making this point, I would like to challenge those who portrayed him as an opportunist. Guizot's example offers us an ideal opportunity to reflect on the difficult apprenticeship of liberty in the aftermath of a momentous revolution that radically changed the social and political map of France. A correct interpretation of Guizot's ideas on the nature of representative government should take into account the dangers that he sought to combat and must also examine his views on constitutionalism that have often been neglected by his interpreters.

In the lectures on the history of representative institutions in Europe, Guizot argued that "the responsibility of power is, in fact, inherent in the representative system; it is the only system which makes it one of its fundamental conditions" (Guizot 2002, 227). The institutions of representative government aim at building a regime of "active liberty" by limiting the power of the monarch who rules but does not govern. "This form of government," added Guizot, "presupposes and declares that no human reason is infallible, that no human will can be arbitrary; it tends to take away from the kings the power to do wrong and to ignore the truth."[42] As we have already seen, a fundamental principle of Guizot's political philosophy was that "no really existing power can be a rightful power, except insofar as it acts according to reason and truth, the only source of right" (Guizot 2002, 67). The essence of a free regime lies precisely in the endless questioning of all powers through publicity, free press, and elections.

For Guizot, the government was, in fact, "*le véritable pouvoir gouvernant*"[43] whose task was to identify and promote the general interests of the country that cut across political lines and did not always coincide with the interests of all the groups and parties represented in the chamber. As such, the executive power was the only "truly active" power in society, the only power capable of governing that is engaged in constant communication with society. At the same time, Guizot emphasized the inviolability of the monarch—he did *not* speak, however, of infallibility!—and granted the king a prominent political role in the direction of political affairs.[44] As a "*gage de sûreté*," the inviolability was supposed to shield the monarch from the pernicious influence of factional interests and revolutionary passions. Guizot also claimed that although in a representative government the ministers do not exercise a power that is distinct from that of the king, they should be held responsible for their own political actions.[45]

The simultaneous affirmation of the individual responsibility of ministers and the inviolability of the king was meant to prevent the monarch from becoming estranged from the policies of the government. In Guizot's opinion, the ministers had both the right and the duty "to enlighten the will of the king" (Guizot 1816, 38–39) and to make sure that their acts did not contradict the intentions and interests of the monarch, whose main role, as a neutral power, was to protect social order and common liberty. Even more important was Guizot's idea that the three powers—the king, the elected chamber, and the hereditary chamber—must work together within a system of checks and balances, in which each serves as a countervailing force that mitigates the tendency of other powers to transgress their boundaries (*"régler le pouvoir par le pouvoir même"* was one of Guizot's favorite phrases).[46] In his opinion, the *union* of these powers—the king, the Chamber of Deputies, and the Chamber of Peers—was the most important prerequisite of order and liberty.[47]

Guizot's views on the institutional framework of representative government evolved over time. Although he continued to believe in the dignity of (limited) executive power and remained committed to the principles of representative government, he eventually revised his ideas on the relations between the elected chamber and the king's government. The articles and reviews published in *Archives philosophiques, politiques et littéraires* (1817–18) illustrate this evolution and allow us to gain a better understanding of Guizot's overall conception of representative government. Responding to a series of theoretical objections raised by Loyson, Guizot claimed that both Parliament and the government had to work together toward the same goals and ought to be able to make the necessary concessions and compromises required by the general interests of the nation.[48] In Guizot's view, political institutions had to be well connected to each other and had to have the same foundation.[49] In practice, this required not only that the elected chamber not impose its own agenda upon the executive power, but also that the legislative initiatives of the majority in Parliament reflect to a certain extent the views of the government. The latter, added Guizot, must constantly justify the legitimacy of its policies and may not force the deputies to pass laws that contradict their interests and beliefs.[50]

It was during these years (1817–20) that Guizot became convinced that the success of representative institutions depended on placing the government "in the middle of the Chambers" in order to test the legitimacy of the executive power and to increase the opportunities for interaction and consultation between government and Parliament.[51] "To deny the Chambers a decisive influence on the formation of government," wrote Guizot in *Du gouvernement de la France*, "or to ask the ministers to be powerful without the support of the Chambers, amounts to rejecting representative government" (Guizot 1820, 283–84). Parliament, he argued, is the most important link between power and society. In the chambers, the most zealous spirits come to moderate their views under the penalty of discrediting themselves in the eyes of the public if they are unwilling to bargain and compromise with their political opponents. As Guizot put it, "It is in the Chambers that the pretensions of coteries, the hopes of factions, and the certainties of parties are submitted to the trial of publicity and debate" (Guizot 1820, 289). Hence, by weakening the influence of the chambers, the government would inevitably become estranged from society, with serious implications on the effectiveness of its policies.[52]

The acknowledgment of the seminal political role played by the chambers underscores the evolution of Guizot's views on representative government and the nature of the process of political learning he underwent during this turbulent period. If, at the beginning of the Restoration, Guizot rejected the idea that the government's survival ought to depend on the majority in the Chamber of Deputies, a few years later he claimed that the government had to maintain a majority of votes in the elected chamber under the penalty of being ousted from power. Once again, it is important to stress that the political context in 1820 significantly differed from that of 1815–16. After the assassination of the Duke of Berry in February 1820, the government veered to the right, and the only chance for liberals to exercise any political influence was to vigorously defend their views in the debates of the Chamber of Deputies.

While it may be tempting to dismiss Guizot's evolution as an expression of opportunism, his change can also be interpreted in a more positive way. It allows us to appreciate the extent to which Guizot, along with the other Doctrinaires caught between the cross fire of political extremes, underwent a significant process of political learning. After all, what is the purpose of experience if not to correct our errors and teach us new things? Guizot's evolution also allows us to see how an imperfect constitution such as the Charter of 1814, which initially arose from the need to find a fragile modus vivendi between various social and political principles and interests, eventually led to the creation of a parliamentary regime. The *ultras* learned to live and work with the institutions of representative government, while their liberal opponents came to understand that alternation in power and regular elections are the fundamental rules of politics in a free society.

It may seem impossible for us to accept that temporary deviations from the principles of representative government can be justified on pragmatic grounds dictated solely by political circumstances is certainly contestable. At first glance, such an approach seems to contradict the very idea of limited government and might come perilously close to justifying a new form of arbitrary power. The crux of the problem lies, of course, in the way in which we are prepared to interpret the notion of "exceptional circumstances." Be that as it may, it is undeniable that by the time Guizot set out to write the history of the origins of representative government, he had already arrived at a conception of parliamentary government that was *consistent* with his theory of sovereignty and publicity. He recognized the principle of the political responsibility of ministers and acknowledged the right of the elected chamber to propose and amend laws and to reject the budget submitted to its examination and approval.

Moreover, in postulating the equality of status between Parliament and government, Guizot's theory went beyond the principle of the strict separation of powers and affirmed that constitutional monarchy is based on the union between executive and legislative power—a union that is *not*, however, incompatible with the existence of a sound division and balance of powers.[53] In this view, Parliament must have not only well-defined legislative functions but also a certain degree of control over the government through the enforcement of the principle of the political responsibility of the king's ministers. Furthermore, the leader of executive power must belong to the majority in the elected chamber. At the same time, the government should not limit itself to purely executive functions, but must also share in the legislative power by retaining the right to dissolve the Parliament and to convoke new elections.[54]

"The Word *Representation* Is a Metaphor"

A more or less similar trajectory can be found in Royer-Collard's case. In 1815–16, he argued against the principle that conditioned the survival of the government on having the majority in the elected chamber. Yet, a decade later, he defended the political responsibility of the ministers and the right of the Chamber of Deputies to propose new laws and to hold the

Pierre-Paul Royer-Collard

executive power accountable for its actions and initiatives.[55] Critics of Royer-Collard such as Michel, Faguet, and Bagge claimed that he, too, was nothing else than an opportunist who changed his ideas as he thought fit. But a closer examination of Royer-Collard's parliamentary discourses reveals that he was and remained to the very end of his life a highly independent spirit, who opposed any form of arbitrary power and consistently endorsed a politics of countervailing or opposing forces—*"une politique de bascule, de contrepoids"*[56]—that sought to create and maintain a balance of powers in an uncertain and volatile political environment. Tocqueville, who was a great admirer of Royer-Collard, correctly grasped this point.

In making the transition from an early period when he defended the authority of executive power to a later one when he advocated a greater role for the elected chamber, Royer-Collard pursued the same political agenda, at the heart of which lay the opposition to absolute and arbitrary power, and a strong commitment to representative government based on the sovereignty of reason. During the early years of the Restoration, Royer-Collard opposed those theories that gave a blank check to the legislative power. He rejected imperative mandate and claimed that the will and opinions of the nation cannot be represented. In an important parliamentary discourse from 1816, Royer-Collard went so far as to argue that the *Chambre introuvable* was *not* representative of the opinions and the will of the nation, a point that echoed Guizot's argument.

To grasp the meaning of Royer-Collard's ideas on representation we must place them in a proper historical context. Like Guizot, Royer-Collard maintained that, during the Revolution, the meaning of representation had been distorted and misinterpreted by Jacobin leaders, who usurped political representation and turned it into a dangerous weapon of destruction. "We have had," he remarked (1861a, 231), "the sad privilege of having learned what nations gain from being fully represented. The Revolution . . . [was] nothing else than the doctrine of representation in action." How was it possible for the principle of representation to be distorted in such a way that it paved the way for a new form of tyranny? What did Royer-Collard mean when claiming that the Revolution was "the doctrine of representation in action"? And, more importantly, what are the conditions under which a nation can be represented in the proper sense of the word?

All these questions were addressed by Royer-Collard in a seminal discourse on representation from 1816, in which he argued that the very word *representation* is nothing other than a "metaphor":

What does it mean to represent a nation? How can a nation be represented? The word *representation* is a metaphor. . . . These are the conditions under which the Chamber of Deputies would be truly representative. First, if each deputy were elected by the entire population of his county, or at least the greatest part of that population. Second, if on each question the vote of each deputy were determined by binding mandate. . . . I do not know if a perfectly representative government exists or could exist on Earth, but there are governments which are imperfect representative governments to various degrees, depending on whether the election of the deputies belongs to a greater or smaller part of the population and whether the mandate is more or less binding. But when the election falls into the hands of a few people and the mandate has fully ceased to exist, and even more, when it is prohibited, then it is clear that representation is nothing more than a chimera, a lie. (Royer-Collard 1861a, 227–28)

Royer's position amounted to claiming that it was meaningless to speak of "true" representation in the absence of imperative mandate and universal suffrage. In order to be truly representative of the nation, the Chamber of Deputies must consist of representatives elected by all citizens of each county or by the majority of the population with the right to vote. Furthermore, on each question the vote of each representative must strictly follow the instructions of his electors. Or, none of the two conditions was met by the Charter of 1814, because the latter was based on limited suffrage and maintained that deputies ought to remain independent from their electors. As a result, in the absence of binding mandate, it was impossible to argue that the decisions of the Chamber of Deputies faithfully represented the opinions and the will of the entire nation.

In its limited representative capacity, the Chamber of Deputies represented "general interests" rather than individual wills, and its own legitimacy derived from the representation of interests rather than particular wills.[57] Another goal was to *limit* the authority of the king and his government. The Chamber of Deputies, argued Royer-Collard, was created by the Charter and electors were nothing else than "functionaries" instituted by the Charter in order to elect deputies to represent and defend their interests. As such, the elected chamber was "*un pouvoir et non une représentation*" (Royer-Collard 1861a, 228), a power rather than a genuinely representative body. Under these circumstances, speaking of representation was nothing else than a "political prejudice" based on a "misleading theory."[58] The most important implication of Royer-Collard's position was that the elected deputies who represented interests and were mandated by the Charter did *not* have the right to speak and act in the name of the entire nation.

As we have already seen, Royer-Collard believed that the effective protection of civil rights and liberties requires pursuing a politics of countervailing forces that aimes at creating a proper balance and a harmonious
cooperation between all powers in the state.[59] In Royer-Collard's view, the
Chamber of Deputies had a well-defined, if limited, role. If we wrote the
elected chamber off the Charter and strengthened the influence of the
monarch and the hereditary chamber, argued Royer-Collard, we would return to a point in time when the nation had no part whatsoever in the direction of political affairs. But, if the power of the elected chamber were
ever to become much stronger than that of the government, the country
would face the equally menacing specter of anarchy.[60] The key point made
by Royer-Collard was that a politics of countervailing forces requires constant efforts to prevent any single power from rising to a position of absolute domination and stifling the development of its rivals.

The clearest formulation of Royer-Collard's theory of constitutional
monarchy as *mixed government* can be found in another important speech
from 1816, in which he drew on the ideas of Cicero and Montesquieu to
develop a modern version of the old theory of *concordia ordinum*. Royer-
Collard spoke of two forms of representation, democratic and aristocratic,
and argued that both of them were indispensable to the proper functioning of the constitutional monarchy instituted by the Charter. The democratic element represented the general interests of the nation, while the
aristocratic element acted as a necessary prerequisite of order and stability.[61] In other words, the hereditary chamber represented the grand and
immutable interests of the nation and reflected the legitimate forms of inequality that existed in the bosom of society. As such, the Chamber of
Peers represented the highest interests of the nation that were not contained within the confines of any single class. In defending a mixed form
of representation, Royer-Collard was alive to the dangers that could arise
from the disappearance of any of the two forms of representation—democratic and aristocratic—and insisted that political liberty depended on
their coexistence.

Underpinning Royer-Collard's *politique de contrepoids* was his belief that in
a constitutional monarchy the government must not be at the discretion of
the majority in the elected chamber. His doctrine of representative government was a middle ground between the traditional thesis "*le Roi en ses conseils*" and the modern conception of elected assemblies.[62] "The equilibrium
between monarchy and popular power," claimed Royer-Collard, "is nothing
other than the equilibrium so difficult to establish between public order and
liberty. If it is broken in favor of monarchy, we incline toward absolute power;

if it is broken in favor of popular power, we incline toward anarchy" (Royer-Collard 1861a, 219). He defended the partial renewal of the Chamber of Deputies (as opposed to its total renewal)[63] and denied that the chamber had the right to reject the ministers proposed by the king and to impose its own candidates. In his famous speech of 1816, he claimed:

> The day when the government will be at the discretion of the majority of the Chamber, the day when it will be established that the Chamber may reject the ministers of the king and impose him its own ministers, that day not only our Charter will be destroyed, but also our monarchy, this independent monarchy which protected our fathers and from which alone France had received its liberty and happiness. That day, we shall be in a republic. (Royer-Collard 1861a, 217)

Like Guizot, Royer-Collard believed that the executive power must be strengthened in order to countervail the predominance of the ultraroyalists in the elected chamber. During the first years of the Restoration (1815–16), he deemed that the Chamber of Deputies had the right to be in opposition to the will of the king and of his ministers. The will of the king, claimed Royer-Collard, is identical with the will of his ministers;[64] the king alone has the right to propose new laws, while the chamber is only entitled to give the monarch its opinion. The two powers ought to govern in concert, but all things considered, the authority of the elected chamber is not equal to that of the king. Commenting on Louis XVIII's decision to dissolve the chamber in September 1816, Royer-Collard remarked: "The dissolution of the Chamber . . . is nothing else than the appeal of the contradicted sovereign to the opinion of his people. . . . The king represents legitimacy; legitimacy is order; order is peace; and peace can be obtained and preserved through moderation" (Royer-Collard 1861a, 268).

As the political context evolved, Royer-Collard changed some of his early views on representative government, in particular his ideas on the proper relation between the government and the Chamber of Deputies. He eventually acknowledged that the gradual consolidation of representative institutions implied a greater role for the elected chamber, including the right to reject the king's ministers or the budget submitted to its approval. In a parliamentary speech given in 1826, he also admitted that the king's ministers had a moral, penal, and political responsibility and must render an account of their actions to the chamber.[65] Furthermore, Royer-Collard came close to acknowledging that the elected chamber represents the will of the nation when arguing that it represents the legitimate interests of the country that are common to all citizens. In 1830, as president of the Chamber of Deputies, he endorsed the *Address of the 221 [deputies]* that challenged the arbitrary policies of Charles X.[66]

By emphasizing the need for a proper balance between the powers in the state, Royer-Collard remained committed to the idea that the essence of political liberty lies in the "multiplicity and opposition of powers, in their defensive and offensive power, in the judicious combination of their mutual energy."[67] He continued to believe that the monarch ought to act as a neutral power that represents the supreme interests of the nation and is placed above all political parties and groups.[68]

Notes

1. I comment on the elitist liberalism of the Doctrinaires in chapter 10. On the relation between democracy and elites, see Sartori 1965, 96–134; Bachrach 1971, 1–48, 69–115; Etzioni-Halevy 1989, 1–90; Etzioni-Halevy 1993, 1–121.

2. On Rémusat's views on the nature and principles of representative government, see Roldán 1999, 133–78 247–63.

3. For more details, see Maistre 1994, 34–38.

4. In the preface to the English translation of *Histoire des origines du gouvernement représentatif*, Guizot explained the relation between his scholarly and political careers as follows: "When in the year 1820, I devoted my energies to this course of instruction, I was taking leave of public life, after having, during six years, taken an active part in the work of establishing representative government in our own land. . . . We had faith in our institutions. Whether they entailed upon us good or evil fortune, we were equally devoted to them. I endeavoured to explain the origin and principles of representative government, as I had attempted to practice it" (Guizot 2002, viii–ix). For more details, see chapter 3.

5. For a defense of mixed government, see the following statement of Cousin: "We have then here, on one hand, an element of the *Ancien Régime* and, on the other, an element of the revolutionary democracy. . . . Their union is so intimate, that the most skillful civilian is much embarrassed to define and limit in theory the proper action of these two branches of sovereign power" (Cousin in Simon 1972, 76).

6. Cousin in Simon 1972, 77, 81; emphasis added.

7. Cousin in Simon 1972, 76, 78.

8. Cousin in Simon 1972, 77.

9. On this issue, see Bastid 1954, 19–32. Similar principles can also be found in the Constitution of 1793 (Year I), which referred to "national representation" and affirmed the sovereignty of the people as the proper foundation of representative government. For more details, see Anderson 1967, 59–66, 171–84.

10. For more details, see Rosanvallon 1989, 416–20. For a comprehensive account of the theories of representation before 1789, see Baker 1990, 224–51. An excellent account of elections during the Revolution can be found in Guéniffey 1993.

11. Constant in Simon 1972, 65.

12. Constant in Simon 1972, 66.

13. Rousseau 1986, 103, 106. Rousseau's views on imperative mandates can be found in *Considérations sur le gouvernement de Pologne* (Rousseau 1986, 187–205). For an excellent account of Rousseau's views on representation, see Fralin 1970, 15–144, and Baker 1990, 235–38.

14. According to Sieyès, the first epoch was characterized by the action of individual wills, while the second was defined by the action of the common will. For an extensive analysis of Sieyès's views on representation, see Forsyth 1987, 128–66. Also see Baker 1989a, 318–22; Baker 1989b, 488–90; Manin 1997, 187–89.

15. Sieyès as quoted in Sewell 1994, 89. Also see Forsyth 1987, 140–41, and Baker 1990, 244–50.

16. Sieyès as quoted in Sewell 1994, 93.

17. Sieyès as quoted in Sewell 1994, 92; emphasis added.

18. See Forsyth 1987, 148.

19. Sieyès as quoted in Forsyth 1987, 138; emphasis added.

20. See Wright 1993, 153, and Rosanvallon 1991, 135–37. Also see the following passage from Sieyès's proposal for the *Declaration of the Rights of Man*: "La loi ne peut être que l'expression de la volonté générale. Chez un grand peuple, elle doit être l'ouvrage d'un corps de représentans choisis pour un temps court, médiatement ou immédiatement par tous les citoyens qui ont à la chose publique intérêt avec capacité" (quoted in Wright 1993, 153).

21. For more details on the image of England in postrevolutionary France, see Reboul 1962; Theis 1997; Kahan 1991; and Bastid 1954, 33–38.

22. For more details, see Maistre 1992, 122–46.

23. For more details, see Chateaubriand 1987, 165–68, and Chateaubriand 1993a, 199–206. In his memoirs, Chateaubriand described this period in the history of France as follows: "La liberté, qui était au fond de cette époque, faisait vivre ensemble ce qui semblait au premier coup d'œil ne pas devoir vivre. . . . Chacun aussi savait mal le langage constitutionnel; les royalistes faisaient des fautes grossières en parlant la Charte; les impérialistes en étaient encore moins instruits; les conventionnels, devenus tour à tour comtes, barons, sénateurs de Napoléon et pairs de Louis XVIII, retombaient tantôt dans le dialecte républicain qu'ils avaient presque oublié, tantôt dans l'idiome de l'absolutisme qu'ils avaient appris à fond" (Chateaubriand 1987, 171).

24. Such an argument was made by Villèle. "Il semble qu'il existe dans les mots de *constitution* et *d'idées libérales* un souffle empoisonné qui détruit au moment où il crée," wrote Marquise de Montcalm (quoted in Oechslin 1960, 102; emphasis added). In turn, Marchand de Chaume argued: "L'existence d'un contrat entre le roi et son peuple sera toujours une supposition absurde tant qu'on ne trouvera pas pour en assurer l'exécution non une autorité de droit mais une puissance de fait supérieure à tous deux" (quoted in Oechslin 1960, 97).

25. Villèle as quoted in Oechslin 1960, 103.

26. Also see Duvergier de Hauranne 1860, 418–20, and Barante 1821, 87–89.

27. Writes Vitrolles: "Nous ne pourrons atteindre les conditions du ministère et compléter le système du Gouvernement, qu'au moment où la Chambre se divisera en deux partis, dont l'un suivra invariablement la bannière du ministère, et l'autre servira sous des couleurs opposées. Cette opposition même est utile, est nécessaire aux Ministres pour les resserrer entre eux, et les forcer à environner toutes leurs disposi-tions de tout le poids de la raison, de toute l'influence des plus grands motifs" (Vit-rolles 1815, 74).

28. Writes Vitrolles: "Si une longue suite de révolutions n'avait pas effacé la trace de nos anciennes institutions, elles auraient pu servir plus directement de bases à la loi qui fixe et détermine nos libertés et la distribution du pouvoir politique, comme il est arrivé en Angleterre" (Vitrolles 1815, 3). This idea can also be found in Necker's political writings.

29. For more details, see Vitrolles 1815, 69.

30. Vitrolles 1815, 30. Also see the following fragment: "Comme cette opinion s'exprime par celle de la majorité dans les Chambres, et en particulier dans la Cham-bre élective, il faut que le ministère ait toutes les conditions qui peuvent lui assurer la majorité de cette Chambre. Ces conditions se trouvent dans les circonstances qui accompagnent sa formation; dans sa conduite plus ou moins conforme à l'opinion publique; enfin dans l'attention qu'il met à attacher à son sort les plus grands et les plus nombreux intérêts politiques. . . . Quand les Ministres ont décidément perdu la majorité dans la Chambre, ils se retirent, et forment le plus souvent une opposition nouvelle: ils essayent ainsi de puiser une nouvelles existence dans l'opinion publique" (Vitrolles 1815, 30, 42).

31. In his memoirs, Chateaubriand described his book as follows: "*La Monarchie selon la Charte* est un catéchisme constitutionnel: c'est là que l'on a puisé la plupart des propositions que l'on avance comme nouvelles aujourd'hui. Ainsi ce principe, que le roi règne et ne gouverne pas, se trouve tout entier dans les chapitres iv, v, vi, et vii sur la prérogative royale" (Chateaubriand 1987, 169). On Chateaubriand's po-litical theory, see Evers 1987 and Clément 1993, 7–46.

32. Writes Chateaubriand: "Il faut donc trouver un mode de gouvernement où la politique de nos pères puisse conserver ce qu'elle a de vénérable, sans contrarier le mouvement des siècles. Hé bien! la Charte présente encore cette heureuse institu-tion: là se trouvent consacrés tous les principes de la monarchie. Elle convient donc, cette Charte, à tous les Français. . . . Les idées nouvelles donneront aux anciennes cette dignité qui naît de la raison, et les idées anciennes prêteront aux nouvelles cette majesté qui vient du temps. *La Charte n'est donc point une plante exotique*, un accident fortuit du moment; c'est *le résultat de nos mœurs présentes; c'est un traité de paix signé entre les deux partis qui ont divisé les Français*" (Chateaubriand 1987, 113–14; empha-sis added).

33. For a synthesis of Chateaubriand's position on this topic, see Chateaubriand 1816, 222–23.

34. For more details, see Chateaubriand 1816, 56, 84.

35. The phenomenon of "parliamentary absolutism" was analyzed by Carré de Malberg 1962.

36. See Guizot 1816, 5–7.

37. In an article published in 1817, Guizot described the two major parties that dominated France as follows: "La France est divisée en deux grands systèmes de principes, d'intérêts et de volontés; d'une part, sont ceux qui ne voulaient pas que la révolution se fît, et qui voudraient la défaire; d'autre part, ceux qui ont fait la révolution ou que la révolution a fait. . . . Le second, par cela seul qu'il est demeuré vainqueur, s'est modifié davantage; trois nuances diverses le constituent. La première, et je lui donne ce rang parce que je la crois appelée à triompher, comprend les hommes qui veulent la charte, c'est-à-dire les principes fondamentaux et les résultats essentiels de la révolution, dans toute sa plénitude et avec toutes ses conséquences; mais qui, ayant appris ce que coûtaient de telles secousses, et convaincus que la France en a obtenu tout ce dont elle a besoin, sont fort disposés à soutenir fermement et loyalement un gouvernement qui, en consommant la révolution, empêchera qu'une autre ne recommence. Non loin d'eux sont d'autres hommes qui partagent au fond leurs opinions et leurs vœux, mais qui, las surtout de tant d'agitations, ou brisés par notre longue servitude, ne demandent que le repos et ne l'espèrent que du pouvoir; honnêtes citoyens . . . qui sont toujours prêts à croire que tout est fini, arrangé, assuré, qu'il n'y a plus qu'à jouir ou à dormir. . . . Au-délà et hors de ces deux classes d'hommes, sont les révolutionnaires, c'est-à-dire ceux qui . . . se réjouissent des fautes du gouvernement . . . et ont placé, dans sa chute, tous leurs désirs comme toutes leurs espérances" (Guizot 1817d, 275–76).

38. See Guizot 1869, xii, and Guizot 1816, 14.

39. See, for example, Guizot 1816, v–viii, 2–3, 13–15, and Guizot 1869, xiv. On this issue, also see Rémusat 1958, 287–92. Here is a revealing passage from his memoirs in which Rémusat commented on the significance of the Ordinance of September 1816: "L'ordonnance de 5 septembre peut être considérée comme un point de partage, d'où les eaux s'écroulérent en sens divers suivant leur pente naturelle. . . . Il se forma décidément un juste milieu qui, victorieux ce jour-là, dura et prévalut pendant environ deux ans avec assez de consistence et de success. Dans la masse générale, l'acte du gouvernement fut approuvé autant qu'il fut compris. . . . On peut dire que *c'est alors seulement que le jour commença à se répandre sur nos affaires.* La Restauration prit quelque chose du vrai caractère qu'elle auraient dû toujours garder" (Rémusat 1958, 288, 292; emphasis added).

40. Writes Guizot: "On persista à voir, dans les assemblées, non un instrument destiné à contenir et à régler le pouvoir même qui s'en sert, mais une puissance *indépendante*, appelée à *contrarier* et à *enchaîner* le gouvernement. Ce principe seul devait conduire à l'anéantissement de l'autorité royale: elle périt en effet; et, comme il fallait bien que quelqu'un gouvernât, les assemblées s'emparèrent du pouvoir exécutif" (Guizot 1816, 54–55; emphasis added)

41. Writes Guizot: "Cette majorité, qu'on a représenté comme une personne réelle, ayant des droits, des volontés et des pouvoirs, n'est donc qu'une force indéterminée

que se disputent les divers partis; considérée en elle-même, la majorité n'est rien ou plutôt elle n'est pas. . . . Si la nécessité imposée au gouvernement d'obtenir, en dernière analyse, la majorité est la garantie la plus efficace des droits des nations, l'invasion violente du gouvernement par la majorité est une des plus dangereuses secousses que puissent éprouver les États et les trônes" (Guizot 1816, 43, 47–48).

42. The paragraph is worth quoting in full: "Les institutions représentatives en général et la responsabilité des ministres en particulier ont en effet pour objet de *contenir le pouvoir royal* dans des bornes légales, et de le placer dans une situation telle qu'il ne puisse se déplacer et agir que *conformément aux véritables intérêts et aux vœux légalement exprimés des peuples.* Cette forme de gouvernement suppose et déclare qu'aucune raison humaine n'est infaillible, qu'aucune volonté humaine ne doit être arbitraire; elle établit, en principe, que l'erreur ou l'excès peut se glisser auprès du trône, et qu'il est nécessaire de les *prévenir*; elle tend à *ôter aux rois le pouvoir de faire le mal* et de ne pas entendre la vérité" (Guizot 1816, 34; emphasis added). On this issue, also see Guizot 1869, xlii–xviii. This view was also held by Royer-Collard.

43. Writes Guizot: "Le pouvoir exécutif est seul dans une communication constante avec les intérêts individuels; lui seul les connaît, les écoute, leur parle, leur applique les règles générales et se prononce sur leur sort; *il est le seul pouvoir matériellement actif dans la société,* et en lui reside nécessairement le principe du mouvement politique. On peut, on doit lui assigner des bornes, lui imposer des conditions; on peut, on doit l'entourer de lumières qui préviennent ses erreurs et de barrières qui répriment ses excès; on n'empêchera jamais qu'il ne soit *le véritable pouvoir gouvernant,* car il est le seul qui puisse gouverner" (Guizot 1816, 46; emphasis added). In this regard, Guizot followed in the footsteps of Necker; for more details, see chapter 6 and Necker 1792.

44. See Guizot 1816, 34–36. Necker, too, affirmed the inviolability of the king and the political responsibility of the king's ministers. On Necker's political legacy, see Grange 1974, 495–502.

45. See Guizot 1816, 32–33.

46. See Guizot 1816, 25, 38.

47. See Guizot 1816, 26–31. On this issue, also see chapter 6.

48. C. Loyson's rejoinder can be found in volume 2 of *Archives philosophiques, politiques et littéraires* (1817); Guizot's response was published in the same issue (Guizot 1817b). In another essay, Guizot explained: "C'est beaucoup *plus que l'union*; disons plus, c'est tout ce dont nous avons un besoin pressant et actuel; que la majorité des chambres s'entende avec le gouvernement, et qu'au moyen de *concessions réciproques,* ces deux forces tendent parallèlement au *même but,* voilà tout ce qui est aujourd'hui possible et nécessaire" (Guizot 1817c, 187; emphasis added). Also see the following revealing passage: "Deux choses importent également au gouvernement: son union avec les chambres, et l'union des chambres avec l'opinion nationale. C'est surtout par l'intermédiaire des chambres que le gouvernement et le public peuvent s'approcher l'un de l'autre, s'entendre et s'allier. Que servi-

raient au gouvernement des chambres impopulaires, sans confiance et crédit" (Guizot 1817c, 188).

49. See Guizot 1817d, 266.

50. See Guizot 1817b, 426.

51. See Guizot 1817b, 427.

52. Writes Guizot: "Mais les chambres sont maintenant *le seul lien qui unisse la société et le pouvoir,* et les contienne l'un par l'autre. Affaiblissez leur influence; la société et le pouvoir s'éloignent, s'isolent, ne se connaissent et ne se pénètrent plus. . . . Est-il un état plus périlleux, plus près de devenir fatal? Et pourquoi donc l'ancienne société française s'est-elle dissoute? Pourquoi la révolution l'a-t-elle brisée avec si peu d'effort? N'est-ce pas parce que tous les liens qui unissaient jadis le gouvernement et les peuples s'étaient dissous eux-mêmes? . . . Nous ne regrettons point que cela soit tombé; nous pensons que les chambres et le gouvernement représentatif valent beaucoup mieux que l'ancien système; mais on ne contestera pas du moins qu'ils en tiennent la place, et que cette place doît être occupée" (Guizot 1820, 287–88; emphasis added).

53. On this point, I disagree with Darío Roldán, who argued that the Doctrinaires did not accept the idea of a division of powers. "Pour les doctrinaires," wrote Roldán, "et étant donné l'imbrication entre le pouvoir et la société, la liberté ne procède ni du contrepoids ni de la limitation que chaque pouvoir est capable d'imprimer aux autres" (Roldán 1999, 157). As I have already demonstrated, both Guizot and Royer-Collard emphasized the importance of a sound division and balance of powers and endorsed a politics of countervailing forces. For them, the division and balance of powers were fundamental conditions of political liberty.

54. I follow here Léon Duguit's definition of parliamentary regime: "Le régime parlementaire repose essentiellement sur l'égalité des deux organs de l'État, le parlement et le gouvernement. . . . Cette collaboration des deux organs, et cette action réciproque qu'ils doivent exercer l'un sur l'autre sont assurés par un element qui est la pièce essentielle de la machine politique, le conseil des ministres, ou ministère, ou cabinet" (Duguit as quoted in Nesmes-Desmarets 1908, 157).

55. For a detailed interpretation of Royer-Collard's theory of representative government, see Nesmes-Desmarets 1908, 93–245, and G. Rémond 1979.

56. See Nesmes-Desmarets 1908, 157.

57. Royer-Collard claimed: "En effet, Messieurs, je vous le demande, que représentez-vous ici? Les personnes et les volontés? Mais ceux qui vous ont envoyés ne forment peut-être pas avec vous la cinquantième partie de la population capable de vouloir. La plus extrême bienveillance, comme la plus haute estime, ne sauraient découvrir en vous qu'une imperceptible oligarchie, en contravention flagrante à la souveraineté du peuple. Votre légitimité ne vient donc pas d'elle; elle vient de ce que, représentant des intérêts, ces intérêts parfaitement exprimés par les votres, vivent, pensent, agissent dans chacun de vous" (Royer-Collard 1861b, 465). Also see Royer-Collard 1861a, 229; Nesmes-Desmarets 1908, 99–113; Bastid 1954, 218–21.

58. The whole passage reads as follows: "*La représentation n'existe nulle part dans notre Gouvernement*. La Chambre, telle que la Charte l'a conçue, est un *pouvoir* et non une représentation. . . . La Chambre est ce que la Charte a fait; rien de plus, rien de moins. Comme *c'est la Charte qui constitue la Chambre, et non l'élection* . . . la Chambre n'exprime jamais *que sa propre opinion* . . . Il est faux en principe, et impossible dans le fait, que l'opinion de la Chambre soit toujours et nécessairement l'opinion de la nation. . . . Si cette opinion existe, elle ne peut être constatée avec certitude que par le mandat. Et puisque le mandat n'est pas admis par la Charte, la Chambre ne peut se dire, et elle ne doit pas être crue l'organe légal et le ministre infaillible de l'opinion nationale. . . . Hors l'élection populaire et le mandat, la représentation n'est *qu'un préjugé politique* qui ne soutient pas l'examen . . . Cette *théorie mensongère* nous a été trop funeste, pour qu'il ne soit pas nécessaire de la combattre partout où elle se présente" (Royer-Collard 1861a, 28–29; emphasis added).

59. "La garantie des libertés nationales réside *dans le Gouvernement tout entier*, dans la royauté, aussi bien que dans les Chambres, et dans la Chambre héréditaire, aussi bien que dans la Chambre élective; elle résulte de l'ensemble et de *l'harmonie des pouvoirs*. Tout accroissement dans l'importance politique de la Chambre élective, loin d'ajouter à cette garantie, *l'affaiblirait*, et d'autant plus, que cet accroissement serait plus considérable; et s'il allait jusqu'à ce point, que, de simple mandataires de la Charte que nous sommes, quoique élus, nous devinssions des mandataires du peuple, ayant droit de parler et d'agir en son nom, c'est alors peut-être que les droits et les libertés de la nation seraient dans *un véritable péril*" (Royer-Collard 1861a, 230–31; emphasis added).

60. For more details, see Royer-Collard 1861a, 219.

61. Here is Royer-Collard's argument: "La Charte a institué deux représentations qui ont chacune leur nature propre, leurs lois, leur destination diverse dans le gouvernement; l'une, la représentation démocratique des intérêts généraux, essentiellement gardienne de la liberté, c'est pourquoi elle est élective; l'autre, la représentation aristocratique des supériorités sociales, essentiellement gardienne de l'ordre qui les protège et de la stabilité qui les conserve; c'est pourquoi elle est ou doit être héréditaire" (Royer-Collard 1861b, 465).

62. For more details on this issue, see Bastid 1954, 220.

63. Also see the following paragraph: "Le jour où la Chambre élective est plus forte, la royauté est plus faible. La théorie decide que, toutes choses égales d'ailleurs, le renouvellement integral appartient advantage au principe républicain, le renouvellement partiel au principe monarchique" (Royer-Collard 1861b, 218).

64. For more details, see the following statement: "Si dans un gouvernement constitutional, le roi n'agit que par des ministres responsables, *dont il ne peut être séparé*, ceux-ci, à leur tour, *ne peuvent être séparés de la volonté royale*, dont ils sont les organs necessaires" (Royer-Collard quoted in Nesmes-Desmarets 1908, 191–92; emphasis added). As Nesmes-Desmarets noted, the confusion between the will of the king and the will of the king's ministers contradicts one of the fundamental principles of parliamentary regime.

65. See Royer-Collard 1861b, 47, 217. On Royer-Collard's view on the political responsibility of the king's ministers, see Nesmes-Desmarets 1908, 227–41.

66. Here is a revealing passage from the Address of the 221 deputies: "Sire, la Charte . . . consacre comme un droit l'intervention du pays dans la deliberation des intérêts publics. Cette intervention devait être, et elle est, en effect, indirecte, sagement mesurée, circonscrite dans les limites sagement tracées . . . ; mais elle est positive dans son résultat, car elle fait du concours permanent des vues politiques de votre gouvernement avec les vues de votre people, la condition indispensable de la marche regulière des affaires publiques (Royer-Collard quoted in Nesmes-Desmarets 1908, 135).

67. Royer-Collard 1861b, 28; 1861a, 230–31. In a letter sent to his electors in 1839, Royer-Collard wrote: "Nous entrons, messieurs, dans une ère nouvelle, de grands maux nous menacent. . . . Qu'avons-nous à faire, dans ces extrémités, nous, gardiens de l'ordre, observateurs de tous les biens péniblement acquis, si ce n'est de nous replier sur nous-mêmes, de nous rallier étroitement et de resister courageusement, comme nous l'avons fait dans d'autres temps, à cette nouvelle anarchie?" (Royer-Collard quoted in Nesmes-Desmarets 1908, 243).

68. Paul Bastid (1954, 220) pointed out that Royer-Collard's theory of representation, most notably his views on the relation between electors and their representatives, found a warm reception around the turn of the century in the works of German legal scholars such as Jellinek and Laband, who argued that representatives must retain their independence from electors. In France, Royer-Collard influenced Duguit's theory of constitutional law and parliamentary regime; among Duguit's most important works were *L'État* and *Manuel de droit constitutionnel*. For more details, see Bastid 1954, 219–21; Rials 1987, 90–92. An excellent discussion of imperative mandates can be found in Manin 1997, 163–67.

~

CHAPTER EIGHT

Representation and Political Capacity

La multitude qui ne se réduit pas à l'unité est confusion. L'unité qui n'est pas multitude est tyrannie.

—Pascal

The Goals of Representative Government

As we have already seen, the Doctrinaires' theory of representation based on the twin notions of political capacity and restricted suffrage was the by-product of their theory of the sovereignty of reason. It rested upon the assumption that representative government does not recognize sovereignty of right as an intrinsic attribute of any person or collective body. In this view, no power should be regarded as legitimate if its actions do not conform to the precepts of reason, justice, and truth. At the same time, the Doctrinaires' views on representation were a typical example of the nineteenth-century skepticism toward political democracy as illustrated by the belief that the most effective security for the people's rights and liberties was not direct political participation but the selection of "a body of able watchmen to guard those invaluable possessions" (Brougham 1860, 63).

The Doctrinaires maintained that the goal of representative government is to provide effective safeguards against any form of arbitrary power. They argued that each appropriation of de facto sovereignty should be regarded as temporary and imperfect. In thier view, the institutions and principles of representative government submit all powers to regular trials and legal obstacles and place them under the obligation of undergoing constant opposition and proving their legitimacy in the eyes of the public. Accordingly, political power ought to be held only by those who demonstrate that they possess the required capacity to act upon the principles of reason, justice, and truth,[1] the decisive factor in granting power being the judgment that electors pass on their representatives. As Bernard Manin pointed out (1997, 158), there is a fine distinction between claiming that only those who are objectively "superior" can hold power and arguing that what grants power to the "capable" individuals is the free and conscious judgment of their electors. The distinction is important because it suggests the possibility that the concept of capacity is not a priori incompatible with the principles of modern democracy.

In the Doctrinaires' opinion, the fundamental purpose of representative institutions was to create a "government by discussion" and to constantly question the legitimacy of all claims to power and sovereignty through debates, publicity (openness), and freedom of the press. In their view, an institutionalized framework for opposition, contestation, and debate, along with liberty of the press, publicity, and trial by jury, were the most effective means of fighting the natural tendency of all powers to extend their authority beyond their legitimate sphere of influence. Representative institutions, argued Guizot, seek to form an alliance between power and liberty by giving publicity and elections a key role in safeguarding civil and political freedoms.[2] Publicity guarantees that power is exercised responsibly by those who have the presumed capacity and are required to constantly prove the legitimacy of their actions to the public at large. As such, the purpose of representative institutions is to simultaneously "constitute" the government through the action of society and to "constitute" society through the intervention of government. This theme is closely related to another idea that loomed large in the Doctrinaires' writings: Power and public opinion must be engaged in a constant dialogue that creates the conditions for a "mutual revelation" between government and society. This dialogue is made possible by the institutions of representative government; that is, publicity, free elections, and open parliamentary debates.[3]

The best illustration of what the Doctrinaires understood by "true" representation can be found in Guizot's *Histoire des origines du gouvernement représentatif en Europe*,[4] which begins with a critique of the theories of political representation advanced during the French Revolution. Guizot denounced those doctrines that affirmed the autonomy of individual will and defined freedom as obedience to the laws to which individuals have consented. In his view, liberty is *not* incompatible with being subject to the precepts of reason, justice, and truth. On this point, Guizot disagreed with Rousseau, who denied that human beings can be free if they obey laws whose legitimacy is independent from their will and consent. Consequently, Guizot rejected the definition of representation as a mechanism of collecting individual wills. He interpreted representation as a natural process by which the fragments of reason and knowledge that exist in society are gathered and brought to form the government of society.

Guizot examined this idea in the second volume of his history of representative government. The functioning of representative institutions is based on the assumption that in every society there is a sum of just ideas and legitimate wills that are unequally dispersed among individuals. The institutions of representative government must collect from the entire society all the scattered and incomplete fragments of reason and knowledge (social power) through elections and publicity. As such, political representation can no longer be defined as "an arithmetical machine employed to collect and count individual wills, but [as] a natural process by which public reason, which alone has a right to govern society, may be extracted from the bosom of society itself" (Guizot 2002, 295–96). Thus, the concept of "representation" undergoes a significant conceptual transformation. According to previous theories of representation, to "represent" meant to make present something that was, in fact, absent. In practice, this amounted to claiming that a representative must do whatever his electors would choose if they were (physically) present. In this view, political representation was seen as a mechanism of collecting and counting individual preferences and was associated with institutional arrangements allowing deputies to deliberate, reason, and act on behalf of those whom they represented in such a way that they acted *in their stead,* or as they would have acted had they been able to participate directly in the making of decisions.[5]

Guizot and Royer-Collard opposed this notion of representation based on the delegation of individual will and imperative mandate. They claimed that electors are not entitled to enjoin their delegates, "*This is our will and that ought to be the law.*" All they can do is to confer upon their representatives the mission of examining and deciding upon the best course of action according to their own reason and judgment. In this view, representation, in the proper sense of the word, ultimately becomes impossible if electors retain an absolute control over their deputies. As Lord Brougham argued (1860, 34), "it is not a representation if the constituents so far retain a control as to act for themselves." They retain, however, the right to communicate with their representatives and to convey to them their opinions and interests. Nonetheless, upon receiving this information from their electors, the deputies are supposed to exercise their own judgment and are free to decide what is, in their opinion, the best course of action for their constituency. They represent their electors *as if* they express their interests but, in fact, they are free to exercise their representative capacity as they think fit. That is why electors "must necessarily trust in the enlightenment of those whom they elect; election is . . . a sovereign but limited right exercised by those who confer political power upon such of the claimants as they may select" (Guizot 2002, 54). It is tempting to ask if Guizot abused the concept of *representation* by redefining representative government apart from any substantive notion of representation.[6] At first glance, it seems that his definition of representation contains the following paradox. Once we discard the theory of representation based on imperative mandate, there is nothing left to "represent" in the original etymological sense of the word. How can we solve this puzzle?

In a famous passage from *Histoire des origines du gouvernement représentatif*, Guizot defined the goals of representative government as follows:

> Pascal has said, "Plurality which does not reduce itself to unity, is confusion. Unity which is not the result of plurality is tyranny." This is the happiest expression and the most exact definition of representative government. The plurality is society; the unity is truth, is the united force of the laws of justice and reason, which ought to govern society. If society remains in the condition of plurality, if isolated wills do not combine under the guidance of common rules, if they do not equally recognize justice and reason, if they do not reduce themselves to unity, there is no society, there is only confusion. And the unity which does not arise from plurality, which has been violently imposed upon it by one or many . . . is a false and arbitrary unity; it is tyranny. The aim of representative government is to oppose a barrier at once to tyranny and to confusion, and to bring plurality to unity by presenting itself for its recognition and acceptance. (Guizot 2002, 52–53)

This long and abstract passage reveals the core of the Doctrinaires' theory of political representation. Borrowing a famous aphorism from Pascal, Guizot argued that representative government is nothing other than a means of combining various social interests to form a genuine unity reflecting the complex nature and composition of modern society. In this view, the purpose of representative government is to bring plurality to "true" unity and to avoid the imposition of a fallacious social unity. The institutions of representative government publicly recognize and sanction the existence of social and political pluralism, which plays a key role in the preservation of political freedom by allowing different ideas, interests, and principles to peacefully coexist in society. Where this pluralism is lacking, confusion and anarchy will inevitably ensue in the long term. As we have already seen, Guizot also developed this theme in *Histoire de la civilisation en Europe*. In the infancy of society, he argued, there is no single general principle ruling over the entire society. The beginning of society is a time when individuality reigns supreme and man considers no one but himself and obeys nothing but his own passions and instincts. An extended and permanent society is then impossible, because there is no general rule or principle regulating social interaction. Social progress consists precisely in substituting public powers for particular wills and achieving genuine unity in plurality through the institutions of representative government.[7] This unity represents the fundamental condition of the creation of a legal order that prevents any power in the state from encroaching upon its rivals and usurping their prerogatives.[8]

A clearer sense of the Doctrinaires' reinterpretation of the meaning of representation may be obtained by examining their views on the relation between *civil equality* and *political inequality*. According to Guizot, in every society there are two trends that work in opposite directions. The first one produces "legitimate" forms of inequality, while the second one maintains (or restores) civil equality between individuals. Both trends are natural, inevitable, and legitimate. Their effects are also salutary insofar as their coexistence tends to mitigate each other's excesses. The degree of legitimate inequality may vary over time and may differ from one society to another, but its underlying principle—political capacity—applies to all societies, regardless of their level of civilization and development. In Guizot's opinion, the emergence of "legitimate" forms of political inequality must always be countervailed by the equally important trend toward civil equality. On the one hand, in the absence of "legitimate" forms of inequality, society would eventually stagnate, because there is no competition between ideas and interest in society. On the other hand, in the absence of civil equality, society in the proper sense of the word cannot be established, since "might alone would dominate, and right would for ever be suppressed" (Guizot 2002, 370). The emergence of "legitimate" forms of inequality can be explained by the natural and beneficial desire to elevate ourselves, to extend our influence, and to bring to light that portion of moral power placed by God in each individual. The tendency to equality has a different origin, being derived from the right of every man not to live under the potentially arbitrary power of other individuals. As such, it has an element of universality pertaining to those rights that are common to all individuals, such as the right not to live under unequal and unfair laws imposed and maintained by force.[9]

Hence, in the Doctrinaires' view, the main object of representative government is to discover the "natural superiorities" of society and to involve them in the direction of public affairs. This idea was clearly conveyed by Victor de Broglie, who argued that "the very essence of representative government is to extract from the bosom of the nation the elite of the most enlightened men, to gather them at the top of the social edifice in a sacred place, which is not accessible to the passions of the multitude, and to make them deliberate on the interests of the state" (Broglie 1863b, 78). Worth noting is the difference between representative government and oligarchy as illustrated by the following passage in which Guizot discusses the conditions of political legitimacy:

> The conditions of legitimacy . . . may be reduced to two: the first, that the power should attach itself to and remain constantly in the hands of the best and most capable, as far, at least, as human imperfection will allow of its doing so; that the truly superior people who exist dispersed among the society should be sought for there, brought to light, and called upon to unfold the social law, and to exercise power. The second, that the power legitimately constituted should respect the legitimate liberties of those over whom it exercises itself.[10]

True legitimacy, argued Guizot, is incompatible with physical force or wealth and is intimately connected with a moral idea, the idea of reason, truth, and justice. The debates in the elected chamber and the free press ought to bring to the fore the main interests and opinions of society that are engaged in constant competition for power.[11] The emphasis on pluralism and contestation underscores the Doctrinaires' belief that the "natural superiorities" should always be challenged to prove their legitimacy in the eyes of the public and may never be allowed to exercise power absolutely in society. The goal of representative government is to constantly search for the superiorities of all kinds that exist in society, to elevate them to positions of power, and after having placed them in those positions, to constrain them to use power only publicly and by means that are accessible to everyone.[12]

To conclude, the principles and institutions of representative government foster concern for the public good and promote moderation. They institutionalize and regulate political opposition and place rival parties and interests into a proper framework by providing room for deliberation and allowing the opposition to express and publicly justify its views.[13] Representative government is a regime that requires mutual sacrifices and transactions among various social interests and provides an arena in which these interests are publicly expressed, debated, and opposed, while all parties involved in the struggle for power learn how to bargain, compromise, tolerate, and reconcile their differences.[14] In *Des moyens de gouvernement et d'opposition*, Guizot described the nature of representative government as follows:

> It forms the parties, but it does not leave them alone. It places the public between them and forces them to get closer to the latter, to recruit themselves in its bosom, and to triumph only if sanctioned by the public. If at the beginning, the parties have a strong interest in constituting themselves and are strongly divided, they are eventually obliged to modify and give up some of their excessive claims, and to dedicate themselves to the service of the country rather than to the exclusive pursuit of their particular interests. Thus, power acquires clear and resolute opinions; and these opinions are at the same time constrained to moderate and adapt themselves to general needs and sentiments. (Guizot 1821, 318)

As such, representative government is a regime of debate, compromise, moderation, and restraint, a regime whose institutions are instrumental in revealing and discarding false political ideas and principles regarding the organization of society. It is not only a "turbulent and noisy regime," but also one of "patience and prudence,"[15] based on discussion, publicity (openness), contestation, and negotiation.

Political Capacity

Let us reconsider for a moment the relation between political democracy and representative government. In Guizot's view, political democracy admits that the right of sovereignty resides in the numerical majority, while representative government is the government by the majority of those who are presumed to have the "the capacity to act according to reason, truth, and justice" (Guizot 2002, 61). A similar dichotomy can be drawn between democracy and liberalism. "Democracy," wrote nineteenth-century French liberal Auguste Nefftzer, "considers only the right, while liberalism also takes into account capacity."[16] Since reason, justice, and truth are never fully embodied in any single institution or person, representative government only presumes that reason is likely to be found in the majority of the "capable" individuals but stops short of assuming that the decisions of the majority are always right. Nineteenth-century liberals believed that the principle supporting a sound electoral system is that only those who are presumed to have the required political capacity can be granted full political rights. Capacity, argued Guizot, is a fact "independent of law, which law cannot create or destroy at will, but which it ought to endeavor to recognize with precision, that it may at the same time recognize the right which flows from it."[17] Political capacity can never be proved or tested once for all and should therefore remain open to "legal suspicion" and contestation.

It is important to stress that the discourse of political capacity was the language used by *all* prominent nineteenth-century European liberals, including Constant and Tocqueville in France, Cattaneo in Italy, and J. S. Mill in England. The language of capacity calls our attention to the *aristocratic* nature of elections that were originally supposed to select representatives who were perceived as different from and superior to their electors. This elitist element was highlighted by Guizot, who claimed that the aim of elections is to discover and to constitute "the *true legitimate aristocracy*, that which is freely accepted by the people over whom it should exercise its power."[18] Far from being reactionary, this argument was in line with a long tradition of thinking in political philosophy that affirmed the fundamental *dissimilarity* between electors and representatives. In spite of the ambiguities associated with its definition, the concept of capacity allowed nineteenth-century liberals to legitimize a new economic, social, and political hierarchy based on a novel set of values and principles.[19] Even left-of-center liberals such as Tocqueville and Barrot considered political capacity as the most appropriate means of giving the "necessary elasticity"[20] to the right to vote that allowed the gradual extension of the franchise. Nineteenth-century liberals expressed skepticism toward large-scale political participation and universal suffrage and feared that, by giving equal weight to every vote, elections would reward ignorance and prejudice instead of knowledge and reason. Liberals opposed universal suffrage because they viewed it as a rudimentary political instrument that contained the seeds of anarchy and destruction.[21] Moreover, when it was not rejected as a dangerous political idea, the introduction of universal suffrage was seen as premature. In liberal circles, the fear was that universal suffrage would become a means by which people would give vent to unruly instincts and passions that would threaten social order.[22]

Hence, to claim that the language of capacity was conservative or reactionary simply because it rejected universal suffrage would be inaccurate since, by using the discourse of capacity, liberals looked *forward*, not backward. They accepted the rising equality of conditions as an accomplished fact and maintained that the only way to adjust political institutions to the new social order was by means of gradual reform. The corollary of this idea was that the main elements of capacity—that is, the property and the education required for the exercise of political rights—vary to a significant extent with the nature of social condition, being determined by the traditions, customs, mores, laws, education, and the structure of property of each society.[23] As such, the discourse of capacity was the foundation of nineteenth-century liberal political culture. It gave European liberals the opportunity to pursue progressive reforms, while striking a middle ground between the radical left and the extreme right. Liberals paid special attention to the conditions that made possible the progressive extension of the suffrage but disagreed on the speed with which electoral reforms were to be carried out in practice. Through the language of capacity, they were able to legitimize a new political hierarchy in accord with the new spirit of the age.[24] Political capacity was seen as a "filtration of democracy"[25] that was supposed to reconcile order, tradition, and political inequality with liberty, progress, and civil equality.

Nonetheless, the actual definition of capacity and the interpretation of its components triggered vigorous controversies in Parliament and the press. What entitles an individual to exercise full political rights? Should capacity be defined on the basis of class criteria or individual criteria? What is the relation between capacity, property, and education? How does this relation change over time? The answers given to these questions highlighted the key role played by property and education in the definition of capacity. In *Principes de politique* (1815), Benjamin Constant considered property qualifications as indispensable to the proper functioning of representative government. He believed that property alone made men capable of exercising political rights,[26] because it established and preserved between individuals stable and uniform ties, protected their interests, and taught them how altruism and self-interest could be combined. "Property," argued Constant (1988, 212), "sets [people] on guard against the imprudent sacrifice of the happiness and tranquility of others by including in that sacrifice their own well-being and forcing them to calculate for themselves. It forces them to descend from the heights of chimerical theories and impracticable extravagances by reestablishing between them and the other members of the association numerous relations and common interests." While rejecting strong property qualifications for the exercise of public functions, Constant acknowledged that it was desirable that representative offices be occupied "by men, if not from the wealthy classes, at least in easy circumstances" (Constant 1988, 212). Constant's argument overlapped with the justification of capacity advanced by other nineteenth-century liberals, who argued that those who are kept in eternal dependence by poverty are "neither more knowledgeable than children in public affairs, nor more interested than foreigners in national prosperity" (Constant 1988, 214).

Capacity also played a central role in J. S. Mill's writings, most notably in his essays "The Spirit of the Age" and "Civilization," as well as in *Considerations on Representative Government* (1861). Mill was concerned that wealth alone might be mistaken for true political capacity. In wrestling with the tension between liberalism (defined as a discourse about capacity) and political democracy (defined as universal suffrage), he reached a set of conclusions that were more or less similar to Guizot's and Constant's ideas on this topic. To be sure, Mill thought that in the "natural" state of society, those who have a superior moral and intellectual education ought to be given greater say in the direction of political affairs than those who lack education. "Society may be said to be in its *natural* state," argued Mill (1986a, 252), "when worldly power and moral influence, are habitually and undisputedly exercised by the fittest persons . . . by those of its members who possess the greatest capacity for such management." The opposite situation occurs in a transitional state, when "world power and the greatest existing capacity for worldly affairs are no longer united but severed" (Mill 1986a, 252).

In *Utilitarianism, Liberty, Representative Government*, Mill defended a voting-plurality scheme according to the principle "every one is entitled to some influence, but the better and wiser to more than others" (Mill 1972, 288). In his opinion, this was the path that would lead to the fulfillment of the true ideal of representative government. Distinguished individuals must command a superior degree of respect and should be have numerous opportunities to participate in the government of society. Mill argued:

> If, with equal virtue, one is superior to the other in knowledge and intelligence—or if, with equal intelligence, one excels the other in virtue, the opinion, the judgment, of the higher moral or intellectual being is worth *more* than that of the inferior. . . . One of the two, as the wiser or better man, has a claim to *superior weight* . . . a *higher* figure being assigned to the suffrages of those whose opinion is entitled to greater weight. There is not, in this arrangement anything invidious to those to whom it assigns the lower degrees of influence. Entire exclusion from a voice in the common concerns is one thing: the concession to others of a *more potential voice*, on the ground of *greater capacity* for the management of the joint interests, is another. (Mill 1972, 283–84; emphasis added)

Mill's real position on voting and capacity was, however, more nuanced and complex than this passage suggests. He not only denied that property alone suffices to confer political rights, but also insisted that those who have superior education ought to be held under tight(er) public scrutiny, in such a way that they would be unable to pass legislation that could strengthen their privileges at the expense of other social classes.

Needless to say, the concept of "natural aristocracy" was not a discovery of Mill. In a famous letter sent to John Adams in 1813, Jefferson referred to two forms of aristocracy, *natural* and *artificial*, and argued that privileges based on wealth and birth constitute "artificial" aristocracy, while virtue and talent create "natural" aristocracy. "The natural aristocracy," wrote Jefferson, "I consider as the most precious gift of nature, for the instruction, the trusts, and government of society."[27] The idea of granting political power to those who displayed superior talent and virtue also loomed large in the *Federalist Papers*. In *Federalist* 57, Madison argued that the aim of every political constitution ought to be the elevation into positions of power of those "men who possess most wisdom to discern, and most virtue to pursue, the common good of the society."[28] To his credit, Madison added that it was necessary to take the most effectual precautions for keeping these prominent individuals virtuous while they continued to hold the trust of the public. The Anti-Federalist writers also acknowledged the importance of social (natural) superiorities created by wealth, talent, birth, and education. As Melanchthon Smith put it, "the author of nature has bestowed on some greater capacities than on others—birth, education, talents, and wealth create distinctions among men as visible and of as much influence as titles, starts, and garters."[29] It is in the "natural" course of things, he added, that the government of society falls into the hands of "natural superiorities" who command a superior degree of respect.

The point that tends to be neglected today is that education, talent, virtue, and wealth create important distinctions and differences among human beings *even* in a modern democratic society in which hereditary aristocratic privileges no longer obtain. Representative institutions must publicly sanction these differences, but they must do it *only* in such a way that the principle of distinction underpinning representative government does *not* lead to new and illegitimate forms of aristocratic privileges incompatible with the principles of modern democracy.

The Triumph of the Middle Class

Not surprisingly, the Doctrinaires also considered education and property as the most important components of political capacity. They believed that it would be better to have a limited number of individuals capable of exercising political rights than a despondent mass of illiterate citizens invested with full political rights, but who are prone to succumb to ruthless political demagogues and mob flatterers. As Victor de Broglie once argued, "A hundred and twenty thousand French citizens who are represented are worth more than two million individuals who alienate their rights without reflecting on what they actually do."[30]

The focus on the *quality* of political representation was a recurrent theme in the Doctrinaires' writings. In every society, claimed Guizot, there are natural electors, "*des électeurs tout faits*," whose existence ought to be properly acknowledged and protected by the legislator. Referring to the qualities that made citizens capable of exercising political rights, Guizot argued that those who have the right to vote ought to be individuals capable of understanding the general interests of society and who are free to dispose of their person and wealth as they think fit. In addition to property, political capacity also requires a certain level of knowledge and education. It will be remembered that Guizot defined capacity as the faculty of acting according to the precepts of reason, truth, and justice in the pursuit of the general interests of society. His approach rests upon the assumption that the true law of government is the law of reason, truth, and justice, which no one fully possesses, "but which certain men [were] more capable than others of seeking and discovering" (Guizot 2002, 61).

A similar point was made by Royer-Collard in his parliamentary speeches. As the sole principle supporting a sound electoral system,[31] capacity grants full political rights only to those individuals presumed capable of using them reasonably and withdraws it from those presumed to lack this capacity. As such, political capacity must *not* be conceived of as an inherited class privilege, and the lack of capacity in an individual case should *not* be interpreted as a permanent characteristic. The nature of capacity, argued Royer-Collard, is such that it changes over time as the equality of conditions becomes more widespread in society. "Our country," he argued, "which had been the domain of privilege for a long time, has been conquered by equality. . . . Privilege has descended into the grave and no human effort could bring it back to life."[32] Yet, continued Royer, it is undeniable that even modern democratic society needs a class of enlightened and independent individuals, "*une élite de citoyens éclairés et independents*,"[33] that cuts across social classes and groups. In a democratic regime, this natural elite is constantly recruited and extracted from society by the institutions of representative government. In the Doctrinaires' opinion, what defines *le citoyen capacitaire* is neither the membership in a certain social group or class nor wealth in itself, but the degree to which an individual possesses a certain "social intelligence,"[34] defined as the capacity to form clear and coherent ideas about public interest and social order.

All these ideas underlay the legislative initiatives of the Doctrinaires during the Restoration. Guizot and his friends explicitly opposed a proposal seeking to create special electoral colleges that would have represented in the elected chamber (only) two great social interests, the landed property and the industrial property. The Doctrinaires argued that the predominance of the middle classes must *not* lead to the prevalence of a narrowly defined class interest; on the contrary, it should express the predominance of reason, which, in their view, could never be contained within the limits of any single class. At the same time, the Doctrinaires went to great length to argue that, far from being arbitrary and transitory, the rise of the middle class was an inevitable social fact with strong historical roots. "The influence of the middle class is a fact," claimed Royer-Collard, "a powerful and impressive fact; it is a living theory. . . . The centuries had prepared it; the Revolution had declared it. The new interests belong to this class. Its security cannot be affected without also endangering at the same time the established order."[35] At the same time, the Doctrinaires maintained that the purpose of the Charter of 1814 was *not* to create an oligarchy of wealth.[36] To be sure, they denounced *l'oligarchie de la richesse* as "the most absurd of all types of oligarchy," lacking any moral and political authority (Royer-Collard 1861a, 409–10). The bourgeoisie, argued Guizot, must remain an open and inclusive class whose strength was expected to increase with the rapid diffusion of property in society and the growth of industrial and liberal professions.[37] It is worth noting that Guizot and his friends often used the two terms *middle class* and *bourgeoisie* interchangeably. One might speculate that for Guizot, *bourgeoisie* was a more historical term, while *middle class* represented a more present-oriented notion.[38] What is beyond dispute, however, is the intentional vagueness of his definition of the middle class (bourgeoisie, third estate).

In a famous parliamentary discourse from May 1837 that was printed and distributed in approximately thirty thousand copies, Guizot acknowledged: "Today as in 1817, as in 1820 or 1830, I want, seek, and serve with all my efforts the political preeminence of the middle classes in France, the definitive organization of this great victory which the middle classes won against privilege and absolute power from 1789 to 1830."[39] In his memoirs, he described the middle class as the most powerful defender of the new social interests and argued that its social mission, properly understood, prevented it from becoming a new type of aristocracy that could exercise an exclusive domination in modern society:

Two ideas constitute the great features of modern civilization; I sum them up in these terms. There are certain universal rights inherent in man's nature, and which no system can legitimately withhold from any one; there are individual rights which spring from personal merit alone, without regard to the external circumstances of birth, fortune, or rank, and which every one who has them in

himself should be permitted to exercise. . . . Which of these two principles promotes or even permits the exclusive supremacy of the middle classes? Assuredly, neither the one nor the other. . . . Such principles are irreconcilable
with exclusive supremacy. That of the middle class as of every other, would be
in direct contradiction to the ruling tendencies of modern society. The middle
classes have never, amongst us, dreamed of becoming privileged orders.
(Guizot 1858b, 164–65)

Once again, Guizot resorted to the lessons of history in order to justify the
political claims of the bourgeoisie. In the seventh chapter of *Histoire de la
civilisation en Europe*, Guizot drew a parallel between the third estate (the
commons), the middle class, and the burgesses of the Middle Ages. He argued that the commons and the third estate of 1789 were the heirs to an
older tradition of self-government whose roots could be traced back to the
twelfth century. Guizot described the administration of the free towns that
fixed their own taxes, elected their own magistrates, and held their own public assemblies for deliberating upon public matters. While praising the
burghers' passion for liberty, he also pointed out their "prodigious timidity, .
. . their humility, the excessive modesty of their pretensions as to the government of the country" (Guizot 1997a, 131) that limited their political influence. The modern bourgeoisie gradually emerged as the result of the progressive enfranchisement of the burghers. If in the twelfth century "it
consisted almost entirely of merchants traders carrying on a petty commerce,
and of small proprietors either of land or houses," three centuries later the
bourgeoisie also included "advocates, physicians, learned men of all sorts,
and all the local magistrates" (Guizot 1997a, 129–30).

The modern bourgeoisie, continued Guizot, is of an entirely different
character. It has a certain loftiness of ambition and determination that was
not to be found six centuries earlier. The new class is aware of its power and
seeks to exercise it with great resolution; its political views are bold and
wide and its desire to be employed in public affairs sincere and ardent. This
class is placed in the middle of society, at equal distance between the lower
and upper classes. As Royer-Collard claimed, above the middle class one
finds a dangerous tendency to absolute domination and arrogance against
which society must protect itself; below the middle class, there is ignorance,
passivity, and dependence.[40] In turn, Rémusat argued: "The aristocracy of
capacity and services, with the middle class as judge: this is, in our opinion,
the regime that is most appropriate to France."[41] On this point, the Doctrinaires' views on the middle class had a clear Aristotelian ring. They claimed
that the middle class is the repository of common sense and distinguishes it-

self through hard work, practical virtue, and sound judgment. In other words, in the middle condition of life, individuals are most ready to follow rational principles and are inclined toward social peace more than any other class in society, whereas those who live in luxury or extreme poverty find it difficult to follow rational principles in their lives. The members of the middle class are more likely to obey the laws, to submit to legitimate authority, and to pursue interests that also serve and promote the general interests of the community.[42]

The Electoral Law of 1817

The electoral law of 1817 was one of the most important pieces of legislation passed during the Bourbon Restoration. What were its underlying principles and what was its symbolical meaning? The debates triggered by the various drafts of this bill marked a turning point in the politics of that time and highlighted the complex nature of elections and representative government that combine both democratic and aristocratic elements.[43] The law of 1817 sought to "cure" the country of the revolutionary spirit that was regarded as the primary cause of political instability in France. As Guizot explained in his memoirs:

> A ruling idea inspired the bill of the 5th of February, 1817—to fix a term to the revolutionary system, and to give vigour to the constitutional Government. At that epoch, universal suffrage had ever been, in France, an instrument of destruction or deceit: of destruction, when it had really placed political power in the hands of the multitude; of deceit, when it had assisted to annul political rights for the advantage of absolute power, by maintaining, through the vain intervention of the multitude, a false appearance of electoral privilege. To escape, in fine, from that routine of alternate violence and falsehood, to place political power in the region within which the conservative interests of social order naturally predominate with enlightened independence, and to secure to those interests, by the direct election of deputies from the country, a free and strong action upon its Government,—such were the objects, without reserve or exaggeration, of the authors of the electoral system of 1817. (Guizot 1858b, 161–62)

The Doctrinaires maintained that all those presumed to have the required political capacity should be recognized as equal among themselves. The law, claimed Royer-Collard, does not—and cannot—grant capacity by itself; it is only supposed to identify what makes individuals capable of exercising full political rights.[44] In modern society based on civil equality and publicity, careers ought to be open to everyone and must reward talent, not birth. The symbolical meaning of the law was nicely conveyed by Guizot, who argued that "in principle, this bill cut short the revolutionary theories of the supremacy of numbers, and of a specious and tyrannical equality; in fact, it brought the new society under the shelter from the threats of counterrevolution."[45]

To be sure, the electoral law of 1817 abolished the system of indirect election favored by the *ultras* that provided for two degrees of election and two types of electoral colleges: *collèges électoraux de canton* and *collèges électoraux de département*. The first type of colleges consisted of the sixty wealthiest individuals, in addition to various categories of functionaries who were electors by right. These colleges nominated the departmental electors according to a fixed criterion determined by the monarch. At the second level, the group of electors included prominent ecclesiastical figures (archbishops, bishops), the sixty wealthiest individuals of each county, and those functionaries who were electors by right. The new law adopted the system of *direct election* according to which every French citizen of at least thirty years of age, who paid at least 300 francs of direct taxes, had the right to vote. The candidates had to be forty or over and had to pay at least 1,000 francs of taxes. A fifth of the chamber was renewed annually and the government had the right to appoint the presidents of each electoral college.[46] The law also stipulated the formation of a single electoral college supposed to meet in the chief town of each department. It established the direct nomination of deputies by departmental colleges by means of a multiple vote system (*scrutin de liste*).

Guizot favored direct elections because they gave to all those who had the required capacity the opportunity to make an informed decision about who would best represent their interests. Indirect elections placed an unnecessary screen between electors and Parliament and weakened the electors' ability to have a significant influence on public and political affairs. "The result," argued Guizot (2002, 350), "is distant and uncertain and inspires little interest; and the same men who will unitedly display great discernment and animation in the choice of their municipal officers, would give their suffrage blindly and coldly to subsequent electors whom their thoughts never follow into the future in which they interfere so little." In Royer-Collard's opinion, too, there was a necessary relation between the equality of electors and the system of direct election, the latter being a direct consequence of the Charter: "The equality of electors, the equality of votes, and direct elections, are all one and the same thing" (Royer-Collard 1861b, 23).

The main limitation of the electoral law of 1817 lay in the small size of the French electorate. Out of a population of 29 million, only approximately

90,000 citizens had the right to vote (in his memoirs, Guizot gave 140,000 as the correct figure, but this figure is open to discussion). It would be interesting to compare the provisions of new law to the legislation adopted during the early years of the Revolution. As Patrice Guéniffey demonstrated in his magisterial study of elections during the French Revolution (1993, 96–97), in 1789, the number of those who were given the right to vote suddenly rose to 300,000, representing 15.7 percent of the entire population and 61.5 percent of the adult population. In comparison, at the same time, England had only 338,000 electors, representing 4 percent of the entire population and 17.2 percent of the adult population. The system set up in France in 1789 distinguished between the right to elect deputies and the right to be elected and endorsed by indirect elections and certain property qualifications.[47] In August 1792, property or tax qualifications were abolished, but the principle of indirect election was retained. Universal suffrage was established, but women, servants, and individuals with no permanent place of residence were excluded from the vote. Two years later, the right to vote was made dependent on the ability to read and write; during Thermidor, the electorate rose to more than five million.[48]

Needless to say, it is possible to interpret the law of 1817 as extremely conservative because of the limited franchise that denied a significant part of the adult population the right to vote. Nonetheless, in spite of this obvious limitation, the law acquired a fundamental symbolical dimension and was regarded as a significant triumph of the liberal camp. "From the public," wrote Guizot (1858b, 162), "and even from what was already designated the liberal party, it encountered but slight opposition. [There was] no declared or active hostility." The law sanctioned the rise and preponderance of the middle class, consisting mostly of electors who paid between 300 and 500 francs in taxes. The meeting of voters in the capital of each department favored the liberals and the urban bourgeoisie, because it limited the political influence of the landed property in the countryside, traditional supporters of the ultra-royalists. The landed gentry continued to play an important role in politics, but the law made no distinction between great and small proprietors. It gave the same political rights to those who paid as little as 300 francs in taxes as to those who paid as much as 6,000 francs in taxes. The goal of the law was to strengthen the influence, "not exclusive, but preponderating,"[49] of the middle classes, that was in keeping with—and demanded by—the spirit of free institutions and the interests of the "new France" that had emerged from the ruins of the Revolution.

The *ultras* were quick to understand that the future of representative government depended to a great extent on the intricate details of the new electoral law. They mounted a strong parliamentary opposition by arguing that that law was too democratic because it endorsed an artificial equality among electors.[50] Using a good dose of skillful rhetoric and political opportunism, the ultraroyalists claimed that the new legislation violated the equality of electors by promoting the interests of a limited group of electors—those paying between 300 and 500 francs in taxes—at the expense of other social categories. The *ultras* maintained that the law must represent all social interests and argued that the true object of representation is not the individual, but the community.[51] They also opposed the formation of large local electoral assemblies, because they feared that the latter would diminish the influence of local landlords (landed gentry) over peasants.

Finally, the ultraroyalists denounced the middle class as the "revolutionary" element of society and ridiculed it for its alleged semi-ignorance, heterogeneity, and lack of a true esprit de corps. "It is above all this middle class," wrote Villèle, "that must be annihilated, because it is entirely revolutionary and semi-ignorant."[52] In turn, Bonald warned that the law would bring forth and legitimize the triumph of a despicable "aristocracy of mediocrity"[53] and money. "You are degrading all citizens," protested La Bourdonnaye; "it is the entire population that you enslave to the golden veal, the aristocracy of wealth, the most powerful and violent of all types of aristocracy."[54] The *ultras* also took liberals to task for allegedly fostering new and pernicious forms of social exclusion by creating a disproportion between that part of the nation which was admitted to vote and those citizens who were excluded from voting altogether.[55] Needless to say, the objections raised by ultraconservatives to the new law were far from being consistent and were motivated in large part by their own political agenda. It would be difficult, for example, to reconcile the argument that one hundred thousand electors could not be considered as the true interpreters of the interests of the people with the warnings against the potential dangers to social order arising from the extension of suffrage. Similarly, their claims against the new form of social exclusion generated by the law of 1817 sound demagogical in the mouths of those who praised the values and principles of the Old Regime.

Hence, describing the Doctrinaires as defenders of a "reactionary" regime that denied political rights to large strata of the population would not render justice to their political philosophy. It must be emphasized again and again that they championed an open meritocratic system based on upward social mobility, civil equality, and the diffusion of education and property in society. Within the Doctrinaires' group, there were, however, significant nuances that reflected their different views on the extension of suffrage. In this respect, Rémusat[56] ultimately proved to be more democratic than Guizot and

Royer-Collard. At the same time, true to their belief in the need for fostering social pluralism that would prevent any one single group or class from imposing its absolute domination in society, the Doctrinaires stopped short of espousing the elitist-technocratic conceptions of Comte and his disciples. Such attempts at creating new scientific-industrial elites would have been, to use Guizot's own words, "strangely ignorant and insane" (Guizot 1858b, 162), because they contradicted the fundamental principles of modern society: political freedom, civil equality, and social pluralism.

Rights and Capacity

What place do rights occupy in the Doctrinaires' writings? Did Guizot and his colleagues lack a full-fledged theory of rights? How are we to interpret the relation between publicity defined as the cornerstone of representative government and elections? What is the relation between capacity, rights, and elections? To answer all these questions, we must return to Guizot's essay on elections (originally published in 1826) and his forays into the history of representative government.

Let us begin by considering the following passage that sums up a long discussion of the English electoral system in volume two of *Histoire des origines du gouvernement représentatif*:

> The true way to diffuse political life in all directions, and to interest as great a number of citizens as possible in the concerns of the State, is not to make them all combine in the same acts, although they may not all be equally capable of performing them; but to confer upon them all those rights which they are capable of exercising. Rights are worth nothing unless they are *full*, *direct*, and *efficacious*. In place of perverting political rights by weakening them, under the pretext of giving them diffusion, let local liberties everywhere exist, guaranteed by *real rights*. (Guizot 2002, 350; emphasis added)

What did Guizot intend to say when claiming that "rights are worth nothing unless they are full, direct, and efficacious" and that "liberty cannot exist except by possession of rights, and rights are worthless if they are not themselves powers" (Guizot 2002, 331)? His position on this issue sought to strike a middle ground between two rival conceptions of rights. On the one hand, he maintained that the principle attaching electoral right to political capacity is universal and applies to all societies regardless of their level of civilization and development. On the other hand, Guizot argued that, while all individuals have equal rights with regard to liberty, there are only limited political rights in matters pertaining to the government of society regardless of the form of government.[57] As "social powers," these rights are part of the government of society and therefore ought to be distributed according to each person's presumed political capacity.

Worth noting is the emphasis on the existence of "legitimate" forms of inequality that nineteenth-century liberals regarded as *compatible* with the principles of representative government and modern society. The liberals' position on this issue was a nuanced one. As we have already seen, Guizot stressed that "it would be dangerous and vain to pretend to regulate, beforehand and for ever, this part of the electoral system of a free people" (Guizot 2002, 337). No law should attempt to define capacity once and forever, because the conditions of capacity and the external signs by which it can be recognized are essentially *variable*. "New capacities form and declare themselves by new symptoms" (Guizot 2002, 337) and the distribution of political rights must follow and reflect the formation of new capacities in society. That is why Guizot and his fellow Doctrinaires regarded the right to vote as a variable and complex right that depends on the social condition, the moral and material development of society, and the progress of civilization:

> This is a variable and complex right. It is neither inherent in all human beings nor independent of the various stages of society. Its original and constant principle is capacity. This right varies according to the relation between the capacity of individuals and the affairs of society in which it must be exercised. If capacity becomes more general, the right to vote will spread as well. It will be more widespread in the case of an enlightened people than an ignorant people. Its legitimate boundary constantly moves depending on the material and moral development of society. This boundary has often been fixed by arbitrary or violent means, rarely according to justice and truth. . . . It must be determined based on facts and . . . according to the nature and degree of civilization. In the midst of a large and civilized society, political capacity is manifested by various signs. As society develops and becomes more complex, the number of these signs increases. Sometimes, the presence of certain material conditions presumes the existences of moral conditions to which capacity is attached; other times, the profession suffices to prove that the moral conditions are fulfilled. (Guizot 1862, 391–92)

Guizot criticized those natural-rights theories based on the questionable assumption that individuals live as monads in a fictitious state of nature. These theories neglect the fact that human life and action are always embedded in complex social relations and exchanges. "It is not by considering man in isolation, in his single nature and individually, that his rights may be discovered," wrote Guizot. "The idea of right implies that of relation. Right can be declared only when relation is established. The fact of a connection, of an approximation, in a word, of society is implied in the very word right" (Guizot 2002, 361). Consequently, Guizot rejected the abstract, ahistorical justification of individual rights and preferred a more sociological and historical explanation that took into account the social, cultural, and political transformations brought forth by the progress of civilization. In his essay on elections, he made a seminal distinction between *permanent* (universal) and *variable* (nonuniversal) rights. Permanent rights belong to all human beings since all individuals are endowed with reason and the capacity to search for truth, reason, and justice. These rights include, for example, the right to obey only legitimate laws and the right not to be subject to arbitrary power. The most important variable right is the right to vote that belongs only to certain categories of individuals who have the capacity of exercising them. These rights evolve over time as old rights are constantly being replaced by new ones that reflect better the composition of society, its mores, social relations, and the changes in property relations.[58]

Guizot emphasized that all universal rights are *civil* rights whose main role is to protect individual liberties and to create an environment in which individuals are free to pursue their own interests while respecting the equal rights and freedoms of other citizens. As such, civil rights serve as the foundation of liberty and must be equal for all individuals. They include the right to assemble and to form associations, the right to practice the religion of one's choice, and so forth. The attempt to reconcile the two types of rights was bound to create significant and ultimately insurmountable tensions in the Doctrinaires' writings. In his memoirs, Guizot recognized the difficulty of finding an adequate solution to this problem. "There are certain universal rights inherent in man's nature," he argued (1858b, 164), "which no system can legitimately withhold from any one; there are individual rights which spring from personal merit alone, without regard to the external circumstances of birth, fortune, or rank, and which every one who has them in himself should be permitted to exercise." Modern legislators, added Guizot, must not commit the same mistakes as their ancient predecessors, who considered individuals only with regard to the social context in which they lived and refused to acknowledge the existence of individual rights.[59]

It is interesting to note in passing that, on this view, the right to property does not (should not) trump other rights; the importance of property derives mainly from the fact that it contributes to the protection of other civil rights. But rights, affirmed Guizot, can never be ends in themselves. In an important parliamentary discourse of October 5, 1831, Guizot advocated a position similar to the one advanced in 1826. His argument can be summarized as follows. There are universal rights that must be protected and strictly enforced, because they constitute the foundation of civil equality and equal moral dignity. They include the right to be protected by public authorities against the injustice done by other persons, the right to live one's life as one pleases, as long as one does not harm the life of other persons or does not encroach upon their rights. Political rights must be granted, however, only according to capacity, because prudence requires that the extension of political rights be accompanied by solid guarantees for the stability of social order.[60]

The main problem that the Doctrinaires' theory of capacity left unsolved was the potential deficit of legitimization at the heart of their doctrine of representative government. The resistance mounted by Guizot to the extension of suffrage in the last years of the July Monarchy, when he came to espouse strong conservative views, illustrates the tensions inherent in the Doctrinaires' elitist liberalism. From a theoretical point of view, it might even be argued that there was nothing, strictly speaking, "inevitable" about the Revolution of 1848 that put an end to the constitutional monarchy supported by the Doctrinaires. Had Guizot's cabinet not sought refuge in a conservative politics of resistance out of touch with the spirit of the age, and had he accepted the extension of suffrage to all citizens who paid 100 francs in taxes, things might have taken a different turn and constitutional monarchy might have survived in France after all. Let us finally turn to examining the Doctrinaires' views on publicity and freedom of the press.

Notes

1. For more details, see Guizot 2002, 370–71. Also see the following passage from Rémusat: "Nulle souveraineté absolue n'est realisée en ce monde; mais, invisible et présente, la raison suprême parle à la raison humaine, et ne parle qu'à elle. . . . *À qui donc appartient le pouvoir politique? Aux plus capables de faire prévaloir la loi commune de la société, à savoir, la justice, la raison, la vérité.* Quelle est la meilleure constitution politique? La plus propre à mettre en lumière la vérité sur chaque chose, et à faire arriver le pouvoir dans les mains de ceux qui sauront le mieux exercer" (Rémusat 1829, 157; emphasis added).

2. A critique of the "natural vice" of power can be found in chapter 14 of Guizot's *History of Civilization in Europe* (Guizot 1997a, 228–45). Also see Guizot 2002, 371–76.

3. Writes Guizot: "C'est le propre du système représentatif, et c'est aussi son plus grand bienfait, de révéler sans cesse la société à son gouvernement et à elle-même, et le gouvernement à lui même et à la société. Le pouvoir et le public viennent sans

cesse s'y présenter l'un à l'autre, pour apprendre à connaître à la fois, et leur propre état intérieur, et leur situation réciproque" (Guizot 1817d, 257).

4. See especially Guizot 2002, 285–97. On the "true" principles of representative government, see Guizot 2002, 52–54, 226–27, 345–47.

5. On this issue, see Friedrich 1948.

6. See Pouthas 1923a, 322. On this issue, also see Rosanvallon 1989, 420–28, and Rosanvallon 1991, 137.

7. Pace Rosanvallon (1985, 60–61), I would like to argue that, in Guizot's opinion, this process did not necessarily entail centralization. Note that Guizot referred to *unity in plurality*, not centralization.

8. For more details, see Guizot 1997a, 47–63, 79–81.

9. For more details, see Guizot 2002, 369–70.

10. Guizot 2002, 89. On legitimacy, also see Guizot 1997a, 50, where Guizot spoke of the "true" legitimacy that belongs only to reason, justice, and right.

11. See Guizot 2002, 348–49; Guizot 1862, 412.

12. See Guizot 1821, 165–66; Guizot 1862, 406.

13. See Guizot 1821, 306–7, 318.

14. Writes Guizot: "Le régime représentatif est, en dernière analyse, un régime de *sacrifices mutuels* et de *transactions* entre les intérêts divers qui coexistent dans la société. En même temps qu'il les met en presence et aux prises, il leur impose l'absolue necessité d'arriver à un certain *terme moyen,* à une certaine mesure d'*entente* ou de *tolérance réciproque* qui puisse devenir la base des lois et du gouvernement" (Guizot 1858a, 190–91; emphasis added).

15. The whole passage is worth quoting: "Le régime de la liberté politique a ses défauts comme ses mérites. Sous ce regime . . . les rivalités des partis ou des personnes, la discussion préalable retardent quelquefois des résolutions et entravent des entreprises grandes et utiles. Mais, en revanche, *que des fautes et des maux épargne,* au pouvoir et au pays, la liberté politique! *Que d'idées fausses elle dévoile et écarte!* Que de résolutions égoïstes, que d'entreprises étourdies elle étouffe dans leur germe, avant que le pouvoir et le pays s'y soient compromis sans retour! Ce *régime orageux et bruyant* est, au fond et dans la pratique définitive des affaires, *un régime de patience et de prudence*; et ses deux libertes fondamentales, la liberté de la tribune et la liberté de la presse, qui font dire et croire dans le public tant de sottises, en préviennent bien plus encore, et de bien plus graves, dans le gouvernement" (Guizot 1863a, 187–89; emphasis added).

16. Nefftzer 1997, 559. In his essay, Nefftzer gave an excellent summary of nineteenth-century liberalism as *juste milieu* between Revolution and Reaction. With regard to the gradual extension of capacity, he wrote: "[Le libéralisme] n'est pas plus réactionnaire que révolutionnaire, mais il s'efforce d'introduire par l'instruction la capacité dans les droits prématurément conquis. . . . Le libéralisme ne suppose pas chez tous les électeurs la capacité de gouverner; il ne leur reconnaît que la capacité de discerner ceux qui paraissent capables de prendre part au gouvernement" (Nefftzer 1997, 560).

17. Guizot 2002, 334. A similar argument can be found in Guizot's essay on elections (Guizot 1862, 385) and Royer-Collard's parliamentary speeches (Royer-Collard 1861b, 20–25, 35).

18. Guizot 1862, 395; emphasis added. On the aristocratic nature of elections, see Manin 1997, 132–60. On the identity between electors and representatives as a fundamental assumption of a democratic regime, see Schmitt 1996, 9–14, 26–29.

19. For more details on this issue, see the introduction in Kahan 2003.

20. The phrase is taken from Odillon Barrot's memoirs. Here is the whole passage: "Si j'insistais tant sur le principe des capacités, c'est que j'y voyais le plus sûr moyen de donner au droit électoral une élasticité nécessaire pour qu'il pût s'éteindre à mesure que l'intelligence et l'éducation politique des masses se répandaient, et en même temps pour rattacher à nos institutions toutes les influences réelles qui se produiraient dans la société. Ainsi, le principe une fois accepté, il eût été facile de faire arriver successivement au droit électoral les syndics des caisses d'épargne, les prud'hommes et autres chefs des travailleurs et de faire entrer ainsi par voie de représentation dans l'exercise actif des droits politiques toute la classe ouvrière, de manière à la faire participer au gouvernement du pays sans aucun danger" (Barrot as quoted in Rosanvallon 1985, 134).

21. This point was made by Guizot in his lectures on the origins of representative government (Guizot 2002). Also see Rosanvallon 1985, 133–40.

22. Guizot, too, referred to universal suffrage as an instrument of destruction and deceit. This view was also held during the July Monarchy and after 1848. "Le suffrage universel," wrote Joseph Ferrari in 1849, "livré à l'ignorance élèvera et brisera les hommes au hasard. . . . Le suffrage de l'ignorance fera du peuple un monster" (quoted in Rosanvallon 1985, 137). On this topic, also see Hazareesingh 1998, 42–51, 152–56, 222–27, 245–48.

23. On this point, see Guizot 2002, 33–38.

24. For an extensive treatment of this issue, see Kahan 2003.

25. I borrow this phrase from Guéniffey 1993, 41.

26. On the role of property in preserving order and liberty, also see Constant 1988, 221, 261–64.

27. The whole passage is worth quoting: "I agree with you that there is a natural aristocracy among men. The grounds of this are virtue and talents. Formerly, bodily powers gave place among the *aristoi*. But since the invention of gunpowder has armed the weak as well as the strong with missile death, bodily strength, like beauty, good humor, politeness, and other accomplishments, has become but an auxiliary ground of distinction. There is also an artificial aristocracy, founded on wealth and birth, without either virtue or talents; for with these it would belong to the first class. The natural aristocracy I consider as the most precious gift of nature, for the instruction, the trusts, and government of society. And indeed, it would have been inconsistent in creation to have formed man for the social state, and not to have provided virtue and wisdom enough to manage the concerns of the society. May we not even say that that form of government is the best, which provides the most

effectually for a pure selection of these natural *aristoi* into the offices of government?" (Jefferson to John Adams, October 28, 1813, quoted in Peterson 1975, 533–35). On the principle of distinction supporting of representative government, see Manin 1997, 94–131.

28. Rossiter 1961, 350.

29. These words are taken from a speech of Melanchthon Smith given in June 1788 and are quoted in Storing 1981, 16.

30. Victor de Broglie as quoted in Rosanvallon 1992, 214.

31. See Guizot 1862, 385, and Guizot 2002, 334.

32. Royer-Collard 1861b, 25. Auguste Nefftzer gave a concise formulation of the liberal credo: "*Tout ce qui favorise l'éducation, le travail, l'épargne et l'acquisition de la propriété est libéral.* . . . Un gouvernement libéral, le parti libéral, les esprits libéraux doivent s'appliquer, avant tout, à instruire le suffrage universel, à l'éclairer, à l'élever, à l'armer, en un mot, de capacité" (Nefftzer 1997, 562, 566; emphasis added). For an instructive discussion on the meaning of the word *liberal* during the first years of the Restoration, see Vaulabelle 1856, 33–34.

33. The phrase belongs to Barante.

34. See Royer-Collard 1861a, 276: "Un certain degree de richesse personnelle étant nécessaire aux yeux de la loi pour fonder la presumption d'un jugement libré et éclairé, c'est-à-dire la presumption du jugement politique, partout où cette presumption se rencontre elle declare l'aptitude personnelle, et l'aptitude est le fondement unique du droit; elle est le droit lui-même." According to Rosanvallon, "l'idée de capacité ne se réduit pas à la notion de cens électoral, elle est beaucoup *plus large* et presque d'une *autre nature*. Elle renvoie à une faculté indivisible d'appréhender, pour aider à le réaliser, le travail de la raison dans l'histoire, bien au-delà, donc, de la sphère de l'expérience personnelle de ceux qui en sont dotés. . . . Elle définit une '*société des intelligences*' supérieure à toutes les distinctions professionnelles de ceux qui la composent" (Rosanvallon 1985, 101; emphasis added). It is worth pointing out that Pareto applauded Guizot's ideas on the circulation and transformation of elites. Yet, the Doctrinaires' notion of elite was primarily *political* and differed from the specialized and technocratic elites advocated by Comte or Pareto.

35. Royer-Collard 1861a, 454. For a powerful defense of liberty of industry and commerce, see Barante 1821, 115–31.

36. On this issue, see Pouthas 1923a, 148–50.

37. See Royer-Collard 1861a, 289–91. Guizot held a similar view: "Il faut que la majorité d'entre eux ait, outre ses intérêts personnels, des intérêts communs et inséparables de l'intérêt de tous, afin que les élections soient nationals" (Guizot as quoted in Pouthas 1923a, 148). For a discussion of the image and social construction of the middle class in postrevolutionary France (and England), see Wahrman 1995, 273–89.

38. For more details, see Wahrman 1995, 277–80; Guizot 1863c, 74; Royer-Collard 1861a, 456.

39. Guizot 1863c, 74. Also see the following passages from *Des moyens de gouvernement et d'opposition*: "Loin de vous montrer si inquiets de l'influence de la classe

moyenne, adoptez cette influence; aidez-la à s'étendre, à se constituer. Au lieu de comprimer timidement le mouvement ascendant de cette classe, secondez-le; ce qui lui manque c'est précisément d'être accomplie. Elle est assez haut pour ne plus descendre, pas assez encore pour fournir à la société et au pouvoir cette véritable, cette légitime aristocratie dont l'un et l'autre ont besoin. . . . Voyez l'ardeur avec laquelle les jeunes gens de cette classe se précipitent vers les études sérieuses, vers les professions qui procurent la considération. Emparez-vous de cette ardeur; élevez seulement le but où elle aspire, et que, pour l'atteindre, elle ait à soutenir de plus grands travaux. . . . Montez-vous aussi bienveillans, aussi empressés pour aider et lier à vous la classe qui s'élève. Elle ne vous demande pas le privilége; c'est le concurs qu'elle réclame; qu'il soit sévère et libre" (Guizot 1821, 217–19).

40. Here is the original passage: "C'est, en effet, dans la classe moyenne que tous les intérêts peuvent trouver leur représentation naturelle. Au-dessus est un certain besoin de domination contre lequel il faut se tenir en garde; au-dessous, l'ignorance, l'habitude, inaptitude complète aux fonctions dont il s'agit" (Royer-Collard 1861a, 290).

41. Rémusat quoted in Roldán 1999, 141.

42. See, for example, Aristotle *Politics* 1295b.

43. On the aristocratic character of elections, see Manin 1997, 132–56. The importance of the French debates on the electoral law of 1817 can be compared, *toutes proportions gardées*, to the famous American debates of 1787.

44. See Royer-Collard 1861b, 20–22. Also see the following fragment: "Remarquez que les électeurs et les éligibles de la Charte, ce n'est pas tel ou tel nombre de *plus* imposés, mais tous ceux qui sont *assez* imposés pour être présumés capables de ces fonctions. . . . La présomption de capacité étant attachée à une certaine contribution, tous ceux qui l'atteignent sont *également capables*. La loi politique n'est point attributive de la capacité, mais seulement *exclusive de l'incapacité*. Ce sont là nos garanties inexpugnables et contre l'oligarchie, et contre la démocratie" (Royer-Collard 1861a, 410; emphasis added).

45. Guizot 1858b, 166. Also see the following paragraph: "Si j'ai fixé une limite à la capacité d'élire, c'est uniquement pour écarter des élections, dans l'intérêt de tous, ceux en qui cette capacité ne m'a pas paru probable, et non pour créer en faveur de quelque-uns un privilège; en fixant cette limite, je n'ai pas cherché les plus riches, j'ai cherché tous ceux dont la richesse offrait une garantie suffisante. Ce n'est pas en partant des fortunes les plus elevées que je suis descendu jusqu'à cette limite à laquelle s'arrête la capacité d'élire, c'est en m'élevant des petites fortunes jusqu'aux fortunes qui m'ont donné les garanties qu'éxigeait le bien de l'État." This fragment is taken from an article of Guizot published in *Le Moniteur* in January 1817 and is quoted in Pouthas 1923a, 149.

46. For more details on the electoral law of 1817, see Guizot 1858a, 164–71; Rosanvallon 1992, 209–30; Vaulabelle 1855, 392–99; Duvergier de Hauranne 1860, 21–60; Charléty 1939, 111–12; Hall 1909, 205–6; Bastid 1954, 221–25; Lucas-Dubreton 1929, 53–55. The electoral system is discussed in Bastid 1954, 211–40.

47. For more details on the electoral system implemented in the autumn of 1789, see Guéniffey 1993, 32–33.

48. For more details, see Guéniffey 1993, 31–105, and Manin 1997, 98–102.

49. The phrase is from Guizot 1858a, 166.

50. See Bonald 1982, 106–22. Bonald denounced the main spirit of the new electoral law in the following terms: "Si l'on adopte la loi, on aura une Chambre démocratique prise dans les classes inférieures de la propriété, et l'équilibre entre les pouvoirs sera rompu. Par cette loi, née des habitudes révolutionnaires, on exclut de fait les chefs de la propriété, et, dans l'armée destinée à repousser l'invasion des prolétaires, on place l'autorité dans la main des simples soldats" (Bonald as quoted in Charléty 1939, 111).

51. For more details, see Rosanvallon 1992, 227–28. Bonald was a leading spokesman of the *ultras* in these debates: "Si, par des lois nées des habitudes révolutionnaires, en appelant les *petits* et les *moyens* proprietaires, vous excluez de faits les *chefs de la proprieté*, c'en est fait de l'ordre social. Si, au contraire, par le sage rétablissement des *corporations*, vous rendez à la proprieté toute son influence, vous sauvez la patrie de tout danger. Je vote pour quele projet de loi soit rejeté comme anticonstitutionnel et antisocial" (Bonald as quoted in Vaulabelle 1855, 396; emphasis added).

52. Villèle as quoted in Rosanvallon 1992, 223. On this issue, also see Wahrman 1995, 285–88.

53. Bonald as quoted by Duvergier de Hauranne 1860, 37. La Bourdonnaye held a similar view: "Voyez quels sont les hommes dont vous allez réveiller l'ambition et l'audace. Ce sont des hommes que leur éducation et l'habitude des affaires portent à se croire propres à tout; ils verront la barrière levée, la carrière ouverte, et ils s'y précipiteront avec cet amour de richesses et de pouvoir qui les caractérise" (Duvergier de Hauranne 1860, 40).

54. La Bourdonnaye as quoted in Rosanvallon 1992, 220–21.

55. On this topic, see Oechslin 1960 and Duvergier de Hauranne 1860, 32–40.

56. For a similar argument, see Roldán 1999, 164–67. Here is a revealing passage from one of Rémusat's articles published in Le Globe in the 1820s: "Puisque la raison n'est ni dans une famille seule ni dans un corps héréditaire et privilégié, où donc est-elle? Dans le nombre, dit-on, dans les majorités? . . . Nous espérons qu'elle y viendra. *Un jour peut luire où la société presque entière sera éclairée, et capable de juger par elle-même.* Alors, sans distinction de fortune ou de situation, il suffira de compter les voix. Mais si nous n'en sommes plus aux temps où la société tout entière avait besoin de tuteurs, nous n'en sommes pas encore au temps où tout entière elle pourra s'en passer" (Rémusat as quoted in Roldán 1999, 174; emphasis added).

57. "En matière de liberté, il y a des droits universels, des droits égaux; en matière de gouvernement, il n'y a que des droits spéciaux, limités, inégaux" (Guizot 1863b, 309).

58. Writes Guizot: "Il y a des droits permanents et des droits variables, des droits universels et et des droits qui ne le sont pas. Tout individu possède et porte partout les premiers, à ce titre seul qu'il est né de l'homme et dresse son front vers les cieux. Les seconds ne s'attribuent à l'individu qu'à d'autres conditions; et il peut, sans que

la raison ni la justice soient offensées, faire partie d'une société où il ne les possède pas. . . . Les droits permanents et universels aboutissent tous au droit de n'obéir qu'à des lois légitimes. Les droits variables sont tous contenus dans le droit de suffrage, c'est-à-dire le droit de juger en personne, directement ou indirectement, de la légitimité des lois au pouvoir" (Guizot 1862, 386–87).

59. Here is an interesting statement of Guizot from an essay published in *Archives politiques, philosophiques et littéraires* in 1818: "L'injustice envers l'individu se produit nécessairement lorsque la législation politique et civile ne prend pas les droits personnels de l'individu pour premier fondement. . . . *Les individus seuls possèdent des droits.* Le vice des législations anciennes a été de ne considérer les individus que par les situations, et de sacrifier ainsi les droits aux faits. Le principe des législations modernes sera de reconnaître les droits là où ils existent réellement, *c'est-à-dire dans les individus*" (Guizot 1818a, 408; emphasis added).

60. Here is a fragment from this important parliamentary discourse of Guizot: "[Ces droits universels, égaux pour tous] se résument dans deux-ci: le droit de ne subir, de la part de personne, une injustice quelconque, sans être protegé contre elle par la puissance publique; et ensuite le droit de disposer de son existence individuelle selon sa volonté et son intérêt, en tant que cela ne nuit pas à l'existence individuelle d'un autre. Voilà les droits personnels, universels, égaux pour tous. De là l'égalité dans l'ordre civil et dans l'ordre moral . . . Les droits politiques, ce sont des pouvoirs sociaux; un droit politique, c'est une portion du gouvernement: quiconque l'exerce décide non seulement de ce qui le regarde personnellement, mais de ce qui regarde la société ou une portion de la société. Il ne s'agit donc pas là d'existence personnelle, de liberté individuelle; il ne s'agit pas de l'humanité en général, mais de la société, de son organisation, des moyens de son existence. De là suit que les droits politiques ne sont pas universels, égaux pour tous; ils sont spéciaux, limités. Consultez l'experience du monde; . . . des garanties ont été partout et de tout temps attachées aux droits politiques comme preuve ou présomption de la capacité nécessaire pour les exercer dans l'intérêt de la société, qui est la sphère que ces droits concernent, et sur laquelle ils agissent. . . . Les droits politiques sont nécessairement inégaux, inégalement distribués" (Guizot 1863b, 308–9).

CHAPTER NINE

~

Publicity and Representative Government

La liberté de la presse servira à la fois les souverains et les peuples; à ceux-ci elle sera une garantie, à ceux-là un moyen de gouvernement.

—Guizot

As we have already seen, the theory of representation advanced by the French Doctrinaires marked a significant departure from previous conceptions of representation. The Doctrinaires defined the latter as a dynamic process of collecting all the fragments of reason and knowledge from the bosom of society.[1] In so doing, Guizot and his colleagues assigned an important role to publicity and freedom of the press in the context of the emergence of a new social condition characterized by high social mobility, freedom of inquiry, and civil equality.

Accordingly, the Doctrinaires established the liberal definition of parliamentarism as government by discussion and highlighted the centrality of openness (publicity) to the functioning of representative institutions. The emphasis on publicity is worth underscoring for us today, since we usually define representative government by referring to free elections (competition for power) and thus tend to downplay or take for granted to a certain extent the role of publicity. What this chapter will attempt to do is to shed fresh additional light on the original relations between liberalism, the belief in discussion and openness, representative government, and democracy.

Public Opinion and Publicity:
The Eighteenth-Century Background

Before we examine in detail the Doctrinaires' ideas on publicity and freedom of the press, a few words about the emergence of public opinion and publicity in the eighteenth century are in order. As Jürgen Habermas noted (1991), the words *public*, *publicity*, and *public sphere* have a multiplicity of concurrent and overlapping meanings. Publicity can be defined as a fundamental organizational principle of modern political order; its object is the public as the carrier of public opinion in the public sphere. The latter is governed by a set of norms and rules that allow individuals to pursue common goals, to establish and modify the principles underpinning the constitution of the social, economic, and political order.

Although the notion of public opinion was slow to appear in dictionaries, its presence came to be widely felt in the eighteenth-century cultural and political European life marked by a growing tendency to individualism and equality of conditions. The concept first gained currency in England around 1730, before it appeared in the writings of the French *philosophes*. In one of his essays, entitled "Whether the British Government Inclines More to Absolute Monarchy or to a Republic," published in 1741, David Hume noted that in modern European society human affairs were entirely governed by opinion, which had replaced force. He remarked that there had been a "sudden and sensible change in the opinions of men within these last fifty years, by the progress of learning and of liberty" (Hume 1985, 51), thereby suggesting that public opinion was no longer under the control of political authorities. At the beginning, however, public opinion was closely associated with the opinion of enlightened individuals rather than with the opinion of the masses; moreover there was a clear distinction between "common opinion" and "public opinion."[2]

Across the Rhine, although the debates on liberty of the press and the meaning of *Aufklärung* addressed the issue of publicity in an oblique way,[3] its full political implications were spelled out in a more systematic manner only later, in the political writings of Kant and Hegel. It will be recalled that Kant acknowledged that in the modern world, political problems could no longer be settled by force, which was another way of arguing that in the absence of publicity, every claim upon right is bound to lose its legitimacy. Kant defined publicity as a transcendental principle of public law that can be applied to issues regarding both domestic policy and international relations. He maintained that all actions affecting the rights of other human beings ought to be compatible with the demands of publicity and pointed out that individuals have the right to form and express tentative opinions on public matters and must be allowed to revise and change their views through public debates.[4]

The framework in which Hegel discussed the role of public opinion and publicity in his *Elements of a Philosophy of Right* was different from Kant's. While claiming that public opinion deserves to be simultaneously respected and distrusted, Hegel regarded it as an essential element of modern society in which freedom of the press has become a powerful vehicle for publicly expressing the opinions and interests of society. Through public opinion, the universal is connected to the particular—in this case, the particular opinions of the many—in such a way that their synthesis reflects the eternal principles of justice in accord with the legitimate tendencies of reality.[5] As such, the growth of public opinion triggers important changes in modern society. The key point made by Hegel (and, as we shall see later, by Guizot) was that in modern society public opinion has definitively replaced coercion and is instrumental in creating a new public sphere and social power protected by freedom of speech, liberty of the press, and freedom of association. "Whatever is to achieve recognition today," argued Hegel (1991, 353; emphasis added), "no longer achieves it by force, and only to a small extent through habit and custom, but mainly through insight and *reasoned argument.*" Furthermore, argued Hegel (1991, 352), in a country where public opinion is vigorous and free, "there is a much more lively attitude towards the state than in one where the Estates have no assembly or where such assemblies are not held in public."

Nonetheless, for Hegel, public opinion defined as "the unorganized way in which the will and opinions of the people make themselves known" (Hegel 1991, 353) retained an element of uncertainty, fickleness, and subjectivity and connoted the possibility of fragmentation of the social bonds.[6] Hegel maintained that sometimes public opinion deserves to be distrusted and despised, because "it contains no criterion of discrimination and lacks the ability to raise its own substantial aspect to [the level of] determinate knowledge" (Hegel 1991, 355). In other words, public opinion lacks the rationality, universality, and objectivity that belong only to reason or the Spirit. In holding this view, Hegel voiced an older suspicion toward public opinion seen as a "feeble and imperfect light, which reveals things only by conjecture and leaves them always in uncertainty and doubt,"[7] thus being unable to protect social unity. The political implication of Hegel's statement was that public opinion cannot be the foundation of stable government as long as it wavered and is in constant flux.

From a sociological point of view, the gradual emergence of public opinion as a key political factor in modern society in general and in France in particular can be interpreted as the outcome of significant social and economic changes, such as the growth of commerce and industry. As Keith Baker demonstrated, the rise of public opinion in the French context can also be seen as a distinctively *political* invention in the larger context of the crisis of absolute monarchy. Yet, this was a slow process, which took decades to unfold. Historians have demonstrated that in eighteenth-century France, the absence of an active legislative assembly thwarted for a long time the political influence of public opinion. In 1764, a royal declaration explicitly forbade the printing of any writings that critically discussed and analyzed the fiscal practices and the administrative procedures of the kingdom of France. Open political debates were seen as "an irremediable evil"[8] that threatened social order and the foundations of the state. As a result, until as late as 1770, public opinion did not manage to articulate a new political space for itself. Nonetheless, it eventually came to be seen as the expression of a new form of social power, which developed into a powerful opponent of political absolutism.

In the last four decades of the eighteenth century, public opinion gradually acquired the status of a universal tribunal sui generis before which citizens, magistrates, and governments were called to appear and were held accountable.[9] The widespread use of notions such as *esprit public, opinion publique, bien public, cri public, conscience publique,* and *la voix du public* demonstrates the growing influence of public opinion as illustrated by many political writings of that period. For example, in an important text published in 1770, Raynal wrote that "in a nation that thinks and talks, public opinion is the rule of government, and government must never act against it without giving public reasons."[10] Twelve years later, Mercier made a similar remark: "In the last thirty years alone, a great and important revolution has occurred in our ideas. Today, public opinion has a preponderant force in Europe that cannot be resisted."[11] In his secret correspondence with Louis XVI from 1790, Mirabeau expressed a similar point of view: "Public opinion has destroyed everything; public opinion must rebuild everything."[12] He went on to qualify his statement by adding that public opinion was not always the outcome of the most enlightened minds and warned that the masses were often swayed by false ideas and principles.

This position marked a clear departure from earlier conceptions of public opinion such as Rousseau's definition of public opinion as the collective expression of the ideas, sentiments, and values embodied in a nation's customs and manners.[13] Not surprisingly, public opinion was represented as a court that enlightened and purified ideas through public discussion. In an often quoted passage, Malesherbes described public opinion as "a tribunal independent from all powers, and respected by all powers . . . that tribunal of the public . . . the sovereign judge of all the judges of the earth,"[14] to which all magistrates and politicians were accountable. His contemporary Linguet, the author of a famous pamphlet *La France plus qu'anglaise* (1788), also defined public opinion as a "supreme judge to which the most absolute tribunals are subordinated."[15] The important point made by both Malesherbes and Linguet was that public opinion functioned as an independent power, invested with an authority similar to that of a judge. This explains why public opinion was often depicted as a judge sitting on a throne in a court of last resort, supposed to redress offenses and offer comfort to the injured.

In 1781, eight years before the French Revolution, Jacques Necker, Louis XVI's finance minister, became famous when he made public the state budget for the first time in the history of the French monarchy. The public success of Necker's *Compte rendu* was tremendous: over three thousand copies were sold the first day of its publication. Justifying his decision, Necker wrote: "Darkness and obscurity favor carelessness, [while] publicity can only become an honor and a reward" (Necker 1781, 1–2). Furthermore, while in England the publicity surrounding the finances of the kingdom increased the confidence of the people in the king's government, in France the practice had always been to make a mystery of the state of finances, a strategy that had perverse effects. Necker thought that this practice was both illegitimate and ineffective and pointed out that public opinion had become "an invisible power which, without any treasury, guard, or army, legislates over the city, the court, and even the king's palaces."[16] It is worth noting that Necker, too, compared public opinion to a court of appeal before which all citizens were held accountable, regardless of their social rank or position. Nonetheless, a clear distinction must be made between Necker's argument for publicity as a useful tool for reform and later, more radical claims that publicity was incompatible with absolute monarchy. When advocating a greater role for publicity, Necker did not see publicity as a power that was supposed to replace or reverse the then existing government.

Publicity, Elections, and Political Representation

A satirical poem circulating in Germany in 1789 conveys the influence acquired by public opinion and publicity on the eve of the French Revolution: "The magic word before whose power / Even the people's masters cower, / Flapping their wigs officiously— / Prick up your years; the word—it is publicity."[17] In revolutionary France, those who opposed the principles of 1789 were publicly denounced as "poisoners" of public opinion. As Bergasse, a member of the National Assembly, put it, "before public opinion all authorities become silent, all prejudices disappear, all particular interests are effaced."[18] The laws and norms of social cooperation had to be justified in the eyes of the public through publicity, that is to say through free discussion and contestation, and were expected to be the outcome of a public competition of private arguments.

Furthermore, public opinion was regarded as the guarantee of a new set of rights, including the right to assembly, to publish, and to express freely one's political and religious views. At the same time, public opinion and publicity were also supposed to bring forth greater enlightenment and accountability and to instill sound habits of reasoning and discussion. Across the Channel, Jeremy Bentham advanced a similar argument in a piece published in 1816. "Among a people who have been accustomed to public assemblies," wrote Bentham, "the general feeling will be raised to a higher tone—sound opinion will be more common—hurtful prejudices, publicly combated, not by rhetoricians but by statesmen, will have less dominion. . . . A habit of reasoning and discussion will penetrate all classes of society."[19]

All these ideas also appeared, albeit in a different form, in Restoration France. In his political writings, Benjamin Constant elaborated on the complex relations between power and public opinion and maintained that in modern society the voice of the public or nation acts like an independent actor, whose interests can no longer be overlooked by those who hold political power. In modern society, claimed Constant, the weight of public opinion plays a seminal role in the limitation of sovereignty and the protection of individual rights, acting like a "mysterious power, present everywhere and yet invisible."[20] In turn, by drawing on his firsthand experience of American democracy, Tocqueville understood that political life in modern democratic regimes is characterized by transparency and unfettered communication of ideas made possible by freedom of the press. Yet, he also realized that public opinion cannot be regarded as an infallible judge in political, intellectual, and moral matters, because it is not entirely free from common prejudices and narrow private concerns.

As Carl Schmitt pointed out (1996, 35), Guizot's writings provided the classical formulation of parliamentarism that emphasized the central role played by publicity in modern politics. (Similar ideas can also be found in Rémusat's texts written during the Restoration.) In *Histoire des origines du gouvernement représentatif en Europe*, Guizot defined the principles of representative government as follows: (1) the powers are always forced to discuss and seek the truth together; (2) publicity and openness place the powers under the control of citizens; (3) freedom of the press allows citizens to seek the truth for themselves and to make it known to the powers that be. Since the main goal of representative government is to provide the conditions for an unfettered confrontation of interests and opinions, Guizot regarded publicity and debates as essential to creating a public sphere partly similar to the economic market, based on a free competition of interests and ideas. He referred to publicity as the most important of the "new means of government" that guarantees the constant intervention of the country in the direction of political affairs through debates, free press, and elections. Thus, publicity alters the nature of the interaction between government and society and brings forth more transparency in the social and political sphere.[21] Rémusat echoed this point. He argued that in both its forms—debates in the press and debates in Parliament—publicity is instrumental in facilitating the circulation of information between society and power in such a way that the communication between the two never comes to an end.

Publicity, added Guizot, also plays a key role in limiting and moderating political power. Since the fundamental principle of representative government is the destruction of absolute and arbitrary power, representative institutions places all those who hold power under the obligation to stand constant trials and to face legal opposition. As we have already noted, this liberal suspicion of power is engraved in the very principles of representative government, which recognizes that no power or individual should be allowed to say, "This is good and just because I have so decided it." The main pillars of representative government—free debates, publicity, liberty of the press, and elections—make the legitimacy of those who exercise power contingent upon their demonstrating the conformity of their actions to the precepts of reason, truth, and justice. As Guizot remarked,

> The principle of the representative system is the destruction of all sovereignty of permanent right, that is to say, of all absolute power upon earth. . . . And it is the formal design of the representative system to provide against the existence of such a power, and to take care that every power shall be submitted to certain trials, meet with obstacles, undergo opposition, and, in fine, be deprived of sway until it has either proved its legitimacy, or given reason for presuming it. (Guizot 2002, 371)

As such, the institutions and principles of representative government compel the whole body of citizens to seek after reason, justice, and truth through public debates and freedom of the press. They provide fora for open debates and place all powers under public scrutiny, thus ensuring that all powers are politically responsible, under penalty of being taxed with illegitimacy.[22]

The most original aspect of Guizot's theory of publicity was arguably the definition of publicity as the cornerstone of representative government. "Theoretically, publicity is perhaps the most essential characteristic of representative government," wrote Guizot (2002, 69). "We have seen that it has for its object to call upon all individuals who possess rights, as well as those who exercise power, to seek reason and justice, the source and rule of legitimate sovereignty. In publicity consists the bond between a society and its government." But what did Guizot actually mean when claiming that publicity must be regarded as the most significant feature of representative government? How can this claim be reconciled with his argument that "publicity has not been invariably attached to a representative government" (Guizot 2002, 70)?

Certainly, Guizot's aim was *not* to downplay the importance of elections and parliamentary debates. His real intention was to rethink the essence of representative government by focusing above all on publicity as its *normative* principle. To be sure, Guizot drew a seminal distinction between two different procedures of legitimization of power: through elections and publicity. While publicity—that is, openness and debate—must be seen as the true foundation of representative government, it cannot serve as a substitute for elections. The particular attention paid by the Doctrinaires to elections is demonstrated by the key role Guizot and his friends played in the drafting of the electoral law of 1817 as well as by the numerous articles and speeches in which they discussed the nature of elections and the relation between elections and publicity. Guizot, for example, stressed again and again that elections must be conceived of as part of a larger political system that provides for free debates and free circulation of ideas and persons:

> Where publicity is lacking, there might be elections, assemblies, and deliberations, but people do not believe in them and they are right to do so. Haven't we seen that without publicity, [elections, assemblies, and deliberations] are nothing else than a vain simulacrum, an insulting comedy? . . . Publicity alone corrects to a great extent the pernicious effects of a bad political machine. England offers a great example in this regard. (Guizot 1818c, 186–87)

In Guizot's view, only publicity could correct the malfunction of political institutions by opening new channels of communication and placing those who hold power under the obligation of justifying their actions under the eyes of public opinion. Moreover, Guizot saw publicity as a powerful and effective *means of government* whose aim is not only to limit and moderate power, but also to call upon all individuals to seek in common reason, truth, and justice.

What made Guizot's approach original was his sociological approach, which highlighted the connection between publicity and the new social condition based on equality of conditions. "The need for publicity in the administration of public affairs," claimed Guizot, "is the essential feature of the social state and the spirit of the age. It is a necessary condition of all institutions; without it, these institutions are incapable of meeting the demands of modern societies."[23] In other words, publicity is not only an important *prerequisite* of political liberty, but also the necessary *outcome* of liberty, as well as the expression of a new type of social power. It is not a mere coincidence that the good itself had always been associated with light (the characteristic of publicity), while the evil had always sought shelter in darkness, the opposite of publicity.

The relation between publicity and elections stands in need of further clarification. As the government by the majority of "capable" citizens, representative government seeks to concentrate all the scattered elements of reason and knowledge that exist in society and to form with them the government. Elections are instrumental in achieving this goal, their object being "to obtain the most capable and best accredited men in the country" (Guizot 2002, 340), who are called to participate in the direction of society on the basis of their (presumed) political capacity. As such, elections serve not only as a procedure of selection of new political elites, but also as a means of legitimization and political control.

In Guizot's view, the effectiveness of elections depends on publicity and the confrontation of differences and opinions that create the conditions for constant communication between society and government, between electors themselves, and between the latter and their representatives. In the absence of publicity and debates, there can be no genuine representative government, because representation, elections, and assemblies would become mere forms devoid of substance and could not fulfill their raison d'être.[24] Voting, argued Guizot, is a limited political act, subject to numerous external influences that might easily distort its true meaning and goal. It is not sufficient to call for elections and ask electors to choose whom they will. They must also be thoroughly familiar with the object of elections and ought to be capable of acting in concert to pursue and achieve common goals. "If they do not know each other," wrote Guizot (2002, 340), "and are equally unacquainted with the men who solicit their suffrages, the object is evidently defeated. You will have elections which will result neither from the free choice nor the actual wishes of the electors" (Guizot 2002, 340).

What this passage highlights is the importance of *deliberation* and *informed choice* as prerequisites of sound ("true") elections, along with openness and debates. This point has been neglected even by the most astute interpreters of the Doctrinaires, who denied that they had anything meaningful to say about deliberation, apart from "confounding" it with elections.[25] In reality, both Guizot and Rémusat stressed the importance of *deliberation* in elections. "Deliberation," wrote Rémusat, "is what constitutes the character and excellence of representative government. From all sides, people demand and expect that the government truly become a public entity by means of a free press, common deliberation, and popular elections."[26] By deliberating on issues of common interest in a regime of publicity and open confrontation of ideas and interests, individuals and their representatives participate in the process of discovering and applying the precepts of reason, truth, and justice.

To be sure, Guizot made a clear distinction between voting and deliberation and insisted that the main limitation of elections derives from the fact that they are a sudden and temporally limited act which usually leaves little room for deliberation. Electors must not blindly follow their momentary passions and impulses which might impair their political judgment. Moreover, they must be united by common ties and interests and ought to be accustomed to peacefully conduct their affairs among themselves. Therefore, the act of election should not take them out of the sphere of their daily lives. It "only assembles them at the centre of that sphere, to obtain the . . . summary of their opinions, their wishes and the natural influence which they exercise over each other" (Guizot 2002, 340).

The crux of Guizot's argument is that the election of representatives must *not* be the work of a small assembly of individuals extraordinarily or arbitrarily convened, among whom no "well-tried and freely accepted influences" (Guizot 2002, 341) exist and who possess no regular common interests. To ensure the veracity and legitimacy of elections, the latter must be "the fruit of ancient relations" between individuals united in the conduct of common affairs and the possession of functions, rights, and interests. In other words, elections must bring to fore those who are deemed capable of recognizing and advancing the general interests of society: "The election must be made by electors capable of choosing wisely and must supply . . . men capable of thoroughly comprehending the interests that they will have to administer" (Guizot 2002, 342).

Guizot feared that coteries, factions, and personal intrigues would appear in the place of political parties which, in turn, would be tempted to give vent to deep-seated animosities by allowing particular interests and opinions to prevail over common ideas and interests. This was another way of saying that elections, too, could be corrupted by lack of experience, poor judgment, and blind passions. Guizot warned that, if political life came to be dominated by personal intrigues and particular interests, a struggle would ensue between social and political interests that lack universality and cannot form strong bonds among citizens. Then, the interests and influences competing for power would not reflect the general views and interests of society and, as a result, "general interests, expansive ideas, and public opinions [would] cease to be the motive and regulative power" (Guizot 2002, 347), and elections would fail to achieve their main goal.

Guizot admired the English electoral system, whose main strengths he outlined in volume two of *Histoire des origines du gouvernement représentatif*. The fact that the entire second volume was devoted to England illustrates Guizot's strong interest in English institutions. The English system successfully brought together the main interests and opinions of the entire society and allowed them to compete for power in a free environment. From the very beginning, English political institutions were connected with local institutions and powers and were an extension of local liberties and customs.[27] Based on direct elections and open voting, the system avoided the main limitations of secret ballots and indirect elections, which eliminate beforehand a certain number of electoral capacities, annul the influence and participation of the minority in the final result of the election, and create "a means of tyranny for the benefit of the majority" (Guizot 2002, 349).

Moreover, in England, the right to vote had always been inseparable from the free exercise of other civil rights. Decentralization, publicity, and self-government created a sound political structure that allowed the same citizens who elected their representatives to have a part in the administration of local affairs and the process of rendering justice. County courts and municipal corporations with deep roots in local communities were constituted into electoral colleges.[28] Hence, the right to vote was deeply rooted in mores and social practices and the whole system was founded upon respect for natural influences and relations:

> The freeholders, that is to say, every free and veritable landowner, used to assemble in the county-courts, to administer justice and to treat together of common interests; and these county-courts were charged with the nomination of representatives. In towns of any importance, the citizens, under forms more or less liberal, regulated their own affairs, chose their own magistrates, and exercised in common certain rights and powers; and these municipal corporations were required to send members to Parliament. . . . Thus the electoral system from its origin was united with every right and institution, and with almost every local and real power. It was the extension and development of existing liberties, a powerful force added to other forces previously in action and exercising government over other interests. (Guizot 2002, 330)

As a result, in England electoral assemblies did not develop into artificial aggregates or coteries for pursuing particular interests. Furthermore, the division of the country into counties allowed citizens to conduct local business by drawing upon their local knowledge and expertise. For Guizot, the English electoral system was the model that France had to imitate in its attempt to build representative government. This model was based on the recognition of "natural superiorities," the bestowal of electoral rights upon capacity, the close union of electoral rights with all other rights, direct election, and open voting.[29] In many ways, this model was completely different from the electoral system unsuccessfully tried in the early 1790s in France. The French electoral system had serious defects that led to the isolation of electoral rights from other civil rights and provided for the creation of electoral assemblies that had very little involvement in local affairs and administration.

Freedom of the Press

After 1789, freedom of the press came to be regarded as one of the most enduring achievements of the French Revolution and was included among the fundamental individual liberties. The wording of Article 11 of the *Declaration of the Rights of Man* was unambiguous: "Free communication of ideas and opinions is one of the most precious rights of man. Consequently, every citizen may speak, write, and print freely, subject to responsibility for the abuse of such liberty in the cases determined by law."[30]

Nonetheless, during Napoléon's reign, this freedom was curtailed. The press was placed under strict surveillance and dissenting journalists were persecuted (the same strict regime applied to books and other publications). The censorship prevented the publication of Madame de Staël's *De l'Allemagne*, which was seen as an indirect critique of the Emporer. Napoléon saw the press as belonging to the public domain and believed that it was "an arsenal reserved for those who enjoy the confidence of the Government."[31] It is true, however, that during the Hundred Days, the Emperor changed his position and recognized the inevitability of freedom of the press. In a private conversation with his former opponent, Benjamin Constant, who had just been entrusted with the task of drafting the Additional Act, Napoléon said: "See what seems possible to you and bring me ideas: public discussions, free elections, responsible ministers, freedom of the press: I want all this! . . . Above all, freedom of the press: it would be absurd to stifle it, I am convinced of this."[32]

Not surprisingly, freedom of the press became the subject of intense political debates and controversies after the fall of Napoléon. The Bourbon

Restoration represented a great age for the press, above all for literary journals, pamphlets, and brochures. In his excellent history of the press in France, Eugène Hatin underscored the importance of the Restoration in the development of the press. "I don't know," he wrote, "what destiny is reserved to the press; but nobody can doubt that it will never live again its wonderful days of the Restoration" (Hatin 1861, 143). It was as if after a long period of oppression, the public suddenly acquired and manifested a great voracity for information and communication, facilitated by the growth of literacy and significant advances in printing techniques and advertising. As already mentioned, many prestigious journals and reviews were founded during this period: *L'Avenir; Minerve; Le Conservateur; Le Constitutionnel; Journal des débats; Archives philosophiques, politiques et littéraires; Tablettes universelles; Le Globe; Revue française; Revue des deux mondes;* and the list goes on.[33]

Undoubtedly, it was the free press and the free expression of ideas that set the pace of political change. In a relatively short period of time, journalists rose to a high social status and their public influence was sometimes equal to that of many members of Parliament. Article 8 of the Charter of 1814 recognized freedom of the press as one of the fundamental principles of the new political order: "Frenchmen have the right to publish and to have printed their opinions, while conforming to the laws, which are necessary to restrain abuses of that liberty."[34] Nonetheless, the Charter left open the possibility of temporary (preventive) forms of censorship in order to prevent and/or punish certain abuses of freedom of the press committed by those who sought to use the press in order subvert the foundations of the new political order.

French liberals regarded liberty of the press as the most important component of publicity and argued that there can be no public opinion without freedom of the press. When newspapers are censored, wrote Constant, and the voice of the nation cannot be heard in the press, the political institutions of the country become isolated from the nation and lack force and vitality.[35] The inevitability of freedom of the press in modern society was also stressed by Guizot, who remarked that liberty of the press "rendered publicity easy without resorting to tumultuous meetings."[36] Guizot's first essays on this topic, "Quelques idées sur la liberté de la presse" and "Sur le nouveau projet de loi relatif à la presse," appeared as early as 1814. He published two other important articles on freedom of the press in *Archives philosophiques, politiques et littéraires*. The first one was a review of Benjamin Constant's "Annales de la session de 1817 à 1818" (Guizot 1817d) and the second one was a longer seventy-page article entitled "Des garanties légales de la liberté de la presse" (Guizot 1818c). Royer-Collard's views on freedom of the press can be found in his parliamentary speeches during the Restoration (January 1817, April 1819, March 1820,

January 1822, February 1827). His magisterial discourse of January 1822 is seminal for anyone who seeks to understand his views on liberty of the press as a form of resistance and an effective means of limiting political power.[37]

Since the Doctrinaires' attitude toward the press generated conflicting interpretations, it is appropriate to examine how Guizot and his colleagues understood the role of the press in the consolidation of representative government. In so doing, we might be able to separate the circumstantial arguments from the more substantive ones, which had significant institutional implications. Let us begin with the following statement of Guizot:

> I am one of those who have been much assisted and fiercely attacked by the press. Throughout my life, I have greatly employed this engine. By placing my ideas publicly before the eyes of my country, I first attracted her attention and esteem. During the progress of my career, I have ever had the press for ally or opponent; and I have never hesitated to employ its weapons, or feared to expose myself to its blows. It is a power which I respect and recognize willingly, rather and compulsorily, but without illusion or idolatry. (Guizot 1858b, 170)

Note the language used by Guizot in this fragment. He described freedom of the press as a social power that demands universal recognition and respect, but which must be respected without illusion or idolatry. What does it mean to recognize freedom of the press without idolizing it or entertaining false illusions about it?

To answer this question, we must examine Guizot's article "Quelques idées sur la liberté de la presse" published at the beginning of the Restoration (1814).[38] The key point addressed by Guizot in this essay was whether any restrictions on freedom of the press could be justified on prudential grounds without jeopardizing the essence of this freedom. The question was not new in France and the fundamental distinction between *restreindre, prévenir,* and *réprimer* had already loomed large in the debates on the articles of the *Declaration of the Rights of Man.*[39] The authors of the Charter of 1814 also struggled with the meanings of these concepts. Montesquieu, who was then minister of the interior, claimed that there was no distinction between prevention and repression, while Bossy d'Anglas demanded the suppression of the word *prévenir* which, in his view, was incompatible with liberty of the press.[40] In the end, a distinction was made between liberty of journals and freedom of the press that it limited in practice the applicability of the new freedom recognized by the Charter. A month after the proclamation of the constitution, Montesquieu presented in the Chamber a bill that reintroduced various forms of censorship. The text formed the basis of the law that was finally adopted on October 21, 1814.

Guizot and Royer-Collard participated in the elaboration of the new bill. They started from the assumption that the political and social context of the Restoration called for prudence and firmness in drafting the new legislation on the press.[41] In particular, the Doctrinaires feared that unlimited liberty of the press would offer radicals a chance to settle past scores. Guizot and his colleagues endorsed a cautious approach that put certain limits on freedom of the press without endangering its ultimate goal—to contribute to the building and consolidation of representative government. The law of October 21, 1814, was justified as a preventive temporary measure meant to protect liberty of the press against its own abuses. Special attention was devoted to issues such as press offenses (*délits de presse*) and trial by jury (the latter had been introduced by the Constituent Assembly in 1790). All journals had to obtain the authorization of the king and all presses were required to have a royal license (*brevet royal*). The new law considered any publication as a specific activity and a potential source of "specific offenses," rejected the trial by jury in cases regarding the press, and allowed for temporary censorship for all journals and writings of less than 320 pages in octavo (twenty *feuilles d'impression*). Three other similar restrictive laws were passed during the Restoration—November 9, 1815; February 28, 1817 (presented by Decazes); December 30, 1817 (presented by Pasquier)—before a new liberal legislation sponsored by de Serre, Guizot, and Royer-Collard was finally adopted in 1819.[42]

It should surprise us to learn that a declared partisan of freedom of the press like Guizot defended the law of October 21, 1814. The justification he gave, not devoid of a few sophisms, is worth examining in detail, because it sheds light on the process of political learning that Guizot and his colleagues underwent during the Bourbon Restoration. Liberty, argued Guizot, is placed between oppression and license. After decades of despotism in which the French nation had been a stranger to the habits of true liberty, the apprenticeship of liberty required caution and prudence. But, continued Guizot, like any other freedom, the implementation of liberty of the press depended on the historical and political context in which it was exercised and had to be learned from experience. In an established government the tendency of those who hold power is to abuse it, and "the danger against which the friends of liberty have to contend is oppression; the function of government is to support order; that of the governed to watch over liberty" (Guizot 1858b, 394–95). In this case, the law should recognize freedom of press, since most citizens have a stake in the system and are not easily swayed by extremist theories that pose a threat to political stability.

The situation is, however, entirely different when a new government is established after a long period of social and political turmoil, when individual interests and passions diverge from the public interest and citizens are "neither instructed by prosperity nor enlightened by experience" (Guizot 1858b, 396). Given the general uncertainty, the public spirit is weak and there are only few barriers against license and anarchy: "All seek their place, without being sure of finding it; common sense . . . has no fixed rule upon which to act; the bewildered multitude . . . know not what guide to follow" (Guizot 1858b, 396). Under these circumstances, freedom of the press is likely to become an obstacle to progress, because the right to publish freely one's views brings forth a host of ideas that fuel the general confusion of theories and principles. The friends of liberty have to fight against license and are called to protect liberty, including freedom of the press, against its own excesses. "Thus," concluded Guizot (1858b, 395), "it becomes necessary to protect liberty from the outrages of license, and sometimes to prevent a strong government from being reduced to defense when uncertain of commanding obedience."

While defending the idea that liberty of the press ought to be protected against its potential excesses (in this case, the publication of seditious writings and appeals to overthrow social order), Guizot warned, however, that any preventive measure had to be taken with utmost care, in such a way that it would not jeopardize liberty altogether. In establishing a barrier against license, a door must always remain open for freedom. Liberty, maintained Royer-Collard, always involves a certain degree of license and the interpretation of what constitutes an abuse of liberty of the press is open to question. Moreover, the nature of the abuse itself changes over time; what was seen as an abuse of freedom of expression in the past might be regarded later as a perfectly legitimate use of this liberty.[43]

Four decades later, Guizot stood by his original justification. He argued that in its original conception, the object of the law was to consecrate by legislative enactment liberty of the press as a permanent institution of the country. But, given the specific political context in the aftermath of a violent revolution and a long despotism, the introduction of representative institutions had to be done gradually. "I decided at once," wrote Guizot (1858b, 47–48), "that a temporary limitation of liberty, in respect to journals and pamphlets alone, was not too great a sacrifice for the removal of such perils and fears." Unfortunately, when the bill was introduced, its true intent was not clearly conveyed and some members of the government appeared as more disposed to control liberty of the press in fact than to acknowledge it in right.

Not surprisingly, the provisions of the new law triggered vigorous reactions from various writers and thinkers such as Constant, Lamennais, and C. Comte, who criticized the attempt to restrict freedom of the press.[44] In an important article published in 1814, "Observations sur le discours prononcé par S. E. le ministre de l'intérieur en faveur du projet de loi sur la liberté de la presse," Benjamin Constant denounced censorship on both practical and theoretical grounds. In his opinion, the arguments invoked in order to restrict liberty were the expression of the slavery and oppression in which the country had previously lived. "It is remarkable," wrote Constant (1957, 1253), "that in a discourse on freedom of the press, the word *individual liberty* whose first guarantee is freedom of the press, is not pronounced one single time." He also pointed out that it made little sense to draw an artificial distinction between publications that had less or more than 320 pages in octavo, since seditious theories were often advanced in longer books that would not have been subject to censorship according to the new law. The only reasonable solution, concluded Constant, was to set up a free constitution that guaranteed unrestricted freedom of the press: "Establish a free constitution and everyone will be interested in maintaining it. . . . The love of liberty motivates those who enjoy freedom to voluntarily cooperate with each other in order to punish license, because the latter discredits liberty."[45]

The Doctrinaires conceived of publicity and liberty of the press not only as effective means of *resistance* to arbitrary power, but also as means of *government*, instrumental in establishing a new type of relations and communication between society and government. The element of resistance is more or less straightforward and has a clear liberal connotation. By giving all citizens an opportunity to criticize the errors made by those who hold power, freedom of the press is one of the most effective weapons against injustice and oppression; if this liberty is lost, argued Royer-Collard, the return to serfdom is inevitable.[46] In the absence of free journals, free assemblies, free elections and ballots, power is absolute and liberty has no guarantees. Elections, parliamentary debates, and the free press place those who hold public office under constant public scrutiny and constrain them to become familiar with the demands of the public, to modify their views accordingly, and to justify them to the public at large.[47] Nonetheless, added Guizot, the goal of representative government is not only to provide the framework for a constant questioning of power, but also to create the conditions for a superior type of communication between government and society as well as between citizens themselves.

This point was underscored by Guizot in an important essay on the legal guarantees needed to protect freedom of the press in modern society (this long article was published toward the end of 1818). Far from fearing or ignoring public opinion, those who hold power ought "to multiply the points of contact between opinion and power" (Guizot 1818c, 234). They must consult public opinion, which acts like a "legal thermometer" indicating the pulse of the nation. If power is not continuously aware of public opinion and its demands, it was bound to pursue obsolete policies that could bring its ruin: "No material entity can resist such an opponent for a long time. The representative system, the trial by jury, and liberty of the press are today the only sources from which the government can derive its power, that is to say, its life" (Guizot, 1818c, 234). Those who believed in the right to free speech ought to allow all individuals to freely express their opinions in print. The social condition of modern society, added Guizot, makes freedom of the press a necessity and any attempt to reject it would be futile and illegitimate.[48] Liberty of the press is a political institution as well as a social necessity that guarantees freedom of thought and freedom of association:

> For modern societies that aspire to political liberty, freedom of the press is an essential need, a true necessity. The need produced the fact; freedom of the press became indestructible because it was necessary. . . . The Charter consecrated it. . . . Freedom of the press is simultaneously a social need, an inevitable fact, and an acknowledged right. . . . Regardless of how one conceives of it, as a need, fact, or right, freedom of the press is only one of the elements of this new social state. . . . The same causes have imposed or will impose . . . civil equality, liberty of conscience, individual freedom, the responsibility of executive power, freedom of the press, and all the institutions which must guarantee them. (Guizot 1817d, 258–59)

Freedom of the press facilitates free debates and contributes to the enlightenment of the general public. It warns those who hold power against their own shortcomings and errors and gives them an opportunity to familiarize themselves with the dominant ideas and interests of society.[49] Freedom of inquiry and freedom of expression also force rulers to hear not only the voice of sycophants, but also the claims of dissenters. More importantly, Guizot argued that as a means of government that expresses a new form of social power, liberty of the press creates the conditions for a "mutual revelation" between government and society and plays the role of "a means of conversation"[50] between the interests of various groups in society.

In an article published in 1819, Guizot argued that the purpose of freedom of the press is to "reveal" the country to itself and to bring society in closer contact with the government.[51] In turn, Charles de Rémusat referred to the press as a means by which society "se fait spectacle à elle-même"[52] and explained the relation between liberty of the press and social condition in terms that recalled Guizot's argument. In modern society, claimed Rémusat, the press is the only means that allows isolated individuals to form sound judgments on public matters, to exchange ideas with one another, and to communicate their opinions to public officials and civil servants.[53] As such, journals and newspapers are the only available means of communication and information for individuals who rarely, if ever, have the chance to meet each other face-to-face. Only by reading the press can they become informed about the political affairs of the country at large and are able to acquire a sense of larger vistas that go beyond their private affairs.[54] Moreover, as a new means of government that manifests the diverse opinions of society, the press also organizes and channels the political influence of society and gives voice to public reason and the general interests of society.[55] Newspapers, journals, and books, along with parliamentary debates, contribute to the enlightenment of the general public and perform the function of a public institution that guarantees civil freedoms and helps extract from the bosom of society the scattered fragments of reason and knowledge.

In his parliamentary discourses, Royer-Collard advanced similar arguments on the nature and the role of freedom of the press. He regarded liberty of the press as a political institution as well as an effective means of connecting government to society and vice-versa. The free exchange of ideas, argued Royer-Collard, is instrumental in the formation of public opinion, and freedom of the press plays a key role as the condition of and the necessary principle of liberty.[56] Moreover, liberty of the press watches over the established powers, enlightened them, and effectively opposes their tendency to overstep their boundaries. As such, concluded Royer-Collard, it is the *crowning* freedom, because without it, society would become powerless and vulnerable. Hence, special guarantees for freedom of the press are required, since the survival of other rights and liberties, such as freedom of expression and association, depends on it.[57]

All these ideas formed the vision undergirding the three laws of the press passed in 1819, which were the work of the Doctrinaires, most notably of Hercule de Serre, assisted by Guizot and Royer-Collard.[58] Two of de Serre's draft bills dealt with the crimes and offenses committed by the press in general, while the third bill referred specifically to journals and periodical writings. The laws of May 17, May 26, and June 9, 1819 freed the press from its previous shackles and acknowledged the seminal role played by the press in the direction of public affairs. As Lucien Jaume pointed out, the laws of 1819 represented a remarkable achievement that was supplanted only by the law of the press passed in July 1881 that abolished the caution-money system and stopped short of recognizing any type of press offenses.[59] For the French press, argued Eugéne Hatin (1861, 315–16), the debates that took place in 1819 were remarkable. After four years of struggles and hesitations, freedom of the press was ready for a definitive settlement. In his memoirs, Guizot commented on the laws of 1819 in similar terms:

> Liberty of the press is human nature displaying itself in broad daylight, sometimes under the most attractive, and at other times under the most repelling aspect. . . . I have always advocated a free press; I believe it to be, on the whole, more useful than injurious to public morality; and I look upon it as essential to the proper management of public affairs, and to the security of private interests. But I have witnessed too often and too closely its dangerous aberrations as regards political order, not to feel convinced that this liberty requires the restraint of a strong organization of effective laws and of controlling principles. In 1819, my friends and I clearly foresaw the necessity of these conditions; but we laid little stress upon them. . . . And we thought, moreover, that the time had arrived when the sincerity as well as the strength of the restored monarchy was to be proved by removing from the press its previous shackles, and in risking the consequences of its enfranchisement. (Guizot 1858b, 170–71)

The laws of 1819 placed the press under the jurisdiction of the common law, recognized trial by jury, and no longer considered the press as a specific activity but as an instrument with a well-defined and limited social function. A journal, it was argued, is a tribune from which individuals speak to thousands of readers and attempt to shape their opinions and ideas.[60] That is why the abuses of the press should not be entrusted to permanent courts (*tribunaux de police correctionnelle*), because such courts, if invested with power, might exercise power arbitrarily. It was decided that these courts could only prosecute press offenses in those cases involving insult and defamation against private persons. The laws of May and June 1819 also abolished the obligation for each paper to obtain a license and asked instead that a simple notification be sent in advance that declared the name of the owners of the journal in question.

The new legislation maintained the caution-money system, which required newspapers to post a certain sum of money in order to obtain an official permit. These requirements were as follows: 10,000 francs for daily journals published in the departments of Seine, Seine-et-Oise, and Seine-et-Marne; 2,500 francs for daily journals published in towns with at least 50,000 inhabitants; 1,500 francs for all other towns. Periodical journals were required to depose only half of these amounts, depending on the region in which they were published.

For Guizot, the real purpose of the caution-money system was *not* to restrict freedom of the press, but to place the newspapers in the hands of responsible individuals, whose views expressed the opinions and interests predominant in society.[61] In turn, in an important speech in the Chamber of Deputies from 1819, Royer-Collard argued: "Subject or not to the caution-money system, people will always write what they want; no direct or indirect prevention will ever constrain writers. Liberty of the press is beyond discussion" (Royer-Collard 1861a, 482). Royer-Collard made a distinction between the act of publishing one's opinions and the act of founding a journal or newspaper. The latter was regarded as a public enterprise and, as such, involved an element of political and commercial speculation. Journals were considered an integral part of representative government that exercised a strong influence over the entire society. Or, like all social and political influences, journals had to offer a number of reasonable guarantees that required a certain social position determined by property or its equivalents. The caution-money, concluded Royer-Collard, regarded only the financial aspect of journals and left more or less intact their freedom to publish ideas and opinions.[62]

The debates on the laws of the press triggered vigorous controversies in the Chamber of Deputies. The discussions focused on the four types of offenses acknowledged by the bills proposed by Hercule de Serre: the public provocation to crimes and offenses; the attacks on the person of the king; the offenses to public morality and good mores; defamation and public insult.[63] Even those liberals who supported unrestricted freedom of the press agreed that the law must prosecute insults directed at the person of the monarch and should punish any encouragement to murder and other crimes.[64] Some ultraroyalists proposed that an additional article be added that condemned press offenses against the religion of the state, while other *ultras* went further to demand the condemnation of any writings attacking the doctrines and the morality of Christianity. The right feared that the new legislation did not adequately protect the interests and rights of religion and of the Catholic Church. The deputies also discussed whether or not to hold accountable the editors who published writings found guilty of specific press offenses. In the end, the majority decided against prosecuting the publishers unless it could be proved that they acted with the clear intention of violating the law.

On a more general level, the source of disagreement can be traced back to the different views on the role of the press in modern society. The Doctrinaires believed that newspapers fulfilled a unique social function—to assist in the government of society—that required a certain *capacity* for its proper discharge. To this effect, they argued that most of the opinions communicated through the press ought to be selected from the educated strata of society that enjoyed economic independence and had a strong interest in promoting the general interests of society. The aim of liberty of the press, wrote Guizot, is "to develop and manifest public reason, which wants all that is necessary and which is equally favorable to the reasonable needs of power as well as to the legitimate rights of citizens" (Guizot 1817d, 262). This position marked an interesting contrast to Benjamin Constant, who opposed some of the provisions of the laws of 1819[65] and took the Doctrinaires to task for proposing an elitist view of the press which, in his opinion, was the reflection of a long tradition of centralization in France. Constant claimed that it would be futile to attempt to create a division between elites and ordinary citizens in modern society in which the information circulate freely and quickly because of the new means of communication. Moreover, Constant argued that freedom of the press ought to be considered as the exercise of a natural right that legislators must acknowledge as sacred and inalienable. Echoing Constant's point, Charles Comte ironically remarked that proposing a law on liberty of the press was as meaningless as drafting a bill regulating the liberty to use one's voice or hands.[66] Constant and Comte feared that the new laws would contribute to the formation of a new form of "intellectual aristocracy"[67] engaged in sophisticated but ultimately futile intellectual discussions.

There was a certain truth in this critique. For the Doctrinaires, as a new means of government, the press was supposed to contribute to the education of society by disseminating general knowledge and information and was expected to play an important role in the creation of new political, intellectual, and economic elites.[68] But the Doctrinaires' own views on the nature and role of the press did change over time. The full extent of Guizot's political learning can be gleaned from the following important passage taken from his memoirs:

> The liberty of the press, that stormy guarantee of modern civilization, has already been, is, and will continue to be the roughest trial of free governments, and consequently of free people. . . . Free nations and governments have but one honourable and effective method of dealing with liberty of the press: to adopt it frankly, without undue complaisance. . . . Liberty of the press . . . is simply the right of all citizens to give their opinions upon public affairs and the conduct of the government, a powerful and respectable privilege, but one . . . which, to be made salutary, requires that the constituted authorities should never humiliate themselves before it, and that they should impose on it that serious and constant responsibility which ought to weigh upon all rights, to prevent them from becoming at first seditious, and afterwards tyrannical.[69]

Moreover, Guizot emphasized that, in order to be effective, the principles and institutions of representative government—the chambers, the jury, publicity, and liberty of the press—must have solid foundations and should be properly linked to each other. In his view, the lack of harmony between these institutions and the absence of a unifying political vision could jeopardize the consolidation of representative government. The example of other European countries proved that the conflict between institutions and mores as well the lack of harmony between institutions delayed their political development for many centuries.[70] In the context of Restoration France, added Guizot, representative institutions had to be brought back to their first principle, "intervention of society itself in public affairs"[71] through publicity and liberty of the press. Neither the legislative nor the executive power could effectively function in the absence of liberty of the press any more than freedom of the press was able to fulfill its role as a mediator between society and government and guarantee of rights if freedom of assembly, freedom of thought, and freedom of expression were not duly protected.

Notes

1. On this issue, see Rosanvallon 1989, 423, and Rosanvallon 1991, 137.

2. For more details, see Ozouf 1987, 420–34, and Ozouf 1989, 771–79.

3. Two important works were Schlözer's *Letters to Eichstädt in Vindication of Publicity* (1785) and Bahrdt's *On Freedom of the Press and Its Limits* (1787). A translation of Bahrdt's *Edict of Religion* has recently appeared in English (2000).

4. For more details on Kant's theory of publicity in relation to his skepticism, see Laursen (1989), for whom Kant's politics of publicity was a response to the tradition of philosophical skepticism.

5. For more details, see Hegel 1991, 353.

6. Also see Ozouf 1989, 773.

7. This passage is from an article on "opinion" in the eleventh volume of the *Encyclopédie* (as quoted in Baker 1990, 167).

8. Madame d'Epinay as quoted in Baker 1990, 171.

9. For a good account of the growth of public opinion in France, see Baker 1990, 167–99; on public opinion after the Revolution, see Rosanvallon 1985, 64–72. The concept of "public opinion" is also discussed by Gunn 1989, 247–65.

10. Raynal as quoted in Baker 1990, 187.

11. Mercier as quoted in Baker 1990, 187.

12. Mirabeau 1986, 87. The secret correspondence between Mirabeau and Louis XVI was published and edited by Chaussinand-Nogaret in 1986.

13. For a comprehensive treatment of this topic, see Ganochaud 1980.

14. Malesherbes as quoted in Baker 1990, 189.

15. Linguet as quoted in Baker 1990, 189.

16. Necker as quoted in Baker 1990, 193; also see Habermas 1991, 263.

17. This satirical poem is quoted in Habermas 1991, 70.

18. Bergasse as quoted in Habermas 1991, 99.

19. See Bentham as quoted in Habermas 1991, 100.

20. The phrase is from Constant's 1805 draft of his *Principes de politique* (as translated in Fontana 1991, 83). For more details on Constant's ideas on public opinion, see Fontana 1991, 81–97.

21. See Guizot 2002, 53–55, 345–46. The important contribution of Guizot to the development of the theory of publicity was acknowledged by Habermas 1991 and Schmitt 1996.

22. For more details, see Guizot 2002, 226–28.

23. Guizot 1818c, 86–87. This passage is taken from an important article of Guizot, "Des garanties légales de la liberté de la presse," published in *Archives philosophiques, politiques et littéraires*, vol. 5 (1818).

24. On the centrality of publicity to representative government, also see Guizot 1818c, 184–86.

25. See, for example, Jaume 1997a, 134–37. Jaume claimed that, in accord with French political tradition, Guizot identified the vote with deliberation.

26. The passage is from Rémusat's text "Situation de la royauté" quoted in Roldán 1999, 168.

27. According to Guizot, "Le système électoral se trouva ainsi, dès l'origine, lié à toutes les institutions, à tous les droits, à tous les pouvoirs locaux et réels. Il fut l'extension, le développement des libertés existantes, une force ajoutée à des forces déjà actives" (Guizot 1862, 382).

28. See Guizot 1862, 382–83.

29. For a summary of Guizot's views on this topic, see Guizot 2002, 351. Royer-Collard's ideas on elections can be found in Royer-Collard 1861a, 459–60.

30. Stewart 1965, 114–15.

31. Napoléon as quoted in Lucas-Dubreton 1929, 57; also see Jardin 1985, 178–79.

32. Napoléon as quoted in Hatin 1861, 132.

33. For a comprehensive analysis of the diversity of the press under the Restoration, see Hatin 1861, 64–110, 168–214, 244–70, 443–510. Also see Vaulabelle 1856; Avenel 1900; Livois 1965.

34. Anderson 1967, 459.

35. See, for example, Constant 1957, 1260–61.

36. Guizot 2002, 70; also see Guizot 1817d, 258.

37. "Quelques idées sur la liberté de la presse" was republished in an abbreviated form in the final section of volume one of Guizot's *Mémoires* (Guizot 1858a, 408–16). For more information, see Pouthas 1923a, 49–52; Rosanvallon 1985, 64–72; Tudesq 1993, 2–3; Jaume 1994a, 113–14. Most of Royer's discourses on freedom of the press (January 1817, April 1819, March 1820, January 1822, February 1827, and August 1835) were collected in Royer-Collard 1949. For an interpretation of Royer-Collard's views on freedom of the press, see Nesmes-Desmarets 1908, 294–312 and G. Rémond 1979, 96–106. For more details on the Doctrinaires' view on liberty of the press, see

Rosanvallon 1985, 64–72. Also worth mentioning is Rémusat's text "De la liberté de la presse et des projets de loi présentés à la Chambre des députés" (1819).

38. For more details, see Guizot 1858a, 408–15; Guizot 1858b, 391–97; Hatin 1861, 45–46.

39. Mirabeau commented: "C'est à tort que tous les projets portent le mot *restreindre*; le mot proper est *réprimer*. La liberté de la presse ne doit pas être restreinte; les délits commis par la voie de la presse doivent être réprimés" (quoted in Hatin 1861, 13; emphasis added).

40. For more details, see Hatin 1861, 41–44.

41. See Guizot 1858a, 409–11.

42. For more details, see Hatin 1861, 46–53, 156–66; Jaume 1997b, 43–59.

43. Here is what Royer-Collard said: "Le bien et le mal sont partout inséparables; il n'y a pas de liberté sans quelque license; le délit échappe à la définition, l'interpretation reste arbitraire. Le délit lui-même est inconstant; ce qui est délit dans un temps ne l'est pas dans un autre" (Royer-Collard 1861a, 500). Also see Royer-Collard 1861a, 341–42; Royer-Collard 1861b, 291–309.

44. For more details, see Hatin 1861, 47–53.

45. Constant 1957, 1259. Constant also published "De la liberté des brochures, des pamphlets, et des journeaux, considérée sous le rapport de l'intérêt du gouvernement."

46. See the following revealing passages from Royer-Collard: "Ainsi, dans l'état des choses, la démocratie ne se protége que par la liberté de la presse. Si elle la perd, elle tombe dans l'esclavage politique le plus absolu" (Royer-Collard 1861b, 138). Also: "Il est vrai que la liberté de la presse a le caractère et l'énergie d'une institution politique; il est vrai que cette institution est la seule qui ait restitué à la société des droits contre les pouvoirs qui la régissent; *il est vrai que le jour où elle périra, ce jour-là nous retournerons à la servitude*" (Royer-Collard 1861b, 133; emphasis added). Also see Nesmes-Desmarets 1908, 308–9, and G. Rémond 1979, 98–99.

47. See Guizot 1985, 375–79.

48. See Guizot 1818c, 188–89.

49. Writes Guizot: "Ce n'est pas du tout pour procurer à quelques hommes l'agrément de dire leur avis qu'un people demand et defend la liberté de la presse; c'est pour se procurer à lui-même tous les moyens possibles de connaître, sur ses affaires, la vérité et son intérêt" (Guizot 1818c, 186).

50. See Guizot 1818c, 187.

51. Writes Guizot: "La liberté des journaux doit avoir pour effet de révéler sans cesse la France à elle-même; de rendre constamment présent, en quelque sorte, la patrie tout entière aux yeux du gouvernement, le gouvernement tout entier aux yeux de toute la patrie" (Guizot as quoted in Tudesq 1994, 3–4).

52. Rémusat as quoted in Rosanvallon 1985, 68.

53. Writes Rémusat: "Dans nos empires modernes, avec leurs grandes populations, les citoyens ne peuvent que par la presse communiquer entre eux, et prendre acte de leur opinion; par elle seule l'autorité peut recevoir d'eux et leur rendre la lumière, et

cet échange est nécessaire pour que les citoyens et l'autorité marchent dans les mêmes voies: ainsi le véritable office de la liberté de la presse est de servir à gouverner" (Rémusat 1819, 12).

54. Writes Guizot: "C'est dans la liberté publique qu'il faut puiser l'énergie vitale que tout gouvernement a besoin d'emprunter à la société; c'est la raison publique qu'il faut demander la protection première de l'ordre et des lois. Ainsi la liberté de la presse servira à la fois les souverains et les peuples; à ceux-ci elle sera une garantie, à ceux-là un moyen de gouvernement" (Guizot 1817d, 261, 265).

55. Writes Guizot: "La liberté de la presse n'est encore considérée que comme une arme offensive, bonne seulement pour l'attaque et contre le pouvoir. L'autorité songe moins à s'en servir qu'à s'en défendre, et l'esprit de faction la réclame avec une ardeur qu'il est mal-aisé de croire sans objet. Il n'y a rien là qui doive alarmer sur le sort ni l'emploi de cette liberté; mal comprise aujourd'hui de ceux qui la redoutent, et destinée par plusieurs de ceux qui la demandent, à atteindre un but qui n'est pas le sien, elle surmontera ces vaines terreurs et trompera ces amitiés intéressées" (Guizot 1817d, 261–62).

56. See Royer-Collard 1861a, 340–41; Royer-Collard 1861b, 134–36.

57. See Royer-Collard 1861b, 131–33. Also: "Ce n'est qu'en fondant la liberté de la presse comme droit publique que la Charte a véritablement fondé toutes les libertés, et rendu la société à elle-même. . . . La liberté de la presse doit fonder à son tour la liberté de la tribune, qui n'a pas un autre principe ni une autre garantie" (Royer-Collard 1861b, 132–33). In turn, Guizot commented on the seminal role played by liberty of the press as follows: "Ce qu'il faut bien comprendre, c'est que . . . ce n'est pas seulement un droit privé, mais encore une liberté publique, et non seulement la liberté de la presse en particulier, mais la liberté de la pensée et de la parole en general, qui sont en question. . . . On ne peut contester ou restreindre un des moyens d'exercer le droit, sans contester ou restreindre le droit lui-même, dans tous les moyens par lesquels son exercice est possible. Et entre ces moyens, quelque divers qu'ils puissent paraître, l'union est si étroite, la solidarité si complete, qu'il n'en est pas un qu'on puisse dire licite et libre, s'ils ne le sont pas tous également" (Guizot 1818c, 189).

58. On the laws of the press of 1819 and the seminal contribution of the Doctrinaires in the drafting of this legislation, see Hatin 1861, 315–36; Vaulabelle 1856, 26–39; Gorce 1926, 153–57.

59. See Jaume 1994a, 114–16.

60. For more details, see Hatin 1861, 317–25; Jaume 1994a, 111. Volume four of Hatin's history of the French press includes generous and valuable excerpts from Hercule de Serre's interventions in the Chamber as well as from the reactions of Constant, Lally-Tollendal, Guizot, and Royer-Collard. In Hatin's opinion, the laws of 1819 formed "une législation complète, conçue d'ensemble et par avance, conformément à certains principes généraux, définissant à tous leurs degrees les délits ou les peines, réglant toutes les conditions comme les formes de l'instruction, et destinée à fonder la liberté de la presse aussi bien qu'à defendre de ses écarts l'ordre et le pouvoir" (Hatin 1861, 332). Also see Chateaubriand 1819b.

61. Note the defense of the caution-money system in the following fragment of Guizot: "L'objet du cautionnement est surtout de ne placer l'influence des journeaux qu'entre les mains d'hommes qui donnent à la société quelques gages de leur existence sociale et lui puissant inspirer quelque confiance. Les journeaux ne sont point l'expression pure et simple de quelques opinions individuelles; ils sont les organs des parties, ou si l'on veut, des diverses opinions, des divers intérêts auxquels se rallient des masses plus ou moins nombreuses des citoyens. Il ne convient pas que ces organs publics soient pris et placés dans la region inférieure des opinions et des intérêts qu'ils expriment" (*AP,* XXIV, p. 167; also quoted in Rosanvallon 1985, 72).

62. "Avons-nous besoin des journeaux? Oui, sans nul doute. Ils sont l'une des conditions du gouvernement représentatif, l'un de ses principes de vie. Un journal est-il une influence? Oui, et peut-être la plus puissante des influences. *Or l'influence politique appelle une garantie*; la garantie politique ne se rencontre, selon les principes de notre Charte, que dans une certaine *situation sociale*; cette situation est determinée par la propriété, ou par ses equivalents. Voilà le principe du cautionnement" (Royer-Collard 1861a, 486; emphasis added). A similar position was held by another liberal, Lainé (see Nesmes-Desmarets 1908, 306–7).

63. On this point, see Guizot 1858a, 177–84; Vaulabelle 1856, 27–28.

64. For more details, see Constant's "De la liberté des brochures, des pamphlets, et de journaux, considérée sous le rapport de l'intérêt du gouvenement" (1818), reedited in Constant 1957, 1219–43.

65. Constant criticized the provisions of the laws regarding the journals. In his view, journals did not have to be subject to special jurisdiction: "Dès que la presse est un instrument, elle doit rentrer dans le droit commun" (quoted in Hatin 1861, 327).

66. Charles Comte argued that "la faculté de divulguer ses opinions est aussi naturelle à l'homme que la faculté de faire usage de ses mains. . . . Une loi sur la liberté des opinions ou sur la liberté de la presse sera donc aussi ridicule qu'une loi sur la liberté de la voix, sur la liberté de la plume, ou sur la liberté des mains: il n'y a qu'une longue tyrannie qui ait pu faire demander des lois sur un tel sujet" (Comte as quoted in Jaume 1994a, 116, fn. 10).

67. Writes Constant: "Je me refuse à cette sorte d'aristocratie intellectuelle qui ferait regarder les lumières et la raison comme le partage exclusif d'une partie de la société. . . . Le véritable objet d'utilité des journaux est de dénoncer les abus, d'accueillir la plainte, d'appeler l'attention sur l'arbitraire et les excès du pouvoir. Les journaux ne sont pas des recueils de philosophie" (*AP,* XXIV, p. 168; also quoted in Jaume 1997b). For more details on the liberals' critique of the Doctrinaires, see Harpaz 1968, 122–28.

68. See Guizot 1858a, 179. For a more critical reading of the Doctrinaires, see Jaume 1997b.

69. Guizot 1858b, 49–50. The original French text contains a few passages that were not included in the English translation (see Guizot 1858a, 45–50).

70. For more details, see Guizot 1817d, 263–65.

71. Guizot 1817d, 265. Writes Guizot: "La liberté de la presse, où quelques personnes ne voulaient voir que l'exercise d'un droit individuel, a été rappelée à sa destination nationale, qui est de garantir tous les droits en assurant l'expression de toutes les pensées, patrimoine commun de la société toute entière. . . . C'est là ce qui importe: *des institutions bien comprises et bien liées entr'elles*" (Guizot 1817d, 266; emphasis added).

CHAPTER TEN

The Elitist Liberalism of the French Doctrinaires Revisited

Ideas perish from inanition far more frequently than as a result of being refuted by argument.

—Isaiah Berlin

Summary

Political theory is usually construed as the study of canonical authors and texts. As such, it seeks to illuminate those ideas that allegedly have perennial importance and transcend the limits of a particular historical context. But there is another way of thinking about the task of political theory, namely, as an in-depth investigation of the multifarious political languages in which different societies articulate their problems and attempt to solve them. Since these political vocabularies are the outcome of particular historical evolutions, in order to examine them we must behave like archaeologists who believe that the past is not a mere repository of obsolete values, but a place where buried intellectual treasures are waiting to be discovered.[1] Such a treasure, I have argued in this book, is the political thought of the French Doctrinaires.

The main goal of this study is to reveal the main aspects of the Doctrinaires' political philosophy that help us rethink the nature and the limits of the political. Isaiah Berlin once claimed that ideas often perish from inanition rather than as a result of being properly refuted. It would be fair to say that the Doctrinaires suffered from an unusual and unfair process of "starvation" at the hands of unsympathetic historians. Hence, this book attempted to change the conventional image of the French Doctrinaires as uninspiring, second-rate minds by concentrating on their most important works, published or written during the Bourbon Restoration, such as Guizot's *Histoire de la civilisation en Europe*, *Histoire des origines du gouvernement représentatif en Europe*, *Philosophie politique: de la souveraineté*, *Des moyens de gouvernement et d'opposition*, Barante's *Des communes et de l'aristocratie*, and Royer-Collard's parliamentary discourses. I argued that the fall of the July Monarchy in 1848 should not be regarded as a sufficient argument to dismiss the entire political thought of the Doctrinaires, in particular their liberal writings published during the Restoration.

The book closely followed the sometimes clear, sometimes cryptic ways in which the French Doctrinaires accepted, tested, or challenged the conventions of their own age, introduced new concepts and principles, and offered propositions and guidelines for political action. In this study, I also challenged the standard image of the Bourbon Restoration (1814–30) and demonstrated that its unique intellectual and political climate created a new vocabulary and agenda for political theory. More specifically, I claimed that this period did not contribute to the narrowing of political outlook (as Roger Soltau claimed),[2] but represented a true golden age of political thought that was characterized by a unique cross-fertilization of ideas and theories. This was an age of great hopes and great battles, a period characterized by an extraordinary revival of arts and sciences that radically transformed the institutional framework of postrevolutionary France. Key issues such as the reorganization of the electoral system and the army, freedom of the press, and the prerequisites of representative government were openly discussed in Parliament and the press. I placed the Doctrinaires in their historical and political environment, outlined their major theoretical innovations, and when appropriate, compared their political and philosophical views to those of other prominent political thinkers such as Tocqueville, Constant, Chateaubriand, Vitrolles, Ancillon, and Cortés.

Moreover, I argued that, in addition to being a leading historian, Guizot was also a major political theorist, comparable in many ways to Madame de Staël, Tocqueville, and Constant (my preferred thinker remains, however, Tocqueville). I commented on the main themes of Guizot's major works such as *Histoire de la civilisation en Europe*, *Histoire de la civilisation en France*, and *Histoire des origines du gouvernement représentatif en Europe*, as well as on his ideas that can be found in lesser-known writings such as *Du gouvernement de la France*, *Des moyens de gouvernement et d'opposition dans l'état actuel de la France*, *De la peine de mort en matière politique*, and *Philoso-*

phie politique: de la souveraineté. Special attention was paid to Guizot's articles published in *Archives philosophiques, politiques et littéraires* and *Revue française*. In particular, I highlighted a dimension of Guizot's thought that has usually been downplayed or overlooked by his interpreters, namely his idea that true freedom can survive only in a pluralist society in which various principles, ideas, and interests, coexist and are engaged in constant competition for power in a regime of publicity.

This book also demonstrated the existence of a strong affinity between the political vision of the French Doctrinaires and Tocqueville's ideas, an affinity that went much deeper than it has been assumed thus far. The Doctrinaires initiated a new way of thinking about democracy (as social condition) that exercised a seminal influence on Tocqueville's method of analyzing democracy and its fundamental principle, the equality of conditions. I examined the close intellectual dialogue between Tocqueville, Guizot, and Royer-Collard and concluded that in order to fully understand the conceptual framework of Tocqueville's *De la démocratie en Amérique*, we must first read Guizot's *Histoire de la civilisation en Europe* and Royer-Collard's parliamentary speeches during the Restoration. I also argued that Guizot's theory of pluralism and civilization suggested to both Tocqueville and Mill the ways in which democracy can be purified, "tamed," and channeled into stable institutions. By reflecting on Guizot's lectures on civilization, Tocqueville and Mill understood that the survival of democratic society depends on its ability to foster and sustain a free competition for power ("systematic antagonism") between rival ideas, principles, forces, modes of life, and interests. They also came to distrust the influence of any power that reigns uncontrolled in society.

Furthermore, I claimed that the Doctrinaires' theory of the sovereignty of reason did *not* lead to the emptying of sovereignty of practical content. The Doctrinaires emphasized that popular sovereignty and popular will must be constrained by pregiven moral principles and values. As such, their theory of the sovereignty of reason had a *liberal* character, although it was not predicated upon the inviolability of individual rights as was the case, for example, with Constant's doctrine of sovereignty. Guizot relied upon the assumption that human beings are fallible and are always inclined to abuse power if allowed to do so. He emphasized the relativity of *all* human claims to legitimate power and sovereignty and maintained that none of these claims should be privileged. All powers are relative, and their legitimacy must be made contingent upon their demonstrating the conformity of their actions to the precepts of reason, truth, and justice. Finally, by comparing Guizot's theory of the sovereignty of reason with Constant's ideas on sovereignty, I concluded that their views on this topic should be seen as two overlapping strategies of criticizing absolute and arbitrary power.

On a more general level, by adding a new flavor—the elitist liberalism of the French Doctrinaires—to the already bewildering diversity of the liberal family, this book also attempted to contribute vicariously to contemporary debates on liberalism and the historical evolution of liberal democracy. At a point in time when the old belief in discussion seems outmoded and the confidence in parliamentary politics has substantially declined in the West, the Doctrinaires' definition of publicity as the cornerstone of representative government ("government by discussion") reminds us that parliamentary debates and the press can play a key role in the general education and improvement of society. The Doctrinaires' writings point out that freedom depends on the existence of a free competition of ideas, opinions, and interests in society. They also teach us a timely lesson about the importance of studying the role of elites in shaping and changing political institutions. Studying political elites and the norms governing their actions does not a priori have antidemocratic connotations. If political science is to become once again relevant to society's problems, students of politics must broaden their outlook and should avoid working with rigid or unrealistic assumptions about the functioning of political institutions.

Furthermore, the Doctrinaires' sociological and historical approach made their liberalism different from the utilitarian and analytical type of liberalism predominant in the English-speaking world (then and now).[3] Guizot and his colleagues emphasized that the most important issues in political theory ought not to be divorced from questions regarding the social condition as illustrated by mores, customs, property, and class relations. Finally, this book also explored the uneasy alliance between liberalism and democracy and the ways in which the tensions between the two were addressed by Guizot and the other Doctrinaires. The next sections of this concluding chapter will discuss the nature of French liberalism and the elitist liberalism of the Doctrinaires in the context of contemporary debates on liberal democracy.

French Liberalism: An Oxymoron?

"I have never met a Frenchman who was a liberal," Émile Faguet once ironically remarked. What today seems merely a witty remark was, in fact, a commonplace in France one century ago, when liberal principles were rejected as inadequate or hypocritical, and liberalism was seen as a mere oxymoron or an exotic eccentricity. This attitude had deep roots in French political culture. For example, in the 1830s, Tocqueville declared himself a "liberal of a new kind," while claiming at the same time that the liberal party to which he belonged did not exist.

Fortunately, a lot has changed in France in the last three decades of the twentieth century. As a result of a "velvet revolution,"[4] liberalism has become a fashionable political ideology, signaling a momentous intellectual change away from Marxism, which Sartre regarded as the unsurpassable horizon of our times. In the footsteps of Raymond Aron and François Furet, contemporary French political philosophers, historians, and sociologists such as Pierre Rosanvallon, Pierre Manent, Lucien Jaume, and Marcel Gauchet have contributed to the rediscovery of a rich tradition of nineteenth-century French political thought and thus managed to exorcise the specter of their country's illiberal past.[5]

The complex legacy of the French Revolution and its internal contradictions explain why French liberals grappled with a particular set of challenging issues and why their solutions and approaches to topics such as rights, individualism, and the market were often found to be unorthodox and unconventional when compared to those advanced by English liberals across the Channel. It has been noted that in France important liberal principles such as limited power and the rights of man were rooted in their moment of origin and were associated with the "movement of rage" of 1789. Right-wing critics of liberalism accused French liberals of disseminating revolutionary doctrines and ideas and drew a parallel between liberal principles and the theories of the *philosophes*, claiming that postrevolutionary liberals recycled the ideas of Voltaire and Diderot. The very word *libéral* was ironically interpreted as "*homme libéré.*" Not surprisingly, an article published in *Le drapeau blanc* in 1818 defined liberalism as "*la religion des gens qui fréquentent les galères.*"[6] A few years later, when the liberals were no longer in power, the incriminatory tone remained unchanged. "Let us read the writings that seep from the pen of liberalism," wrote Abbé Beauchamp in 1822, "listen to the speech of its orators, and everywhere we will see that they profess the same principles. . . . Liberalism will admit into its ranks and under its banner anyone who . . . abjure[s] Catholicism and . . . swear[s] an eternal war not only against royalty, but against all kings."[7] Furthermore, some ultraroyalists denounced liberalism as a disguised form of political Protestantism and took it to task for furthering egoism and anarchy in society. As such, explained an ultraconservative contributor to *Mémorial catholique*, liberalism "carries death to the heart of society"[8] because it sanctifies the individual along with one's desires and rights and makes one neglect one's duties toward his Creator and society.

If many peculiar features of French liberalism can be attributed to its historical origins and the context in which it developed, its strengths and weaknesses along with its protean and sometimes ambiguous qualities require further explanation. To be sure, if many French thinkers were renowned for their rich theoretical imagination, their political theories were often found wanting by more pragmatic spirits concerned to a greater extent with the practical implications of political ideas and principles. French ideas and slogans such as the famous *"Liberté, Fraternité, Égalité"* were bold and marvelous creations of the human mind, but they were used to legitimize political regimes that proved to be inimical to individual freedom and happiness. Too often, French thinkers shunned moderation and opted instead for various forms of radicalism that displayed a disquieting propensity to excess and perfectionism. Where, after all, one might rhetorically ask, are the French equivalents of Benjamin Franklin, George Washington, and James Madison?

As Edouard Laboulaye once acknowledged, the propensity to perfectionism had always been a prominent feature of modern French political culture.[9] But in France, perfectionism has often gone hand in hand with a particular concern with style and rhetoric. A seventeenth-century writer, Béat-Louis de Muralt, candidly acknowledged: "Style, whatever it expresses, is an important thing in France. Elsewhere, expressions are born of thoughts . . . , here it is the reverse; often it is the expressions that give birth to thoughts."[10] A century later, Tocqueville conveyed a similar idea in his *Souvenirs*. He argued that the French display an unusual propensity to radicalism and tend to judge by impressions rather than reasons. As such, the French look for what is novel and ingenuous rather than for what is true and show themselves sensible to the playing and elocution of the actors without regard to the results of the play.[11]

Time has proved Tocqueville right again and again. In the last century, disenchanted with the "decadent" bourgeois world in which they lived, and thirsting for new certainties that were expected to free them from the shackles of the "rotten" capitalist world, many French intellectuals often indulged in vitriolic critiques of Western liberal democratic regimes and exaggerated the accomplishments of Soviet-style communism. Of course, none of the *bien-pensant* intellectuals moved permanently to Moscow or Beijing to enjoy, live, the "marvelous" accomplishments of the actually existing communism. Instead, they spent long hours chatting in the pleasant cafés on Boulevard Saint-Michel in Paris and paid occasional visits to their heroes in the East, when they became bored with the "unbearable lightness of being" in the decadent capitalist world.

To this day, French liberalism has not fully shed some of its peculiar features that have made it so different from its counterpart across the Channel or the Ocean.[12] To quote again Tocqueville, "in France there is only one thing we can't set up: that is free government; and only one institution we can't destroy: that is centralization" (Tocqueville 1959, 189–90). Not surprisingly, skeptical observers of the French scene such as Jack Hayward have claimed that in France "liberalism still remains something of an alien import, accepted with a reluctant resignation rather than enthusiasm, damned by its Anglo-Saxon connotations and feared as a threat to French exceptionalism" (Hayward 1998, 241–2). In Françoise Mélonio's opinion, France has had liberal practices and liberal sensibilities on both the left and the right, but not a "true" liberalism similar to the English liberalism grounded in constitutionalism, decentralization, and self-government.[13] This point was echoed by Pierre Rosanvallon, who remarked that nineteenth-century French liberalism lacked many of the principles and ideas that were central to eighteenth- and nineteenth-century English liberalism. For historian Sudhir Hazareesingh, French liberalism has always been an intrinsically contradictory phenomenon, mysterious and elusive at the same time. "On the one hand," he wrote, "French political history . . . can be read in terms of a progressive development of liberal ideas and liberal institutions. On the other hand, this strength is often difficult to isolate with precision. For one thing, it is obscured by the apparent inability of liberals to recognize the central elements of their own doctrine, or indeed even each other" (Hazareesingh 1998, 166; 163). Hazareesingh also noted that the very idea that the state should be neutral among competing versions of the good life has not been well received in France.

Tony Judt went even further to claim that France has always lacked the building blocks of a genuine liberal political vision, such as a strong emphasis on individual rights and the separation between the public and private spheres. French thinkers, argued Judt, often succumbed to the seductions of civic virtue, civic duties, and statism and the language of rights underwent an important conceptual transformation in France. From a protective device designed to defend individuals against the encroachment of the state, it evolved into the basis for justifying the claims and actions of those in power. The enjoyment of civil liberties and rights was sometimes made dependent on the need for preserving social and political order. As a result, abstract or natural rights were displaced in favor of positive and concrete rights that could be forfeited in exceptional or emergency situations. According to Judt, to speak of natural rights or rights against the interference of the state in private affairs has never been a favorite topic in France.[14]

Moreover, the French also displayed a strong propensity toward a strong executive power that, in turn, engendered a particular type of liberalism *through* the state, not against the state as in the Anglo-American liberal tradition. The habit of looking to the state for assistance was accompanied by a nuanced form of skepticism toward individualism and utilitarianism and a certain distrust of the market. "The indivisibility of the State," wrote Soltau, "the supremacy of its rights, the dependence on it of any individual or association, all this is taken as axiomatic [in France]" (Soltau 1959, xxii). According to Rosanvallon, most of these attitudes can be found in the writings of the French Doctrinaires, whose "anti-individualistic" liberalism espoused a monist view of the social, had little interest in the subject of civil society, and granted priority to executive power.[15]

Finally, in *L'individu effacé ou le paradoxe du libéralisme français*, undoubtedly the most comprehensive history of nineteenth-century French liberalism to date, Lucien Jaume identified the existence of three major strands of liberalism in France: *elitist liberalism* to be found in the Doctrinaires' writings; *individualistic liberalism* associated with Constant and Madame de Staël and predicated upon the inviolability of individual rights and personal autonomy; and *Catholic liberalism*, which sought to reconcile the doctrines of the Catholic Church with the claims of the modern state. Jaume attributed the shortcomings of French liberalism to the alleged domination of the former (statist) type of liberalism over the last two versions of liberalism. As a result, argued Jaume, "France did not have a philosophic resource to think through a liberalism comparable to Locke in England" (Jaume 1997a, 14). French thinkers have too often been inclined to speculate on concepts such as the sovereignty of reason or *gouvernabilité* and downplayed equally important issues such as individual rights, the economic market, and the separation of powers.

He who insists too much on the alleged incoherence of French liberalism risks overlooking, however, not only its key features, but also its unique virtues. It is important to remember that in eighteenth-century France there was a tradition of fighting against absolute power, as illustrated, for example, by the works of Boullainvillers and Le Paige, who sought to limit the power of the monarchs by increasing the influence of the nobles, Parliament, and the magistrates.[16] From the very beginning, liberalism became a synonym for opposition to political absolutism and administrative tyranny and was equated with open-mindedness (in the nineteenth century, the liberal motto was "liberty without anarchy, order without despotism"). Most liberals were in favor of a constitutional monarchy consisting of a king (performing the function of a neutral power), an upper Chamber of Peers, and an elected

Chamber of Deputies. Eventually liberalism came to be identified with the defense of the values and interests of the middle class and acquired a clearer social profile and identity, thus becoming "a form of education, a *Bildung* of personality, and a political culture" (Jaume 1997a, 18).

At the same time, it is important to acknowledge the tensions between the different types of French liberalism that might account to a certain extent for its elusive and protean quality. For example, during the Restoration, there was a variety of liberal attitudes and ideas that included left-wing liberals such as La Fayette, Manuel, and Constant and *juste milieu* liberals such as Cousin, Guizot, and the other Doctrinaires.[17] They all shared a common allegiance to the principles of representative government and constitutionalism but held different views on issues such as the organization of power, individual rights, and liberty of the press. Furthermore, it is worth pointing out that during the Restoration both the left and the right advanced a certain number of liberal claims. It will be recalled that Chateaubriand's *De la monarchie selon la Charte* made a series of liberal arguments that articulated a coherent theory of constitutional monarchy. Moreover, during the first years of the Bourbon Restoration, the ultraroyalists defended decentralization, even if their political project was ultimately antiliberal.

Perhaps even more significantly, the link between political and economic liberalism has always been tenuous in France, compared to England or the United States. From its inception, French liberalism has been *political* and *historical*, not economic. It will be recalled that Tocqueville was skeptical toward some principles of commercial society and did not share many ideas that loomed large in the writings of prominent economic liberals such as Bastiat and Say. Along with Royer-Collard, he denounced the crass materialism of the July Monarchy in harsh words worthy of Flaubert or Marx. The reign of the middle class, wrote Tocqueville, was exclusive and corrupt, public morality was degraded, and a general flatness and mediocrity threatened to create a flaccid humanity, incapable of great heroic actions.[18] A few decades later, Taine expressed a similar discontent in the following terms: "A society is like a garden: it can be laid out to produce peaches and oranges, or else carrots and cabbages. Ours is entirely laid out for carrots and cabbages."[19]

At the same time, many French liberals were critical of the radical tendencies associated with socialism and political democracy. The Doctrinaires, for example, advocated moderate reforms, went to great length to separate themselves from rival doctrines, and developed a prudent and flexible approach that regarded politics as an open-ended exercise, in which rules and procedures ought to be constantly adapted to the necessities of the moment. Their opponents charged them with political opportunism and often found them guilty by association with the dominant *juste milieu* of the July Monarchy. Yet, the proverbial flexibility of the Doctrinaires was an outcome of their skepticism toward radical forms of democracy (socialism) and must be linked to their awareness of the limitations of the anachronistic politics advocated by radicals on both ends of the political spectrum. Be that as it may, the ability to adapt itself to circumstances came to be regarded as the hallmark of French liberalism, and the French liberals were eventually pushed to the fringes of political life, being condemned to marginal positions, unable to influence the major political and intellectual debates of their country.[20] Nonetheless, it must be reiterated that this was *not* the case during the Restoration and the July Monarchy, when liberals of various persuasions managed to exercise a significant influence on the political and cultural agenda of that time.

Hence, it would be an exaggeration to affirm that a political and social center "between a utopian future and a nostalgically reclaimed past . . . did not exist in France" (Judt 1992, 242). During the Restoration, the Doctrinaires occupied precisely such a fragile space between prophets of the past and left-wing radicals and faced a set of challenges that taught them timely lessons about the fragility of political institutions in a conflict-ridden political environment as well as about the fundamental antinomies at the heart of modern society. This unique situation created a *liberalism under siege* that forced the Doctrinaires to be at the same time partisans and critics of democracy, aristocracy, and the French Revolution. This context also explains how the Doctrinaires, who were no friends of absolute power, sometimes arrived at conclusions about the organization of power and the status of individuals that differed from what we regard today as self-evident principles in the Anglo-American political tradition.

The Liberalism of the French Doctrinaires

It would be tempting to argue that the liberalism of the French Doctrinaires was in many ways a liberalism *extra muros*.[21] But, as we familiarize ourselves with their writings and learn more about their historical context, we realize that the Doctrinaires, too, defended the main principles associated with nineteenth-century (European) liberalism: opposition to absolute power, gradual reform, freedom of thought and freedom of movement, limited power, publicity, division of powers, civil rights, liberty of the press, freedom of speech, and trial by jury.[22]

Nonetheless, the Doctrinaires' liberalism was unconventional if compared to the ideas held by classical liberals. Guizot and his colleagues developed an original theory of sovereignty and the "new means of government" based on an original, if controversial, understanding of the relation between state and society. Without being anti-individualist, their liberalism was critical of certain forms of individualism and paid less attention to economic issues than did other liberals across the Channel. At the risk of abusing our contemporary language, we might characterize the eclectic liberalism of the Doctrinaires as an original mixture of "perfectionist" and "agonistic" liberalism grounded in a "liberalism of fear" *avant la lettre*.[23] The perfectionist strand is demonstrated by the Doctrinaires' belief that the goal of the state is to create the conditions for the harmonious moral and intellectual development of individuals in accord with the progress of civilization. The agonistic strand of the Doctrinaires' liberalism was related to their belief that, since liberal institutions are the outcome of both historical contingency and conscious design, rights and liberties could never be made fixed, being the contested product of conflict and various political settlements. If the Doctrinaires often regarded themselves as the "party of resistance," their position was not reactionary, since their main concern was not to restore the Old Regime, but "to end" the Revolution by building representative institutions. Yet, theirs also was a "liberalism of fear" haunted by the specter of the Revolution starting over and over again. Historical memory is the faculty of mind on which this type of liberalism draws most heavily and seeks to avoid the evils of the past by keeping the memory of past tragedies alive as a source of instruction and an appeal to moderation.

Nonetheless, there was much more to the Doctrinaires' liberalism than this fear of revolution. Their own version of perfectionist liberalism rested upon the assumption that cultivating a society of responsible agents is dependent upon individuals having the opportunity to develop proper capacities for moral and personal autonomy. As such, the Doctrinaires' political vision was based upon an enlightened pedagogy of the nation and an ambitious *gouvernement des esprits*. As we have already seen, they believed that the state has a certain moral purpose *beyond* the protection of property rights and the creation of the conditions for the individual pursuit of material goals. At the same time, the Doctrinaires maintained that this ought to be done in a constitutional framework whose main purpose is to prevent the usurpation of the sovereignty of right and to create and sustain a vibrant social and political pluralism. As Guizot pointed out, legitimate sovereignty must endlessly be sought and all those who exercise power must always be constrained to demonstrate the legitimacy of their claims to power. This could be achieved by allowing for "the confrontation of independent and equal powers capable of reciprocally imposing on each other the obligation of seeking the truth in common" (Guizot 1985, 343).

Another striking feature of the Doctrinaires' liberalism was its *sociological* and *historical imagination;* that is, the ability to determine certain structural traits of modern society, to examine the primary elements of social structure (beliefs, property, institutions, rules, and the like), and to explore their relations to political institutions in historical comparative perspective.[24] The Doctrinaires' writings provided a detailed analysis of the interplay between institutions, religious creeds, political and philosophical ideas, and social structure. They regarded the development of civil life as being linked to the moral development of individuals and the type of relations they establish among themselves. Guizot and his colleagues made of the distinction between political institutions and social structure a central tenet of their political thought and grounded the latter in a comprehensive theory of social and historical change. They combined the analysis of institutions, structures, practices, mores, beliefs, culture, property and class relations, and habits sustaining various modes of life with a critical examination of the key features of modernity relevant to political life.

In addressing these questions, Guizot and the other Doctrinaires argued that theory and political action must be based on a *theory of society* (encompassing the facts that constitute the state of society and the laws that bring these facts together and allow them to coexist), a *theory of principles* (defined as the ensemble of the principles to which the institutions are related and which form their foundation and determine their nature), and a *theory of morality* (defined as the totality of the ideas and moral sentiments of society).[25] As Guizot pointed out in *Histoire de la civilisation en France,* any study of civilization should consider the latter both as a social and moral development in the history of mutual relations among individuals. The most important issues in political theory cannot be divorced from questions regarding the social condition as illustrated by mores, customs, property, and class relations. Social state, argued Guizot, is closely linked to the moral state of nations, which includes creeds, feelings, ideas, manners that precede the external condition, social relations, and the political institutions of each society. That is why in order to determine the nature of any political regime, we must first examine the state of the people, the collective beliefs, the fabric of society, its composition, the manner of life, the relations between different classes, the patterns of authority, the ways in which individuals live together and pursue both individual and common goals, and the distribution and circulation of property.[26]

Hence, the Doctrinaires proposed a more sociological and historical mode of political argument that focused on social and institutional change in historical perspective. As we have already seen, central to their political thought was a long-term view of history based on a theory of civilization and progress that emphasized the interaction between various social and individual activities, between modes of behavior, philosophical ideas, religious creeds, sciences, letters, and arts. In their view, the study of the social state had to be supplemented by the investigation of the internal state of individuals, that is, the state of souls, the ideas, doctrines, and the whole intellectual life of individuals, along with the relations between ideas and actions. The moral state, argued Guizot, ought to be seen as distinct from and, to a certain point, independent of the social state; as such, it exercises a strong influence on institutions that reflect the moral state of society and are dependent on it.[27]

Accordingly, what Guizot and his friends had to say about liberty and authority, power, representation, and sovereignty derived from a preliminary analysis of the types of society to which these concepts were related. The Doctrinaires pointed out the existence of different types of society (aristocratic, democratic) and examined the ways in which political concepts reflect and spring out of various social structures. In so doing, they drew upon and brought together a number of different intellectual traditions by combining insights from history, sociology, philosophy, and theology. While making a seminal distinction between social, moral, and political order, Guizot and his colleagues underscored the complex and unique nature of the *political* as a distinctive dimension of human life that cannot be reduced to a mere epiphenomenon of economics, as Marx famously claimed. It is also worth pointing out that the Doctrinaires' approach was qualitatively different from the scientism and positivism of Saint-Simon, Comte, and their disciples.

A brief comparison between the Doctrinaires' conception of the political with the views on this topic held by two prominent nineteenth-century English liberals, Jeremy Bentham and James Mill, is also useful. The main contrast I have in mind is between a theory of politics that emphasizes its relation to and dependence on a combination of social and historical factors and an alternative conception that regards politics as autonomous and seeks to discover its laws by using apodictic methods similar to those of natural science. Drawing inspiration from Hobbes's deductive approach to politics and society, the utilitarianism of Bentham and Mill[28] aspired to create a new science of politics that sought to eliminate from politics "vague" and ill-defined notions such the rights of men and natural laws. To this effect, they postulated a priori principles and worked from basic and allegedly immutable features of human nature in order to reach "rigorous" conclusions about individual desires, passions, and feelings. To Mackintosh, who objected to this type of argument, James Mill reiterated his belief that the man who subjected the largest province of human knowledge to the fewest principles was to be esteemed the most successful philosopher. Moreover, Mill and Bentham developed a predominantly static mode of argument that paid relatively little attention to institutional change in historical perspective.

The French Doctrinaires opposed this mode of argument. They believed that the concepts used to describe human actions cannot be defined with a mathematical precision that would yield apodictic axioms regarding human behavior in general. Guizot and his colleagues regarded history and sociology as indispensable to their intellectual and political agendas. They started from the assumption that all questions concerning political institutions are relative to the society in which they operate, which was another way of claiming that different stages of human progress inevitably have different political institutions. For example, the nature of the checks on government and their effectiveness cannot be decided once for ever in light of an allegedly immutable theory such as the separation of powers. It is determined by the social condition of each society and the ways in which the private and the public spheres are linked to each other.

In politics as well as in human affairs in general, remarked Guizot, a priori reasoning and deduction cannot grasp the bewildering variety displayed by social and individual life. Political life is more or less intractable to large-scale rational construction that ignores the basic truth that the each type of polity has its own set of manners, values, norms, and modes of behavior. In the Doctrinaires' view, it was impossible to deduce a science of government from a narrow set of principles governing human nature, entirely detached from a preliminary knowledge of history and society. Instead, a general theory of politics must rely on the insights and lessons provided by a philosophy of history that accounts for the development of political institutions over time and highlights their complex relations with a wide range of cultural, economic, and social factors.

The same conclusions can be reached from a cursory examination of the articles published in the *Edinburgh Review*. Jeffrey, Horner, Mackintosh, Brougham, and Macaulay shared a common interest in analyzing the profile of modern commercial society through the lenses of history, economics, and philosophy. Macaulay believed that, in order to explain contemporary political phenomena, one should study how social and institutional change occurs and must descend into the fabric of society instead of remaining on its surface. Like Guizot, Macaulay was persuaded that the most important revolutions in the history of mankind were "noiseless" phenomena consisting of gradual and peaceful changes in manners and morals. In his opinion, "he alone reads history right, who, observing how powerfully circumstances influence the feelings and opinions of men . . . learns to distinguish what is accidental and transitory in human nature from what is essential and immutable."[29] Macaulay encouraged politicians and historians to spend more time studying and understanding the life of society and the general moral and cultural spirit of each period, which, in turn, exercises a powerful influence on social and political institutions.[30]

Rethinking Liberalism

Unconventional cases such as French nineteenth-century liberalism should be of particular interest to all scholars who wish to explore the tensions between liberal and illiberal principles in the history of modern Europe. Unfortunately, there is a tendency among historians of political thought—at least, in the English-speaking world—to shy away from examining those forms of liberalism which have developed in cultures with seemingly fragile liberal traditions. How many studies of Italian, French, or German liberalism(s) have been published in the past five decades? The question is far from being rhetorical, and the difficulty in answering it indicates a failure of political theorists to come to grips in a meaningful way with the complexity of the liberal tradition in all its manifestations.

To be sure, the paucity of studies of nineteenth-century European political thought in comparative (cross-national) perspective continues to be a serious problem confronting all students of liberalism. The notorious ambiguity of the concept of *liberalism* also comes into play here. As James Sheehan once argued (1984, 44), "no term within the vocabulary of politics is more difficult to define than liberalism," which is a many-sided tradition that has produced a rich variety of emphases and approaches. Moreover, there are many competing definitions of liberalism and there is surprisingly little agreement about its boundaries and meanings. Too often, one type of liberalism—the Anglo-American type—has been emphasized at the expense of other strands of liberalism, and the outcome has been an impoverished understanding of the internal diversity of liberalism.

The foray into the history of nineteenth-century French liberalism gives us the opportunity to address this problem and to reflect on the complex alliance between liberalism and democracy. At the same time, it warns us against the tendency to draw simplistic conclusions regarding the evolution of liberalism and to conflate the principles of liberalism and democracy. The orthodox view of liberalism that can be found in many textbooks locates the origins of liberalism in the seventeenth-century theories of the state of nature and the social contract. It regards Hobbes and Locke as forefathers of Adam Smith and J. S. Mill and explains the rise of a particular type of liberalism whose central values are individualism, rationalism, and utilitarianism and whose main actors are autonomous rational individuals seeking to maximize the satisfaction of their personal wants.[31] "Strange" liberals such as Tocqueville and Humboldt rarely figure in these anthologies, because their ideas do not always fit the general profile of liberalism.

This interpretation deserves to be revised, since it offers a unidimensional and, ultimately, misleading account of the nature and evolution of liberalism. We must study the ways in which beleaguered liberals responded to the challenges mounted by their opponents in countries with fragile liberal traditions. The retrieval from oblivion of the liberalism of the French Doctrinaires can heighten our awareness of the internal diversity of liberalism and prevents us from drawing a simplistic contrast between liberalism and conservatism in a way that neglects not only the richness of nineteenth-century liberal thought, but also the extent to which liberal themes were sometimes advanced by conservative thinkers.

The unique political and social situation of the nineteenth century, so different from ours today, makes the task of intellectual historians even more difficult. "The contours of the liberal movement in the nineteenth century," argued Alan Kahan, "are still too hazy for a definitive study to be undertaken with substantial hope of success" (Kahan 1991, 3). That is why we need more historical investigations of the different kinds of liberalism that have existed in the past two centuries. A historically informed approach could offer a useful typology that would allow us to perceive the essence of liberalism in its various manifestations over time. Furthermore, it would also allow us to apprehend the boundaries of liberalism vis-à-vis its main political opponents, conservatism and socialism. Hence, we should firmly resist the temptation of attributing to liberalism a uniform and monolithic worldview that cannot be found in liberal discourses, particularly in nineteenth-century writings that encompassed a bewildering variety of ideas, principles, values, discourses, practices, and rhetoric.

In my opinion, nineteenth-century French liberalism should be described as a network of overlapping similarities and family resemblances or, to put it differently, as a multivocal system of ideas, discourses, practices, and institutions in which it is difficult to discern a hegemonic voice.[32] That is why we must explore family resemblances and differences between the various types of liberalism that have existed in the past. We must also point out the ways in which these types continue to be part of the larger liberal family whose richness comes from the many dialects that have been spoken by liberals of all kinds over time. To this effect, we need extensive historical comparative investigations of the various types of liberal ideas and practices that would also shed light on unorthodox forms of liberalism, such as that of the Doctrinaires. Since French liberals held widely different views on topics such as the Enlightenment and the French Revolution, religion and modern commercial society, the nature of parliamentary (as opposed to merely representative) government, reform from above as opposed to emancipation from below, class struggle, political democracy, civil and political rights, it behooves us to explore the entire gamut of these views and to assess the similarities and differences between them.

But, one might ask, why is it so important to highlight the internal diversity of liberalism? Does it really matter if we refer to "liberalisms" rather than "liberalism"? And why do we need a typology of liberalism after all? These are important and legitimate questions that ought to be properly addressed by all historians of liberalism. It has been remarked that liberal democracy enjoys today a paradoxical status in the Western world: It is both quasihegemonic and jeopardized.[33] On the one hand, it can be argued that there is no serious ideological challenger to the triumph of liberal democracy at the end of this century (at least in the West), after the exhaustion of Marxism. One could even argue that we are all liberal democrats today. On the other hand, because of the triumph of liberal democratic principles, there is a tendency to conflate liberalism with Anglo-American rights-based political liberalism, whose core is a theory of justice that purports to be neutral between various conceptions of the good life. The predominance of one type of liberalism, if it becomes an academic fashion, inevitably contributes to the neglect of other unconventional types of liberalism, which draw upon alternative conceptions of rights and sovereignty and do not seek to justify institutions and practices that claim to be neutral between rival versions of the good life.

Personal considerations and polemics aside, this issue has far-reaching implications that are worth examining in further detail. As Michael Freeden once argued (1999, 38), the deontological type of liberalism that is fashionable in contemporary academic circles has a weak *political* element and an "etiolated understanding of the political." It is excessively concerned with articulating abstract principles of social and political organization and applying them to contemporary moral dilemmas in a more or less rigid manner that takes noncontroversiality and neutrality as ideals that ought to be pursued in politics.[34] In John Gray's opinion, "in political liberalism what justice demands is a matter not for political decision but for legal adjudication. The central institution of Rawls's political liberalism is not a deliberative assembly such as a parliament. It is a court of law" (Gray 2000, 16).

A cursory look at the writings of contemporary liberals who draw inspiration from Rawls's approach to justice seems to buttress Gray's view (I should add that I am referring here only to the general ethos supporting the approaches of contemporary political theorists working within this paradigm). Using a specific vocabulary that sometimes turns into an esoteric jargon unlikely to appeal to a general audience, these theorists avoid thinking (as a matter of principle) about larger visions of moral and political order, which are allegedly beyond their legitimate sphere of inquiry. Yet, this neglect has its own price. The outcome is an idealistic and ultimately inadequate understanding of the political, based on the questionable assumption that both social and political life ought to be regulated by a general agreement on a set of abstract principles and rules, which are supposed to be the outcome of rational deliberation or a new form of social contract among individuals. Consequently, these theories couched in procedural terms tend to reduce politics to an arena in which individuals rationally choose what kind of society they would like to live in.

The French Doctrinaires belonged to an older and arguably richer tradition of thought, one that combined historical analysis, sociological typology, and constitutional design and did not remain estranged from the great political and social transformations of the past. As historians, journalists, political philosophers, and politicians, Guizot and his colleagues sought to understand the cultural and institutional prerequisites of political life and reflected on the multifarious ways in which social and moral factors affected the functioning of political institutions. The central question with which they wrestled (even if they did not manage to fully solve it) was how to design a political system that would work efficiently and respect civil liberties, while also promoting the ideal of a harmoniously developed individual. For them, the central institution of political life was Parliament, not a supreme court.

As such, the Doctrinaires' writings help us rediscover the dignity of political power and invite us to reexamine the important role of elites in political life. Liberal democracy is *not only* about justifying norms and principles that can be accepted by any rational individual. It is *also* a method of making effective and timely decisions, often based on limited information and in a conflict-ridden environment of structural uncertainty. The presence of elites is an undeniable and inevitable fact of political life in liberal democratic regimes. As Joseph Schumpeter pointed out, contrary to common beliefs, elites do not a priori undermine the functioning of democratic institutions; democracy is as much about individual freedom as about free competition for free votes. In a democratic regime, the primary function of the electorate, noted Schumpeter (1950, 273), is "to produce government," a thesis that bears striking similarities with the ideas of Guizot and Royer-Collard. The most important issue is not to eliminate political elites, but to create institutions that would ensure that elites, too, are held politically accountable and are not immune to democratic standards and practices.

The merit of the Doctrinaires is to have highlighted two fundamental facts about what constitutes good government in modern society: (1) publicity— openness, debates, and contestation—ought to be seen as the cornerstone of representative government; (2) the quality of government depends on the quality of the men who form the government as well as on the pattern of public opinion. Once again, the similarity with Schumpeter's theory of democracy is worth noting and proves that the Doctrinaires' ideas can bring an interesting contribution to our debates on liberal democracy, even if today the very notion of elitist democracy has become problematic and unpopular. It will be recalled that Schumpeter listed "democratic self-control" among the conditions of good government in modern society. In his view, this implied two things. First, "electorates and parliaments must be on an intellectual and moral level high enough to be proof against the offerings of the crook and crank" (Schumpeter 1950, 294). Second, "the voters outside of parliament must respect the division of labor between themselves and the politicians they elect" (Schumpeter 1950, 295), which, in turn, means that they must refrain from instructing their representatives about what they ought to do. While it would be easy to dismiss Schumpeter's realism as a covert manifestation of his own antidemocratic (Central European) prejudices, we should applaud his courage to affirm the need for an enlightened electorate and political class. In many ways, his views on the prerequisites of democracy appear as a twentieth-century elaboration of some themes that were central to the Doctrinaires' understanding of the functioning of representative government.

Last but not least, the case of the Doctrinaires proves that ideas can make a difference in practice and reminds us of a bygone time in which political theorists were read by a large audience and were also political actors whose ideas had a strong impact on society at large. It is equally refreshing and important to remember that the political theories advanced by many thinkers in the past were not disengaged from political facts (as it is often the case today), but were written with a clear practical purpose in mind. Their object was to design and change institutions and to offer effective blueprints for political action.

"Gray Is Beautiful"

Finally, the writings of the Doctrinaires can teach us timely lessons about the virtues and limitations of moderation in politics.[35] If anything, the case of the Doctrinaires shows that moderates are exposed to the relentless and often ruthless cross fire of extremists, who know how to play with human emotions and passions. Too often, moderates gain the reputation of indecisive spirits lost in a gray area, and their initiatives and ideas are usually dismissed as an expression of political opportunism or weariness.[36]

The political context of the Bourbon Restoration offers numerous examples that allow us to test the validity of these views. In a polemical article published in *Le Conservateur* in 1820, the ultraroyalist Marquis Coriolis d'Espinouse condemned the abuse of the word *moderation* and denounced the *modérantisme* of those who feared the presence of strong passions in politics. For Coriolis, moderation was an ill-defined and ambiguous concept that lent itself to misinterpretations which, in fact, reflected the moral confusion of French society under the Restoration.[37] Nonetheless, it would be a serious mistake to assume that moderation can be nothing more than a synonym for lukewarm and inconsistent beliefs. It is sometimes the only position that allows centrist politicians to promote contested reforms that would otherwise have been blocked or imperiled by overzealous radicals. But moderation can also lead to a peculiar form of exile, and this has been overlooked by political philosophers.

Take, for example, Nietzsche's diatribe against moderation and the mean. "The instinct of the herd," he wrote, "considers the middle and the mean as the highest and most valuable: the place where the majority finds itself; the mode and manner in which it finds itself. It is therefore an opponent of all orders of rank. . . . The herd feels the exception as something opposed and harmful to it. . . . Fear ceases in the middle: here one is never alone, here there is little room for misunderstanding; here there is equality" (Nietzsche 1967, 159). Is this a fair characterization of political moderation? Rather, is it not the case that fear does not necessarily cease in the middle and moderation is not inevitably an expression of cowardice and herd mentality?

Douglas Johnson once claimed that, from a theoretical point of view, the middle-of-the-road liberalism of the Doctrinaires was weak because it lacked those uplifting dreams which alone can inspire individuals in politics. Yet, a closer look at the environment of the Restoration demonstrates the reasonableness of *juste milieu* liberalism, which arose out of the need to achieve a decent compromise between various social and political interests. As such, the Doctrinaires' moderation did not lack political vision, courage, and practical wisdom, even when it appeared to be less inspiring and appealing than millenarian and radical movements searching for ultimate certainties and solutions on Earth. Furthermore, Guizot's own political trajectory from the liberalism of the 1820s to the conservatism of the late 1840s illustrates the difficult apprenticeship of liberty in postrevolutionary France.

More cautious than utopian thinkers, the moderates demonstrate that prudence, patience, and reliance on compromise are valuable and indispensable political virtues in any political environment. As sociologist Alan Wolfe once argued, "marginalized in the middle is perhaps the best place for the social critic to stand, for the middle looking out gives a clearer perspective than the sidelines looking in. One usually thinks of the center as solid and the extremes as precarious, but in the ideological climate of today the reverse seems more accurate; the extremes of right and left know where they stand, while the center furnishes what is original and unexpected" (Wolfe 1996, 18). The same conclusion might be applied to political actors as well.

In my view, it is the Doctrinaires' *moderation* that makes them relevant today, in an eclectic age when doctrines and ideas are again mixed, after having lost their previous sharp contours and identities. The age of extremes, one can only hope, is over, and with it also disappears the notion of politics as "the pursuit of certainty." Much like the Doctrinaires two centuries ago, we are again called to philosophize with the compass[38] and must find our way in the middle of a dark and thick forest, guided only by a few basic truths. After decades marked by utopian experiments that ended in oppression and poverty, we are now rediscovering the virtues of gray and the primacy of practical thought over utopianism. That is why, to paraphrase Adam Michnik, we must acknowledge today that "gray is beautiful" after having suffered from the tyranny of sharper and bolder colors.[39] The collapse of communism should teach us an important lesson about the need for humility and moderation in politics. If Marxism was a form of Promethean hubris, then the principles of liberal democracy, defined as a mixture of "sinfulness, saintliness, and monkey business" (Michnik 1998, 326), can immunize the body politic against the seductions of perfectionism and the tyranny of abstractions in politics.

Yet, because of its many imperfections, to love democracy well or, to put it differently, to fall in love with the subtle beauty of gray is no easy task. It demands not only passion but also moderation and prudence, as well as a certain political imagination that is prepared to swim against the current (if necessary).[40] The encounter with the Doctrinaires' works shows the errors made by the "prophets of the past" who defiantly opposed the principles of democracy and equated the latter with chaos, anarchy, and atheism. But, as Charles de Rémusat put it, to love democracy well also means to attempt to "moderate" it. Hence, the Doctrinaires' writings warn us against the errors made by the immoderate friends of liberal democracy, who forget that democracy must not be sheltered behind the rhetoric of democracy and who idolize its values and principles instead of attempting to "purify" them.

Lionel Trilling once argued that "a criticism which has at heart the inter-est of liberalism might find its most useful work not in confirming liberalism in its general sense of rightness but rather in putting under some degree of pressure the liberal ideas and assumptions of the present time" (Trilling 1953, viii). Taking this claim seriously requires that we no longer assume that the manner in which we conceptualize our own social and political problems to-day is the only adequate way of dealing with those issues. We must also ac-knowledge that liberal democracy should not be sheltered behind the reas-suring rhetoric of democracy. Many friends of democracy are still reluctant to recognize that the proper functioning of democratic institutions depends on a certain degree of virtue, capacity, and wisdom that may sometimes be en-dangered by the rigid application of the principle of equality to all spheres of social and political life.

The study of nineteenth-century (French) liberals offers valuable lessons about how to "tame" and "educate" democracy and reminds us that, in spite of our wishful thinking, liberalism and democracy do not always make in practice for a perfect marriage. As Tocqueville demonstrated, left to its own inclinations, democracy tends to engender apathy, bureaucratic despotism, individualism, and materialism. Maybe, in spite of his well-known propensity to hyperbole, Carl Schmitt was on to something important when claiming that there is no liberal politics, but only a liberal critique of politics. It is highly important that liberalism remain true to its original spirit and mission and continue to question the legitimacy of the claims made in the name of the good or just society. Like Mill and Tocqueville, Guizot and his fellow Doctrinaires believed that the "taming" of democracy could only be done gradually through education and publicity and required the formation of a new "clerisy" that was supposed to play an important role in the general (moral and material) improvement of society. In their view, democracy (as social condition) possessed the spirit of fecundity and progress, while politi-cal democracy lacked the spirit of conservation and prudence. The insights of these nineteenth-century liberals seem to contradict our democratic sen-sibility, but we would be well-advised not to dismiss them too quickly. After all, it may be true that under certain circumstances, liberalism must remain, to quote Guy Sorman (1994, 198), "*une affaire des minoritaires*" (not to be confounded, however, with a new form of technocratic elitism!), that seeks to preserve and nurture the pluralism of ideas, principles, and interests that is essential to freedom in modern society. To constitute democracy means to moderate it.

Boredom with established truths, Bernard Crick once said, may be a great enemy of free men. In turn, Isaiah Berlin, confessed: "I am bored by reading people who are allies, people of roughly the same views, because by now these things seem largely to be a collection of platitudes because we all accept them, we all believe them."[41] If we believe that imagination is (and must remain) a vital component of the liberal spirit, then we must take time to visit every now and then exotic intellectual landscapes that might provide the best cure for boredom and complacency. We should attempt to retrieve from oblivion those political philosophers who thought creatively about their world and played an important role in the transfer of ideas, but who, for various reasons that do *not* have to do with the quality of their work, have not been incorporated into the canon of political thought (yet). Reading the writings of the French Doctrinaires is a unique opportunity for such a rewarding intellectual journey that might expand our liberal imagination and might offer, as Ortega y Gasset once promised, rare and exquisite pleasures of the mind.

Notes

1. See, for example, Pocock 1971, 1–41, and Skinner 1998, 101–20.

2. See Soltau 1959, xx–xxii.

3. A comprehensive examination of the relation between liberalism and democracy in historical perspective is beyond the scope of this book. The reader can find such an analysis in the French context in Jaume 1997a.

4. I borrow the phrase from Lilla 1994a.

5. Mark Lilla summarized this change of heart as follows: "The Mitterand era has also represented the final rapprochement of the French revolutionary tradition with the liberal institutions of the Fifth Republic . . . [and] it has marked the end of a long tradition of political illiberalism and the birth of what François Furet has called a 'centrist republic'" (Lilla 1994a, 149). For a presentation of the new French thought, see Lilla 1994b, 3–34. On the place of French liberalism in the larger context of liberalism, see Manent 1994 and Manent 2001.

6. See Vaulabelle 1856, 53. Vaulabelle quoted the following (most likely, imaginary) dialogue between two former prisoners: "Quoi! Je te vois, ami, loin du bagne fatal! / Es-tu donc libéré?—Non, je suis libéral" (Vaulabelle 1856, 53).

7. The passage is taken from Beauchamp's *Du libéralisme,* as quoted in McMahon 2001, 167.

8. Quoted in McMahon 2001, 168.

9. Laboulaye 1861, xlvi.

10. Béat-Louis de Muralt as quoted in Judt 1992, 248–49. On French politics and society, see Judt 1992, 229–74, and Judt 1998, 3–27.

11. See Tocqueville 1959, 70.

12. As Bertier de Sauvigny notes, the word *liberal* appeared for the first time in a proclamation of Bonaparte from 19 Brumaire, Year VIII: "Les idées conservatrices, tutélaires, *libérales,* sont rentrées dans leurs droits par la dispersion des factieux qui opprimaient les conseils" (Sauvigny 1979, 422; emphasis added). Bertier de Sauvigny comments: "*Idées liberales,* c'était un equivalent *d'idées généreuses,* c'était la générosité appliqué au domaine de la politique" (idem emphasis added). The transition from "liberal ideas" to "liberalism" occurred later. The word *liberals* appeared in the title of a pamphlet "Les Capucins, les libéraux et les canards" (Sauvigny 1979, 423). A journal entitled *Le Libéral* was published for a short period of time in 1819.

13. See Mélonio 1994a, 38–39.

14. For more details, see Judt 1992, 233–43.

15. For more details, see Rosanvallon 1994b, 133–39.

16. For more details, see Grange 1974, 275–78.

17. For a detailed discussion, see Thureau-Dangin 1876 and Harpaz 1968.

18. See Tocqueville 1959, 1–15, 76–77.

19. Taine 1897, 33 (as quoted in Hazareesingh 1998, 171).

20. For a similar argument, see Hazareesingh 1998, 171–74.

21. Lucien Jaume claimed that the elitist liberalism of the Doctrinaires dominated nineteenth-century French liberalism: "Depuis le siècle dernier, la figure de Guizot a été advantage mise en lumiére que celle de Benjamin Constant; malgré l'échec de 1848, le group doctrinaire . . . a attire à lui le label même de 'libéralisme' (Jaume 1997a, 119). In my view, the opposite holds true: Constant and Tocqueville have received much greater attention than the Doctrinaires.

22. On freedom of movement of persons and ideas, see Guizot 1821, 157–58. On limited power, division of powers, and constitutionalism, see Guizot 1821, 172, 277–81, 299; Guizot 1985, 326–27, 343–45, 359, 375–79; and Guizot 2002, 68–69, 328–76.

23. I borrow the term *agonistic liberalism* from Gray 1995. The term *liberalism of fear* was coined by Shklar; her essay "Liberalism of fear" was republished in Shklar 1996, 3–20. For a presentation of perfectionist liberalism and its relation to other strands of liberalism, see Johnston 1994, 68–99.

24. I borrow the term "sociological imagination" from Mills 1959. I developed a similar argument in Craiutu 1998. More than two decades ago, Larry Siedentop claimed that the Doctrinaires were the "originators" of this sociological approach. In his book on Tocqueville published in 1994, he qualified this view by suggesting that Montesquieu and the Scottish philosophers ought to be seen as the precursors of the Doctrinaires. But the Scots were more interested in the nature and direction of social change than in constitutional issues. On the contribution of the Scottish Enlightenment to the development of modern social thought, see Burrow 1988, 21–49.

25. For more details, see Guizot's third note in the appendix to his translation of Ancillon's treatise on sovereignty (Ancillon, 1816).

26. See Guizot 1859c, 30–31.

27. See Guizot 1859c, 99–100. Here is what Guizot had to say at the outset of the fourth lecture of volume one of *Histoire de la civilisation en France:* "Nous nous sommes occupés jusqu'ici de l'état social de la Gaule, c'est-à-dire des relations des hommes entre eux, de leur condition extérieure et matérielle. Cela fait, les rapport sociaux décrits, les faits dont l'ensemble constitue la vie d'une époque sont-ils épuisés? Non, certes: il reste à étudier l'état intérieur, personnel des hommes, l'état des âmes, c'est-à-dire, d'une part les idées, les croyances, toute la vie intellectuelle de l'homme; de l'autre, les rapports qui lient les idées aux actions" (Guizot 1859c, 99).

28. See, for example, Bentham's *An Introduction to the Principles of Morals and Legislation* and James Mill's essay, "Government," which triggered a famous response from Macaulay in the *Edinburgh Review.*

29. Macaulay as quoted in Clive 1973, 109.

30. An excellent and informed discussion of Macaulay's contribution to the *Edinburgh Review* can be found in Clive 1973, 96–141. Also see Hamburger 1976, 49–72; Lively and Rees 1978, 1–130; Letwin 1965, 127–202. On the politics of the *Edinburgh Review* (1802–1832), see Fontana 1985b, 11–45, 112–185; Starzinger 1991.

31. For such an approach, see Wolin 1960. To his credit, Wolin has eventually turned to Tocqueville, in whom he has found a reliable guide for the exploration of modernity.

32. I draw here on a similar argument made by Kahan 1992. For an application to the French context, see Jaume 1997a, 7–21, and Sauvigny 1979. A general discussion of liberalism from a historical perspective can be found in Sheehan 1984 and Kahan 2003. A useful presentation of the nineteenth-century liberal creed in France can be found in Auguste Nefftzer's article "Libéralisme," originally published in 1863. The text was reissued as an appendix to Jaume 1997a, 557–67. It is worth noting that Nefftzer defined liberalism, first and foremost, as a discourse about *political capacity.*

33. See, for example, Berkowitz 1996 and 1997.

34. On this topic, also see Berkowitz 1996; Beiner 1992 and 1996; Gray 1990 and 1997; Wolin 1996. A more detailed critique can be found in Gray 2000. Here is a passage that summarizes Gray's argument: "There was a time when political philosophers were also political economists, historians, and social theorists, concerned—as were Smith, Hume, and John Stuart Mill, for example—with what history and theory had to teach us about the comparative performance of different institutions and the constraints of feasibility imposed on human institutions of all sorts by circumstances of any realistically imaginable world. When these political philosophers of an older tradition were liberals, they were deeply concerned with the cultural and institutional preconditions of liberal civil society, preoccupied with threats to its stability, and anxious to understand the deeper significance of the major political developments of their time" (Gray 1995, 10).

35. Norberto Bobbio made an interesting distinction between the "included" and "inclusive" middle. While the first attempts to find its own space between two opposites and without seeking to eliminate them altogether, the inclusive middle tends to go beyond the two opposites, by incorporating them into a higher synthe-

sis. In political debates, writes Bobbio, the "inclusive" middle is often presented as a third way that transcends both the left and right. "The included middle is essentially practical politics without a doctrine, whereas the inclusive middle is essentially a doctrine in search of a practical politics" (Bobbio 1996, 8).

36. For more details, see Block 1863, 734–35.

37. Coriolis d'Espinouse ironically remarked: "Du moment qu'on vous accuse d'être absolu dans votre sentiment, de manquer de moderation, vous êtes dès-là mal placé pour vous defender" (Coriolis d'Espinouse 1820, 560).

38. Diez del Corral found, in my view, the perfect expression: *brujulear* (from the Spanish, *brújula*, compass). *Brujulear* means to search with the compass, without ever been able to perfectly know the right way that must be looked for at every step.

39. For a spirited defense of liberal democracy, see Michnik 1998, 317–27.

40. I follow here a suggestion from Manent 1993.

41. Berlin 1998, 90. This is an excerpt from a posthumously published interview with Steven Lukes (in *Salmagundi*).

~

Bibliography

I. Primary Sources

1. Works of the French Doctrinaires

Barante, Prosper de. 1821. *Des communes et de l'aristocratie*. Paris: Ladvocat.

———. 1849. *Questions constitutionnelles*. Paris: Victor Masson.

———. 1875. *Notes sur la Russie, 1835–1840*. Paris: Michel-Lévy Frères.

———. 1892. *Souvenirs du baron de Barante*. Vol. 2. Paris: Calmann-Lévy.

———. 1893. *Souvenirs du baron de Barante*. Vol. 3. Paris: Calmann-Lévy.

Broglie, Victor de. 1863a. *Écrits et discours*. Vol. 1: *Philosophie-Littérature*. Paris: Didier.

———. 1863b. *Écrits et discours*. Vol. 2: *Discours*. Paris: Didier.

———. 1863c. *Écrits et discours*. Vol. 3: *Discours et Éloges*. Paris: Didier.

———. 1870. *Vues sur le gouvernement de la France*. 2d ed. Paris: Michel-Lévy Frères.

———. 1887a. *Personal Recollections of the Late Duc de Broglie*. Vol. 1. Translated by Raphael Ledos de Beaufort. London: Ward & Downey.

———. 1887b. *Personal Recollections of the Late Duc de Broglie*. Vol. 2. Translated by Raphael Ledos de Beaufort. London: Ward & Downey.

Guizot, François. 1814a. *Quelques idées sur la liberté de la presse*. Paris: Lenormant.

———. 1814b. *Sur le nouveau projet de loi relatif à la presse*. Paris: Lenormant.

———. 1816. *Du gouvernement représentatif et de l'état actuel de la France*. Paris: Maradon.

———. 1817a. Review essay: "Manuel des Electeurs." "Des prochaines élections." *Archives philosophiques, politiques et littéraires* 1: 137–48.

———. 1817b. Response to Loyson. *Archives philosophiques, politiques et littéraires* 1: 418–27.

———. 1817c. "Session de 1817—Débats des Chambres." *Archives philosophiques, politiques et littéraires* 2: 183–208.

———. 1817d. Review of Benjamin Constant, "Annales de la session de 1817 à 1818." *Archives philosophiques, politiques et littéraires* 2: 257–77.

———. 1817e. Review of Vicomte de Chateaubriand, "Du système politique." *Archives philosophiques, politiques et littéraires* 2: 278–96.

———. 1818a. Review of Montlosier's *De la monarchie française. Archives philosophiques, politiques et littéraires* 3: 385–409.

———. 1818b. Review essay: "Troubles et agitations du department du Gand." "Précis de ce qui s'est passé en 1815." "Dissentions et persecutions dans l'arrondissement du Vigan." "De l'état des protestans en France." *Archives philosophiques, politiques et littéraires* 4: 141–57.

———. 1818c. "Des garanties légales de la liberté de la presse." *Archives philosophiques, politiques et littéraires* 5: 184–238.

———. 1820. *Du gouvernement de la France depuis la Restauration et du ministère actuel.* Paris: Ladvocat.

———. 1821. *Des moyens de gouvernement et d'opposition dans l'état actuel de la France.* Paris: Ladvocat.

———. 1822. *De la peine de mort en matière politique.* Paris: Béchet.

———. 1826–27. *Histoire de la révolution d'Angleterre depuis l'avènement de Charles I jusqu'à la restauration de Charles II.* Paris: Leroux et Chantepie.

———. 1829. Review of "Correspondance littéraire, philosophique et critique de Grimm et Diderot," *Revue française,* no. 11 (September): 214–50.

———. 1830. "Du vrai caractère de la crise actuelle." *Revue française,* no. 14 (March): 225–34.

———. 1836. *Essais sur l'histoire de France.* 4th ed. Paris: Ladrange.

———. 1837. "De la démocratie dans les sociétés modernes." *Revue française* 3 (November): 139–225, n.s.

———. 1849. *De la démocratie en France.* Paris: Victor Masson.

———. 1851. *Histoire des origines du gouvernement représentatif en Europe.* Paris: Didier.

———. 1858a. *Mémoires pour servir à l'histoire de mon temps.* Vol. 1. Paris: Michel-Lévy Frères.

———. 1858b. *Memoirs to Illustrate the History of My Time.* Vol. 1. Translated by J. W. Cole. London: R. Bentley.

———. 1859a. *Mémoires pour servir à l'histoire de mon temps.* Vol. 2. Paris: Michel-Lévy Frères.

———. 1859b. *Memoirs to Illustrate the History of My Time.* Vol. 2. Translated by J. W. Cole. London: R. Bentley.

———. 1859c. *Histoire de la civilisation en France depuis la chute de l'empire romain.* Vol. 1. Paris: Didier.

———. 1859d. *Histoire de la civilization en France depuis la chute de l'empire romain.* Vol. 2. Paris: Didier.

———. 1859e. *Histoire de la civilization en France depuis la chute de l'empire romain.* Vol. 3. Paris: Didier.

———. 1859f. *Histoire de la civilization en France depuis la chute de l'empire romain.* Vol. 4. Paris: Didier.

———. 1860a. *Mémoires pour servir à l'histoire de mon temps.* Vol. 3. Paris: Michel-Lévy Frères.

———. 1860b. *Memoirs to Illustrate the History of My Time.* Vol. 3. Translated by J. W. Cole. London: R. Bentley.

———. 1862. *Discours académiques.* Paris: Didier.

———. 1863a. *Trois générations: 1789, 1814, 1848.* Paris: Michel-Lévy Frères.

———. 1863b. *Histoire parlementaire de France.* Vol. 1. Paris: Didier.

———. 1863c. *Histoire parlementaire de France.* Vol. 3. Paris: Didier.

———. 1864. *Méditations sur l'essence de la réligion chretienne.* Paris: Michel-Lévy Frères.

———. 1867. *Mémoires pour servir à l'histoire de mon temps.* Vol. 8. Paris: Michel Lévy Frères.

———. 1869. *Mélanges d'histoire et de politique.* Paris: Ladvocat.

———. 1872. *Méditations et études morales.* Paris: Didier.

———. 1873. *The History of Civilization from the Fall of the Roman Empire to the French Revolution.* Translated by William Hazlitt. London: Bell & Daldy.

———. 1882. *The History of France from the Earliest Times to the Year 1789.* Vol. 8. Translated by Robert Black. London: Sampson Low, Marston, Searle, & Rivingston.

———. 1884. *Lettres de M. Guizot à sa famille et à ses amis.* Edited by Mme de Witt. Paris: Hachette.

———. 1892. *The History of Civilization from the Fall of the Roman Empire to the French Revolution.* Translated by William Hazlitt. 3rd American edition. New York: Appleton.

———. 1972. *Historical Essays and Lectures.* Edited by Stanley Mellon. Chicago: University of Chicago Press.

———. 1984. *Des conspirations et de la justice politique. De la peine de mort en matière politique.* Paris: Fayard.

———. 1985. *Histoire de la civilisation en Europe: depuis la chute de L'Empire romain jusqu'à la Révolution française; suivie de Philosophie politique: de la souveraineté.* Edited by Pierre Rosanvallon. Paris: Hachette.

———. 1997a. *The History of Civilization in Europe.* Edited by Larry Siedentop. Translated by William Hazlitt. London: Penguin.

———. 1997b. *Historie de la Révolution d'Angleterre.* Edited by Laurent Theis. Paris: Robert Laffont.

———. 2002. *The History of the Origins of Representative Government in Europe.* Edited by Aurelian Craiutu. Translated by Andrew R. Scoble. Indianapolis: Liberty Fund.

Jordan, Camille. 1817. *La Sesion de 1817, aux habitans de l'Ain et du Rhône.* Paris.

———. 1825. *Discours de Camille Jordan, precede de son éloge by M. Ballanche et d'une Lettre de M. le baron de Gérando sur sa vie privée.* Paris: Henouard.

Rémusat, Charles de. 1819. "De la liberté de la presse et des projets de lois présentés à la Chambre des députés." Paris: Delaunay.

———. 1829. Untitled article. *Le Globe* (March 11): 156–57.

———. 1847. *Passé et présent.* Paris: Ladrange.

———. 1853a. "Burke, sa vie et ses écrits." *Revue des deux mondes* (January 15): 209–61.

———. 1853b. "Burke, sa vie et ses écrits." *Revue des deux mondes* (February 1): 435–90.

———. 1856. "L'Ancien Régime et la Révolution." *Revue des deux mondes* (August 1): 652–70.

———. 1861. "L'esprit de réaction: Royer-Collard et Tocqueville." *Revue des deux mondes* (October 15): 777–813.

———. 1875. *Politique libérale, ou Fragments pour servir à la defense de la Révolution française* (new edition). Paris: Michel-Lévy Frères.

———. 1958. *Mémoires de ma vie.* Vol. 1. Edited by C.-H. Pouthas. Paris: Plon.

———. 1959. *Mémoires de ma vie.* Vol. 2. Edited by C.-H. Pouthas. Paris: Plon.

———. 1962. *Mémoires de ma vie.* Vol. 4. Edited by C.-H. Pouthas. Paris: Plon.

Royer-Collard, Pierre-Paul. 1861a. *La vie politique de M. Royer-Collard: ses discours et ses écrits.* Vol. 1. Edited by Prosper de Barante. Paris: Didier.

———. 1861b. *La vie politique de M. Royer-Collard: ses discours et ses écrits.* Vol. 2. Edited by Prosper de Barante. Paris: Didier.

———. 1913. *Les fragments philosophiques de Royer-Collard.* Edited by André Schimberg. Paris.

———. 1949. *De la liberté de la presse.* Paris: Médicis.

2. Other Primary Sources

Ancillon, Frederick. 1816. *De la souveraineté et des formes de gouvernement.* Translated by François Guizot. Paris: Lenormant.

Benjan. 1838. *Des doctrinaires et de l'article de M. Guizot sur la démocratic daus les sociétés modernes.* Paris: Des Fonges.

Bonald, Louis de. 1817. *Pensées sur divers sujets.* Vol. 2. Paris.

———. 1818. "Sur un écrit de M. Camille Jordan, ayant pour titre: La Session de 1817, aux habitans de l'Ain et du Rhône." *Le Conservateur,* no. 1: 249–73.

———. 1819a. "De la chambre de 1815." *Le Conservateur,* no. 4: 158–71.

———. 1819b. "Sur les parties." *Le Conservateur,* no. 5: 590–607.

———. 1982. *Œuvres completes.* Vols. 6–7. Paris: Slatkine.

———. 1988. *Réflexions sur la Révolution de juillet 1830 et autres inédits.* Edited by Jean Bastier. Paris: Duc/Albatros.

Brougham, Henry Lord. 1860. *The British Constitution: Its History, Structure, and Working.* Works of Brougham. Vol. 11. London: Charles Griffin & Co.

Chateaubriand, François-René de. 1814. *Réflexions politiques sur quelques écrits du jour et sur les intérêts de tous les Français.* Paris.

———. 1816. *The Monarchy According to the Charter* [*De la monarchie selon la Charte*]. London: John Murray.

———. 1819a. "Politique." *Le Conservateur,* no. 4: 353–75.

———. 1819b. "De la liberté de la presse." *Le Conservateur,* no. 5: 62–72.

———. 1951. *Mémoires d'outre tombe.* Vol. 2. Edited by Maurice Levaillant and Georges Moulinier. Paris: Bibliothèque de la Pléiade.

———. 1987. *Chateaubriand politique.* Edited by Jean-Paul Clément. Paris: Hachette.

———. 1993a. *Grands écrits politiques*. Vol. 1. Edited by Jean-Paul Clément. Paris: Imprimerie Nationale.

———. 1993b. *Grands écrits politiques*. Vol. 2. Edited by Jean-Paul Clément. Paris: Imprimerie Nationale.

Constant, Benjamin. 1861. *Cours de politique constitutionnelle*. Edited by Edouard Laboulaye. Paris: Guillaumin.

———. 1979. *Œuvres*. Edited by Alfred Roulin. Paris: Bibliothèque de la Pléiade.

———. 1980. *De la liberté chez les modernes*. Edited by Marcel Gauchet. Paris: Librairie Générale Française.

———. 1988. *Political Writings*. Edited and translated by Biancamaria Fontana. Cambridge: Cambridge University Press.

———. 1989. "De la souveraineté." In *Ideology and Religion in French Literature*, edited by Harry Cockerham and Esther Erman, 173–79. Camberley: Porphyrogenitus.

Coriolis d'Espinouse, Marquis de. 1820. "Si ce qu'on nomme aujourd'hui moderation est la moderation." *Le Conservateur*, no. 6: 558–63.

Cortés, Donoso. 1991. *A Defense of Representative Government*. Translated by Vincent McNamara. North York, Ontario: Captus Press.

Cousin, Victor. 1851. "Nouvelle défense des principes de la Révolution française et du gouvernement représentatif." *Revue des deux mondes* (April 1): 5–46.

———. 1856. *Du vrai, du beau, et du bien*. Paris: Didier.

Crignon d'Auzouer. 1818. "Sur les élections." *Le Conservateur*, no. 1: 49–60.

Destutt de Tracy. 1819. *Commentaire sur l'esprit des lois de Montesquieu*. Paris: Théodore Desoer.

D'Herbouville, Marquis de. 1819. "Sur l'harmonie sociale considérée relativement à notre situation." *Le Conservateur*, no. 2: 385–98.

Genoude, M. 1819. "D'un manifeste des Doctrinaires." *Le Conservateur*, no. 2: 150–55.

Lahaye de Cormenin, Louis-Mariè de (Timòn). [1844] 2000. Le livre des orateurs. Edited by E. Harpaz. Genève: Slatkine.

Maistre, Joseph de. 1971. *The Works of Joseph de Maistre*. Translated and edited by Jack Lively. New York: Schocken.

———. 1980. *Considérations sur la France*. Edited by Jean-Louis Darcel. Geneva: Slatkine.

———. 1992. *De la souveraineté du peuple: un anti-contrat social*. Paris: PUF.

———. 1994. *Considerations on France*. Translated by Richard Lebrun. Cambridge: Cambridge University Press.

Mill, John Stuart. 1963. *Collected Works*. Vol. 12: *The Early Letters of John Stuart Mill, 1812–1848*. Edited by John Robson. Toronto: University of Toronto Press.

———. 1969. *Autobiography*. Boston: Houghton Mifflin.

———. 1972. *Utilitarianism, Liberty, Representative Government*. Edited by H. B. Acton. London: Dent.

———. 1977. *Collected Works*. Vol. 18: *Essays on Politics and Society*. Edited by John Robson. Toronto: University of Toronto Press.

———. 1985. *Collected Works*. Vol. 20: *Essays on French History and Historians*. Edited by John Robson. Toronto: University of Toronto Press.

——. 1986a. *Collected Works*. Vol. 22: *Newspaper Writings*. Edited by Ann Robson and John Robson. Toronto: University of Toronto Press.

——. 1986b. *Collected Works*. Vol. 23: *Newspaper Writings*. Edited by Ann Robson and John Robson. Toronto: University of Toronto Press.

Montlosier, Comte de. 1814. *De la monarchie française*. Paris.

Mounier, Jean-Joseph. 1789. *Considérations sur les gouvernements, et principalement sur celui qui convient à la France*. Versailles: P. D. Pierres.

Necker, Jacques. 1781. *Compte rendu*. Paris: Imprimerie royale.

——. 1792. *Du pouvoir exécutif dans les grands états*. Paris.

Staël, Madame de. 1818. *Considerations on the Principal Events of the French Revolution*. London: Bladwin, Cradock & Joy.

——. 1979. *Des circonstances actuelles qui peuvent terminer la Révolution et des principes qui doivent fonder la république en France*. Edited by Lucia Omacini. Geneva: Slatkine.

Tocqueville, Alexis de. 1866. *Œuvres*. Vol. 5. Edited by Gustave de Beaumont. Paris: Michel-Lévy Frères.

——. 1958. *Democracy in America*. Vol. 1. Translated by Phillips Bradley. New York: Vintage.

——. 1959. *Recollections*. Translated by A. Teixeira de Mattos. New York: Meridian.

——. 1968. *Democracy in America*. Edited by J. P. Meyer. Translated by George Lawrence. New York: HarperPerennial.

——. 1970. *Œuvres Complètes*. Vol. 11. Edited by A. Jardin. Paris: Gallimard.

——. 1977. *Œuvres Complètes*. Vol. 13. Edited by A. Jardin. Paris: Gallimard.

——. 1985a. *Œuvres Complètes*. Vol. 3: *Écrits et discours politiques*. Edited by A. Jardin. Paris: Gallimard.

——. 1985b. *Selected Letters on Politics and Society*. Edited by Roger Boesche. Translated by Roger Boesche and James Toupin. Berkeley: University of California Press.

——. 1988. *L'Ancien Régime et la Révolution*. Edited by Françoise Mélonio. Paris: Flammarion.

——. 1989. *Œuvres complètes*. Vol. 16: *Mélanges*. Edited by Françoise Mélonio. Paris: Gallimard.

——. 1990. *De la démocratie en Amérique*. Edited by Eduardo Nolla. Paris: Vrin.

——. 1998. *The Old Regime and the Revolution*. Translated by Alan S. Kahan. Chicago: University of Chicago Press.

——. 2003. *Lettres choisies. Souvenirs*. Edited by Françoise Mélonio. Paris: Gallimard.

Vitrolles, Baron de. 1815. *Du ministère dans le gouvernement représentatif*. Paris: Dentu.

——. 1952. *Mémoires*. Vol. 2. Edited by Eugené Forgues. Paris: Gallimard.

3. Nineteenth-Century Newspapers, Reviews, and Journals Consulted

Archives Parlementaires (second series, from the year 8 to 1938). Paris (abbreviated *AP*).

Archives philosophiques, politiques et littéraires (*APPL*), 1817–1818. Paris. Vols. 1–5.

Le Conservateur, 1819–1820. Paris. Vols. 1–6.
Revue française, 1828–1830. Paris. Vols. 1–14. New series: Vol. 3, 1837.
Le Globe, 1824–1830. Paris.

II. Secondary Literature

Acton, Lord. 2001. *Lectures on the French Revolution*. Indianapolis: Liberty Fund.

Allier, Jacques. 1976. "Esquisse du personnage de Guizot." In *Actes du colloque François Guizot*, 27–45. Paris: Société de l'Histoire du Protestantisme Français.

Anderson, Frank Maloy, ed. 1967. *The Constitutions and Other Select Documents Illustrative of the History of France, 1789–1907*. New York: Russell & Russell.

Antoine, Agnès. 1997. "Maine de Biran et la Restauration." *Commentaire* 19, no. 76 (Winter): 931–38.

Aquinas, Thomas. 2000. *Treatise on Law*. Translated by Richard Regan. Indianapolis: Hackett.

Artz, Frederick B. 1934. *Reaction and Revolution, 1814–1832*. New York: Harper & Brothers.

Avenel, Henri. 1900. *Histoire de la presse française depuis 1789 à nos jours*. Paris: Flammarion.

Bachrach, Peter, ed. 1971. *Elites in a Democracy*. New York: Atherton Press.

Bagge, Dominique. 1952. *Les idées politiques en France sous la Restauration*. Paris: PUF.

Baker, Keith, ed. 1987. *The French Revolution and the Creation of Modern Political Culture*. Vol. 1: *The Political Culture of the Old Regime*. Oxford: Pergamon.

———. 1989a. "Sieyès." In *A Critical Dictionary of the French Revolution*, edited by François Furet and Mona Ozouf, 313–23. Translated by Arthur Goldhammer. Cambridge, Mass.: Harvard University Press.

———. 1989b. "Constitution." In *A Critical Dictionary of the French Revolution*, edited by François Furet and Mona Ozouf, 479–93. Translated by Arthur Goldhammer. Cambridge, Mass.: Harvard University Press.

———. 1990. *Inventing the French Revolution*. Cambridge: Cambridge University Press.

Balmes, Jaime Luciano. 1850. *Protestantism and Catholicity Compared in Their Effects on the Civilization of Europe*. Baltimore: John Murphy & Co.

Balzac, Honoré de. 1869. *Essais historiques et politiques*. Paris: Calman-Lévy.

Barbé, Maurice. 1904. *Étude historique sur des idées sur la souveraineté en France de 1815 à 1848*. Paris: Librairie générale de droit et de jurisprudence.

Barberis, Mauro. 1985. "Constant, Guizot e il liberalismo preso sul il serio." *Materiali per una storia della cultura giuridica*, no. 15: 465–81.

———. 1989. *Sette studi sul liberalismo rivoluzionario*. Torino: G. Giappichelli.

Barbey, Jean. 1936. *Le Conseil des Ministres sous la Restauration*. Faculté de droit, Université de Paris. Paris: Domat-Montchrestien.

Bardoux, M. A. 1894. *Guizot*. Paris: Hachette.

Barthélemy, J. 1904. *L'introduction du régime parlementaire en France sous Louis XVIII et Charles X*. Paris: Giard & Brière.

Bastid, Paul. 1954. *Les institutions politiques de la monarchie parlementaire française, 1814–1848*. Paris: Sirey.

Beaud, Oliver. 1996. "Souveraineté." In *Dictionnaire de philosophie politique*, edited by Stéphane Rials and Philippe Raynaud, 625–33. Paris: PUF.

Beik, Paul, ed. 1970. *The French Revolution*. New York: Walker & Co.

Beiner, Ronald. 1992. *What's the Matter with Liberalism?* Berkeley: University of California Press.

———. 1996. "What Liberalism Means." *Social Philosophy and Policy* 13, no. 1 (Winter): 191–206.

Beiser, Frederick. 1996. *The Sovereignty of Reason: The Defense of Rationality in the Early English Enlightenment*. Princeton: Princeton University Press.

Bellamy, Richard. 1992. *Liberalism and Modern Society*. University Park: Pennsylvania State University Press.

Bellanger, Claude, Jacques Godechot, Pierre Guiral, and Fernand Terrou, eds. 1969. *Histoire générale de la presse française*. Vol. 2: *De 1815 à 1871*. Paris: PUF.

Bénichou, Paul. 1977. *Le temps des prophètes: doctrines de l'âge romantique*. Paris: Gallimard.

Berlin, Isaiah. 1991. *The Crooked Timber of Humanity*. New York: Knopf.

———. 1998. "Isaiah Berlin in Conversation with Steven Lukes." *Salmagundi*, no. 120 (Fall 1998): 52–134.

Berkowitz, Peter. 1996. "The Debating Society." *The New Republic*, November 25, pp. 36–42.

———. 1997. "Liberalism Strikes Back." *The New Republic*, December 15, pp. 32–37.

Billard, Jacques. 1998. *De l'École à la République: Guizot et Victor Cousin*. Paris: PUF.

Birnbaum, Pierre. 2001. *The Idea of France*. New York: Hill & Wang.

Block, Maurice, ed. 1863. *Dictionnaire général de politique*. Vol. 1. Paris: Lorenz.

Bobbio, Norberto. 1990. *Liberalism and Democracy*. London: Verso.

———. 1996. *Left and Right*. Cambridge: Polity.

Boesche, Roger. 1987. *The Strange Liberalism of Alexis de Tocqueville*. Ithaca: Cornell University Press.

Bouretz, Pierre. 1991. "L'héritage des Lumières." In *François Guizot et la culture politique de son temps*, edited by Marina Valensise, 37–67. Paris: Gallimard.

Bramsted, E. K., and K. J. Melhuish, eds. 1978. *Western Liberalism: A History in Documents from Locke to Croce*. London: Longman.

Broglie, Gabriel de. 1979. *Histoire politique de la Revue des deux mondes de 1829 à 1979*. Paris: Perrin.

———. 1990. *Guizot*. Paris: Perrin.

Brush, Elizabeth Parnham. 1974. *Guizot in the Early Years of the Orleanist Revolution*. 2d ed. New York: Howard Fertig.

Burdeaux, Georges. 1953. *Traité de science politique*. Vol. 5. Paris: Librairie générale de droit et de juris prudence.

Burrow, J. W. 1988. *Whigs and Liberals*. Oxford: Clarendon Press.

Calhoun, Craig, ed. 1992. *Habermas and the Public Sphere*. Cambridge, Mass.: MIT Press.

Carré de Malberg, R. 1962. *Contribution à la théorie générale de l'État*. Vol. 2. Paris: Éditions du CNRS.

Chabanne, Robert. 1977. *Les institutions de la France de la fin de l'ancien régime à l'avènement de la troisième République (1789–1875)*. Lyon: L'Hermes.

Charléty, Sébastien. 1939. *Histoire de la Restauration*. Paris: Hachette.

Chevalier, Jean-Jacques. 1964. "La pensée politique des doctrinaires de la Restauration." In Conseil d'État, *Études et documents*, 13–29. Paris.

Clément, Jean-Paul. 1993. "Présentation." In Chateaubriand, *Grands Écrits Politiques*, 7–46. Vol. 1. Paris: Imprimerie Nationale.

Clive, John. 1973. *Macaulay: The Shaping of the Historian*. Cambridge, Mass.: Harvard University Press.

Coco, Antonio. 1983. *François Guizot*. Napoli: Guida.

Collingham, H. A. C. 1988. *The July Monarchy: A Political History of France, 1830–1848*. London: Longman.

Collini, Stefan, Donald Winch, and John Burrow. 1983. *That Noble Science of Politics*. Cambridge: Cambridge University Press.

Collins, Irene. 1957. *Liberalism in Nineteenth-Century Europe*. London: Wyman & Sons.

———, ed. 1970. *Government and Society in France, 1814–1848*. London: Edward Arnold.

Craiutu, Aurelian. 1998. "Between Scylla and Charybdis: The 'Strange' Liberalism of the French Doctrinaires." *History of European Ideas* 24, nos. 4–5: 243–65.

———. 1999. "Tocqueville and the Political Thought of the French Doctrinaires." *History of Political Thought* 20, no. 3 (Fall): 456–94.

———. 2002. Introduction to *The History of the Origins of Representative Government in Europe*, by François Guizot, vii–xvi. Indianapolis: Liberty Fund.

———. 2003. "Rethinking Political Power: The Case of the French Doctrinaires." *European Journal of Political Theory* 2, no. 2: 125–55.

Curtius, Ernst Robert. 1932. *The Civilization in France*. Translated by Olive Wyon. New York: Macmillan.

Deguise, Pierre. 1989. "Albertine de Staël, Duchesse de Broglie, et Prosper de Barante. Amitié, politique, et religion." In *Ideology and Religion in French Literature*, edited by Harry Cockerham and Esther Erman, 111–32. Camberley: Porphyrogenitus.

Denis, Antoine. 2000. *Amable-Guillaume Prosper Brugière, Baron de Barante (1782–1866). Homme politique, diplomate et historien*. Paris: Honoré Champion.

Derathé, Robert. 1950. *Jean-Jacques Rousseau et la science politique de son temps*. Paris: PUF.

Diez del Corral, Luis. 1956. *El liberalismo doctrinario*. Madrid: Instituto de Estudios Políticos.

———. 1960. "Tocqueville et la pensée politique des Doctrinaires." In *Alexis de Tocqueville: Livre du Centenaire, 1859–1959*, 57–70. Paris: CNRS.

———. 1989. *El pensamiento político de Tocqueville*. Madrid: Alianza Editorial.

Dodge, Guy H. 1980. *Benjamin Constant's Philosophy of Liberalism*. Chapel Hill: University of North Carolina Press.

Drentje, Jan. 2003. *Thorbecke (1798–1872), the Outsider in Dutch Liberalism: Politics on the Cusp of Philosophy and History*. Amsterdam: Damon Publishers.

Drescher, Seymour. 1964. "Tocqueville's Two *Démocraties*." *Journal of the History of Ideas* 25 (April–June): 117–27.

———. 1968. *Dilemmas of Democracy*. Pittsburgh: University of Pittsburgh Press.

Duvergier de Hauranne, Prosper. 1860. *Histoire du gouvernement parliamentaire en France, 1814–1848*. Vol. 4. Paris: Michel-Lévy Frères.

Eckermann, Johann Peter. 1892. *Conversations of Goethe*. Translated by John Oxenford. London: George Bell & Sons.

———. 1949. *Gespräche mit Goethe in den letzten Jahren seines Lebens*. Edited by H. H. Houben. Wiesbaden: Eberhard Brockham.

Eötvös, József. 1996. *The Dominant Ideas of the Nineteenth Century and Their Impact on the State*. New York: Columbia University Press.

Etzioni-Halevy, Eva. 1989. *Fragile Democracy: The Use and Abuse of Power in Western Society*. New Brunswick: Transaction Publishers.

———. 1993. *The Elite Connection: Problems and Potential of Western Democracy*. Cambridge: Polity Press.

Evers, Frank. 1987. *Die Staatstheorie Chateaubriands im Spiegel der deutschen Konstitutionalismus-Diskussion*. Frankfurt am Main: Peter Lang.

Faguet, Emile. 1890. *Politiques et moralistes au dix-neuvième siècle*. Paris: Lecène, Oudin & Co.

Fasnacht, G. E. 1952. *Acton's Political Philosophy: An Analysis*. London: Hollis and Carter.

Fontana, Biancamaria. 1985a. "The Shaping of Modern Liberty: Commerce and Civilization in the Writings of Benjamin Constant." *Annales Benjamin Constant, 3–15*. Vol. 5. Paris: Institut Benjamin Constant; Voltaire Foundation; Jean Touzot Libraire-Éditeur.

———. 1985b. *Rethinking the Politics of Commercial Society: The Edinburgh Review, 1802–1832*. Cambridge: Cambridge University Press.

———. 1991. *Benjamin Constant and the Post-Revolutionary Mind*. New Haven: Yale University Press.

Forsyth, Murray. 1987. *Reason and Revolution: The Political Thought of the Abbé Sieyès*. Leicester: Leicester University Press.

Fossaert, Robert. 1955. "La théorie des classes chez Guizot et Thierry." *La Penseé*, no. 59 (January–February): 59–69.

Fralin, Richard. 1970. *Rousseau and Representation*. New York: Columbia University Press.

Freeden, Michael. 1999. "Helping Us To Be Perfect." *Times Literary Supplement*, January 29, p. 38.

Friedrich, Carl J. 1948. "Representation and Constitutional Reform." *Western Political Quarterly* 1, no. 2 (June): 124–30.

Furet, François. 1978. *Penser la Révolution française*. Paris: Gallimard.

———. 1985–86. "The Intellectual Origins of Tocqueville's Thought." *The Tocqueville Revue/La Revue Tocqueville* 7: 117–27.

———, and Mona Ozouf, eds. 1989a. *A Critical Dictionary of the French Revolution*. Translated by Arthur Goldhammer. Cambridge, Mass.: Harvard University Press.

———, and Mona Ozouf, eds. 1989b. *The Transformation of Political Culture, 1789–1848*. In *The French Revolution and the Creation of Modern Political Culture*. Vol. 3. Oxford: Pergamon Press.

———, and Mona Ozouf, eds. 1993. *Le siècle de l'avènement républicain*. Paris: Gallimard.

———. 1995. *Revolutionary France: 1770–1880*. Oxford: Blackwell.

Ganochaud, Collete. 1980. *L'opinion publique chez Jean-Jacques Rousseau*. Lille: Bibliothèque Universitaire.

Gargan, Edward. 1955. *Alexis de Tocqueville: The Critical Years, 1848–1851*. Washington, D.C.: Catholic University of America Press.

———. 1962. "The Formation of Tocqueville's Historical Thought." *Review of Politics* 24, no. 1 (January): 48–61.

Gauchet, Marcel. 1989. "Rights of Man." In *A Critical Dictionary of the French Revolution*, edited by François Furet and Mona Ozouf, 818–28. Translated by Arthur Goldhammer. Cambridge, Mass.: Harvard University Press.

Gengembre, Gerard. 1989. *La Contre-Révolution ou l'histoire désespérante*. Paris: Imago.

Girard, Louis. 1976. "Le régime parlementaire selon Guizot." In *Actes du Colloque François Guizot*, 121–33. Paris: Société de l'Histoire du Protestantisme Français.

———. 1985. *Les libéraux français*. Paris: PUF.

Goblot, Jean-Jacques. 1995. *La jeune France libérale: le Globe et son groupe littéraire, 1824–1830*. Paris: Plon.

Godechot, Jacques. 1961. *La contre-révolution: Doctrine et action, 1789–1804*. Paris: PUF.

Gontard, Maurice. 1976. "Guizot et l'instruction populaire." In *Actes du Colloque François Guizot*, 49–62. Paris: Société de l'Histoire du Protestantisme Français.

Gorce, Pierre de la. 1926. *La Restauration: Louis XVIII*. Paris: Plon.

———. 1928. *La Restauration: Charles X*. Paris: Plon.

Graham, John. 1974. *Donoso Cortés: Utopian Romanticist and Political Realist*. Columbia: University of Missouri Press.

Grange, Henri. 1974. *Les idées politiques de Necker*. Paris: Klincksieck.

Gray, John. 1990. *Liberalisms: Essays in Political Philosophy*. London: Routledge.

———. 1995. *Enlightenment's Wake*. London: Routledge.

———. 1996. "The Derelict Utopia." *Times Literary Supplement*, May 24, p. 29.

———. 1997. "Autonomy Is Not the Only Good." *Times Literary Supplement*, June 13, p. 30.

———. 2000. *Two Faces of Liberalism*. New York: The New Press.

Griffo, Maurizio. 2001. "Sovvranità e governo limitato in François Guizot." *Il pensiero politico*, no. 1: 95–104.

Guéniffey, Patrice. 1993. *Le nombre et la raison. La révolution française et les Elections*. Paris: Éditions de l'École des Hautes Études en Sciences Sociales.

Guiral, Pierre. 1960. "Le libéralisme en France." In *Tendances politiques dans la vie française depuis 1789*, edited by Guy Michaud. Paris: Hachette.

Gunn, J. A.W. 1989. "Public Opinion." In *Political Innovation and Conceptual Change*, edited by Terrence Ball, James Farr, and Russell Hanson, 247–65. Cambridge: Cambridge University Press.

———. 2000. "Conscience, Honour, and the Failure of Party in Restoration France." *History of Political Thought* 21, no. 3 (Autumn): 449–66.

Guyon, Bernard. 1969. *La pensée politique et sociale de Balzac*. 2d ed. Paris: Armand Colin.

Habermas, Jürgen. 1991. *The Structural Transformation of the Public Sphere*. Translated by Thomas Burger and Frederick Lawrence. Cambridge, Mass.: MIT Press.

———. 1998. *Between Facts and Norms*. Translated by William Rehg. Cambridge, Mass.: MIT Press.

Hall, John R. 1909. *The Bourbon Restoration*. London: Alston Rivers.

Hamburger, Joseph. 1976. *Macaulay and the Whig Tradition*. Chicago: University of Chicago Press.

Harpaz, Ephraïm. 1968. *L'École libérale sous la Restauration*. Paris: Droz.

Harrison, Carol. 1999. *The Bourgeois Citizen in Nineteenth-Century France*. Oxford: Oxford University Press.

Hatin, Eugène. 1861. *Histoire politique et littéraire de la presse en France*. Vol. 8. Paris: Poulet-Malassis et de Broise.

Hayward, Jack. 1991. *After the French Revolution*. New York: New York University Press.

———. 1998. Review of *L'individu effacé*, by Lucien Jaume. *History of European Ideas* 24, no. 3: 239–42.

Hazareesingh, Sudhir. 1998. *From Subject to Citizen*. Princeton: Princeton University Press.

———. 1999. "Theory without Heroes." *Times Literary Supplement*, October 29, p. 26.

Hegel, G. W. F. 1991. *Elements of the Philosophy of Right*. Edited by Allen Wood. Cambridge: Cambridge University Press.

Herrera, R. A. 1996. *Donoso Cortés: Cassandra of the Age*. Grand Rapids: Eerdmans.

Hoeges, Dirk. 1974. "Guizot und Tocqueville." *Historische Zeitschrift* 218, no. 2 (April): 338–53.

———. 1981. *François Guizot und die französische Revolution*. Frankfurt am Main: Peter Lang.

Holmes, Stephen. 1984. *Benjamin Constant and the Making of Modern Liberalism*. New Haven: Yale University Press.

———. 1995. *Passions and Constraint*. Chicago: University of Chicago Press.

Hume, David. 1985. *Essays: Moral, Political, and Literary*. Edited by Eugene Miller. Indianapolis: LibertyClassics.

Jardin, André, and André Tudesq. 1983. *Restoration and Reaction, 1815–1830*. Paris: Éditions de la Maison des Science de l'Homme.

Jardin, André. 1984. *Alexis de Tocqueville, 1805–1959*. Paris: Hachette.

———. 1985. *Histoire du libéralisme politique*. Paris: Hachette.

Jaume, Lucien. 1990. *Échec au libéralisme: Les Jacobins et l'État*. Paris: Kimé.

———. 1992. "Guizot et la philosophie de la représentation." *Droits*, no. 15: 141–52.

———. 1993. "Garantir les droits de l'homme." *La Revue Tocqueville/The Tocqueville Review* 14, no. 1: 49–65.

———. 1994a. "La conception doctrinaire de la liberté de la presse." In *Guizot, les Doctrinaires et la presse, 1820–1830* edited by D. Roldán, 111–24. Val-Richer: Fondation Guizot.

———. 1994b. "La raison politique chez Victor Cousin et Guizot." In *La pensée politique*, edited by P. Manent, P. Rosanvallon, and M. Gauchet, 242–53. Vol. 2. Paris: Gallimard & Seuil..

———. 1997a. *L'individu effacé, ou le paradoxe du libéralisme français*. Paris: Fayard.

———. 1997b. "Heurs et malheurs de la liberté de la presse." In *Liberté, libéraux et constitutions*, edited by J.-P. Clément, L. Jaume, and M. Vespaux, 43–59. Paris: Presses Universitaires d'Aix-Marseille & Economica.

Jennings, Jeremy R. 1986. "Conceptions of England and Its Constitution in Nineteenth-Century French Political Thought." *Historical Journal* 29, no. 1: 65–85.

Johnson, Douglas. 1963. *Guizot: Aspects of French History, 1787–1874*. London: Routledge & Kegan Paul.

———. 1967. "A Reconsideration of Guizot." In *European Political History, 1815–1870; Aspects of Liberalism*, edited by Eugene C. Black, 84–102. New York: Harper & Row.

———. 1976a. "Allocution de clôture." In *Actes du colloque Guizot*, 479–84. Paris: Société de l'Histoire du Protestantisme Français.

———. 1976b. "Guizot et l'Angleterre." In *Actes du colloque Guizot*, 111–20. Paris: Société de l'Histoire du Protestantisme Français.

Johnson, Paul. 1991. *The Birth of the Modern: World Society, 1815–1830*. New York: HarperCollins.

Johnston, David. 1994. *The Idea of Liberal Theory*. Princeton: Princeton University Press.

Jouvenel, Bertrand de. 1993. *Power*. Indianapolis: Liberty Fund.

———. 1997. *Sovereignty: An Inquiry into the Political Good*. Indianapolis: Liberty Fund.

Judt, Tony. 1992. *Past Imperfect: French Intellectuals, 1944–1956*. Berkeley: University of California Press.

———. 1998. *The Burden of Responsibility: Blum, Camus, Aron and the French Twentieth Century*. Chicago: University of Chicago Press.

Kahan, Alan. 1991. "Guizot et le modèle anglais." In *François Guizot et la culture politique de son temps*, edited by M. Valensise, 219–31. Paris: Gallimard.

———. 2000. *Aristocratic Liberalism*. 2d rev. ed. New Brunswick: Transaction Publishers. Originally published in 1992 (New York: Oxford University Press).

———. 2003. *Liberalism in Nineteenth-Century Europe: The Political Culture of Limited Suffrage*. New York: Palgrave.

Kale, Steven D. 1992. *Legitimism and the Reconstruction of French Society*. Baton Rouge: Louisiana State University Press.

Kant, Immanuel. 1991. *Political Writings*. Edited by Hans Reiss. Cambridge: Cambridge University Press.

Katznelson, Ira. 1994. "A Properly Defined Liberalism." *Social Research* 61, no. 3 (Fall): 611–30.

Kelley, Donald R. 1984. *Historians and the Law in Postrevolutionary France*. Princeton: Princeton University Press.

Kelly, George Armstrong. 1965. "Liberalism and Aristocracy in the French Restoration." *Journal of the History of Ideas* 26, no. 4 (October–December): 509–30.

———. 1986. "Constant and His Interpreters: A Second Visit." *Annales Benjamin Constant*, no. 6: 81–89. Lausanne: Institute Benjamin Constant.

———. 1992. *The Humane Comedy: Constant, Tocqueville, and French Liberalism*. Cambridge: Cambridge University Press.

Kelsen, Hans. 1969. "Sovereignty and International Law." In *In Defense of Sovereignty*, edited by W. J. Stankiewicz, 115–31. New York: Oxford University Press.

Keohane, Nannerl O. 1980. *Philosophy and the State in France*. Princeton: Princeton University Press.

King, Preston. 1987. "Sovereignty." In *The Blackwell Encyclopedia of Political Thought*, edited by D. Miller, 492–95. Oxford: Blackwell.

Kirschleger, Pierre-Yves. 1999. *La religion de Guizot*. Geneva: Labor et Fides.

Laborie, Lanzac de. 1930. "L'amitié de Tocqueville et de Royer-Collard." *Revue des deux mondes* (August 15): 876–901.

Laboulaye, Edouard. 1861. Introduction to *Cours de politique Constitutionnelle*, by Benjamin Constant, viii–li. Edited by E. Laboulaye. Paris: Guillaumin.

Lacorne, Denis. 1993. "Le débat des droits de l'homme en France et aux États-Unis." *La Revue Tocqueville/The Tocqueville Review* 14, no. 1: 5–31.

Lamberti, Jean-Claude. 1983. *Tocqueville et les deux démocraties*. Paris: PUF.

Langeron, Roger. 1956. *Un conseiller secret de Louis XVIII: Royer-Collard*. Paris: Hachette.

Laquièze, Alain. 2002. *Les origines du régime parlementaire en France (1814–1848)*. Paris: PUF.

Larmore, Charles. 1996. *The Morals of Modernity*. Cambridge: Cambridge University Press.

———. 2000. "Le 'nous' moral que nous sommes." In *Comprendre*, no. 1: 219–34.

Laski, Harold J. 1917. *Studies in the Problem of Sovereignty.* New Haven: Yale University Press.

———. 1919. *Authority in the Modern State.* New Haven: Yale University Press.

Laurent, Marcel. 1972. *Prosper de Barante et Madame de Staël.* Saint-Laure, Maringues: Clermont, 1972.

Laursen, John Christian. 1989. "Scepticism and Intellectual Freedom: The Philosophical Foundations of Kant's Politics of Publicity." *History of Political Thought* 10, no. 3 (Autumn): 439–55.

———. 1993. "Publicity and Cosmopolitanism in Late-Eighteenth-Century Germany." *History of European Ideas* 16, no. 1–3: 117–22.

Lawler, Peter. 1993. *The Restless Mind: Alexis de Tocqueville on the Origin and Perpetuation of Human Liberty.* Lanham: Rowman & Littlefield.

Lebrun, Richard A. 1988. *Joseph de Maistre: An Intellectual Militant.* Montreal: McGill-Queen's University Press.

Lecky, W. E. H. 1981. *Democracy and Liberty.* Indianapolis: Liberty Fund.

Lefort, Claude. 1988. "Le libéralisme de Guizot." In François Guizot, *Des moyens de gouvernement et d'opposition dans l'état actuel de la France,* 7–34. Paris: Belin.

———. 1994. "Libéralisme et démocratie." In *Les libéralismes, la théorie politique et l'histoire,* edited by Siep Stuurman, 3–16. Amsterdam: Amsterdam University Press.

Letwin, Shirley Robin. 1965. *The Pursuit of Certainty.* Cambridge: Cambridge University Press.

Lilla, Mark. 1994a. "The Other Velvet Revolution: Continental Liberalism and Its Discontents." *Daedalus* 123, no. 2 (Spring): 129–57.

———, ed. 1994b. *New French Thought: Political Philosophy.* Princeton: Princeton University Press.

Littré, Émile. 1889. *Dictionnaire de la langue française.* Vol. 1. Paris: Hachette.

Lively, Jack, and John Rees, eds. 1978. *Utilitarian Logic and Politics: James Mill's 'Essay on Government,' Macaulay's Critique and the Ensuing Debate.* Oxford: Clarendon.

Livois, René de. 1965. *Histoire de la presse française.* Vol. 1: *Des origines à 1881.* Paris: Les Temps de la Presse.

Logue, William. 1983. *From Philosophy to Sociology: The Evolution of French Liberalism, 1870–1914.* DeKalb: Northern Illinois University Press.

Lough, John. 1982. *The Philosophes and Post-Revolutionary France.* Oxford: Clarendon.

Lucas, Colin, ed. 1988. *The French Revolution and the Creation of Modern Political Culture.* Vol. 2: *The Political Culture of the French Restoration.* Oxford: Pergamon Press.

Lucas-Dubreton, J. 1929. *The Restoration and the July Monarchy.* New York: G. P. Putnam's Son's.

Lutaud, Olivier. 1976. "Guizot historien, politique, écrivain devant les revolutions d'Angleterre." In *Actes du colloque François Guizot,* 239–72. Paris: Société de l'Histoire du Protestantisme Français.

Manent, Pierre. 1991. "Guizot et Tocqueville devant l'ancien et le nouveau." In *François Guizot et la culture politique de son temps,* edited by Marina Valensise, 147–59. Paris: Gallimard.

———. 1993. *Tocqueville et la nature de la démocratie*. 2d ed. Paris: Fayard.

———. 1994. *An Intellectual History of Liberalism*. Princeton: Princeton University Press.

———. 1996. "The French Revolution and French and English Liberalism." In *The Legacy of the French Revolution*, edited by Ralph Hancock and Gary Lambert, 43–78. Lanham: Rowman & Littlefield.

———, ed. 2001. *Les libéraux*. 2d ed. Paris: Gallimard.

Manin, Bernard. 1997. *The Principles of Representative Government*. Cambridge: Cambridge University Press.

Mansfield, Harvey C., Jr. 1989. *Taming the Prince: The Ambivalence of Modern Executive Power*. New York: The Free Press.

Maritain, Jacques. 1951. *Man and the State*. Chicago: University of Chicago Press.

Marcel, Pierre Roland. 1910. *Essai politique sur Alexis de Tocqueville*. Paris: Alcan.

Mazzini, Giuseppe. 1984. *Dei doveri dell'uomo; Fede e avvenire*. Edited by Paulo Rossi. Milano: Mursia [English translation: *The Duties of Man*. New York: Harper, 1963].

McMahon, Darrin. 2001. *Enemies of the Enlightenment*. Oxford: Oxford University Press.

McNamara, Vincent. 1992. "Juan Donoso Cortés: un doctrinario liberal." *Revista de Filosofia de la Universidad de Costa Rica* 30, no. 72: 209–16.

Mellon, Stanley. 1958. *The Political Uses of History: A Study of Historians in the French Restoration*. Stanford: Stanford University Press.

———. 1972. Introduction to *Historical Essays and Lectures*, by François Guizot, xvii–xlv. Chicago: University of Chicago Press.

Mélonio, Françoise. 1993. *Tocqueville et les Français*. Paris: Aubier.

———. 1994a. "Les libéraux français et leur histoire." In *Les libéralismes, la théorie politique et l'histoire*, edited by Siep Stuurman, 35–46. Amsterdam: Amsterdam University Press.

———. 1994b. "L'histoire à l'avant du pouvoir: Le Globe de 1820 à 1830." In *Guizot, les Doctrinaires et la presse, 1820–1830*, edited by D. Roldán, 77–96. Val-Richer: Fondation Guizot.

Merriam, C. E. 1968. *History of the Theory of Sovereignty since Rousseau*. 2d ed. New York: AMS Press. (1st ed., 1900.)

Merquior, J. G. 1991. *Liberalism, Old and New*. Boston: Twayne.

Michel, Henry. 1896. *L'idée de l'État*. Paris: Hachette.

Michnik, Adam. 1998. *Letters from Freedom*. Berkeley: University of California Press.

Migniac, Louis. 1900. *Le régime censitaire en France*. Paris: Arthur Rousseau.

Mills, C. W. 1959. *The Sociological Imagination*. New York: Oxford University Press.

Mirabeau. 1986. *Notes à la cour suivies de Discours*. Edited by Guy Chaussinand-Nogaret. Paris: Hachette.

Mouffe, Chantal. 1995. "À propos d'un libéralism qui se dit politique." *Esprit*, no. 208 (January): 202–29.

Nefftzer, Auguste. 1997. "Libéralisme." Appendix to *L'individu effacé, ou le paradoxe du libéralisme français*, by Lucien Jaume, 557–67. Paris: Fayard.

Neidleman, Jason. 2001. *The General Will Is Citizenship*. Lanham: Rowman & Littlefield.

Nemoianu, Vurgil. 2001. "From Goethe to Guizot: The Conservative Contexts of 'Wilhelm Meisters Wanderjahre,'" *Modern Language Studies* 31, no. 1 (Spring): 45–58.

Nesmes-Desmarets, Robert de. 1908. *Les doctrines politiques de Royer-Collard*. Paris: Girard & Brière.

Nietzsche, Friedrich. 1967. *The Will to Power*. Translated by Walter Kaufmann. New York: Vintage.

———. 1980. *On the Advantage and Disadvantage of History for Life*. Translated by P. Preuss. Indianapolis: Hackett.

Nique, Christian. 2000. *L'École au service du gouvernement des esprits*. Paris: Hachette.

Nisbet, Robert. 1976–77. "Many Tocquevilles." *The American Scholar* (Winter): 59–75.

Nolla, Eduardo. 1990. Introduction to *De la démocratie en Amérique*, by Alexis de Tocqueville, edited by Eduardo Nolla, i–lxxxi. Vol. 1. Paris: Vrin.

———, ed. 1992. *Liberty, Equality, Democracy*. New York: New York University Press.

O'Connor, Mary C. 1955. *The Historical Thought of François Guizot*. Ph.D. diss. Washington, D. C.: Catholic University of America Press.

Oechslin, J.-J. 1960. *Le mouvement ultra-royaliste sous la Restauration*. Paris: Librairie générale de droit et de jurisprudence.

Ortega y Gasset, José. 1962. *History as a System, and Other Essays Toward a Philosophy of History*. New York: Norton.

———. 1964. *Obras Completas*. Vol. 5. Madrid: Revista de Occidente.

Ozouf, Mona. 1987. "L'opinion publique." In *The French Revolution and the Creation of Modern Political Culture*. Vol. 1: *The Political Culture of the Old Regime*, edited by K. Baker, 420–34. Oxford: Pergamon Press.

———. 1989. "Public Spirit." In *A Critical Dictionary of the French Revolution*, edited by François Furet and Mona Ozouf, 771–79. Translated by Arthur Goldhammer. Cambridge, Mass.: Harvard University Press.

Pasquino, Pasquale. 1991. "Sur la théorie constitutionnelle de la monarchie de Juillet." In *François Guizot et la culture politique de son temps*, edited by Marina Valensise, 111–28. Paris: Gallimard.

Pénault, Pierre Jean, ed. 1987. *Guizot et le Val-Richer*. Association "Le Pays d'Auge."

Peterson, Merrill D., ed. 1975. *The Portable Jefferson*. New York: Penguin.

Philippe, Adrien 1857. *Royer-Collard, sa vie publique, sa vie privée, sa famille*. Paris: Michel-Lévy Frères.

Pierson, George Wilson. 1996. *Tocqueville in America*, 2d ed. Baltimore: Johns Hopkins University Press.

Pilbeam, Pamela M. 1991. *The 1830 Revolution in France*. London: Macmillan.

Pire, Jean-Miguel. 2002. *Sociologie d'un volontarisme culturel fondateur: Guizot et le gouvernement des esprits, 1814–1841*. Paris: L'Harmattan.

Pitkin, Hannah F. 1967. *The Concept of Representation*. Berkeley: University of California Press.

Pocock, J. G. A. 1971. *Politics, Language, and Time: Essays on Political Thought and History*. New York: Atheneum.

Pouthas, Charles H. 1923a. *Guizot pendant la Restauration*. Paris: Plon.

———. 1923b. *Essai critique sur les sources et la bibliographie de Guizot pendant la Restauration*. Paris: Plon.

———. 1936. *La jeunesse de Guizot*. Paris: Alcan.

Raynaud, Phillippe. 1989. "The American Revolution." In *A Critical Dictionary of the French Revolution*, edited by François Furet and Mona Ozouf, 595–98. Translated by Arthur Goldhammer. Cambridge, Mass.: Harvard University Press.

———. 1991. "La Révolution anglaise." In *François Guizot et la culture politique de son temps*, edited by Marina Valensise, 69–81. Paris: Gallimard.

———, and Stéphane Rials, eds. 1996. *Dictionnaire de philosophie politique*. Paris: PUF.

Reboul, Fabienne. 1991. "Guizot et l'instruction publique." In *François Guizot et la culture politique de son temps*, edited by Marina Valensise, 163–86. Paris: Gallimard.

Reboul, Pierre. 1962. *Le mythe anglais dans la littérature française sous la Restauration*. Lille: Bibliothéque Universitaire.

Rees, J. 1969. "The Theory of Sovereignty Restated." In *In Defense of Sovereignty*, edited by W. J. Stankiewicz, 209–40. New York: Oxford University Press.

Reizov, B. 1962. *L'historiographie romantique Françoise*. Moscow: Editions en langues e'trangères.

Rémond, Gabriel. 1979. *Royer-Collard: Son essaid'un système politique*. 2d ed. New York: Arno Press.

Rémond, René. 1976. "Le philosophe de l'histoire chez Guizot." In *Actes du colloque François Guizot*, 273–86. Paris: Société de l'Histoire du Protestantisme Français.

Renan, Ernest. 1859. "De la philosophie de l'histoire contemporaine." *Revue des deux mondes* (July 1): 179–209.

Rials, Stéphane. 1987. *Révolution et Contre-Révolution au XIXème siècle*. Paris: Albatros.

Richter, Melvin. 1969. "Comparative Political Analysis in Montesquieu and Tocqueville." *Comparative Politics* 1, no. 2: 129–60.

———. 1970. "The Uses of Theory: Tocqueville's Adaptation of Montesquieu." In *Essays in Theory and History*, edited by Melvin Richter, 74–102. Cambridge, Mass.: Harvard University Press.

Ripley, George, ed. 1838. *Philosophical Miscellanea of Cousin, Jouffroy, and Constant*. Boston: Hilliard, Gray & Co.

Roldán, Darío, ed. 1994. *Guizot, les Doctrinaires et la presse,1820–1830*. Val-Richer: Fondation Guizot.

———. 1996. "La 'démocratie mouvante' et le gouvernement représentatif. Politique et société dans la pensée politique doctrinaire: Charles de Rémusat." Paper delivered at the Fifth Conference of the International Society for the Study of European Ideas, Utrecht, August 1996.

———. 1999. *Charles de Rémusat: certitudes et impasses du libéralisme doctrinaire*. Paris: L'Harmattan.

Rosanvallon, Pierre. 1985. *Le moment Guizot*. Paris: Gallimard.

———. 1986. "Pour une histoire conceptuelle du politique." *Revue de synthèse* 1–2 (January–June): 93–106.

———. 1989. "Les Doctrinaires et la question du gouvernement représentatif." In *The French Revolution and the Creation of Modern Political Culture*. Vol. 3: *The Transformation of Political Culture, 1789–1848*, edited by François Furet and Mona Ozouf, 411–31. Oxford: Pergamon Press.

———. 1991. "Guizot et la question du suffrage universel au XIXème siècle." In *François Guizot et la culture politique de son temps*, edited by Marina Valensise, 129–46. Paris: Gallimard.

———. 1992. *Le sacre du citoyen: histoire du suffrage universel en France*. Paris: Gallimard.

———. 1993. "L'histoire du mot démocratie à l'époque moderne." In *La pensée politique*. Vol. I: *Situations de la démocratie*, edited by M. Gauchet, P. Manent, and P. Rosanvalon, 11–29. Paris: Gallimard.

———. 1994a. *La monarchie impossible: les Chartes de 1814 et de 1830*. Paris: Fayard.

———. 1994b. "Les Doctrinaires sont-ils des libéraux?" In *Guizot, les Doctrinaires et la presse, 1820–1830*, edited by D. Roldán, 133–39. Val-Richer: Fondation Guizot.

———. 1995. "Faire l'histoire du politique." *Esprit*, no. 209 (February): 25–42.

Rossiter, Clinton, ed. 1961. *The Federalist Papers*. New York: New American Library.

Rousseau, Jean-Jacques. 1964. *Œuvres complètes*. Vol. III: *Du contrat social. Écrits politiques*. Edited by B. Gagnebin and M. Raymond. Paris: Bibliothèque de la Pléiade.

———. 1986. *Political Writings*. Translated by Frederick Watkins. Madison: University of Wisconsin Press.

Roussel, Jean. 1972. *Jean-Jacques Rousseau en France après la Révolution, 1795–1830*. Paris: Armand Colin.

Ruggiero, Guido de. 1959. *The History of European Liberalism*. Boston: Beacon Press.

Ryan, Alan, ed. 1979. *The Idea of Freedom*. Oxford: Oxford University Press.

———. 1993. "The Liberal Community." In *Democratic Community: Nomos XXXV*, edited by John W. Chapman and Ian Shapiro, 91–114. New York: New York University Press.

Sainte-Beuve, C. A. 1874. *Nouveaux Lundis*. Vol. 10. Paris: Michel-Lévy Frères.

Sartori, Giovanni. 1965. *Democratic Theory*. New York: Praeger.

Sauvigny, Guillaume de Bertier de. 1959. *Metternich et son temps*. Paris: Hachette.

———. 1966. *The Bourbon Restoration*. Philadelphia: University of Pennsylvania Press.

———. 1979. "Le libéralisme. Aux origines d'un mot." *Commentaire*, no. 7 (Autumn): 420–24.

Schleifer, James T. 2000. *The Making of Tocqueville's Democracy in America*. 2d expanded edition. Indianapolis: Liberty Fund [1st ed. University of North Carolina Press, 1980].

Schmitt, Carl. 1928. *Verfassungslehre*. München: Von Duncker & Humbolt.

———. 1996. *The Crisis of Parliamentary Democracy*. Translated by Ellen Kennedy. Cambridge, Mass.: MIT Press.

Schumpeter, Joseph A. 1950. *Capitalism, Socialism, and Democracy*. New York: Harper & Row.

Sewell, William H., Jr. 1994. *A Rhetoric of Bourgeois Revolution: The Abbé Sieyes and What Is the Third Estate?* Durham: Duke University Press.

Sheehan, James J. 1984. "Some Reflections on Liberalism in Comparative Perspective." In *Deutschland und der Westen*, edited by Henning Köhler, 44–58. Berlin: Colloquium Verlag.

Shklar, Judith. 1996. *Political Thought and Political Thinkers*. Edited by Bernard Yack. Cambridge: Cambridge University Press.

Siedentop, Larry. 1979. "Two Liberal Traditions." In *The Idea of Freedom*, edited by Alan Ryan, 153–74. Oxford: Oxford University Press.

———. 1994. *Tocqueville*. Oxford: Oxford University Press.

———. 1997. Introduction to *The History of Civilization in Europe*, by François Guizot, edited by Larry Siedentop, vii–xxxvii. London: Penguin.

Simon, Jules. 1885. *Thiers, Guizot, Rémusat*. Paris: Calmann-Lévy.

Simon, Walter, ed. 1972. *French Liberalism, 1789–1848*. New York: John Wiley & Sons.

Skinner, Quentin. 1998. *Liberty before Liberalism*. Cambridge: Cambridge University Press.

Smithson, Rulon Nephi. 1972. *Augustin Thierry: Social and Political Consciousness in the Evolution of a Historical Method*. Geneva: Droz.

Soltau, Roger. 1959. *French Political Thought in the Nineteenth Century*, 2d ed. New Haven: Yale University Press.

Sorman, Guy. 1994. "Le libéralisme face à la dynamique de la société moderne." In *Les libéralismes, la théorie politique et l'histoire*, edited by Siep Stuurman, 187–98. Amsterdam: Amsterdam University Press.

Spitzer, Alan B. 1987. *The French Generation of 1820*. Princeton: Princeton University Press.

Spuller, E. 1895. *Royer-Collard*. Paris: Hachette.

Stankiewicz ,W. J., ed. 1969. *In Defense of Sovereignty*. New York: Oxford University Press.

Starzinger, Vincent. 1991. *The Politics of the Center: The Juste Milieu in Theory and Practice, France and England, 1815–1848*. 2d ed. New Brunswick: Transaction Publishers.

Stern, Fritz, ed. 1956. *The Varieties of History*. New York: Meridian Books.

Stewart, John H., ed. 1965. *A Documentary Survey of the French Revolution*. New York: Macmillan.

Storing, Herbert, ed. 1981. *The Complete Anti-Federalist*. Vol. 6. Chicago: University of Chicago Press.

Stuurman, Siep. 1994. "Le libéralisme comme invention historique." In *Les libéralismes, la théorie politique et l'histoire*, edited by Siep Stuurman, 17–32. Amsterdam: Amsterdam University Press.

Taine, Hippolyte. 1897. *Carnets de voyage: Notes sur la province, 1863–1865*. Paris: Hachette.

Terral, Hervé. 2000. *Les savoirs du maître: Enseigner de Guizot à Ferry*. Paris: L'Harmattan.

Thadden, Rudolf von. 1991. "Guizot et la pensée allemande." In *François Guizot et la culture politique de son temps*, edited by Marina Valensise, 83–92. Paris: Gallimard.

Theis, Laurent. 1994a. "La revolution d'Angleterre dans *le Globe.*" In *Guizot, les Doctrinaires et la presse, 1820–1830*, edited by D. Roldán, 97–110. Val-Richer: Fondation Guizot.

———. 1994b. "Les libéraux français et la Révolution anglaise." *Commentaire* 17, no. 68 (Winter): 963–70.

———. 1997. "Présentation de 'L'histoire de la revolution d'Angleterre.'" In *François Guizot, Histoire de la Révolution d'Angleterre*, xxxv–lxxiv.

Thierry, Augustin. 1866. *Lettres sur l'histoire de France*. Paris: Garnier frères.

Thureau-Dangin, Paul. 1876. *Le parti libéral sous la Restauration*. Paris: Plon.

Toulazin Muret, Charlotte. 1972. *French Royalist Doctrine since the Revolution*. 2d ed. New York: Octagon.

Trilling, Lionel. 1953. *The Liberal Imagination: Essays on Literature and Society*. Garden City, N.Y.: Doubleday.

Tudesq, André-Jean, and André Jardin. 1973. *La France des notables, 1815–1848*. Paris: Seuil.

Tudesq, André-Jean. 1994. "Guizot et la Presse sous la Restauration." In *Guizot, les Doctrinaires et la presse, 1820–1830*, edited by D. Roldán, 1–10. Val-Richer: Fondation Guizot.

Tulard, Jean, ed. 1990. *La Contre-révolution*. Paris: Perrin.

Valade, Bernard. 1990. "Les théocrates." In *La Contre-Révolution*, edited by B. Yvert, 286–309. Paris: Perrin.

Valensise, Marina, ed. 1991. *François Guizot et la culture politique de son temps*. Paris: Gallimard.

Varouxakis, Georgios. 1999. "Guizot's Historical Works and J. S. Mill's Reception of Tocqueville." *History of Political Thought* 20, no. 2 (Summer): 292–312

Vaulabelle, Achille de. 1855. *Histoire des deux Restaurations jusqu'à l'avénement de Louis-Philippe*. Vol. 4. Paris: Perrotin.

———. 1856. *Histoire des deux Restaurations jusqu'à l'avénement de Louis-Philippe*. Vol. 5. Paris: Perrotin.

Vermeren, Patrice. 1994. "Les têtes rondes du Globe et la nouvelle philosophie de Paris: Jouffroy et Damiron." In *Guizot, les Doctrinaires et la presse, 1820–1830*, edited by D. Roldán, 59–76. Val-Richer: Fondation Guizot.

Wahrman, Dror. 1995. *Imagining the Middle Class*. Cambridge: Cambridge University Press.

Waresquiel, Emmanuel de. 1993. "Les doctrinaires ou l'éloge du centre." *Commentaire* 6, no. 2 (Summer): 349–57.

——. 1996. "Quand les doctrinaitres visitaient l'Angleterre au début du XIXe siècle." *Commentaire* 18, no. 66 (Summer): 361–67.

Weber, Eugen. 1997. "The man who tamed the past." *Times Literary Supplement,*
April 25, p. 11.

Welch, Cheryl B. 1984. *Liberty and Utility: The French Ideologues and the Transformation of Liberalism.* New York: Columbia University Press.

Weintraub, Karl J. 1966. *Visions of Culture.* Chicago: University of Chicago Press.

Wolfe, Alan. 1996. *Marginalized in the Middle.* Chicago: University of Chicago Press.

Wolin, Sheldon S. 1960. *Politics and Vision.* Boston: Little, Brown & Co.

——. 1996. "The Liberal/Democratic Divide: On Rawls's *Political Liberalism.*" *Political Theory* 24, no. 1 (February): 97–119.

Woodward, E. L. 1930. *Three Studies in European Conservatism.* London: Constable
and Company.

Wright, Kent J. 1993. "Les sources républicaines de la Déclaration des droits de
l'homme et du citoyen." In *Le siècle de l'avènement républicain,* edited by F. Furet
and M. Ozouf, 127–64. Paris: Gallimard.

Yvert, Benoît, ed. 1990. *La Contre-Révolution.* Paris: Perrin.

——. 1994. "Aux origines de l'orléanisme. Les Doctrinaires, le Globe et les Bourbons." In *Guizot, les Doctrinaires et la presse, 1820–1830,* edited by D. Roldán,
11–34. Val-Richer: Fondation Guizot.

Zetterbaum, Marvin. 1967. *Tocqueville and the Problem of Democracy.* Stanford: Stanford University Press.

Zuckert, Michael. 1993. "On Social State." In Tocqueville's *Defense of Human Liberty,* edited by Peter A. Lawler and J. Alulis, 3–21. New York: Garland.

Index

Note: The terms democracy, Doctrinaires, France, French Revolution, government, Guizot, history, institutions, law, liberalism, monarchy, order, political, political thought, political theory, power, representative government, Restoration, society, state, *and will appear frequently in the text and were indexed only in connection with main themes. Most sources cited in the endnotes were not indexed. Main works are listed with author's name.*

sovereignty, 2, 7–10, 17, 35, 43, 61, 73, 124–48, 156, 159, 165, 188–91, 217–18, 223, 250–51, 275, 283, 285, 289; absolute, 129, 132, 137–38, 158; and authority, 147n3; of intelligence, 141; of justice, 142; limited, 127, 137, 142, 150n32; of the nation, 73; of the people (popular sovereignty), 5, 38, 42, 81, 88, 99, 104–5, 114–15, 124, 126–27, 130–33, 136–39, 141–43, 145–47, 190, 198, 208n9, 275; royal, 72–74
sovereignty of reason, 10, 15, 30, 44, 91, 105, 115, 123, 127, 133, 135–36, 141–47, 170, 187, 204, 217, 275, 280; history of the concept of, 128–29, 148n9; institutional implications of, 142–47, 152n58
Spark, Jarred, 69
Staël, Madame de, 23, 28–29
Stapfer, Paul-Albert, 33
Starzinger, Vincent, 144, 152n52
social state, 100, 120, 240, 253, 262, 284–85. See also social condition
state, 23, 42, 81, 105, 113, 124, 140, 143, 146, 157, 165, 168, 170, 172, 174, 176, 178, 247, 279, 280, 283; of nature, 159, 236, 287; and society, 17, 113; of society, 113, 284; task of, 161–62, 168, 178, 283
Stoffels, Charles, 99, 119n39
Stoffels, Eugène, 92, 116n10, 117n19
suffrage, 38, 225, 232, 234, 238; limited, 14, 205, 217; universal, 5, 31, 41, 81, 99, 105, 114–15, 137, 145, 177, 205, 224, 226, 231, 233, 240
Suleau, Vicomte de, 24
superiorities: natural, 91, 159–60, 222, 227, 256; social, 227
Surville, Laure, 25

Tablettes universelles, 23, 257
Taine, Hyppolite, 36, 281

Terral, Hervé, 53n62, 182n35
Terror (of 1793–1794), 2, 19, 21, 27, 30, 32, 57–59, 105, 112, 126, 131, 156, 190
Theis, Laurent, 6, 119n43, 209n21
Thierry, Augustin, 24, 60–61, 82n8
Thiers, 28, 40, 42, 91, 175
third estate, 60–61, 64, 72, 93, 95–97, 104, 229–30. See also bourgeoisie; middle class
Third Republic. See Republic, Third
Thorbecke, Johan Rudolf, 44, 55n87
Thureau-Dangin, Paul, 27, 84n40, 296n17
tiers état. See third estate
Tocqueville, Alexis de, xi, 1, 2, 5–7, 9, 14–15, 21, 23–25, 28–29, 36–38, 40, 42–43, 47, 59–60, 62, 78, 103–4, 113–15, 116n4, 116n6, 116n8, 116n9, 116n11, 117n13, 117n14, 117n15, 117n19, 117n21, 117n23, 117n25, 118n29, 118n30, 118n34, 118n36, 119n39, 119n40, 119n47, 119n49, 119n53, 121n67, 121n70, 122n78, 122n81, 122n82, 163, 166, 177, 204, 224, 250, 274, 275, 277–79 281, 288, 294; *L'Ancien Régime et la Révolution*, 2, 95, 97–98, 100, 102; on the Charter of 1814, 73–74, 84n38; *De la démocratie en Amérique*, xi, 1–2, 5, 7, 29, 38, 47, 88–90, 94–96, 99, 104, 106–7, 111, 116n5, 116n10, 119n40, 122n78, 122n81, 163, 275; and Guizot, xi, 92–102; on moderating democracy, 111–12, 121n70; and Royer-Collard, 89–90
Tracy, Destutt de, 128
trial by jury, 17, 218, 259, 262, 264, 282
Trilling, Lionel, 294
Turgot, 103
tyranny, 67–68, 81, 105, 110, 129, 130–31, 134, 138, 190, 199, 204, 220, 255, 280, 293

~

About the Author

Aurelian Craiutu (Ph.D., Princeton University, 1999) is Assistant Professor of Political Science at Indiana University, Bloomington, where he teaches history of political thought and modern political theory. He has previously taught at Duke University and University of Northern Iowa. His research interests include French political and social thought, varieties of liberalism and conservatism, democratic theory, as well as theories of transition to democracy and democratic consolidation in Eastern Europe. Craiutu's dissertation, *The Difficult Apprenticeship of Liberty: Reflections on the Political Thought of the French Doctrinaires,* won the American Political Science Association's Leo Strauss Award for the best doctoral dissertation in the field of political philosophy in 2000.

Aurelian Craiutu is the editor of Guizot's *History of the Origins of Representative Government in Europe* (Liberty Fund, 2002) and the author of *In Praise of Liberty: Essays in Political Philosophy* (Polirom, 1998; in Romanian). He also translated into Romanian Edmund Husserl's *Cartesian Meditations* (Humanitas, 1994) and coedited (with Sorin Antohi) *Dialogue and Liberty: Essays in Honor of Mihai Sora* (Nemira, 1997; in Romanian). Dr. Craiutu's articles have been published in *History of Political Thought; Political Theory; Review of Politics; European Journal of Political Theory, History of European Ideas; Historical Reflections/Reflexions historiques; Ethics; Rhetoric and Public Affairs; Government and Opposition;* and *East European Constitutional Review.* He is currently working on a book on political moderation.